DATE DUE

'JG 1971   S K P

BISMARCK, GLADSTONE,
AND THE CONCERT OF EUROPE

Bismarck, Gladstone,
and the
Concert of Europe

by

W. N. MEDLICOTT

STEVENSON PROFESSOR OF
INTERNATIONAL HISTORY IN THE
UNIVERSITY OF LONDON

GREENWOOD PRESS, PUBLISHERS
NEW YORK

Reprinted with the permission of the Athlone Press

First Greenwood Reprinting, 1969

Library of Congress Catalogue Card Number: 69-13931

PREFACE

WHEN before the Second World War I published a study of the Congress of Berlin and its aftermath I found it convenient to end the story in April 1880, for it seemed to me that the acute phase in the Near Eastern settlement had ended with the fall of Disraeli. But it is far from being the case that the Turkish Empire was allowed at that point a period of rest and oblivion, and during the next two years the problems of Montenegro, Greece, Bulgaria, Tunis, Armenia, and Egypt rivalled in their complexity and publicity the Near Eastern 'question' of the late 'seventies. Yet something was different, and it was in the attempt to understand the changed attitude of the greater powers towards Balkan and Mediterranean problems that I began to see this period of European diplomacy in terms of conflicting German and English programmes, and in a personal sense in terms of the Bismarck-Gladstone rivalry. Accordingly my study of the completion of the Berlin settlement soon broadened into an examination of the Gladstonian programme of the Concert of Europe and the Bismarckian alternative of close alliances, and this in turn called for some assessment of the fundamental mistrust which separated the great English Liberal from the German master of *Realpolitik*.

This is, in fact, one of the major turning-points in the history of European diplomacy. During the short period from 1879 to 1882 Bismarck's new course gave Germany the mechanism of security while imposing on Europe a deadlock which was a preventive of war rather than a guarantee of peace; Gladstone's search on the other hand for a revived Concert of Europe was the last attempt before 1914 to achieve a permanent relaxation of tensions in a united Europe. The story is that of Bismarck's success in negotiating and concluding the Three Emperors' Alliance of 18 June 1881 while accepting with ostensible sincerity Gladstone's leadership of the Concert; the Concert was thus used as a cover for negotiations in which the Concert itself was destroyed.

The source material needed for a study of modern European diplomacy on these lines is widely dispersed, and has sometimes to be looked for in unusual places. As long ago as 1924 I had the opportunity, through the kind offices of Dr. Meyendorff and of M. Sablin, to make transcripts for this period from the archives of the Russian embassy in London. I have been able to make use in this book of the unpublished correspondence of de Giers, the acting Russian Foreign Minister, with P. A. Saburov, the chief Russian negotiator of the Three Emperors' Alliance. In Vienna during several visits I transcribed the complete Austro-Hungarian documentation of the negotiations for the alliance; this is, as far as I am aware, the first time that this material has been used for this purpose by an historian. More recently I have had the opportunity to read through the entire German Foreign Office documentation for the alliance nego-tiations, which has come to London as a result of the exigencies of the Second World War. Some, but not all, of this material was available to, and used by, Wolfgang Windelband, one of the few German historians who was able to supplement the very inadequate German publication of Foreign Office docu-ments for this period; but there are some important gaps in Windelband's account. In using this material I am indebted to Mr. E. J. Passant, Librarian of the Foreign Office, and the Hon. Margaret Lambert, the British editor in chief of the *Documents on German Foreign Policy, 1918–1945*. I have also to acknowledge the help and efficient service of the staffs of the Staatsarchiv in Vienna and of the Public Record Office in London. For the chapters on the Montenegrin and Greek questions I have drawn largely on the voluminous British Foreign Office corres-pondence, and on the Gladstone and Granville private papers. A visit to Princeton and Washington in the second half of 1952 enabled me to fill gaps in my reading of recent American and continental historical literature; some of this is still not avail-able (as far as I know) in any British library. The writing of this book was largely completed at the Institute for Advanced Study in Princeton, where I was privileged to enjoy the Insti-tute's unique hospitality and to have the benefit of conversations with Professor C. E. Black, Sir Llewellyn Woodward, and the late Professor E. M. Earle. I am indebted to Mr. J. A. Finch for the use of transcripts of Austrian documents for 1879, and to my colleague, Miss Hilda Lee, who has read the whole work in manuscript, and made useful comments. I have also to thank my wife for much help in the transcription of documents in Vienna and in proof reading, and for general common sense and encouragement.

29 April 1955   W.N.M.

CONTENTS

CONTENTS

MAPS

ABBREVIATIONS

A.A.   Auswärtiges Amt. Unpublished German Foreign Office correspondence, 1880–1881.

A. & P.   Accounts and Papers.

B.B.M.   A. Brauer, E. Marcks, K. A. Müller, *Erinnerungen an Bismarck*. Berlin, 1924.

B.M. Add. MSS. British Museum, Additional Manuscripts.

B.St.H.   Barthélemy Saint-Hilaire, *Fragments pour l'histoire de la diplomatie française du 23 Septembre 1880 au 14 Novembre 1881*. Paris, 1882.

Busch   L. Raschdau (ed.), 'Die Durchführung der Berliner Kongressakte (1880–1), aus dem literarischen Nachlass des Unterstaatssekretärs Dr Busch', *Deutsche Rundschau*, May 1911.

D.D.F.   *Documents diplomatiques français (Commission de publication des documents relatifs aux origines de la guerre de 1914)*, vol. iii (January 1880–May 1881). Paris, 1931.

F.O.   Foreign Office.

Gladstone   J. Morley, *The Life of William Ewart Gladstone*, 3 vols., London, 1904.

Goschen   A. D. Elliot, *The Life of G. J. Goschen, first Viscount Goschen, 1831–1907*, 2 vols. London, 1911.

G.P.   *Die Grosse Politik der Europäischen Kabinette, 1871–1914* (ed. J. Lepsius, A. Mendelssohn Bartholdy, and F. Thimme), vols. ii, iii. Berlin, 1922.

Granville   Lord E. Fitzmaurice, *The Life of Lord Granville*, 2 vols. London, 1905.

Hohenlohe   Fürst zu Hohenlohe-Schillingfürst, *Memoirs*, 2 vols. London, 1906.

Knaplund Paul Knaplund (ed.), *Letters from the Berlin Embassy, 1871–1874, 1880–1885.* American Historical Association, 1942.

L.J.   *Livre jaune.*

Lucius   R. Lucius von Ballhausen, *Bismarck-Erinnerungen.* Stuttgart and Berlin, 1920.

Lyons   Lord Newton, *Lord Lyons,* 2 vols. London, 1913.

Medlicott W. N. Medlicott, *The Congress of Berlin and After.* London, 1938.

Moüy   C. de Moüy, *Souvenirs et causeries d'un diplomate.* Paris, 1909.

Nolde   Baron Boris Nolde, *L'Alliance franco-russe.* Paris, 1936.

Political Speeches W. E. Gladstone, *Political Speeches in Scotland, November and December 1879 (March and April 1880),* 2 vols. Edinburgh, 1880.

R.E.   Russian Embassy, Chesham House, London. Unprinted correspondence between the embassy and St. Petersburg, 1879–84.

Radowitz H. Holborn (ed.), *Aufzeichnungen und Erinnerungen aus dem Leben des Botschafters Joseph Marie von Radowitz,* 2 vols. Berlin, 1925.

Saburov J. Y. Simpson, *The Saburov Memoirs, or Bismarck and Russia.* Cambridge, 1929.

Schweinitz General von Schweinitz, *Denkwürdigkeiten,* 2 vols. Berlin, 1927.

Skazkin   S. Skazkin, *Konets austro-russko-germanskogo souiza.* Moscow, 1928.

Windelband W. Windelband, *Bismarck und die europäischen Grossmächte 1879–1885.* Essen, 2nd edn., 1942.

W.S.A.   Wiener Staatsarchiv. Unpublished Austro-Hungarian Foreign Office correspondence, 1879–82.

CHAPTER I

Bismarck and Gladstone

'BEHOLD at long last, the realization of the philosophers' dream', wrote the Russian diplomatist, Peter Alexandrovich Saburov, in May 1880. 'The Concert of Europe is established.' After ten years of peculiarly nerve-racking tension, many besides the philosophers of Europe were seeking security for their countries in some system of international collaboration against aggression. In Great Britain the Beaconsfield government, which had steered the country so dramatically for six years through all the crises of its own and its neighbours' creation, had just been defeated at the polls; the election campaign had been largely a personal triumph for the new prime minister, William Ewart Gladstone, who had above all things pledged himself to re-establish the Concert, under English guidance. In his great Midlothian speeches he had defined this policy as 'the bringing about the "common accord" of Europe, embodying in one organ the voice of civilized mankind in the actings and fostering care of England', and he entered on the task with resolution and fervour. 'I do believe that the Almighty has employed me for His purposes in a manner larger or more special than before' he wrote after the opening of Parliament, 'and has strengthened me and led me on accordingly.'

But as it happened the Gladstonian Concert of Europe, and the ordering of European affairs which it implied, were regarded by the powerful German Chancellor, Prince Otto von Bismarck, as a direct challenge to his own plans for Europe. The year 1879 was a turning-point in Bismarck's career as fundamental in its way as 1871 or 1866. It saw his breach with the National Liberals and the beginnings of his alliance with the German Conservatives, the virtual liquidation of his quarrel with the German Catholics and the Papacy, the beginnings of

protection, and the alliance of October 1879 with Austria; a
rapid succession of events which might well be described as his
rejection, in both home and foreign policy, of what were
essentially English conceptions of liberalism. The alliance with
Austria was facilitated on the one hand by the Emperor Franz
Joseph's breach with the Austrian-German Liberals, and on the
other by the relaxing of Bismarck's campaign against the
Roman Church. In the constitutional sphere these developments meant that Germany, already a respectable example of
the *Rechtsstaat*, the state based on legally guaranteed individual
rights, was not to develop, through an alliance with Bennigsen
and his supporters, the additional guarantee of a responsible
and representative government on the English model. In foreign
affairs they meant that Bismarck, after a characteristic phase of
hard thinking and nervous excitement, had abandoned the
policy of the free hand in international affairs which he had
sought to follow since 1862; his commitments to Austria involved the risk of a dangerous admixture in Austrian affairs, but
he had satisfied himself that the risk was worth taking. The
October treaty was soon followed by further developments in
Bismarck's alliance system, which defeated Gladstone's dream
of a united Europe, and were equally opposed both to the
specific programme of Gladstone's second government (1880–5)
and to the somewhat indeterminate 'principles of right policy'
which he expounded in the Midlothian campaigns of 1879–80.

The immediate purpose of both statesmen was the same—to
bring to an end the tension between the powers created by the
long-drawn-out Near Eastern crisis which had followed the collapse of Turkish government in Constantinople and the Balkans
in 1875 and 1876.[1] The six great powers had maintained a
nominal agreement until May 1876, when the hint of a coercion
of Turkey contained in the Berlin Memorandum had led the
British government to separate itself from Russia, Germany,
and Austria, the authors of the memorandum; the Concert had
been recreated in December 1876 at the Constantinople Conference, and remained in formal agreement until the following

[1] The most comprehensive study of this crisis is B. H. Sumner's *Russia and the
Balkans, 1870–1880* (1937). For developments after the Congress of Berlin of 1878
the reader may be referred to the present writer's *Congress of Berlin and After* (1938).

March 1877, when the rejection by the Turks of the innocuous London Protocol had left Russia, with much irritation and some misgiving, to fight Turkey as the distrusted mandatory of the remaining powers. The subsequent events—the insistence of the Russian military leaders on operations sufficiently extensive to ensure victory, the inability of the Russian Chancellor, Prince Gorchakov, to hold the Tsar to the more restricted military and political programme known as the 'petit paix', the growth of nationalist and Panslavist feeling in Russia which, heightened by Russian reverses in the summer of 1877, demanded a correspondingly drastic peace settlement, and finally the preliminary peace of San Stefano of March 1878—brought Russia to the verge of war with Austria-Hungary and Great Britain, and compelled her to accept considerable reductions of her gains at the Congress of Berlin in the summer of 1878. After the Congress Russian irritation showed itself in an injudicious attempt to obstruct the execution of the treaty clauses, and a tendency to blame not only Austria and Great Britain but also Germany for her disappointments; there seemed to be danger of a general European war in the summer of 1879, although in fact this was the last thing that Russia (the ostensible aggressor) desired. Where Gladstone and Bismarck differed was in their interpretation of these facts. Gladstone saw Turkey as an evil thing, encouraged in wickedness by the Beaconsfield government, whose selfish conduct had broken the Concert in May 1876; Russia's crusade was praiseworthy, and should have been supported until her aims were 'visibly turned to evil account'; the powers of Europe, if they once learned to act in concert, would subdue their selfish tendencies, find unity in a common cause, and by their irresistible authority constrain the Turk to behave himself. Bismarck saw Turkey as a bone of contention between the powers, whose appetites, fears, and passions had been dangerously aroused by recent events; he believed that there were dark forces in Russia which must be controlled and appeased within a new Three Emperors' Alliance; and he believed that France, whose hostility to Germany was quiescent but irremovable, must be diverted from dreams of a lost frontier by visions of a future empire at Turkey's expense. His policy was one of controlled tensions which would give Germany the maximum of influence with the minimum of obligation, and he looked with jealousy, but also with good reason, on any programme which offered the powers an alternative to the careful balance of forces under his control.

So although both statesmen agreed that the existing Near Eastern crisis must be brought to an end they differed profoundly in their conception of the European relationships which would result from the liquidation, and this was soon to produce a conflict of wills even in their handling of the Turks. By the spring of 1880 the powers had dealt with those parts of the Berlin Congress settlement which had provided the most serious crises between themselves, and what remained were a number of cases in which the Turkish government had failed to execute the clauses of the treaty of Berlin. It will be the purpose of this book to show how Gladstone sought to make his Concert of Europe a reality through the medium of negotiations over these clauses, and how Bismarck used the same negotiations as a cover for the conclusion of the Three Emperors' Alliance of 18 June 1881, after which Gladstone was told to leave Balkan affairs alone. It is right to speak of this conflict in terms of Anglo-German rivalry, for Bismarck undoubtedly saw in Gladstone the most serious obstacle to his plans; but as the rivalry was unacknowledged on Bismarck's side and, as far as we can see, only dimly perceived by Gladstone, it is easy to underrate its importance in the context of Anglo-German relations. The nature of the struggle was still further concealed by the fact that the more publicized crises of the day (in 1880 and 1881) arose out of the Sultan of Turkey's resistance to the execution of the Berlin treaty, and showed very few signs of strain between the great powers themselves; and also by the fact that the secrecy of the negotiations for the Three Emperors' Alliance was maintained with record efficiency.[2] Bismarck's support of British

[2] The first authentic account of the negotiations appeared in two articles by Professor J. Y. Simpson, 'Russo-German Relations and the Saburov Memoirs' (*The Nineteenth Century*, December 1917 and January 1918), based on a memoir in French, *Ma mission à Berlin, 1879–1884*, by the Russian ambassador, Peter Alexandrovich Saburov. This was later translated and edited by Simpson as *The Saburov Memoirs* (Cambridge, 1929). There was no reference to the alliance in Bismarck's *Reflections and Reminiscences*, or in such English biographies as *The Life of Lord Granville, 1815–1891* (by Lord Edmond Fitzmaurice, London, 1905). The usual view (cf. C. Grant Robertson's *Bismarck*, which is dated February 1918) was that

policy in Egypt in 1882 and 1883 concealed the extent of Anglo-German antagonism a little longer, but its existence became clear enough in the colonial crisis of 1884-5, and by this stage the country had become conscious for the first time of Germany as a serious, and, so it seemed, unscrupulous rival in trade.[3] In both the colonial and commercial spheres a clash of material interests had been added to the unsolved problem of Anglo-German ideological incompatibilities by the time of Gladstone's fall from office in 1885.

But in 1879 Germany, in the eyes of most Englishmen, was still no more than a formidable and temperamental neighbour with whom it was unwise, but also unnecessary, to quarrel. What existed in 1879 was an underlying Anglo-German antagonism which had not yet become a major problem of European politics, and a European distrust of Bismarckian diplomacy which had not yet become a dominant element in British political thought. Gladstone shared this mistrust, but only as one element among many that appeared to him to merit censure in the political conduct of European (including British) politicians of his generation; it was certainly not his intention to put himself forward as the protagonist of international Liberalism against Bismarckian *Realpolitik*, and it is only in retrospect that we can see the issues of the early 'eighties in these terms.[4]

Russia was on the point of returning to the Three Emperors' agreement of 1872 when the assassination of the Tsar Alexander II in March 1881 snapped the wire between Berlin and Petersburg (p. 399). It is interesting to note that there is no reference to the alliance in *The Holstein Memoirs* (ed. N. Rich and M. H. Fisher, 1955), written by Holstein in stages, starting in 1883. The best general introduction to the period is A. J. P. Taylor's *The Struggle for Mastery in Europe* (1954), chs. x–xiii.

[3] A Royal Commission was appointed in 1885 to investigate the causes of the 'depression of trade and industry' resulting from hostile tariffs and foreign competition. It reported in great detail in 1886 on the effect of protection in producing not only a decline of British exports but also a surplus of production in protected countries which could be sent abroad to undersell commodities 'produced under less artificial conditions'. The most serious competitors were Germany and the U.S.A. The whole problem is examined in the authoritative work by J. R. S. Hoffman, *Great Britain and the German Trade Rivalry, 1875–1914* (1933), esp. chs. 1–3.

[4] Indeed, it is so difficult to find direct criticisms of Bismarck in Gladstone's recorded statements that care must be taken to avoid the attribution to him of sentiments which he did not profess. 'Gladstone fühlte sich dem machtpolitischen Realismus Bismarcks und den Wegen seiner Reichsgründung innerlich entgegengesetzt,—eher sah er hier das Prinzip tätig, das seiner insularen Selbstgerechtigkeit nicht als das gute erschien'. H. Oncken, 'Disraeli und Gladstone', in *Menschen, die Geschichte machten* (1933), quoted Baum: see fn. 10 below.

Of these three underlying conditions which influenced, often obscurely and indirectly, the development of Anglo-German relations at this period—the incipient Anglo-German antagonism, Bismarck's European reputation, and Gladstone's Liberal outlook—the first is perhaps the hardest to explain on rational grounds, for before 1880 it was the absence of any serious grounds of political or commercial rivalry that had supplied the real key to Anglo-German relations. There had been a great deal of rather aimless, and often misinformed, comment, friendly and otherwise, by each on the other's policy, methods, and institutions, but there had been no compelling reason for either a serious quarrel or, on the other hand, for close co-operation. During the long years of peace after 1815, while the triumph of political and economic liberalism and the un-challenged security of her empire and her shores were fashioning England into the complete Liberal state, Prussia and the smaller north German states had been vaguely apprehended by Englishmen as forming a kind of political No-Man's-Land between the three great continental powers—France, Russia, and Austria; but this political futility had seemed to English-men to have few compensating attractions. The popular and sentimental view of the kindly, gifted, romantic, unpractical Germans was, as far as it went, entirely friendly, and many Englishmen found much to praise in German culture and edu-cation, while shaking their heads over the incapacity of Prussia and the smaller states to take a strong or independent line in foreign affairs. It was believed that a strong Germany would be a natural ally of Britain in keeping in check the ambitions of Russia and France, and as political disunity resulted from the existence of the numerous ruling families it seemed reasonable to assume that national unity would produce, and result from, some form of national revolution on Liberal lines.[5]

Germans for their part often regarded the development of English Liberalism with admiration, but also with some jealousy and irritation. The association of Liberalism in the

[5] The fullest study of Anglo-German relations before 1878 is the long and lively work of Veit Valentin, *Bismarcks Reichsgründung im Urteil englischer Diplomaten* (1937), a much broader treatment than the title suggests. See especially pp. 1–8, 463–6.

German mind with French politics predisposed many Germans
to seek a model of their own, and the successful association in
England of Liberal institutions with a highly flourishing
national state did not by any means convince all Germans that
what they called Liberalism (the definition was not always very
clear) necessarily provided a solution of their own problems.
Many German Liberals from List to Bennigsen had no doctrinaire objection to protection, regarding a Liberal economy
as a result, rather than a cause, of national greatness; List liked
to point out that England had used very different methods
when her power was still being created. Two partly contra-
dictory views emerged. One was that the English were self-
satisfied, somewhat hypocritical, unwilling in spite of their own
achievement of wealth, empire, and liberty to help or sympathize with the struggles of their less fortunate neighbours.
The other was that England was quick enough to subordinate
Liberal to nationalist ends when her own interests appeared to
be threatened, and that she was at heart no friend of German
unity. Opposition in 1848 to the Frankfurt Parliament's designs
on Schleswig-Holstein strengthened this conception of England
as an enemy of German unity, and of English Liberalism as a
convenient expedient for hamstringing the strength of her
neighbours.[6]

The normal English Liberal view of Bismarck's activities in
1863 and 1864 was that they were risky and unconstitutional
adventures which represented a last desperate attempt of
reaction to oppose the victory of Liberalism in Prussia; as late
as 1866 it was believed that this nightmare could not last long,
that Bismarck was merely a straw in the current of public
opinion, in Sir Robert Morier's words.[7] Criticism of Bismarck,
however, could not easily be distinguished from criticism of
Prussian policy, and so of Prussia, as in *The Times'* comment
of 21 February 1863 on the Russo-Prussian (Alvensleben) con-

[6] Bismarck wrote to Leopold von Gerlach on 11 May 1857: 'Ich habe, was das
Ausland anbelangt, in meinem Leben nur für England und seine Be-wohner
Sympathie gehabt, und bin stundenweis noch nicht frei davon; aber die Leute
wollen sich ja von uns nicht lieben lassen . . .' *Briefwechsel des Generals Leopold von
Gerlach mit . . . Bismarck* (Berlin, 1893), p. 336.
[7] Mrs. Rosslyn Wemyss, *Memoirs and Letters . . . of Sir Robert Morier* (1911), ii,
87. Cf. A. A. W. Ramsay, *Idealism and Foreign Policy* (1925), p. 51.

vention, 'whatever may be our hostility to the bear, there is no
doubt of our feeling towards the jackal'. But the German
achievement of national unification was accepted readily
enough. At the beginning of the Franco-German war public
opinion in England was indeed, for the most part, anti-French;
The Times was violently so, and believed, like Morier, that
Germany was fighting to defend her national existence. The
rapid and overwhelming victories, and what in those days
seemed the unrelenting harshness and brutality of German
conduct throughout, produced a rapid change in English
opinion; the whole affair began to suggest ruthless premedita-
tion, and those who already distrusted Bismarck discovered an
elaborate and farsighted plan behind what had hitherto seemed
to be the haphazard brutalities of an eccentric reactionary.
British Liberals disliked his methods; they were not convinced
that 'blood and iron' was the sole recipe for national greatness,
and they were not at all certain that if it were its use was justified. It was characteristic of mid-Victorian foreign policy that
the British governments of the day should have felt impelled to
give expression to these feelings; but their action in the Polish
and Danish question in 1863–4, in the Luxembourg question in
1867, and in 1870–1 when protests were made against the bombardment of Paris and the terms of peace, was due far more to
the feeling that protests were called for by public opinion than
to fear that any serious threat to the country existed. The effect
on German opinion was, not unnaturally perhaps, to strengthen
the conviction that the British were both hostile and ineffective.

The situation after 1871 was therefore one of considerable
anxiety to the more farsighted in both countries. The British
were, in spite of any appearance to the contrary, willing enough
to accept the new Germany; but the greatest uneasiness was
felt as to Bismarck's character and future plans. Would his conquests continue? Could they continue, without the annihilation
of countries—Belgium, Holland, Denmark, France perhaps—
whose independence was considered vital to Britain's own
security? Gladstone took the unusual course of writing from
10 Downing Street an anonymous article in the *Edinburgh
Review* for October 1870 in which he stated the essential point
explicitly: could France and Germany be relied on to maintain

in future 'a pacific policy on the continent of Europe'? There
was much criticism of French conduct in the article, but he
believed that the French national debt would be so heavy after
the war as to produce a violent reaction against Bonapartism
and so make France the 'head' of this pacific policy. As for
Germany,

> Should the popular constitutional tendencies in Germany prevail;
> should she qualify the principle of universal soldiering, which has
> now worked out its only rational aim, the independence of the
> country; the general establishment of this better policy will be
> easy. . . .

In other words, if Germany knew when to stop, all would be
well. Bismarck was ready enough to offer assurances. When
Lord Odo Russell, an Assistant Under-Secretary in the Foreign
Office, visited him at his headquarters at Versailles in December 1870, Bismarck talked expansively about German policy,
and assured the Englishman that henceforth the Germans
would be 'solely employed in organizing their political strength
at home and will resist any engagements to fight other nations
abroad, and having no conquests to make for themselves will
only care to resist invasion, while the conquest made by others
will be indifferent to them'.[8] This assurance was repeated in
equally unqualified language to other governments, and he
continued to repeat it at intervals until his retirement in 1890.

He could hardly hope to carry immediate conviction: perhaps it is among the major paradoxes of history that this successful author of three aggressive wars should have been able to
establish any reputation at all as a man of peace. In England
during the 'seventies distrust remained, kept alive by the disconcerting moves of his diplomacy, and by the periodic press
campaigns in which the new German nationalism denounced
as envy, hatred, and all uncharitableness the view which the
English were believed to be taking of the new Reich. Bismarck's
own attitude to England at this time is in some ways puzzling.
There is perhaps some truth in the theory that although he

[8] W. E. Gladstone, *Gleanings of Past Years, 1851–1877: Foreign* (1879), p. 246.
Odo Russell to Granville, 18 December 1870, reprinted in *Letters from the Berlin
Embassy, 1871–1874, 1880–1885*, ed. Paul Knaplund (American Historical Associa-
tion, 1942).

thought the popular German view of England silly, without basis in fact or logic, he encouraged the popular attacks in order to awaken the British to a realization of their weaknesses, weaknesses which, in the army and diplomacy, were largely due to their devotion to liberal principles. This apparently quixotic attitude is explainable on the theory that the 'natural ally' would be a useful ally only if she were strong.[9] A more obvious reason is that he was deriding English Liberalism as a means of hitting at English influence at the German Court, and at those aspects of German Liberalism which he regarded as dangerous to the new Germany.[10] It is easy, however, to be a little too subtle in these explanations; many of Bismarck's outpourings were due to nothing more than his own irritability, and right down to the days of his retirement he continued to speak of Gladstone to his confidants in terms which showed as little understanding as the most unsophisticated organs of the 'reptile' press. Gladstone, he said, quibbled with words, and had ended by becoming their victim. 'It is very convenient to have principles which can be made to fit in with and justify your conduct.'[11] His strongest criticism, which recurs repeatedly throughout his comments, was of England's unreliability, a result of political conditions which were particularly accentuated under Gladstone, but which could never be entirely absent from a Parliamentary state.[12]

[9] This theory, for what it is worth, is expounded by R. J. Sontag, *Germany and England, Background of Conflict, 1848–1894* (New York, 1938), p. 136.

[10] Eva Maria Baum, *Bismarcks Urteil über England und die Engländer* (Munich, 1936), pp. 29–33.

[11] The chief critic of England in Bismarck's entourage was probably Lothar Bucher. Sidney Whitman argues however that Bismarck had too great a sense of humour to go the whole length with anyone so uncompromising as Bucher on the subject of Gladstone. S. Whitman, *Personal Reminiscences of Prince Bismarck* (London, 1902), pp. 148–53, 237. Cf. the discussion in E. Eyck, 'Bismarck and Gladstone' (*The Contemporary Review*, June 1946).

[12] Cf. Baum, *op. cit.*, p. 51. It follows that Bismarck, as long as he held these views, was not likely to seek a permanent alliance with England, and therefore that it is no use blaming England for having rejected Bismarck's alleged alliance offers. The statement, in Lucius von Ballhausen's *Bismarck-Erinnerungen* (14 August 1889, p. 500), 'Das ganze Ziel und Objekt der deutschen Politik seit zehn Jahren sei, England für den Dreibund zu gewinnen' is the last of many similar utterances which have produced a considerable body of German works on Bismarck's alliance policy towards England. M. von Hagen, *Bismarck und England* (Berlin, 1943) is a recent and convenient summary, which like many other German studies of this

If Bismarck wanted peace, it was on his own terms; his philosophy of international life remained fundamentally combative and pessimistic, and he could discover no reliable basis for national survival other than the accumulation and manœuvring of superior force. Although he was ready after 1871 to declare Germany a satiated state, and to throw his weight against fresh adventures, tension did not relax; Europe had to struggle for a generation with the problem of a German peace policy which seemed to keep the continent ever on the verge of war.

Criticism of Bismarck's work, which has appeared belatedly but vigorously in Germany since 1948, still shows some uncertainty in its assignment of responsibility for Germany's disasters; partly because while Hitlerism, to which Bismarckism led, is unequivocally condemned, unification, Bismarck's basic achievement, is still generally accepted as an inevitable development justifying whatever methods were necessary for its fulfilment. There has thus been no general acceptance of the view that the decentralized German Confederation of 1815 should have been preserved because, in the words of the historian Georg Gottfried Gervinus in 1871, it 'was created for the very purpose of forming in the centre of Europe a neutral state which would by its federal organization guarantee peace'.[13] As criticism from this federalist point of view has not made much headway, debate has perforce turned to a re-examination of the familiar problem of English classrooms: was there no way but 'blood and iron'? Dr. Eyck, in his exhaustive three-volume life of Bismarck,[14] accepts most of the ends, particularly the unifications of the German nations in a powerful and glorious Empire, and has been able to criticize most of the means of Bismarck's policy, for he believes that unification could have been secured

subject tends to criticize British governments for not responding to German proposals which were, nevertheless, of only tactical importance even to Bismarck (cf. pp. 64 ff.). The problem is correctly stated by Wilhelm Schüssler, *Deutschland zwischen Russland und England* (Leipzig, 1940), pp. 62–8.

[13] Professor Hans Kohn, in quoting this passage, speaks of Gervinus's 'courageous and farsighted words' ('Rethinking Recent German History', in *German History: Some New German Views*, ed. Hans Kohn, 1954), and summarizes recent criticism of Bismarck from the federalist angle (pp. 30–6).

[14] Erich Eyck, *Bismarck, Leben und Werk*, three vols. (1941–4); also *Bismarck and the German Empire* (1950).

without war against France, and that the new Empire could have developed after 1871 without the repudiation of Liberalism, and would have been the better for it. But on the whole Bismarck's present-day critics have hesitated to accept Eyck's consistent Liberalism; their objections are varied, but reduce themselves in the end to the conclusion that it cannot be proved that anything less than Bismarck's methods would have secured the desired ends before 1871,[15] and that he was, in any case, the chief defender of peace in Europe after that date.[16] They are thus half-way towards an acceptance of the means as justified by the ends, and more than half-way, in some cases, to the view that as the 'great architect of European peace' Bismarck as diplomatist after 1871 did in practice satisfy the most exacting Liberal standards.

But the fact is that Bismarck was singularly unconvincing as the great architect of peace: foreign states were mainly conscious of the aggressive potentialities of his diplomacy. Peter Shuvalov, after seeing him in Berlin in May 1875, insinuated to Odo Russell that he thought Bismarck 'a little out of his mind at times'.[17] A considerable problem that faces the student of his later diplomacy is, indeed, to decide how far he was alarmed by nightmares of his own creation.[18] Both German and non-German historians of his Chancellorship have been too ready to accept his own alarmist interpretations of the foreign situation: and if many of his analyses of the intentions of foreign powers do not seem quite to tally with the available evidence the tendency has been to assume that the master diplomatist must have seen further than other people, or that the foreign sources are incomplete. This, however, is argument in a circle. Bismarck is judged to be right because he is the master diplomatist: he is the master diplomatist because he is right. His

[15] 'All the virtuosity of Bismarck's manipulation of the rival powers, his skill in the handling of men and his daring as well, were required to achieve the goal.' Franz Schnabel, 'The Bismarck Problem' in Hans Kohn, *op. cit.*, p. 71.

[16] Cf. Gerhard Ritter, *Europa und die Deutsche Frage* (1948), pp. 97–9.

[17] Lord Newton, *Lord Lyons*, ii, 78.

[18] Examples of Bismarck's tendency to be frightened by his own bogies—to exaggerate for domestic purposes a foreign danger, and later to be convinced of its reality—can be seen in his fear of 'the great Catholic conspiracy' of 1874–5, French preparations for a war of revenge (1875–7), Russian attack in 1879, and Gladstone's leadership of a revolutionary crusade in 1880.

judgments of foreign governments were in fact often wildly wrong. The selective publication of documents in the first six volumes of *Die Grosse Politik der Europäischen Kabinette,*[19] the basis of what we might call the Weimar phase of Bismarckian historiography, has done much to create this idealized picture of the shrewd, objective, Olympian statesman, with the 'uncanny sense of realities', and so on. The printing of a large percentage of the memoranda and despatches in which he gave admirable academic analyses of the international situation showed him at his best, and helped to satisfy the yearning of German writers and people for a justifiable hero in the depressing post-war years. No doubt the contemplation of a recent, triumphant, apparently serene, apparently infallible national leader was some assurance of future greatness, and it would have damaged this legend to have printed much of the correspondence in which Bismarck would be seen in angry, frustrating, day-to-day struggle with difficult colleagues and foreigners. For this more human, passionate, nerve-wracked figure historians have had to await further German material, and the investigation of foreign archives, particularly the British, French, and Austrian; a different, but not less interesting, figure appears, not without its own greatness.[20]

The tendency to speak of Bismarck as a disinterested mediator in other people's disputes ignores, of course, the extent to which

[19] Published in 1922, and covering the years 1871 to 1890. In the period covered by this volume (1879–81) there are two surprising gaps: from 5 January to 8 August 1879, when nothing at all is printed, and from January to June 1881, the period of the negotiation of the Three Emperors' Alliance, when only ten documents are printed. The first was a period of prolonged difference with Russia, the second with Austria. On the other hand the negotiation of the Austro-German alliance of 1879 is fully documented. It is difficult to avoid the conclusion that the editors preferred to dwell on Bismarck's triumphs, rather than on his less dignified struggles with adversity.

[20] Dr. W. Taffs, after studying the War-in-Sight crisis of 1875 in Odo Russell's papers, writes: 'A different Bismarck emerges, whose strange threats and inexplicable demands were inspired by terrors which were as real to his mind as they were exaggerated in fact. . . . That the rumours he circulated were without adequate foundation cannot be denied, but it is equally impossible to deny that he must have been receiving extraordinary reports and that he shaped his conduct accordingly. His complaint of ill-health and sleepless nights was not feigned, though he seems to have been unaware that his policy could only bring about the very state of affairs he wished to avoid.' (W. Taffs, *Ambassador to Bismarck, Lord Odo Russell* (1938), p. 105.)

Germany was directly responsible for the disputes in question, and even interested in preventing their settlement. All the major causes of tension in Europe after 1871 were in some measure the result of the formation of the German Empire, and of the determination of the German government not to surrender any of the recent gains. In place of the German Confederation, whose disunited, militarily weak, politically ineffective condition had placed, as Gervinus had noted, a buffer state on the French, Austrian, and Russian frontiers, there now appeared, tightening everyone's nerves, this vast and mobile armed power, pressing against the three frontiers. There was nothing altruistic in Bismarck's determination to keep the peace with France by preventing France from finding allies for a war of revenge. It is usual to say that Austria, driven out of Germany and Italy, found compensation in a policy of expansion in the Balkans; if this view exaggerates the novelty of Austria's Balkan activity it is nothing but the obvious truth as far as Germany is concerned, and it means that the Habsburg Monarchy, discredited in the eyes of its national minorities and debarred from any *grossdeutsch* solution, had somehow to be assisted, guided, and protected by Germany, and also prevented from seeking security in alternative alliances. It is even more true of Russia than of Austria that she had been turned out of Germany. The sense of responsibility for the peace of Europe which had so strong an influence on the minds of Alexander I and Nicholas I, and which still lingered as a tradition with Gorchakov and Alexander II in the 'seventies, was a challenge to Bismarck's own leadership of Europe; here again his effort to control and canalize Russian activities was anything but a mere genial gesture of disinterested friendliness.

In so far as the new Empire was genuinely threatened by its neighbours Bismarck's diplomacy was necessary in the name of security; and it would be entirely unrealistic to ignore the unusual personal problems that were bound to accompany his transition to any policy of peace. History has few examples of the successful warlord who was allowed to retire, and willing to retire, from the business of war; the element of greatness in his character which enabled him to forgo the personal gratification of continued military success could be demonstrated only by time, and if his conduct after 1870 had been entirely meek he would still have been thought in many quarters to be, in Disraeli's words in 1875, 'really another old Bonaparte again', who 'must be bridled'. He would also, in any circumstances, have had to contend with a fine aftermath of unavoidable hatred and jealousy on the part of both the enemies and friends of the 'sixties; and he would have had to disappoint friends and allies who had an exaggerated idea of his resources, and expected him to work diplomatic miracles on their behalf. Europe, however, needed time to get used to the new Reich, to convince itself that this fearsome new state could indeed become (as Bismarck certainly wished) a tranquillizing factor in international politics. He did less than justice to his own policy when he declared so roundly and so incorrectly that Europe was no more than a geographical expression; it was, in fact, too closely linked and interdependent to be indifferent to the sudden appearance of an incalculable conqueror of genius in its midst, and it desired nothing better after 1870 than to be able to believe that the new Germany was indeed satiated. Nothing could be more calculated than Bismarck's own conduct to destroy such a belief. The fact is that the real danger to his system did not come from his desire to keep Germany at the head of a combination of peacefully inclined states, or from the desire of any state or combination of states to attack Germany: it came above all from the effect of his political philosophy and tortuous diplomacy in keeping alive the profound uneasiness created by his policy in the 'sixties.

The underlying sense of insecurity which was the almost inevitable accompaniment of Germany's sudden new greatness did much to prevent any serious challenge to his diplomatic methods inside the Reich, and this absence of effective internal criticism no doubt accounts in part for his persistent underestimate of the influence of public opinion on the foreign affairs of other countries. He could safely ignore the language in which such contemporaries as Georg Gottfried Gervinus, Jakob Burckhardt, and Constantin Frantz deplored his triumph over the principles of morality, justice, and even stability in international affairs. There is a sense, however, in which public opinion was a determining factor in his policy on many occasions; although he showed great skill in creating support through his control of influential organs of the press he was bound at times to follow, and even to be carried away by, the passion and semi-hysteria which he had himself done so much to arouse. The German people shared with him a sense of the vulnerability of the new Reich with three great powers as neighbours; the startling success of his methods provided a handsome testimony to the profits of astute diplomacy and an effective army, but it did nothing to remove the fear that these methods might be turned in time against the new state. There was a widespread consciousness of foreign enmity which fostered dangerous tendencies to isolationism and persecution mania. A sense of the uniqueness of Germany's position, of its strength and unpopularity, of the jealousies of neighbours who were, nevertheless, believed to be its inferiors in energy, courage, and efficiency, helped to complete the rout of the German Liberals, and fostered a growing arrogance and assertiveness which gave some popular emotional backing to the rather tentative expansionism of the 'eighties. But it was as a defender of the new Empire against internal and external foes that Bismarck appeared indispensable to his countrymen.[21]

So, as the years went by after 1871, the mere absence of war certainly strengthened belief in his peaceful aims, but doubts remained. His personality, which became ever more familiar to diplomatists and the public as the years went by, did not lose its disconcerting features. The particular brand of prudence which commended itself to him was of a short-term character, amounting to little more than an endless series of carefully-planned manœuvres to neutralize or isolate immediate or potential rivals; he seemed unable to visualize any state of international society in which security could exist apart from this unsleeping day-to-day vigilance, or to regard peace, if we may adapt Clausewitz's dictum, as anything but the continuance of war by other means. He was the victim, in part, of his own reputation, in part of his own achievements; but

---

[21] 'The modern man of power in Germany, however, as we have ultimately experienced him with terror, was still far from completed. There were still several intermediate stages between the Goethe period and the Bismarck period and between the Bismarck period and the Hitler period.' F. Meinecke, *The German Catastrophe* (Harvard, 1950), p. 9.

mainly perhaps he was a victim of his own personality, and of his deliberate choice of political methods. His rejection in the 'fifties of the Liberal solution of the problem of unification had been the result of hard thinking based on a careful study of the alignment of political forces in the Germany of his day; but it had also been the natural expression of the ruthless, cynical, pugnacious side of his character, which undoubtedly found much emotional and intellectual satisfaction in self-dramatiza-tion of himself in the rôle of the fighter. His conviction in the 'sixties that every ideal should be subordinated to the needs of the state, the will-power which enabled him to drive relentlessly through the obstructions which even his supporters felt it neces-sary at times to place in his path, were also evidence of political genius forced along certain lines of action by well-marked limitations of character and temperament. For such a man peace could hardly be visualized except in terms of military science; the abandonment of the policy of seeking national greatness through aggressive war must be followed by the em-ployment of military strength to defend the newly-won fortress against all comers. He was unable to carry his analysis of the reasons why Germany needed peace much beyond this point: it was enough that wars were expensive, success not certain, further increases of territory embarrassing—in short, that there was a limit to the profits of forceful acquisitiveness which the astute politician should be able to recognize in due time. For the more positive case for peace—the view that the non-military weapons of persuasion were adequate, if suitably developed and generally accepted, to solve all the outstanding problems of European international relations—he could scarcely conceal his impatience and contempt.[22]

It was, however, just this conception that gave a label to Gladstone's programme of foreign policy. The 'Concert of Europe' seemed to many continental statesmen a mere phrase,

[22] Meinecke, while pointing out that Machiavellianism was not confined to Ger-many, adds: 'Specifically German, however, was the frankness and nakedness of the German power-state and Machiavellism, its hard and deliberate formulation as a principle of conduct', and the pleasure taken in its reckless consequences'. Even in this critical mood, however, Meinecke and other German writers who stress the peaceful nature of Bismarck's diplomacy after 1871 tend to ignore the

a high-sounding nothing reminiscent of the Emperor Alexander's call to the righteous in 1815; and Gladstone, a bewildering figure to most of them, did not make it any more precise. In the ordinary language of continental diplomacy the Concert was something which existed when the great powers sat round a conference table, or found it expedient or convenient to join in collective action; there was a Concert of Europe when the action of the great powers was concerted, and when it was not there was not; any more formal arrangement seemed to be neither expedient nor practicable. Gladstone certainly read more into the phrase, but his programme did not appear to distinguish between the Concert as a tutelage of the great powers over the smaller, and the Concert as a means of preserving the peace of Europe by preventing war between the great powers themselves. In the former sense the Concert had been a reality ever since 1815, and as this period had seen no general European war comparable with those of Napoleon or the eighteenth century it was possible to assume that the Concert had preserved peace between the greater powers as well. But the Concert contained no machinery for coercing or overawing the aggressive big state; smaller powers might be sufficiently cowed to adopt the proposals of a conference of their greater neighbours, and when this happened the Concert could be said to function, but if a great power were not prepared to accept the views of its neighbours a mere majority vote in an international conference would not bind it. The London conference kept the peace between Schleswig-Holstein and the Danes in 1852, but the Vienna conference failed to keep it between the great powers in 1853. As long as Europe remembered the horrors of the Napoleonic wars it remained, for the most part, at peace, and therefore in concert; but it was peace that maintained the Concert, and not the Concert that maintained peace.

Gladstone's basic ideas on foreign policy were formed in the

psychological heritage of his earlier policy: either to see in his mere abstention from war a positive, and by implication, deliberate, contribution to peace, as if the earlier war-making was a sin that had been atoned by 'good service to the Western community of nations' (*op. cit.*, p. 14), or to ignore the connexion altogether, and simply praise him as the honest broker in disputes for which Germany had no interest or responsibility (cf. Gerhard Ritter, *op. cit.*, p. 99). For Meinecke's earlier views, see *Die Idee der Staatsräson* (1929 edn.), pp. 511, 518–23.

'forties and 'fifties, when he and Bismarck and their obstreperous contemporary Karl Marx were men of a new generation who added to the accident of genius a growing dissatisfaction with the conservative achievements of the Metternich era. All three were just of an age in their early manhood to embody the new political exuberance which succeeded the spiritual defeatism of the post-Napoleonic era. A generation of freedom from foreign menace had strengthened the nerves of European peoples and allowed them to turn their restless minds to the contemplation of their own wrongs and virtues; social criticism and rapid economic change, new religious movements and demands for political fulfilment in a liberal or liberal-nationalist form were found in nearly every part of the continent. The period that produced the *Watch on the Rhine*, the 1848 revolutions, and the Crimean and Italian wars of the 'fifties can hardly be regarded as one of complete stability and peace; but it was one in which the best and most energetic minds were passionately seeking the betterment of their neighbours, and in which war could be justified only if it served the same ends.

> Let it flame or fade, and the war roll down like a wind,
> We have proved we have hearts in a cause, we are noble still.

Gladstone's conscience allowed him to support the British government in the early stages of the Crimean War, for he believed that Russia had challenged the 'public law of Europe'.

The peculiar quality of Gladstone's views on foreign affairs is, however, a product of English party politics, and it was the fact that his interest in external affairs was aroused intermittently but powerfully by moral issues (wrongdoing abroad or the condoning of it at home by his colleagues or opponents) which gave it, to continental observers, its puzzling emotionalism.[23] The most complete exposition of his programme came in

[23] 'Of the various and important incidents of my life which associated me almost unawares with foreign affairs in Greece (1850) in the Neapolitan kingdom (1851) and in the Balkan Peninsula and the Turkish Empire (1853) I will only say that they all contributed to forward the action of those home causes, more continuous in their operation, which, without in any way effacing my old sense of reverence for the past, determined for me, by the process I have endeavoured to describe, my place in the present, and my direction towards the future.' ('My earlier political opinions', by W. E. Gladstone, 16 July 1892, B.M. Add. MSS. 44790, fol. 64).

the two series of election speeches which he made to his con-
stituents in Midlothian in the winter of 1879–80, and it was,
incidentally and by implication, a criticism of the diplomatic
practice of foreign governments; directly, however, it was a
majestic indictment of Disraeli at the bar of Gladstone's long-
established convictions. His foreign policy is, in short, better
understood in the light of his earlier contacts with British
external relations than with the contemporary foreign field of
1879 and 1880. In this sense there were perhaps four main and
distinct sources of ideas in the Midlothian speeches.

As early as 1841, when his doubts as to British policy in the
first Chinese war had caused him to hesitate about joining Peel's
administration, he had begun to display scepticism as to the
necessity and morality of war,[24] and this had brought him in the
'fifties closely into sympathy with Richard Cobden and John
Bright. But he was not a pacifist; he differed from Cobden in
supporting the government in the earlier phases of the Crimean
war, and again when he joined Cobden's old enemy, Palmerston, in the Whig government of 1859. On this matter he was
not a doctrinaire, and although he shared with Cobden an
awareness of the psychological factors which might drive his
countrymen into unnecessary war he was very far from claiming
that war in itself was unnecessary. He was not prepared, like
Cobden, to make the preservation of peace the supreme preoccupation of his foreign policy; nevertheless he had been
sufficiently closely identified with the peace movement for his
attitude in this matter to have great importance in the 'seventies, when Bismarck's advertising of the philosophy of force was
beginning to affect the nerves of Europe.

A second and more important source of his ideas on foreign
policy was the long-drawn-out controversy over the limits of
intervention, with which Palmerston was for long associated.
The fact that such a controversy could become a major issue in
English politics was in itself an expression of the lack of a sense
of urgency which prevented clear thinking about many of the

[24] 'Colonial subjects, as I have shown, had made a first breach in my Toryism'
(*ibid.*, fol. 44), but of his threatened resignation in February 1842 he remarks,
'undoubtedly in this proceeding I was absolutely without comprehension of the
political situation, and acted like a schoolboy, which indeed I still was to no small
extent' (fol. 48).

country's external problems. It was easy to make a case against
a policy of 'meddling' over an incident such as Don Pacifico's
compensation in 1850; but the continued popularity of Palmerston's vigorous diplomacy was due to the general acceptance of the belief that he was a robust defender of freedom
abroad and of legitimate British interests, and with these aims
Gladstone himself could hardly disagree. (The events of the
'fifties had, however, deepened his conviction that the only
satisfactory basis for intervention in the affairs of other states
was in collaboration with other powers in the maintenance of
the public life of Europe. This was, in the best sense, a European outlook, and it was an essential part of his political thinking that his own country should not demand advantages which
could not be reconciled with the interests of Europe as a whole.)
It was of course open to continental critics to argue that Britain
had already provided herself with an excessive share of the
world's possessions, and had every intention of retaining it. But
the familiar imputations of hypocrisy were really beside the
point, for the country seemed ready enough to lower tariff
barriers, starve its armed forces, disembarrass itself of colonial
possessions, and accept with respect the popular aspirations of its
neighbours to liberty and national independence. The domestic problem was to decide how far the country should go in
offering active assistance to such movements in Europe; and
Gladstone found the answer in the maintenance of the European Concert. Thus he denied in 1877 that Britain's intervention in the Crimean war in Turkey's defence had been due
either to self-interest or to chivalry; the latter theory 'provokes
the question, how far it is to reach; and whether we, of all mankind, have taken out a general roving commission of knight
errantry—"To ride abroad redressing human wrongs".' No:
the British government was led into the war neither through
'cynical selfishness' nor 'high-flown Quixotry'; the policy 'was
that of repressing an offence against the public law of Europe,
but only by the united authority of the Powers of Europe. Public
law and European concert were in truth its twin watchwords'.[25]
   The European Concert was in this sense his contribution as a

[25] W. E. Gladstone, *Gleanings of Past Years, 1875-8* (1879), pp. 103-4. Cf. Erich
Eyck, *Gladstone* (1938), pp. 211-31.

practical statesman to the problem of promiscuous intervention—for noble or ignoble ends—in continental affairs; he
believed that in concert, but only in concert, with other powers
could Britain play a part appropriate both to her responsibilities
and to her strength. Her responsibility in his eyes derived from
the happy circumstances that had made her the incontestable
protagonist of European Liberalism; she was a member of the
European family of nations, and must play her part in its public
life. Seeing political issues as he so often did in moral terms,
he usually found the desirable course indicating itself clearly to
him as one of right against wrong, justice or freedom against
oppression; moreover the action of the European powers in
unity would automatically make articulate the public voice of
Europe, and the intentions of any government which separated
itself from this concert of powers would be automatically
suspect. When this veto on independent action was found to
exclude 'knight errantry' many of his admirers were chilled and
puzzled, and it cannot be denied that the unrestrained fervour
of his public denunciations of wrongdoing contrasts strangely
at times with his circumspection in action. He believed in the
existence of a European public opinion to which appeal could
be made; publicity was a legitimate and practical weapon in such
circumstances, and one which did not necessarily involve any
threat or use of force by his own government (although he recognized that he must use this weapon more sparingly in office than
in opposition, if only because of the practical difficulty of separating his personal responsibility from that of his government).

The third source of his ideas on foreign policy was his conception of liberty. During the half-century before 1880 he had
become a progressively more ardent admirer and supporter of
political freedom in every sphere; after opposing both parliamentary reform and negro emancipation he was driven by
a noble indignation to speak in support of the Chinese against
war and opium, of the Neapolitan prisoners against their
government, of the Bulgarians against their Turkish masters.
It is probably correct to say, as Mr. J. L. Hammond has suggested, that of the three revolutions in progress in his lifetime it
was the one spreading self-government in Europe which captured his imagination; he was drawn into the second, spreading

democracy in Great Britain, as a result of his discovery after 1865 that the arguments which had failed to move Conservative Europe had a most powerful effect on great political audiences in his own country; he never saw the significance of the third, which was transforming industry and social life in England, Germany, and America.[26] The readiness of English political thought at this period to assume that the best interests of society could be attained by the mere freeing of the individual will made it at times incomprehensible to the continent, which was more often concerned with the search for organized power as a basis for national emancipation or national aggrandizement. While English Liberalism was a formula for the maintenance of liberty, continental Liberals were primarily concerned with its attainment, and found little to help them in the assumption that the preservation and extension of liberty through non-violent struggle was the essential feature of the Liberal creed. The difference, however, was more a matter of objectives than of principles; Gladstone was ready enough to praise freemen fighting for liberty and the English model was widely respected on the continent. But it was inevitable that the continental Liberals should underestimate, and the English Liberal exaggerate, the efficacy of non-violent weapons in the struggle against reaction.

Gladstone's Midlothian speeches were, however, in the fourth place, profoundly influenced by his controversy with Disraeli over external policy during the 'seventies. The most surprising feature of this controversy to a later generation is the narrowness of the ground on which the titanic duel between the two was fought. Gladstone had resigned from the leadership of the Liberal party after his electoral defeat in 1874, and although he returned to the forefront of English politics with his attack on the Conservative government in 1876 he remained a free-lance until after the Liberal victory in April 1880. His policy during the late 'seventies was not always to the liking of the Liberal leaders in Parliament,[27] and as Disraeli also had some difficulty

[26] Cf. J. L. Hammond, *Gladstone and the Irish Question* (1938), ch. v.

[27] 'There is no fear of a return from Elba. He is played out. . . . He has done two good things; he has damaged the Government much and himself still more.' Harcourt to Sir Charles Dilke, 10 October 1876 (A. G. Gardiner, *The Life of Sir William Harcourt* (1921), i, 312).

in imposing his views on his followers the struggle between the two took from the start the character of a personal duel, and tended to obscure the substantial measure of agreement which existed between the two parties. No one can read the letters and speeches of Gladstone during the last months of 1876 without realizing that in his attacks on Disraeli a profound and un-shakable distrust of the Prime Minister formed the starting-point of all his criticisms; it is equally clear that Disraeli had abandoned long since any hope of convincing Gladstone, or even of understanding him.

Yet the specific differences of party programme on which their rivalry had been based during the previous thirty years supply little to explain the intensity of this personal animosity. Much that was incomprehensible to the continent in the English party struggle is indeed explained by the fact that the strength of personal animosities at this period tended to be in inverse, rather than in direct, proportion to the differences in party programme. The basic conservatism of all classes and policies drastically limited the possible grounds of rivalry between parties and individuals; when the struggle became so often a series of manœuvres to obtain exclusive credit for the acceptance of inevitable innovations of a reformist character to meet the slow maturing of public opinion it was difficult to criticize anything except the ability or the sincerity of one's opponents, or the motives determining their actions. It hap-pened also that the contrasting gifts and styles of the two states-men made each an admirable foil for the other; these accidents of manner and physiognomy did much to dramatize and sim-plify the issues in the public mind. In the 'seventies Disraeli, ailing, impassive, and sharp-tongued, had become the em-bodiment of cynicism, or, to his followers, of good sense; the robust and still handsome Gladstone, with his bursts of splen-did but impromptu and sometimes slightly confused eloquence, gave glimpses of a loftier morality, from which good sense seemed, to his rival, to be sadly divorced.

The last phase of this personal struggle in the 'seventies was concerned mainly with questions of foreign and imperial policy. The defeat of Gladstone's great administration in 1874 was due primarily to the alienation of many vested interests by six years of domestic reform, and the government's record abroad formed, perhaps, only a subordinate cause of discontent. Disraeli's success was nevertheless largely the result of his greater skill in anticipating and accommodating himself to tendencies in public opinion which particularly affected foreign and colonial affairs. The overwhelming military strength which Germany had revealed in her defeat of France in 1870, and the success of Russia in repudiating the Black Sea clauses of the Treaty of Paris in 1871, were a reminder of the existence of powerful, and possibly hostile, forces on the continent, and ensured a cool reception for the courageous pacifism which culminated in the embarrassing Alabama award in 1873. Public opinion was turning also on colonial questions; the negative but well-intentioned policy of the Liberal leaders, with the conventional disclaimer of any desire to hold the colonies by brute force, allowed Disraeli to secure to the Conservative Party practically the full strength of the growing—and in a party sense unappropriated—imperial sentiment. What we can see today, however, is that the innovations were slight, and that Disraeli had once more dished the Whigs without promising any very significant changes in external policy. There were already Liberal imperialists in 1874, and Disraeli's mild and admirable sentiments on the subject of the empire in his Crystal Palace speech in 1872 contained no trace of the flamboyancy later associated with Jingoism; his choice of Lord Derby as Foreign Secretary was sufficient proof that no adventures were being planned. The controversies which arose over the Near Eastern question from 1876 to 1880 appeared at first sight to turn on more fundamental issues than those over which the two rivals had struggled during the previous thirty years. Yet neither desired to abandon the broader lines of national policy on the issue in question: and each certainly displayed his old skill in erecting, on the narrow issue of policy which separated them, a dramatic, and apparently comprehensive, statement of policy which commanded a wide measure of popular support.

British policy in the Near East, for half a century before 1875, had been based on the necessity of protecting the route to India by maintaining a Turkish state sufficiently strong and extensive to withstand Russian military and political influence;

but this general aim allowed scope for considerable divergence of opinion as to the nature, and effectiveness, of any attack that Russia might make. It had always been flexible enough to allow for maximum and minimum programmes—the maximum, the maintenance of Turkish sovereignty in its widest extent, being the one for which Britain would struggle diplomatically, but for which she would not necessarily fight. The minimum for which she would fight, as defined by Derby in his memorandum of 6 May 1877, was a Turkish state controlling Constantinople and the Straits and the Moslem provinces, Turkish and Arab, and it would have been impossible for Gladstone to have carried the Liberal Party with him in a demand for the abandonment of this minimum programme. British governments of all parties had made continuous efforts since the 'thirties to induce the Porte to reform and modernize its administration, and had shown that a consciousness of the defects of Turkish government had accompanied the determination to keep a Turkish state in existence; from time to time British governments had acquiesced, more or less unwillingly, in the detaching of provinces from Turkey in Europe to form the new states of Greece, Serbia, and the Principalities. The urgency of the Turkish question for the British in the late 'seventies was due to the fact that the process of Christian emancipation appeared to be threatening the strategic security of Constantinople itself, and if Gladstone had demanded, as he appeared for a time to do, the destruction of Turkey in Europe there would certainly have been at last a fundamental issue of policy between him and Disraeli. But his demand in the autumn of 1876 for the expulsion of the Turks 'bag and baggage' turned out to be a demand, not for the expulsion of Turks from Europe but merely for the expulsion of Turkish officials from Bosnia and Bulgaria, the latter the scene of Turkish massacres in the previous May and June; on subsequent occasions he made it clear in various ways that in spite of his unqualified abhorrence of the Turk, 'the one great anti-human specimen of humanity', he was not demanding the extinction of Turkish rule over, for example, the Sultan's shockingly misgoverned Moslem subjects, or even over the Christians of Macedonia. Even in Bulgaria the Turks were to retain their 'titular sovereignty'. Although there can be no doubt that he would have strongly preferred a more thorough-going solution of the Eastern question he was prepared to recognize the practical difficulties of such a solution; but he had discovered, a few weeks before Disraeli, that the emancipation of the Bulgarians was a political innovation for which public opinion was ripe and which could nevertheless be reconciled with the traditional lines of British foreign policy. Disraeli on the other hand had badly misjudged the situation. He committed himself in July 1876 to the assertion that the 'atrocity' stories were exaggerated and that there was accordingly no need for change; it was indeed some weeks before he discovered how effectively Gladstone had dished the Tories.[28] Within a few months, however, the government had adjusted itself to the new situation, and the solution finally secured by the British representatives at the Congress of Berlin in 1878—the Turkish frontier to run along the Balkan mountains with an autonomous Bulgarian state to the north—was proclaimed to the world by the Conservatives as a triumph for their policy, and by Liberals as proof that 'the bag and baggage policy triumphed at Berlin'.

Thus if we look for the real grounds of difference between Gladstone and Disraeli during this crisis we shall find them once again in genuine mistrust and misunderstanding of each other's character and methods rather than in any fundamental difference of opinion as to the ultimate objectives of British policy. The main specific item in his final public indictment of Disraeli's policy was that he had broken the Concert of Europe by his rejection of the Berlin Memorandum in May 1876; this evidence of the disunity of the powers had encouraged the Turks to refuse to carry out reforms and Russia had been compelled to fight an unnecessary war in 1877 in order to secure Bulgarian emancipation.[29] Gladstone put his case unequivocally

[28] 'Mr. Gladstone had both displayed a sure instinct as to the most effective method of public approach and at the same time did justice to his own burning and innate hatred of all cruelty and oppression.' J. Morley, *The Life of William Ewart Gladstone* (1904), iii, 352. On the whole crisis, D. Harris, *Britain and the Bulgarian Horrors of 1876* (1939).

[29] In private he attributed Disraeli's conduct to hatred of Christians. 'What he hates is Christian liberty and reconstruction.' 'The Jews in the East bitterly hate the Christians.' 'Disraeli may be willing to risk his government for his Judaic feeling,' etc. *Gladstone*, iii, 351–3.

in the first important speech in his Midlothian campaign, delivered at Edinburgh on 25 November 1879.

The point upon which we quarrelled was this: whether coercion was under any circumstances to be applied to Turkey to bring about the better government of that country. . . . But there is an important limitation. We have never given countenance to single-handed attempts to coerce Turkey. We felt that single-handed attempts to coerce Turkey would probably lead to immediate bloodshed and calamity, with great uncertainty as to the issue. The coercion we recommended was coercion by the united authority of Europe, and we always contended that in the case where the united authority of Europe was brought into action there was no fear of having to proceed to actual coercion.[30]

In devising a distinctive and workable foreign policy to place before the electorate in the Midlothian speeches Gladstone had to solve many problems. As it was difficult to say whether the Gladstone or the Disraeli programme had really triumphed at the Congress of Berlin, he could neither repudiate what had been done, nor offer, for the time being, to do more. His policy, moreover, had to be largely his own; the official Liberal opposition, under the leadership of Granville and Hartington, was still decidedly lukewarm in its support of the ex-leader, and found it difficult to share either his confidence in Russia's good-will or his suspicions of Austria's intentions. In other directions a wholehearted repudiation of Conservative policy presented difficulties. Among the younger Liberals, such as Rosebery and Dilke, there was considerable sympathy for the new colonial movement, and although on the whole all sections were prepared to be unpleasant to the Turks the Liberals could not very well be more minatory in tone than Salisbury had been in his attempt to force reforms on the Porte since the Congress. Thus, on the face of things, it would not be easy for a new government to attempt any considerable reversal of Tory policy in the Near East, however much they might like to do so; the official opposition had not even had any very convincing general programme of foreign policy to put forward, and in practice had had to limit its criticism to a series of more or less disconnected attacks on details of the Conservative foreign policy.

[30] W. E. Gladstone, *Political Speeches in Scotland* (1880), i, 53.

There was, therefore, a natural tendency for Gladstone to emphasize the general principles of foreign policy which had been so much in his mind during the past four years, and which seemed to him to summarize the lessons of his forty years' experience of public affairs. But for those who failed to find in his oratory any echo of their own ideas the speeches inevitably appeared a mere repetition of personal invective which had lost by this stage any original merits of spontaneity or relevance. An anonymous versifier wrote at the time in a dialect appropriate to the occasion:

> Has he been reivit? ye weel may speir—
> Ay, o' the place o' the Queen's Premier: . . .
> But Willie was reivit lang years syne,
> Sae he suldna come yammerin' in seventy-nine!

And Disraeli at the end of November 1879 could find little sense in 'his wearisome rhetoric . . . a waste of powder and shot'.[31]

Gladstone introduced the idea of a 'Concert of Europe' in his Edinburgh speech on 25 November 1879, and this was followed by the elaboration of his six 'right principles of foreign policy' at West Calder on 27 November. The first principle was good government at home 'to reserve the strength of the Empire, to reserve the expenditure of that strength, for great and worthy occasions abroad'. The second was to preserve peace 'especially to the Christian nations of the world'. To these may be added the sixth principle, a love of freedom. 'There should be a sympathy with freedom, a desire to give it scope, founded not only upon visionary ideas, but upon the long experience of many generations within the shores of this happy isle, that in freedom you lay the firmest foundations both of liberty and order; the firmest foundations for the development of individual character, and the best provision for the happiness of the nation at large.' The love of freedom, however, was only to inspire foreign policy 'subject to all the limitations that I have described'. These limitations, set forth as the remaining principles, give us therefore the essence of Gladstone's policy.

[31] 'The Hot Trod,' (September 1879), in *The Gladstone Rule* by 'An Outsider', pp. 11, 12; W. F. Monypenny and G. E. Buckle, *The Life of Benjamin Disraeli* (1929 edn.), ii, 1375.

In my opinion the third sound principle is this—to strive to cultivate and maintain, ay, to the very uttermost, what is called the Concert of Europe; to keep the Powers of Europe in union together. And why? Because by keeping all in union together you neutralize and fetter and bind up the selfish aims of each. I am not here to flatter either England or any of them. They have selfish aims, as, unfortunately, we in late years have too sadly shown that we too have selfish aims; but then common action is fatal to selfish aims. Common action means common objects; and the only objects for which you can unite together the Powers of Europe are objects connected with the common good of them all.

The fourth principle was to avoid needless and entangling engagements, and the fifth,

to acknowledge the equal rights of all nations. You may sympathize with one nation more than another. Nay, you must sympathize in certain circumstances with one nation more than another. . . . But in point of right all are equal, and you have no right to set up a system under which one of them is to be placed under moral suspicion and espionage, or to be made the constant object of invective.[32]

Gladstone's opponents cannot, perhaps, be blamed if, with his denunciations of the Turks since 1876 fresh in their ears, they chose to regard the latter sentiment as hypocritical; within a few weeks, following a fancied disparagement of himself by the Emperor of Austria, he was to expatiate on the general unworthiness of that country, with the excellent example of 'moral suspicion and invective': 'there is not an instance, there is not a spot upon the whole map, where you can lay your finger and say, "There Austria did good".'[33]

He professed to see no inconsistency in these pronouncements. Attacks on a foreign government were inexpedient if one were in office; but he was a free-lance; he could therefore speak his mind. He wrote on 9 April to Lord Reay:

[32] *Political Speeches*, i, 115–17.

[33] In the fourth Midlothian speech, at Edinburgh, 17 March 1880. In the printed version of the speech there is more than a page of criticism on these lines. 'Austria has been the steady, unflinching foe of freedom of every country in Europe. Russia, I am sorry to say, has been the foe of freedom too, but in Russia there is one exception—Russia has been the friend of Slavonic freedom' . . . 'in the Congress of Berlin, Austria resisted the extension of freedom', etc. There were further criticisms of Austria in later speeches. *Political Speeches*, ii, 40–1, 263–7, 277–80, 320.

... I think it my duty though I am simply an individual and neither a minister nor a party leader, to cherish respect and sympathy for every foreign state, without exception or distinction.

But, when there is apparent reason to believe that they are prosecuting schemes adverse to liberty beyond their own borders, then, as I have tried in former times, so I will try now to raise up moral forces as far as in me lies, to defeat their aims. . . .

Since I have done my best—little as it may be—to counteract the designs of a British Government, when hostile in my view to liberty abroad, I certainly cannot be more reticent in the case of a foreign state.

He ended the letter with a rousing declaration which would have confirmed Bismarck's gloomiest suspicions of his revolutionary intentions:

Liberty is what I wish to defend, and I care not who is the assailant. . . . My mottoes are 'Hands Off' and 'the soil for the people'; these I think to be principles of law and order, honour and repute, of safety and peace for us all. Beyond this my desire is that we should be the best friends possible with all the world.[34]

But there was always a duality in Gladstone's statements, even if he refused to admit inconsistency. The liberty-loving freelance had also to sketch a programme for his party, if not for himself; and it was for the most part with a due sense of his responsibility as future minister that he was speaking in Midlothian, in spite of tactical denials. In the six principles of West Calder the case against Disraeli-Toryism, as Gladstone understood it, was clearly stated; it was amplified and illustrated by sundry other passages throughout the campaign. From one aspect it can be regarded as an attempt to assert a 'European' in opposition to an imperialistic policy, although here again it was Disraeli's handling of imperial affairs, his bellicose language and selfish nationalism, which formed the real ground of attack. He was careful to dissociate himself from the ultra-pacificism and isolationism of the Manchester School, but he also challenged the ideal of splendid imperial isolation—a negative attitude towards European affairs and a corresponding development of imperial ties—which Disraeli had sketched

[34] Gladstone to Lord Reay, 9 April 1880; Gladstone Papers, B.M. Add. MSS. 44463.

in 1872. Liberalism was ready to act on all important occasions in concert with the other powers, and to go further in a just cause than any Tory contemplated. 'However deplorable wars may be, they are among the necessities of our condition', he said in the fourth Midlothian speech, 'and there are times when justice, when faith, when the welfare of mankind, require a man not to shrink from the responsibility of undertaking them.'[35]

In attacking the new imperialism he criticized more particularly what he considered the excessive fears of Russian threats to India and the route to India, and the likelihood that for reasons of defence, the protection of victims of Turkish oppression, or less worthy motives, Britain would be led to acquire control in the Middle East. Throughout the Eastern crisis indeed he had shown curiously little interest in the government or misgovernment of the non-Christian subjects of the Sultan, saying in 1877 in an article on Egypt that though 'the grievances of the people are indeed great' it was best for them to remain under Turkish rule, and expressing faith in the Turk and suspicion of European 'liberating' efforts in this sphere which contrasted strangely with his abuse of the Turks and support of Russian advance where Bulgaria was concerned. In regard to Egypt he had protested against any attempts to hasten partition: 'I have heard of men on board ship, thought to be moribund, whose clothes were sold by auction in their hearing by their shipmates. And thus, in the hearing of the Turk, we are now stimulated to divide his inheritance. . . . I object to our making him or anybody else a victim to the insatiable maw of these stage-playing British interests.' He had also questioned the whole strategic theory on which Conservative policy was based. 'Suppose the very worst. The Canal is stopped. And what then? . . . It seems to be forgotten by many, that there is a route to India round the Cape of Good Hope.'[36] In the Midlothian campaign came the final stage in the development of this line of argument on imperial questions. England must maintain her power in India as a capital demand upon her national honour, but she had no

[35] *Political Speeches*, ii, 30–1.
[36] 'Aggression on Egypt and Freedom in the East', reprinted from *The Nineteenth Century*, August 1877: *Gleanings of Past Years, 1851–77: Foreign*, pp. 352–4, 364–5.

interest in India except the well-being of India itself; the question, who should have supreme rule in India, was, by the laws of right, an Indian question; India was actually a source of weakness in military affairs. 'The material greatness of our nation lies within the compass of these islands, and is, except in trifling particulars, independent of all and every sort of political dominion beyond them.' 'Whatever is to be done', he said in the first Midlothian speech, 'in defending and governing these vast colonies and their teeming millions; in protecting that unmeasured commerce; in relation to the enormous responsibilities of India—whatever is to be done, must be done by the force derived from you and from your fellow-electors, throughout the land, and from you and from the citizens and people of this country.'

In all this speechmaking there was no hostile reference to Bismarck, no criticism of his aims or methods, and, indeed, no indication that Gladstone regarded the German Chancellor as in any way an obstacle to his plans for the pacification of Europe.[37] In fact, however, Gladstone's programme was highly distasteful to the German Chancellor, who thoroughly regretted the Liberal victory in April 1880, although he was glad when Lord Granville, and not Lord Derby, went to the Foreign Office. This distrust was due in part to misunderstanding of Gladstone's intentions; it was influenced by jealousy of a rival claimant to the leadership of Europe; but it was mainly caused by a quite clearsighted view of the threat that Gladstone was unknowingly offering to Bismarck's immediate plans.

In the first place, Gladstone's Concert, if carried into effect, would completely frustrate the alliance plans on which Bismarck had now embarked after so much painful thought and emotional conflict. For Gladstone, in his strenuous condemnation of Disraeli's conduct, had attacked repeatedly the isolated action of one or more powers, even for what might be considered laudable ends; the Concert would function as an informal consultative body of all the powers, handling each

[37] He wrote, however, to Lord Reay on 9 April: 'Were I disposed to search for causes of complaint, I might find them in the violent articles of inspired papers in Germany.—But for me, except when a practical purpose is in view, all these are in diplomatic phrase *non avenus*' (Gladstone Papers, *ibid.*).

European question as it arose by *ad hoc* discussion, and finding a solution of differences between the great powers themselves in (presumably) the good fellowship and spirit of mutual concession which this friendly collaboration would foster. This view was by no means so utopian as many of Gladstone's critics suggested. He had grasped the point that Cobden had urged so persistently in the period of Anglo-French panics in the early 'sixties: that many international rivalries were the result of nothing more than the vicious spiral of reciprocal fears and defiances, and would disappear if statesmen on both sides resolutely declined to make bogies of each other. Accordingly Gladstone had throughout the Eastern crisis and his Midlothian speeches refused to be panicked by the Conservative fears of a Russian threat to British interests. But if this attitude seemed dangerous even to Englishmen it was bound to seem completely unrealistic to Bismarck, who was quite convinced that such problems as the French desire for *revanche* or Austro-Russian rivalry in the Balkans were no figment of his imagination, and who was in no mood to welcome the view that the 'selfish aims' of the powers would melt away in the mere comradeship of a common mission—such as the coercion of the Porte.

Gladstone's programme was also unwelcome to Bismarck because it seemed to threaten his immediate plans for the liquidation of the Near Eastern crisis, and for the establishment of satisfactory treaty relations with the Russian government. It was not merely that Gladstone was apparently prepared to reverse Conservative policy in certain directions: such changes, although they might necessitate a rearrangement of the pieces, would, if based on some rational conception of national interest, make no excessive demands on Bismarck's skill in controlling the European chess-board. But Gladstone did not seem to him to be a rational being; he found him incalculable, emotional, ready to embark on some erratic course guided only by arbitrary affections and dislikes—at the best an unpractical idealist, at the worst the typical Liberal politician, ever ready to catch votes by irresponsible promises. Bismarck accordingly began to lay his plans to defeat the Gladstonian policy from the moment the success of the new government in England was assured.

CHAPTER II

The Concert Opens

1. PRELUDE BY GRANVILLE

IT was known by the end of the first week of April 1880 that the Conservative government had been defeated. There was some delay on the Queen's part in summoning Gladstone to form a ministry and it needed both Hartington's refusal and his somewhat unconvincing assurances as to the soundness of Gladstone's foreign policy to bring her to the unpalatable decision. 'I alluded to Mr. Gladstone's apparent leaning towards Russia, which Lord Hartington denied, saying he merely objected to the government not taking the line he thought they ought against Russian influence,' she wrote in her diary on 22 April. Accordingly it was Gladstone who met Parliament on 20 May, Prime Minister for the second time at the age of seventy-one, with a majority that left no doubt as to the country's verdict on the Midlothian programme.

The new Foreign Secretary was Lord Granville, an urbane and respected survivor of the first Gladstone administration, too courteous and conventional to make much headway with the inexplicable German or even the insufferable Turk, but a willing, if slightly embarrassed, agent for the mighty task of European conciliation that Gladstone had set himself. For although the Midlothian policy in action began and ended with the intransigence of the Sultan it continued in Gladstone's mind to be charged with wide and lofty ideals: 'the high office of bringing Europe into concert, and keeping Europe in concert, is an office specially pointed out for our country to perform,' as he said during the campaign.[1] Even when all this had faded into the light of common day it meant that the new government desired friendship with all, and was willing to act on the

[1] Gladstone, *Political Speeches in Scotland*, ii, 221.

assumption that England had a special responsibility, in view of the disruptive tactics of the Disraeli administration, in removing obstacles to the agreement of the powers over Near Eastern questions. If the creation of a genuine Concert had been the real goal of Liberal policy Gladstone might have achieved it at the expense of his Turkish programme; but events were to show that Gladstone, in addition to a very vague understanding of the real stresses and strains between the continental powers, had every intention of making the Turk do his duty, even in face of the reluctance of the other powers to co-operate. The Concert served a useful purpose for some months in bringing the acrimonies of the past three or four years to an ostensible end; the powers were able for a time to find agreement among themselves in more or less spontaneous denunciation of Turkish conduct. But when, by the autumn of 1880, Abdul Hamid's stubbornness had begun to threaten new divergences among them, the Concert broke up. Granville's bland and conventional diplomacy was of little avail in these circumstances; and Bismarck, who had viewed the British initiative with no friendly eye, was able to proceed with his own plans.

In April and May, however, all seemed to be going well, and the continental powers made haste to give assurances of their goodwill. A detailed examination by the Foreign Office of the unexecuted clauses of the treaty of Berlin showed that, while there were still points over which the powers might differ, the main problem was now Turkish resistance or procrastination in the execution of the Greek, Montenegrin, Macedonian, and Armenian clauses.[2] This fact in itself was sufficient to ensure a considerable *détente* in the relations of the powers, for no government had any desire to play as truculent a part in Montenegro and Greece as Russia had been playing in Bulgaria; and all the powers had been exasperated in one way or another by Turkish behaviour in the immediate past.[3] Granville indicated the general trend of his ideas at the first of his weekly meetings with members of the diplomatic corps on 30 April. He told Musurus Bey, the Turkish *chargé*, that the new government had found the

---

[2] Cf. *Present State of the Questions arising under the Treaty of Berlin*, by Lord Tenterden, 28 April 1880, F.O. 358/4.

[3] Cf. W. N. Medlicott, *The Congress of Berlin and After* (London, 1938), chs. vi–ix.

Berlin treaty an accomplished fact, but that many of its most important provisions were unexecuted, and they 'hoped to receive the hearty co-operation of Turkey, together with that of the other powers, to give effect to the provisions of the treaty without delay'. A broad hint that they intended to stand no nonsense followed. While they wished 'to abstain from anything like menace, any intimation they gave would be adhered to,—to the letter. But I trusted no such intimation would be required'. Musurus Bey promised to report these observations to his government, but the Porte appears to have been too timid to pass them on to the Sultan.[4]

II. BISMARCK'S FIRST ALLIANCE MOVES

Russia among the European powers appeared to benefit most from the Liberal victory, and Bismarck found it correspondingly disconcerting. But before examining the attitude of the three empires to the new British government it will be useful to glance briefly at their relations during the later winter of 1879–80.

Prince Gorchakov remained formally in charge of Russian foreign policy, but his control had been little more than nominal since the Russo-German crisis had reached its height in August 1879. His policy since the spring of 1879 had been essentially one of self-confessed isolation, justified willy-nilly as a new 'politique de recueillement'.[5] As he had no desire for alliance with republican France, and was persuaded that Austria, England, and Germany were for the time being irreconcilable, there seemed nothing to do but bewail Russia's hard lot. Nikolai Karlovich Giers, Assistant Minister for Foreign Affairs since December 1875, could now be described as the real director of Russian foreign policy, subject to the somewhat unfortunate attempts of the Emperor Alexander II to direct it himself; but Giers' modest and somewhat humdrum personality

---

[4] Granville to Layard, 30 April, F.O. 78/3073, no. 287; Layard to Granville, May, F.O. 78/3085, no. 482. Cf. *Greece Abandoned; or, Three years of Diplomacy on the Greek Question* (London, 1881), published by the Greek Committee.

[5] E. de Cyon, *Histoire de l'entente franco-russe* (1895), p. 211; cf. references in W. N. Medlicott, 'Bismarck and the Three Emperors' Alliance, 1881–87' (*Transactions of the Royal Historical Society, 1945*), pp. 64–6.

led Bismarck for some time to underrate his influence.[6] He accepted the need for an alliance with Germany, and was supported in this aim by the Minister of War, Count Miljutin, and by the new Russian ambassador to Berlin, Peter Saburov, whose instructions on 8 September 1879 to reassure Bismarck as to Russia's attitude had provided the first genuine armistice in the 'two chancellors' war'. Saburov argued that Russia could not struggle successfully against her two opponents, England who threatened her military and political position in the Black Sea, and Austria who threatened the progress of her work in the emancipation and political organization of the kindred races in the Balkan peninsula. Hostility to Austria-Hungary would involve Russia in a probable conflict with Germany; the most elementary prudence counselled her to be satisfied for the time being with the immense progress that she had made recently in the Balkans, and to devote herself to the one which touched her interests and security more directly. 'In other words, let us be less Slav, and more Russian.' The basis of Russo-German agreement had been worked out by Saburov and Bismarck on these lines in discussions in Berlin (19 January–6 February 1880). Bismarck made it clear that he could not abandon the dual alliance of 7 October 1879 with Austria, but he claimed that there was no incompatibility between this and a triple alliance. In St. Petersburg the principle of a triple agreement was accepted during February 1880 in secret deliberations between the Tsar, Giers, Miljutin, and Saburov, without Gorchakov's knowledge. By the beginning of March 1880 both the Russian and German Emperors had accepted the principle of a revived Three Emperors' Alliance.

Thus the Tsar, faced with the need to divide his opponents, had agreed to regard Great Britain (under a Conservative government) as a greater direct menace to Russian security than Austria-Hungary, and to come to terms with Austria on the

[6] Kálnoky reported the following remarks of Baron Jomini on 5 November 1879: 'Fürst Gortschakoff werde zurückkehren und nominell Kanzler bleiben und der Kaiser—qui se plait à être son propre Ministre des Affaires étrangères et qui trouve que depuis ce temps les affaires vont beaucoup mieux—wird fortfahren mit Herrn von Giers zu arbeiten wie bisher. Un détestable arrangement parce que de fait il n'y a plus personne qui dirige notre politique, wie Baron Jomini meint, der es wissen kann.' Kálnoky to Haymerle, 5 November 1879, W.S.A. Politisches Archiv, Geheimakten II.

basis of quiescence in the Balkans. This meant in turn that Russia would make it her main purpose in the alliance negotiations to secure from Germany and Austria a guarantee against any attempt by the British to open the Straits of the Bosphorus and Dardanelles in time of war in order to attack Russia in the Black Sea. Miljutin, supported by Giers, had insisted in the preliminary discussions in 1879 that the Straits question should be given this prominence in the discussions, and Saburov had at first opposed the plan, arguing that it was impracticable and would prejudice the success of the negotiations. He was, however, overruled. Miljutin, who knew that Russia could not afford to risk war, did not propose that Russia should seek the agreement of the other two powers to an occupation of the Straits, and he does not, indeed, appear to have regarded it as a matter of urgency for Russia. The closing of the Straits as a ground for rapprochement between Austria and Russia was, in fact, well chosen, although it was right for Haymerle (and Bismarck) to assume that the Russians were deliberately concealing their ultimate objectives in the Balkans. [7]

To those Russians like Peter Shuvalov who had no desire to see their country exhaust herself in altruistic panslavist adventures in the Balkans the prevention of British control at Constantinople was always the decisive objective of Russia's Near Eastern policy, and the only one indeed that seemed to justify the risk of war. [8] The Austrian government had shown

[7] *Saburov*, pp. 88–92; S. Skazkin, *Konets austro-russko-germanskogo soiuza* (Moscow, 1928), pp. 123 and n., 147–8. See pp. 257–65 below.

[8] This led Peter Shuvalov to write from the London embassy before the Constantinople Conference: 'Il importe surtout d'enlever à l'Angleterre tout prétexte d'occuper seule les Dardanelles. . . . Nous devons craindre à plus d'un titre qu'une fois entrée dans les détroits, l'Angleterre ne veuille pas en sortir. Ce coup porté aux intérêts primordiaux de la Russie en Orient ne pourrait être compensé par aucun succès obtenu ailleurs' (S. to Gorchakov, 22 November/4 December 1876). Similarly, on the eve of the Russo-Turkish war, he spoke of 'les désastres de la guerre infailliblement victorieuse que nous entreprendrions'. He knew that Austria would occupy slav provinces as the price of her co-operation, and he anticipated 'l'établissement des anglais dans les détroits. . . . Prendre des gages matériels, occuper les détroits et venir en troisième pour l'heure de partage, ce sera infailliblement la politique que poursuivra Angleterre. Dieu veuille que ces deux faits ne se passent pas du règne de l'Empereur, ni jamais.' (S. to Gorchakov, 2/14 March 1877). *The Slavonic and East European Review*, iv, no. 11, p. 444; no. 12, pp. 755–6. If the Russians exaggerated the danger of an English advance, the British government equally underrated the Russian desire for security in the Black Sea.

during the recent Near Eastern crisis rather less apprehension than Great Britain at the prospect of a temporary Russian occupation of the Turkish capital, and had joined Russia and the other powers (including Great Britain) at the Congress of Berlin in reaffirming (on 6 July 1878) the maintenance of the *status quo ante* in the question of the Straits. Lord Salisbury had startled the Congress on 11 July by bringing forward a unilateral declaration that the obligations of the British government did not go further than 'an engagement with the Sultan to respect in this manner His Majesty's independent determinations in conformity with the spirit of existing Treaties'. At the next sitting a Russian declaration had affirmed that the 'principle of the closing of the Straits is a European principle', and there the matter had rested. Salisbury's declaration, as he explained in 1885, was intended to make it clear that 'if, in any circumstances, the Sultan should not be acting independently, but under pressure from some other Power, there would be no international obligation on our part to abstain from passing through the Dardanelles'. Continental jurists have not accepted Salisbury's interpretation, if it was meant to deny that Great Britain's engagement, like that of the other signatory powers, was not merely several but joint. On the other hand the London treaty of 1871 allowed the Sultan to admit foreign vessels into the Straits, in the exercise of his judgment, to carry out certain treaty obligations, and it could reasonably be argued that the treaty would be valid only if the Sultan were free to make independent judgments. [9] If Russia bullied the Sultan into admitting a Russian fleet, Great Britain could not accept a Russian veto on intervention. But under the terms of Salisbury's

[9] There is a good discussion of the juristic points in C. Phillipson and N. Buxton, *The Question of the Bosphorus and Dardanelles* (1917), pp. 154–62. Geffcken, Bonfils, Nye, and others treat Salisbury's statement as merely a unilateral declaration which could not modify the consent already given to the unanimous decision of the Congress. Westlake thought that Salisbury was right in substance, because the engagement 'must surely refer to the Sultan's independent judgment' only (pp. 158–9). The best discussion of the problem in its historical setting is in N. Dascovici, *La question du Bosphore et des Dardanelles* (1915), who points out that the extent of the changes brought about by the treaty of 1871 has been underrated, and that Russia herself, as soon as she had restored her naval position in the Black Sea, would find it advantageous to discuss with the Sultan alone the passage of the Straits (pp. 256–8).

declaration Russia would have nothing to fear if she herself did nothing to weaken the Sultan's independence. So Salisbury no doubt argued. Saburov, straining the meaning of Salisbury's words, certainly attributed to Great Britain more aggressive intention than the facts warranted.

Elle ne respectera pas davantage la volonté du Sultan, si celui-ci lui fermait l'entrée des détroits à notre demande; car alors, aux termes de la déclaration anglaise, les déterminations du Sultan ne seraient plus indépendantes.—

En d'autres termes, l'Angleterre se réserve désormais d'entrer dans les détroits *quand bon lui semblera*!

In this deployment of argument there was some evidence of genuine apprehension, but its chief purpose was to provide a basis for amicable discussion between Russia and Germany.[10]

Bismarck's willingness for the agreement was the main reason for the new turn in Russian policy: the Tsar and his advisers saw in an alliance with Germany the sole means of escape from Bismarck's hostility. Although this view was correct it was based in some measure on a misreading, or at least an over-simplification, of Bismarck's attitude. Bismarck had, as ever, only one long-term aim in his foreign policy, namely German security; but the peculiarity of his outlook, as it concerned his two neighbours, can be understood only if one remembers that in the 'seventies the prospect of an Austro-Russian agreement for the amicable division of influence in the Balkans appears to have alarmed him almost more than that of an open quarrel between them. In 1879, distrustful of Russia and not yet finally sure of Austria, he could see many advantages in an alliance which kept his two neighbours passive in the Near East, distrustful of each other, and anxiously competing for his future support. This policy of balanced tensions has its dangers; it could give permanent satisfaction to none of the three. Somewhat similar tactics had certainly not stood the strain of the Eastern crisis of 1876 to 1879; not so much because Austria and

[10] From Saburov's *aide-mémoire*, given to Bismarck on 5 February 1880. *G.P.*, iii, no. 517. On the following day he sent Bismarck a draft of a triple agreement, providing security for Russia in the Black Sea, 'sécurité fortement ébranlée par la nouvelle interprétation que l'Angleterre cherche à donner aux Traités qui règlent la fermature des Détroits'. *Ibid.*, no. 518.

Russia had been disappointed by his limited support, as because they both feared that he might be secretly working against them. The essential basis of the curious and vague Three Emperors' League of 1872-3 had been that Bismarck undertook no obligation to support either of his two allies in any international dispute, and above all did not undertake to support either against the other, but that his mediation and friendly offices were always to be at their disposal. If by a tactful and dignified bearing and a refusal to intrigue with or against either he had been able to create genuine confidence in his impartiality this position might have been indefinitely maintained: even the passive friendliness of the strongest military power in Europe was worth having. But there were constant hints of manœuvres, bargains, animosities; his many displays of suspicion and alarm at Russia's intentions, culminating in his search for an Austrian alliance after the spring of 1879, convinced even the Russians who clung to the policy of Russo-German friendship that Bismarck was neither a loyal friend of Russia nor even a benevolent neutral in Austro-Russian disputes.[11] Austria of course was correspondingly relieved in October 1879 to find that his choice had fallen on her, but she still needed proof that the choice was genuine and permanent. The one unquestionable conclusion that we must

[11] Russian dissatisfaction with Bismarck's more or less passive attitude in 1876 and 1877 is shown in the correspondence of Peter Shuvalov, who had no personal hostility to Bismarck, e.g. 'A Berlin on nous prodigue, il est vrai, beaucoup de bonnes paroles et d'assurances de sympathie, mais les faits ne manquent-ils pas à l'appui?' 'Il semble, mon Prince, que dans la question qui nous occupe, l'entente des trois Cours a offert tous les inconvénients d'une alliance sans en présenter en retour les avantages', etc. (S. to Gorchakov—January 1877, *Slavonic Review*, vol. iv, no. 12, pp. 744-5). The Austrians, however, also complained of the limited extent of Bismarck's support, and Giers and Shuvalov recognized his services to Russia at the Congress of Berlin (cf. Medlicott, pp. 127-35). This judicious attitude can be contrasted with Jomini's explanation to Kálnoky (5 November 1879): 'Fürst Gortschakoff [in 1874-5] habe nicht geglaubt, dass es im Interesse weder Russlands noch Europas sei, wenn Frankreich noch mehr geschwächt werde und habe sich ablehnend verhalten gegenüber den Anträgen des deutschen Reichskanzlers. "C'est ensuite qu'il nous a poussé dans cette guerre avec la Turquie qui a tant éprouvé nos forces, et depuis qu'il nous voit sur le flanc et hors de combat, il est allé s'assurer de l'Autriche-Hongrie toujours dans le même ordre d'idées afin d'assurer la sécurité de son oeuvre—seulement qu'il a trouvé bon d'inventer le spectre de l'invasion slave pour nous marquer ses sentiments".' See also pp. 57-9 below.

draw from the story of Bismarck's recriminations against Russia in the summer of 1879 is that he had made his decision in favour of an Austrian alliance long before the events (such as the Tsar's letter of 15 August) by which he was later to justify the decision. He had already spoken of the need for close relations with Austria to General Schweinitz, the ambassador to Russia, in the autumn of 1878.[12] The conclusion drawn by Giers, Saburov, and Miljutin from the events of 1879 seems to have been that Russia could not afford to quarrel with Germany, and that Gorchakov's policy of trying to bring Bismarck to heel by recriminations and flirtations with France was suicidal: it would, therefore, be wise to enter an alliance with him as a means of neutralizing his hostility, but not in the expectation that much positive advantage could be derived from it.[13]

Bismarck's nerves and his good judgment had not, in fact, been strong enough to allow him to carry out with any conviction the retiring, disinterested, conciliatory rôle in international politics which he had apparently assigned himself under the *Dreikaiserbündnis* of 1872–3. Yet while the decision of 1879 to sign a defensive treaty with Austria satisfied his need for action it also placed him in a false position from which he was never able to escape.[14] It seemed so obviously a proof that he had given his preference to Austria that the Russians had to

[12] A. von Brauer, *Im Dienste Bismarcks* (1936), pp. 59–60; cf. E. C. Corti, *Alexander von Battenberg* (1920), pp. 53–5.

[13] Saburov was more sanguine, but was not typical.

[14] Oncken remarks of Bismarck's decision: 'Es ist die Summe alles dessen, was er in den Jahren 1875 bis 1879 erlebt und jetzt zu einem politischen Axiom verdichtet hatte, mit dem zu siegen oder zu fallen er entschlossen war. . . . Als wenn er auf diese Stunde gewartet hätte, griff er nach dem Zarenbriefe als nach einer Waffe, um alle Widerstände zu überwinden' (Hermann Oncken, *Das Deutsche Reich und die Vorgeschichte des Weltkrieges* (1933), i, 255). German historians do not seem able to decide how far Bismarck's decision was due to genuine (and unjustified) fear of Russian attack, and how far to a desire, independent of possible Russian hostility, to complete the work of German unity by an organic relationship with the Habsburg Empire. In so far as the latter was Bismarck's true purpose his tactics can be criticized for their permanent association of the dual alliance with the Russian quarrel. Heller's view seems to lie between these two extremes: the Eastern crisis in 1877–8 had convinced Bismarck that Germany could not remain indifferent to threats to the integrity and independence of the Danube monarchy (E. Heller, *Das deutsch-österreichisch-ungarische Bündnis* (1925), p. 36, etc.). F. Leidner, *Die Aussenpolitik Österreich-Ungarns . . . 1870–1879* (1936), discusses the alliance solely in terms of Bismarck's 'cauchemar des coalitions' (p. 110). Cf. Hans Rothfels, *Bismarck und der Osten* (1934), p. 35.

assume a permanent anti-Russian bias in his policy as long as it remained in force. Henceforth he faced the dilemma that by admitting his preference for Austria he would alienate the Russians still further, and by denying it he would risk the loss of Austrian confidence. The equivocations of the Reinsurance treaty negotiations of 1887 were implicit in the decisions of 1879, and were anticipated on numerous occasions in the Three Emperors' Alliance negotiations of 1880–1.

Russia's decision to enter this alliance meant, therefore, that she was seeking her own form of reinsurance against German and Austrian hostility: it was an attempt to neutralize the October treaty by postponing the problem that the October treaty was intended (in her belief) to solve. The decision was not, however, by any means a difficult one for her to make: indeed, it offered certain immediate advantages in addition to her reconciliation with Bismarck and assurance concerning the Straits. The internal situation demanded peace, and the *status quo* position, if established just at this moment, would enable her to consolidate a not disadvantageous position in the Near East. She had struggled since the autumn of 1878 to secure the abandonment or the indefinite postponement of the more obnoxious clauses of the Berlin treaty, and it would suit her very well from this point of view to put the Eastern question into cold storage at this point. The Russian army of occupation had, in accordance with Article XXII of the treaty, retired from the area of the Balkan mountains by July 1879, and Turkish troops should then have advanced to garrison the mountains; but the Sultan had not had the courage to send his troops forward. If he could be prevented from doing so he would lose his last good military frontier in Europe, and the chance of preventing the eventual union of Bulgaria and Eastern Rumelia. Then, again, Austria had the right under the treaty to occupy the sanjak of Novipazar, the small Turkish enclave between Serbia and Montenegro, and her troops had occupied the area in September 1879; if she could be prevented from consolidating her legal and administrative hold on the sanjak the possibility would remain that some day a joint Serbo-Montenegrin frontier could be secured, and a barrier placed in the way of Austria's expansion into Macedonia. The position in Asia Minor was similar. The unwelcome interest shown by the British government in administrative reforms in Turkey's Anatolian provinces, and the recent appointment of military consuls, had alarmed both the Russians and the Turks (although for rather different reasons) at the prospect that this would develop into some form of British protectorate.[15]

As Russia had had to evacuate Bulgaria and accept the clauses of the Berlin treaty which most directly limited her aspirations in the Near East she had thus every reason to welcome an arrangement which would result in postponing the execution of those clauses which would benefit, or appear to benefit, Turkey, Austria, and Great Britain. Prince Lobanov-Rostovski had already received instructions on these lines in January 1880, when he succeeded Peter Shuvalov as ambassador in London.[16]

The success of Bismarck's programme depended on the continuance of Anglo-Russian antagonism, and it had hitherto been easy to persuade the Russians, who needed little convincing, that the British reform programme was both sinister and aggressive. Austria-Hungary had been correspondingly hard to convince. Even before the dual alliance had been signed, Bismarck in various conversations with Saburov during September 1879 had spoken of the Austro-German agreement as the first act of a political system which would be completed by the reconstitution of the *Dreikaiserbund*; and after telling Saburov on 29 September that 'an Empire like Russia cannot let herself be cooped up by England in the Black Sea',[17] he had sent a private letter to Andrássy reporting the readiness of the Russians to accept the dual alliance and to proceed to form an *entente à trois*. But in a comment on this letter for the Emperor Andrássy flatly rejected, both as a minister and as a gentleman, the idea of any such understanding with Russia.[18] During the

[15] If Salisbury had had any serious thoughts about establishing a formal protectorate he had abandoned them before the end of 1878. Reforms were pressed energetically by Layard in 1879 for humanitarian and strategical reasons: to satisfy British opinion and to increase Turkish powers of resistance to Russia. This phase of British policy is described in some detail in Medlicott, ch. viii.

[16] Medlicott, pp. 395–6.   [17] *Saburov*, p. 81.

[18] Bismarck to Andrássy, 29 September 1879, letter with the following pencil note (1 October) by Andrássy for the Emperor: 'Habe diesen Brief heute erhalten. Was Bismarck betrifft, bin ich vollkommen zufrieden. Was die Russischen Auffas-

following months Bismarck on the one hand encouraged Salisbury to maintain British influence at Constantinople,[19] and on the other encouraged Saburov to assume that Russia could count on the benevolent neutrality of Germany in a war with England over Near East affairs, and that such a war was ultimately inevitable.[20] But he made no progress in his attempts to interest Austria-Hungary in an agreement with Russia. Freiherr von Haymerle, the new Austro-Hungarian Foreign Minister, was a cautious, correct, unadventurous official, who had played a somewhat unhappy rôle at the Congress of Berlin as the third Austrian delegate; his nervousness and his rather woebegone personality had caused his colleagues some embarrassment and irritation, and this reputation clung to him when he was brought from the embassy at Rome to succeed the colourful Count Andrássy in October 1879. But he understood and was determined to continue Andrássy's anti-Russian policy; he believed that Russia's panslavist programme was being pushed as actively as ever in the Balkans, and that Russian agents were working against the Berlin treaty and the interests of Austria in Serbia, Bulgaria, and on the Danube, and he wished to keep her in isolation. The defensive alliance with Germany, and the close co-operation of the last two years with Great Britain, gave Austria the security she needed: why should she weaken them now? Bismarck called him timid, but it was Haymerle's stubbornness in resisting the new understanding with Russia which really annoyed the German Chancellor.

To understand the intensity with which Haymerle clung to the English friendship we must remember that Austria was seeking not only security but also a large measure of preponderance in the Balkan peninsula. Before the Congress the

sungen anbelangt, scheint Fürst Bismarck dieselben kaum *gründlich* aufgefasst zu haben. Dieselben sind voll Perfidie und ich muss gestehen, dass ich nicht nur als Minister, sondern auch als gentleman Bedenken tragen würde, nach den gemachten Erfahrungen Euer Majestät die Erneuerung [eines Dreikaiser-Bündnisses zu empfehlen]—einer Abmachung mit Russland betreffs des Orientes zu empfehlen. Sollte—was ich nicht hoffe—die Annahme "pur et simple" nicht gelingen, so würde ich mir erlauben Euer Majestät meine Bedenken präcise zu motiviren.' The phrase in square brackets deleted by Andrássy. (W.S.A., Politisches Archiv Geheimakten II, Fasz. rot. 454). [19] Medlicott, pp. 343, 395.

[20] He said to Saburov on 20 January 1880: 'There is still too much antagonism between you in the East; you will need a great "Königgrätz" one day in order to settle this great Asiatic dispute.' *Saburov*, p. 111.

Emperor Franz Joseph and some of the military leaders had had hopes of annexations towards Salonica, but these were outside the range of practical politics—especially Magyar politics. The treaty of Berlin had nevertheless given her the opportunity to extend her influence politically and territorially and above all economically, and resistance could be fed only by Russia. In 1879 it had still been possible that Russia would, at a certain point, repudiate the treaty and refuse to evacuate the peninsula, in which case Austria and Great Britain would have found themselves at war with her on the side of Turkey. But by the autumn this danger had passed, and from this point the Austrian complaint became more and more of the obstruction of Austria's legitimate interests by Russian agents throughout the peninsula.

These interests had been vigorously pushed at the Congress by Baron Schwegel, director of the commercial section of the Austrian Foreign Office, with the understanding and support of Andrássy. The occupation of Bosnia and the Hercegovina had opened the way; the pushing back of the Montenegrin frontiers had been influenced by the desire to secure friendly relations with the north Albanian tribes and to open up commercial routes; under Article XXV of the treaty Austria, while leaving the administration of the sanjak of Novipazar to Turkey, had reserved the right to garrison and control military and commercial routes throughout the sanjak, up to the other side of (au dela de) Mitrovica. Serbia and Bulgaria had been required under the treaty to complete the links in the Constantinople railway, and Serbia to link up with the Salonica-Mitrovica line. Thus the prospect opened up was nothing less than the commercial domination of the peninsula through four routes: the Danube valley, the two great rail routes from Vienna via Belgrade to Constantinople and Salonica, and a route through Scutari to the Adriatic.

But there was, not surprisingly, considerable resistance to these ambitious plans. There was a sharp diplomatic struggle with Serbia, which went on until the agreement of the Serbian government to the Austro-Serbian commercial treaty of March 1881 and the secret political treaty of June 1881. Throughout 1879 and the greater part of 1880 the Serbian Prime Minister, Jovan Ristić, had been unable to solve the dilemma that faced him after the Congress. He was, like most of the Serbs, strongly russophil and austrophobe; the distrust of Austria had been increased by the occupation of Bosnia, the Bosnian resistance to the Austrian occupation forces, and the fear of Austrian dominance; on the other hand Russia had so clearly washed her hands of Serbia that self-interest demanded friendly, even subservient, relations with Vienna. Ristić had been told at the Congress by Peter Shuvalov that Russia could do nothing for him, and that he should address himself to Andrássy. He had with evident distaste signed a convention with the Austrians on 8 July 1878, when it had appeared that otherwise Serbia's territorial claims might be ignored. This convention had provided that Serbia was to construct and exploit the railways from Belgrade to Nish and Alexinac, to work with Austria to secure the construction of the corresponding lines in Bulgaria and Turkey, to join a commission in Vienna for the construction and exploitation of the railways, to agree to Austria's plans concerning the navigation of the Danube at the Iron Gates, and to establish close commercial relations with Austria-Hungary by means of a treaty of commerce. But after the Congress Ristić, who found it hard to abandon his russophil sympathies, and even harder to expose himself and the Liberal party to unpopularity by the increased taxation that would be needed for the railways, delayed the completion of the bargain and with it the commercial treaty which would define its terms. It was not until his resignation in October 1880 that the Progressists, with Milan Pirotchanaz as Prime Minister and Chedomille Mijatović as Foreign Minister, came into office and serious negotiations began. In Bulgaria the Russians were apparently doing their best to delay completion of the railway, and with regard to the Danube valley there was much apprehension in Austria that the Russians, who by their reoccupation of Bessarabia had secured control of all the Kilia mouths of the Danube except one, would divert trade from the Sulina mouth, and perhaps embarrass Austrian commerce and shipping in other ways.[21]

[21] Medlicott, pp. 23–7, 100–1; V. Georgevitch, 'La Serbie au Congrès de Berlin' (*Revue d'histoire diplomatique*, 1891, pp. 483–552); C. Mijatovich, *Memoirs of a Balkan Diplomatist* (1917), pp. 32–7; A. F. Pribram, 'Milan IV von Serbien und die Geheimverträge Osterreich-Ungarns mit Serbien, 1881–1889' (*Historische Blaetter* (1922), i (3), pp. 466–70); H. Hajnal, *Le droit du Danube international* (1929), 129–33.

All this foreshadowed years of intrigue and struggle in the peninsula, at a level and in a form that might escape the notice of more politically minded diplomatists, and the nature of the underlying economic issues was probably not understood by Russians like Miljutin and Saburov, although Giers had an accurate grasp of the essential problem. He was to emphasize later that in the Balkans the political and economic aspects of foreign influence could not be separated; that economic channels were the conductors of political influence.[22] He believed that Russia was at a disadvantage in this struggle; Haymerle, however, believed the reverse. Certainly it seemed to Haymerle essential that the Austro-German alliance, which had already sobered the Russian government, should be strengthened by the support of other powers; and he was determined to perpetuate Russian isolation by every device at his disposal.

Bismarck, however, had exactly the opposite intention. His first task after the conclusion of the October treaty was to disabuse Haymerle of the idea that the next step should be to strengthen the opposition to Russia by bringing Great Britain into closer relations with the Central Powers. On 6 November 1879 Haymerle told Reuss, the German ambassador in Vienna, that he understood that Bismarck and Andrássy had discussed this idea, and he added the argument that if the British cabinet could count on Austro-German support in the Near East it would prefer this support in its foreign policy to that of France.[23] Bismarck on the 10th, after a sour comment on Salisbury's lack of tact in asking for particulars of the dual alliance ('a sign of the lack of breeding so often noticeable among English even of the highest class') reminded Haymerle that the agreement was directed to the defence of the two empires against a Russian attack, and not to the support of any policy whatsoever in the Near East. In view of Layard's activities at Constantinople they would be unwise to give England a blank cheque.[24] This carefully worded statement did not rule out the possibility of co-operation with England against Russia in certain circum-

[22] Skazkin, pp. 159–61; see below, pp. 262–5.
[23] Heinrich VII Reuss to Bismarck, 6 November 1879, *G.P.*, iii, no. 510.
[24] Bismarck, unsigned dictated note, 10 November 1879, *ibid.*, no. 511.

stances, but three months later he had dissociated himself almost completely from any show of sympathy for British policy, speaking of it as provocative and selfish. Haymerle's alarm at Russia's conduct was unabated, and conversations between Bismarck and Kálnoky, the Austrian ambassador in St. Petersburg, served only to underline the difference. Kálnoky saw the Chancellor on 9 February 1880, only three days after the conclusion of the latter's talks with Saburov.

Haymerle's instructions to Kálnoky started with a survey of Austrian relations with Italy: Haymerle wished to allow the Italian situation to develop by itself and to follow a policy similar to that of Bismarck towards France, which events had justified. It was necessary to avoid pressure which would unite parties in nationalist feeling; moves hostile towards Italy would, moreover, alienate liberally disposed England. An Italian campaign would be embarrassing; the terrain would make it protracted, and its conclusion would be difficult, for Austria-Hungary did not wish to occupy the country permanently, and it was not ripe for dissolution into provincial republics. If Russia at the same time should cause trouble in Bosnia and Serbia, Austria-Hungary would face a task which would demand most of her strength. Russia it is true would encounter Germany, but Austria-Hungary might not be able to stand as closely at Germany's side as would be necessary. This led Haymerle to consider the possibility of their being confronted with a Russo-Franco-Italian combination, and brought him back to the question which Bismarck had, he said, raised at Gastein— their relations with England, so deeply engaged in these matters. For Austria-Hungary, Italy was a secondary *Kriegsschauplatz*: her supreme preoccupation was with Russia. Would Bismarck agree to a further sounding of Salisbury and Disraeli, with a view to securing a promise from them to keep Italy neutral in the event of a conflict between the Central Powers and Russia? Haymerle thought that the British government might, in spite of its dislike of binding engagements, agree to a move which would earn so much advantage at such small cost. A coalition of the central powers with England would maintain peace, for it would be so strong that no other grouping would dare to challenge it. Haymerle also discussed the need for, and the difficulties of, an agreement with Rumania in the event of Russian aggression.[25]

Haymerle ended his instructions by warning Kálnoky to allow Bismarck in all circumstances to speak without interruption, and Kálnoky's report[26] on the conversation on the 9th shows that Bismarck did in fact do most of the talking. The gist of it was an emphatic rejection of Haymerle's proposals. Bismarck talked at length about the fear of a coalition against Germany which had disturbed him in the previous autumn, but he believed now that it was Russia which suffered from this *cauchemar de la coalition*. British conduct inspired this fear; if the Russians were now satisfied that the British would not be supported it would be easy for them to return to a temperate policy, and a desirable understanding with Austria-Hungary would not be difficult to achieve.

Today England is the chief cause of the uneasiness of Russian statesmen. And it cannot be denied that the behaviour of England during and after the last Oriental crisis was strangely challenging. One cannot maintain that the attitude of Layard and those agents of his in European and Asiatic Turkey does anything to ease the situation. It appears unnecessary to support England in this case. If she wishes to proceed in this arrogant manner she must do so on her own responsibility. If Russia feels reassured on this point it will not be difficult to bring about again a desirable understanding between her and Austria-Hungary over the Eastern Question, and thereby to strengthen confidence in the maintenance of peace.

Bismarck's words (thus reported by Kálnoky) completely ignore the possibility that British conduct might be no more than a reaction to Russian conduct: this is the more surprising, for Bismarck was himself going through a renewed phase of irritation at Russian military movements on the Polish frontier. Bismarck complained later that Kálnoky had put the case for an English alliance in an almost aggressive form; but there is no trace of this in his report, and he was in any case following instructions.[27]

[25] Vortrag Haymerles, 8 February 1880, W.S.A., Geheimakten II, Fasz. rot. 454.
[26] Kálnoky's report to Haymerle is printed by H. Krausnick, *Neue Bismarck-Gespräche* (1940), pp. 13–28, with useful notes and introduction. Bismarck's rejection of Haymerle's proposals concerning Italy has long been familiar: see A. F. Pribram, *Les traités politiques secrets de l'Autriche-Hongrie* (Paris, 1923), pp. 169–74.
[27] Cf. Krausnick, *op. cit.*, p. 29.

This is the first of a long series of complaints about the Austrian negotiators; Haymerle was the chief target, but he was partly the victim of Bismarck's inability to differ from anyone without impugning the other's intelligence or character or manners. Bismarck could get his way because few people could afford to disagree with him. This did not mean, however, that he had convinced them.

For the time being, the Austro-Hungarian government was not prepared to abandon its co-operation with England, or to draw closer to Russia. Haymerle welcomed Bismarck's peaceful views, but not his 'übermässige Gereiztheit' against England. 'So long as our interests in the East are so closely parallel to those of the English we should be unwise to abandon England', he wrote on 13 February 1880. 'I leave open the question whether the nightmare of a coalition, although unpleasant for Russia, might not have a beneficial rather than a disturbing effect.'[28]

III. Austria and Russia join the Concert

This was the position in March 1880, immediately before the general election in Great Britain. Gladstone's triumph was unexpected in St. Petersburg: as late as 14 March Beaconsfield had spoken optimistically about his prospects, and Lobanov had reported that the question of Home Rule, adroitly exploited by the government, had divided the Opposition and discredited the Liberal party in the eyes of the public. Gorchakov, a few days before, had written somewhat unenthusiastically that a Conservative ministry ought to be of value to Russia in view of the hostile attitude which radicalism was forcing on the French government: 'unfortunately experience has taught us that English policy is prepared to be conservative at home and revolutionary abroad'.[29] The Russians made no attempt to conceal

[28] Haymerle to Kálnoky, 13 February 1880, W.S.A., G. II, 454. A memorandum by Haymerle, dated 21 February, gives details of strongly expressed objections by Andrássy to Reuss against an agreement with Russia. Bismarck knew, he said, the superhuman efforts that it had cost him to maintain a peaceful agreement; Haymerle as a German could not do it for a week. He also spoke bitterly of Russia's professions of loyalty and gratitude before the fall of Plevna, and change of attitude afterwards.

[29] Gorchakov to Lobanov, R.E., 27 February/10 March, 1880; Lobanov to Gorchakov, 2/14 March 1880, no. 10.

their surprise and relief at the election result; it had still to be seen how far the Liberals would go in co-operation with Russia, but it was assumed at once in St. Petersburg that no active British hostility to Russia in the current controversies need now be feared. For a few weeks the possibility of some close co-operation between the two powers was discussed among Russian diplomatists.

It can at least be said of this correspondence that it reveals some genuine understanding as to what Gladstone himself meant by the Concert of Europe. Belief in the need for a federative policy for Europe, judiciously oriented in accordance with the enlightened conservatism of St. Petersburg, had been the guiding principle of Russian foreign policy under Alexander I and Nicholas, and the memory of the Holy Alliance as an attempt to establish the Concert of Europe on a basis of justice, Christian charity, and peace was almost reverently preserved, long after it had become in the West no more than a vague symbol of reaction. Nicholas too had sought for many years a peaceful solution of the Turkish question on a basis of amicable arrangements between the powers, and it was a stock assumption of Russian diplomacy that the troubles of Europe since the Crimean war were due to the rejection of this leadership.[30] However, when the Russians tried to interpret the Gladstonian programme in terms of practical diplomacy they could think of it only as a choice between an Anglo-Russian and a Russo-German alliance, and they were determined not to compromise the latter.

Bismarck, who had been so ready with criticisms of the Conservatives, now produced with remarkable alacrity some even more disturbing comments on their rivals and successors. Almost immediately he sounded the alarm by proclaiming that Gladstone's victory would give encouragement to the republican spirit in every part of Europe, and he continued to push this argument vigorously for some weeks. In a despatch to Schweinitz on 7 April he said that the election result was

[30] The Emperor Nicholas had even offered Constantinople to Austria in December 1845 in the interests of a peaceful settlement of the Near Eastern Question: G. H. Bolsover, 'Nicholas I and the Partition of Turkey', *Slavonic and East European Review* (December 1948), pp. 133–4.

synonymous with the resumption of the antimonarchical continental policy of Lord Palmerston, with the difference that Palmerston had found the means of combating the Emperor Nicholas outside the borders of Russia, whereas a revolutionary policy inspired by Gladstone would find the plotters against the throne of the Emperor Alexander II already assembled in Russia and the neighbouring Slav states under the banner of panslavism.[31] Whether he himself took this rigmarole seriously is difficult to say. With Sir Charles Dilke (as Under-Secretary for Foreign Affairs) and Joseph Chamberlain in the ministry it was possible for the German Junker to believe that anything might happen; he told Prince Hohenlohe on 30 April that the incalculable forces of radicalism made the internal situation in England as unpredictable as that of France.[32] Lord Dufferin, the British ambassador to St. Petersburg, tried to reassure Schweinitz with the observation that the new government was as interested in the Greeks as in the Slavs.[33] Saburov on 9 April showed himself to be quite unimpressed by Bismarck's arguments about the revolutionary danger; he retorted that Gladstone might be Austria's enemy, but he was not the enemy of

[31] Wolfgang Windelband, *Bismarck und die europäischen Grossmächte 1879–1885* (Essen, 1942, 2. Auflage), p. 139. Part II of this important work covers the period of the present volume, and is valuable for its copious quotations from unpublished German Foreign Office papers; it thus supplements the very inadequate collection of documents published in *G.P.* It does not use unpublished material from other governmental archives. Copies of Windelband were almost unprocurable in England for some years after the Second World War; I first read it at Princeton in 1952, when I had already read and transcribed the relevant German diplomatic correspondence (then in the Foreign Office in London) for the period covered by this volume. These transcripts included a number of documents not used by Windelband. Windelband is sparing of comment, orthodox in the acceptance of Bismarck's broader conceptions of policy, but not unduly laudatory. In addition to the *Politisches Archiv* of the Auswärtiges Amt Windelband used material from the *Friedsrichsruher Archiv* and the Schloss Nehmten. The best of the more general surveys is Hermann Oncken, *Das Deutsche Reich und die Vorgeschichte des Weltkrieges* (Leipzig 1933), vol. i.

[32] Windelband, pp. 141–2. Hohenlohe, German ambassador to Paris (1874–85) was acting head of the Foreign Office for a few months in 1880.

[33] 'Als ich Besorgnis äusserte, dass die lebhafte slavische Einbildungskraft durch den Fall Lord Beaconsfields und durch die Reden Mr Gladstone's zu Ausschreitungen verleitet werden könne, sagte der Botschafter: "Die Slaven werden bald erkennen, dass das Wohlwollen, welches die Männer des neuen Cabinets den unterdrückten Christen bezeigt haben, gleichmässig den Griechen wie den Slaven zugewandt ist".' Schweinitz to Bismarck, A.A.: Russland no. 61, 15 April 1880, no. 114.

Russia. He advised Bismarck to make use of his argument in Vienna in order to persuade Haymerle to enter the triple entente before Russia had found a *modus vivendi* with England.[34]

Saburov was shrewd enough to understand Bismarck's real ground for concern at the Liberal victory. It was not that the change of government in London had deprived Germany of a friend or potential ally, for Bismarck had decided six months earlier that he did not wish to develop closer relations between Germany and Great Britain in opposition to Russia. But the success of the programme of negotiation which he had been following depended on the continuance of Anglo-Russian antagonism, and the consequent isolation of both Russia and Great Britain. He had hitherto been able to leave the initiative to the Russians, who had no choice, while faced with British and Austrian hostility, but to seek Bismarck's goodwill. He had been in no hurry to put pressure on the Austrian government, knowing that Haymerle would be difficult to persuade, and that time would be needed to accustom the Russians to their new relationship with Germany. Faced now with the unwelcome prospect of Anglo-Russian agreement he was forced to take the initiative himself, and after his first, and quite futile, attempts to scare the Russians with the bogy of a Red Gladstone, he made what was, for the moment, an equally unsuccessful attempt to hurry the Austrians into acceptance of the alliance plan. When Haymerle proved unresponsive, Bismarck was forced to recognize that his second attempt to isolate Gladstone had failed, and that he must let matters take their course for some months, in the meantime giving lip service to the Concert of Europe.

Giers, like Saburov, had been quick to see the significance of the new turn in British policy. For some weeks the possibilities of an alliance with England were discussed; there seems to have been no doubt at any point that the Three Emperors' Alliance would remain the Russian objective, but the goodwill shown towards the Gladstone programme was considerable, and the discussion throws much light on the real character of Russo-German relations. It will be useful therefore at this point to examine this exchange of ideas in a little detail. Giers' first

<hr />

[34] *Saburov*, pp. 128–31.

detailed comments on the election results were made to
Lobanov on 17 April. He realized that the Liberals would
accept the Berlin treaty and Anglo-Turkish convention; Russia
also regarded the Berlin treaty as the basis of the *status quo* in the
East, and was firmly resolved to respect it and have it respected
by others. 'But this treaty itself needs to be applied and interpreted in a sense which will save it from the consequences of its
own defects. Taken literally it would produce the immediate
occupation of the Balkans by the Turks, the explosion of a
national Bulgarian movement, the entry of Ottoman troops into
Eastern Roumelia, and, in consequence, incalculable complications.' Nothing was more likely to hasten this dangerous
result than antagonism between the great powers, and especially
between England and Russia. He anticipated that the new
government would show a particular interest in the Greeks;
Russia was prepared to support it providing that the interests
of other races were not neglected. Russia also would not offer
any objections if the government sought the serious application of reform in Asia Minor as a condition of the maintenance
of the Anglo-Turkish convention; but if it sought to do so
under the direct and exclusive control of its own agents,
Russia would take her stand on the Berlin and earlier treaties
'which assure the participation of all the great signatory
powers in the supervision of reforms in Armenia, as well as in
the rest of Asia Minor'.

Russia would be disposed to respect the legitimate interests
of England and particularly those which concerned the route to
India; it would facilitate this if the new government would, for
its own part, renounce the menacing and directly aggressive
character which the policy of its predecessors had assumed in
Asia Minor and Armenia.[35] He dealt politely but somewhat
cautiously with the 'Concert of Europe'. Russia, he said, had

[35] A reference to the Cyprus Convention of 4 June 1878, which promised British
support for the Sultan in defending his Asiatic territories against a Russian attack;
in return the Sultan promised to undertake reforms to protect his 'Christian and
other' subjects, and to assign Cyprus to England. Salisbury's appointment of
'military' consuls to supervise the reforms caused both Russian and Turkish apprehensions that a British occupation of Asia Minor was visualized. A threat to send
the British fleet to Constantinople at the end of October 1879 was due to Beaconsfield's fear of a sudden Russian attack, and caused alarm in both Constantinople
and St. Petersburg (Medlicott, pp. 21, 328–32).

sought to establish it for twenty-five years, but for half a century it had had the character of a coalition hostile to her and this character had been accentuated at the time of the Crimean war, the Russo-Turkish war of 1877, and the Congress of Berlin.

But it had then as its aim the maintenance, at any price, of Turkish domination. How far can the new principles, publicly proclaimed by the Liberal party, be reconciled with this past policy? Events will show in the near future. If we can attach a serious value to the declarations of Mr. Gladstone we shall be disposed to attribute to the European concert . . . a significance which we gladly accept. This concert is not applicable only to the affairs of the Near East. Events have shown how necessary it is to the repose and equilibrium of Europe. It is sufficient to survey the course of history to convince oneself how much an entente between England and Russia can contribute to this. It is not we who have disturbed this good understanding. . . . It will be assured the moment we have succeeded in smoothing the differences, more apparent than real, which divide the two governments in the Near East and in Asia. That must be our immediate objective. [36]

The despatch offers striking proof of the willingness for conciliation, and absence of aggressive purpose, of the Russian government at this stage; the closing passages hinted at the possibility of some more permanent understanding after the immediate difficulties had been removed, although without any great expectation of its achievement.

Neither government in fact regarded a formal or far-reaching alliance as practicable. The whole point of the British programme was to avoid anything of the sort, and to work on an equal footing with each of the five other powers. The Russians certainly discussed the possibility; Giers told Baron Mohrenheim in 1882 that Russia had had to choose in 1880 between a serious and solid *rapprochement* with England, and re-entry into the triple alliance with Germany and Austria, and all the ambassadors had been consulted about the choice. There is evidence in Saburov's correspondence that Jomini at least among the senior Russian officials favoured closer relations with England as an alternative to the Three Emperors' Alliance; the habit of peace makes men peaceful, he said, and

[36] Giers to Lobanov, R.E., 5/17 April.

he appeared to see great possibilities in the Gladstonian programme and the action of the British electors in supporting it.[37]

The atmosphere of Berlin, and his own plans for the revival
of the *Dreikaiserbund*, made Saburov more critical of British
policy; he was even opposed, in spite of a recent declaration by
Granville that England would take no action concerning
Herat, to any unilateral attempt at conciliation by Russia in
Central Asia. He wrote to Giers on 10 May that there were two
courses open to the Russian government. It might secure from
Germany and Austria the required guarantee against an entry
of the British fleet into the Black Sea; it could not be denied
that such a treaty would be directed against Great Britain, and
the result would be that both Whigs and Tories would feel
tricked, and say that while negotiating with England for an
agreement Russia was conducting a second negotiation directed
against her. Or the negotiations with Bismarck might fail, and
the question of the Straits would remain in its existing unsatisfactory condition. What means of negotiation would remain
open to Russia if she relinquished her solitary handle, namely
her ability to offer guarantees to the British on the side of
India?[38] He expressed his views more emphatically to Jomini on
the 24th. He believed that even with Gladstone the desire to
maintain the Concert was not sincere. 'The seeming concert
only serves as a transition to groupings, as yet unknown, but at
which the best advised will know how to arrive sooner or later.
. . . I have no hesitation in thinking that . . . for Gladstone himself, who labours for it in the front rank, this concert has only
the value of a clever introduction.'[39]

Saburov in fact remained the champion of the triple agreement, and the Emperor did not take long to decide that a
revival of the *Dreikaiserbund* was preferable to a *rapprochement*
with England. But no one in St. Petersburg seems to have
shared Saburov's facile confidence in Bismarck's goodwill, and
the choice was all too clearly due to the greater capacity of the
Central Powers for unpleasantness: Giers put the position
bluntly in 1883 when he said that Russia's accession to the

[37] *Saburov*, pp. 136–7.
[38] Saburov to Giers, R.E., 28 April/10 May, copy.
[39] *Saburov*, pp. 131, 137.

Austro-German entente 'guarantees us against Germany and saves us from a conflict in the immediate future with Austria'. His comments in his instructions to Mohrenheim in 1882 were on the same lines. A serious *rapprochement* with England would poison Russia's relations with the two central powers. They were neighbours of Russia; their military power, united in the centre of Europe, would enable them to throw two million men across their frontiers, whereas England was far away. 'These reasons, supported by the unanimous opinions of our ambassadors, determined the late Emperor Alexander II to prefer a restoration of the triple understanding with the Imperial Courts.'[40]

Giers set out the Russian government's decision in a long and carefully reasoned reply to Saburov on 18 May. Russia certainly did not intend to abandon or compromise the pursuit of an accord with Berlin and Vienna. Close proximity made close relations with these two powers inevitable. But good relations with England would also be useful, and, whatever the difficulties, both ends must be achieved. There was a third position, neither Austro-German nor British, but Russian. The favourable disposition of England made it possible for Russia to treat on terms of equality with Germany. Asia was, as ever, the stumbling-block; Herat was by no means the only point, for Russia was vulnerable not only in Persia and the Turcoman steppes but also on the side of the Oxus and Turkestan. England however had also much to defend.

I conclude that our interest is to profit from the tendencies of the present government and the apprehension that we can inspire in India, not to prolong the uncertainty or the antagonism of our relations, but on the contrary to enter into agreement with it in order to remove as completely as possible the hitherto incurable mistrust which has divided us. The question of the Straits has an intimate connexion with the Asiatic situation. The security of India and the freedom of communication with India form the final objective of all the Eastern policy of England and it is that which gives the Straits their principal importance for her. The prolongation of her fears in

---

[40] Giers to Mohrenheim, 15/27 August 1882; instructions on his appointment as ambassador to London (Russian embassy archives); *ibid.*, 6/18 August 1883 (Notice and covering letter).

Asia can only perpetuate and amplify her hostility towards us in the Near East, and every Eastern crisis can only be aggravated by diversions in Asia. On the other hand, a satisfactory arrangement in Asia would diminish the keenness of our antagonism in the Near East and in consequence the danger of a violation of the Straits.[41]

Having secured his main point, Saburov was quite content to allow the *Dreikaiserbund* negotiations to hang fire for the moment. He remarked to Lobanov on 23 May that although the laborious efforts of the previous spring to revive the triple understanding had not succeeded he had arrived incidentally at another result which was perhaps of greater practical import-ance, namely a complete *détente* in Russia's relations with Ger-many. Considerable immediate advantage could be expected from the *rapprochement* with England, and the Russian govern-ment would put itself in a false position if it concluded at this stage an agreement about the Straits obviously directed against her. It was on these lines that the Russian government acted during May, June, and July. Its aim was to go as far as it was possible to go in supporting Gladstone's programme without prejudicing relations with Germany and Austria. Lobanov was instructed on these lines on 19 May, and Giers warned him to be on his guard against attempts by the Turkish government to make demonstrations of friendship to Russia as a means of defy-ing the British government. 'Our aim is to re-establish the Con-cert and to see England enter it otherwise than as the declared adversary of Russia.'[42]

Gladstone's startling attack on Austria in his Midlothian speech on 17 March 1880 might well have been expected to destroy all immediate prospect of Anglo-Austrian co-opera-tion.[43] Nevertheless, Bismarck had to admit to Saburov on 21 April that Haymerle had allowed himself to be very speedily reassured. The personal influence of Sir Henry Elliot, the British ambassador in Vienna, appears to have been of con-siderable importance in restoring good relations between the two governments, although there was a preliminary mishap. Immediately after Count Károlyi, the Austro-Hungarian am-

[41] Giers to Saburov, R.E., 6/18 May, 1880.
[42] Giers to Lobanov, R.E., 7/19 May, 1880.
[43] See above, p. 30.

bassador in London, had sent a report on Gladstone's speech Haymerle asked for a contradiction; Elliot accordingly sent two telegrams, the first *en clair*, giving a distinct contradiction and saying that on his own account he wished that it could be made public; the second in cipher, saying that Haymerle was anxious for the contradiction. Both were published, and Elliot expressed his disgust at 'the mess' and his 'extreme annoyance' to Haymerle on 24 March; he pointed out that the second telegram was clearly not intended for publication, and that Sir Stafford Northcote ought never to have said that Haymerle had asked for the contradiction.[44] After the election Granville made haste to send friendly assurances to Vienna; on 30 April he assured the Austrian and German ambassadors that he was glad of the intimate understanding which now existed between Germany and Austria. On the Austrian side Gladstone's hard words were certainly forgiven with surprising readiness.[45] After considerable correspondence with Károlyi, Gladstone was ultimately persuaded to withdraw his observations if assured that he had been misinformed, and on 11 May a letter was published regretting the language which had been used on secondary evidence. Salisbury in the House of Lords expressed wonder that Austria had accepted the apology, and pointed out that Gladstone had withdrawn nothing and had only promised, in recognition of the assurance given him by Károlyi that Austria did not desire to advance beyond where she now stood, that he would not renew the accusation.[46] But the letter made a good impression in court circles in Austria and Germany, and although Bismarck made no attempt to imitate the geniality of the Austrian Emperor, he said he was satisfied with it.[47] Elliot was able to make a further gesture of appeasement when he heard on 6

[44] Károlyi to Haymerle, 18 March, W.S.A., no. 26. Elliot to Haymerle, 24 March, W.S.A. private.

[45] L. Ritter von Przibram, *Erinnerungen eines alten Oesterreichers* (1910), ii, 112–13.

[46] *Hansard*, House of Lords, 174, 21 May. Károlyi to Haymerle, 12 May, W.S.A., no. 40B. Granville to Elliot, 6 May, F.O. 7/985, no. 207. The text of the letters is reprinted in *Political Speeches in Scotland*, ii, 364–6.

[47] *Granville*, ii, 208. A letter to James Bryce (31 May) shows that Gladstone was determined not to be drawn into further criticisms of possible Austrian designs against the rights of the subject races of Turkey. 'I had no option in honour and propriety but to accept Károlyi's explicit declaration on that subject.' (B.M. Add. MSS. 44544).

May that Mr. W. E. Goschen had been appointed a 'special' ambassador to relieve Sir Austin Layard at Constantinople; he suggested to Haymerle that Goschen should be invited to Vienna on his journey out, and that Károlyi should drop a hint in London to this effect. Haymerle telegraphed in this sense on the following day.[48] The conduct of Count Károlyi in London was equally tactful. In his conversations with Gladstone and Granville and in his letters to the former he was careful to represent his desire for a satisfactory settlement of the Mid-lothian incident as personal, in order that his government would not be compromised by a refusal, and he regarded Gladstone's letter not only as a definite solution of the difficulty but as 'an entirely satisfactory starting-point for our new relations'.[49] Haymerle echoed and amplified this note of deliberate optimism in a despatch of 18 May prepared for communication to the British government. He said that Gladstone's explanation had made the best impression on Austrian public opinion, and had been fully comprehended; he believed that the interests of the two powers coincided on many important questions and that no real divergence existed between them, and he was prepared to co-operate wholeheartedly in Gladstone's plans for the execution of the Berlin treaty.[50] An anti-Russian note had already appeared in the relations between the two powers. On 29 April Károlyi gave Granville details of a Russian importation of arms into Bulgaria; on 7 May a note from the Foreign Office to Károlyi stated that one hundred and sixty-three Russian non-commissioned officers, and some rifles, had arrived in Bulgaria early in April.[51]

Bismarck, like Haymerle, was too alarmed at the prospect of

[48] Elliot to Haymerle, 6 May, W.S.A. private. Haymerle to Károlyi, 7 May, tel. no. 33.

[49] Károlyi to Haymerle, W.S.A. 5 May. On 26 May he wrote emphasizing the essential continuity of Gladstone's Near Eastern policy with that of his predecessor. K. to Haymerle, 26 May, W.S.A. no. 45c.

[50] Haymerle to Károlyi, W.S.A. 18 May. As early as 4 May the Emperor told the retiring French ambassador, Teisserenc de Bort, that apprehensions 'which he admitted himself to have felt upon the change of Government in England were already to a great degree removed by reports received of the disposition of Her Majesty's new cabinet'. Elliot to Granville, 5 May, F.O. 7/990, no. 208; cf. 7 May, no. 219.

[51] Granville to Károlyi, W.S.A., 7 May. Károlyi to Haymerle, 12 May, W.S.A., no. 40E.

Anglo-Russian co-operation to be able to afford any public display of hostility to the new British government. He appears, indeed, before the end of April, to have become aware that his own fulminations against the revolutionary plot in Downing Street were not only unconvincing, but were likely to deceive the Austrians as to his intentions. According to a note by Saburov on 21 April Bismarck had done everything he could to persuade Haymerle to accept a Russian alliance. Haymerle had shown himself very timid over the question of the Straits; he had made the objection that it constituted an English interest of very great importance, and that it would be a case of following a course entirely opposed to England, and of forgoing for ever an alliance with her. And Bismarck had replied that this reasoning was ill-timed; the English Liberals had no alliance to offer; the only alliance open was that with Russia; Russia, moreover, sought merely to defend herself in the Straits, and could be aggressive towards England only in Central Asia, in Persia, and in Asia Minor, where Russia asked for support neither from Austria nor from Germany. This was the truth, but not the whole truth, as far as it revealed Bismarck's intentions. It was designed to keep alive the sanguine hopes of the Russian ambassador, who sought throughout the alliance negotiations, as Bismarck well knew, to substitute Russia for Austria as Germany's chief friend and partner. 'Our action is working its way in, like a wedge, between these two Powers', Saburov wrote on 21 April. 'Bismarck, roused for the fight, gets visibly angry under Haymerle's opposition.'[52] Although Bismarck wished to bring Austria into the triple alliance he did not wish to drive Great Britain into the arms of Russia, and his advice to Haymerle was to enter the alliance but at the same time to do enough to maintain British friendship. A despatch which he sent to Reuss on 23 April was in his calmer and more analytical style, and stated his conviction that the tendency of individual personalities in London would not prevail against the weight of British interests: the nation believed in the need to preserve India from dangerous neighbours and to keep safe and open the lines of communication, and all English statesmen were aware that the satisfaction of these needs depended on the relations

[52] *Saburov*, pp. 132-4.

between France and Russia. England needed a strong and *peaceful* continental power between France and Russia; she had found it before 1866 in Austria, and after 1866 had hoped to make use of the *Norddeutscher Bund* for the same purpose. England could not have a fuller and safer guarantee than when Germany and Austria were united in a joint policy of peace. There might of course be great differences in the energy and choice of means of different English governments, and a redoubled vigilance was necessary in view of Gladstone's new experiments with the so-called principle of nationality.[53]

Haymerle, however, did not need any persuading that the essential bases of British policy had not changed: he was so anxious to believe that he could still find in Great Britain a bulwark against Russian aggression that he rebuffed all Bismarck's efforts to secure his acceptance of the Russian programme. The Russian government, in spite of its willingness to examine the possibilities of the new British programme, was careful not to frighten Bismarck by suggesting any cooling of enthusiasm for the triple alliance, and accordingly, on 24 April, Saburov gave Hohenlohe the official Russian proposal for the conclusion of a thoroughgoing agreement between the three empires over Balkan questions. He added the warning that the Emperor might otherwise, in view of Gladstone's pro-Christian and anti-Turkish inclinations, prefer to come to terms with England rather than with Germany and Austria. Bismarck forwarded particulars of this Russian *démarche* to Reuss on the 27th, with an emphatic statement that it was necessary to come to terms with the Russians. But Haymerle refused, and made no attempt to conceal his alarm at Bismarck's attitude. He softened the refusal by conceding that the greatest danger from the British cabinet lay in its possible effect on Russian chauvinism, and that it was necessary to maintain friendship with the Tsar, but he was not prepared to enter into the triple agreement.[54] There were further exchanges during May, but Haymerle would not be persuaded, and tried instead to draw closer to England and to

[53] The essential portions of this interesting despatch are quoted by Windelband, pp. 143–4.
[54] Windelband, pp. 146–7.

arrange for joint Anglo-Austrian consultations on all Balkan questions.[55]

Haymerle's anxiety to resume and continue the co-operation with England had, then, met with a response sufficiently favourable to postpone further negotiations over the *Dreikaiserbund* until the following September. Russia and Austria were both counting on British friendship; both supported, therefore, although with their own reservations and arguments, the British plans for the coercion of Turkey in the interests of Montenegro and Greece. Bismarck was compelled to watch development for some time, and to postpone the treaty negotiations, although he was determined that British policy should not lead to the perpetuation of the Austro-Russian estrangement. But during May and June there seemed no sign that this estrangement had in any way diminished. During June statements appeared in the Russian press suggesting that the real enemy of Russia in the Near East was Austria, and that an Anglo-Russian agreement on current Near Eastern problems could be secured.[56]

IV. FRANCE, BISMARCK, AND ENGLAND

The British programme also received a satisfactory enough reception from the French and Italian governments, although there was a distinct cautiousness in the attitude of de Freycinet, who combined the offices of President of the Council and Minister of Foreign Affairs after Waddington's fall in December 1879. The French problem for some years had been to recover the standing and self-confidence of a great power without taking the risk of positive action in doing so, and Thiers' maxim, 'être ami de tout le monde', had been an adequate guide to conduct. In the spring of 1880 the official policy was still one of 'reserve'. It had in fact been anything but a negative policy, and had necessitated the establishment of well-defined relations with all the great powers: the question before de

[55] See p. 83 below. Schüssler, who should know better, follows earlier writers in assuming that after the fall of the Beaconsfield government Haymerle abandoned hope of agreement with England, and agreed early in May to enter a new Three Emperors' Alliance (W. Schüssler, *Deutschland zwischen Russland und England*, p. 59).

[56] *Golos*, 2/14 June; *Moscow Gazette*, 31 May/12 June (extracts in F.O. 65/1080, no. 256).

Freycinet was whether the time had not come for the discreet exploitation of these contacts to France's advantage.[57]

To do so it was necessary to find some sphere of activity which would supply gains without embarrassing France's relations with the great powers, and which would also not alarm the French public. France had traditional interests in Egypt which might be exploited with England's support, and she had an established position in Algeria which made it desirable that she should extend her own control, or at least prevent any extension of control by other European powers, in Morocco to the west and Tunis to the east. The internal condition of all three countries—Egypt, Tunis, and Morocco—invited foreign intervention, but in each case French aggression would be challenged. In Tunis her opponent was Italy but she could count, at any rate until the fall of the Beaconsfield government, on both British and German acquiescence in her plans. Waddington, Freycinet's predecessor, had, however, been unable to take advantage of the hints about Tunis dropped by Salisbury and Bismarck at the Congress of Berlin, owing to the veto of Léon Gambetta on immediate action. Gambetta made it a condition that Italy's agreement should be secured before a French intervention took place; he told the Italian ambassador in August 1878 that the French government had never contemplated the occupation. Waddington also failed to secure a formal guarantee after the Congress of British support, although Salisbury's passive acquiescence was not withheld; the able British consul-general, Sir Richard Wood, a great opponent of French influence, was recalled.[58] Since 1877 France and Great

[57] Perhaps the best introduction to French foreign policy in this period is Baron Boris Nolde's *L'alliance franco-russe* (Paris, 1936), which makes use of the private papers of Giers, de Staal, and Alexandre Nelidov. See particularly Part I, ch. iii. A shorter survey is that of Raymond Recouly, *De Bismarck à Poincaré* (Paris, 1931), pp. 88–128.

[58] Nolde, pp. 73–8; cf. Medlicott, p. 206, on Salisbury's suspicions of French policy in the Near East in 1879. Salisbury left Wood in ignorance of his encouragement of the French initiative in Tunis; Wood followed the traditional policy of encouraging Tunisian resistance to French influence, and Waddington's consequent protests forced Salisbury to recall him in January 1879. Wood's official retirement, after 53 years' service, dated from 1 April 1879. The excuse was the need for a reorganization of the British consular service in the Orient as a result of the Berlin treaty. Tunis was placed on a reduced footing, under a consul, Reade, son of a former consul-general, Sir Thomas Reade.

Britain had acted as mandatories for the powers in Egypt, had joined in pressing financial reforms on the Khedive Ismail, and had brought about the Khedive's deposition by the Sultan in July 1879, after his dismissal of his British and French advisers. But the Conservative government had had no desire for a mere 'bondholders' policy' or for more direct control of Egyptian affairs, and Salisbury had made it clear to Waddington in August 1878 that anything in the nature of an Anglo-French condominium was out of the question. After the accession to office of Prince Tewfik, Sir Rivers Wilson and M. de Blignières were restored to their portfolios in the Egyptian cabinet, but Egypt drifted towards bankruptcy and army rule throughout 1880. There was a similar, but less advertised, problem in Morocco. The British government, supported by that of Spain, favoured internal reforms which would, it was hoped, make the Sultan of Morocco master in his own house. The French sought to perpetuate the corrupt system of protection which left the door open for foreign interference.

France indeed, in March 1880, was potentially the most aggressive of the European powers. While the three empires were each ready for a period of quiescence in European and Near Eastern affairs; while Great Britain was concerned only with the stabilization of the Moslem world through internal reform; and while Italy, in spite of her longing for expansion, was too weak and timid to act, France was preparing for a forward move in any sphere which would give her prestige without embarrassment.

Germany of course was the real problem. The victory of the Moderate Republicans in France in October 1877 had brought about no obvious change in French foreign policy except a new note of reticence about Alsace-Lorraine; the Monarchists, although they had felt it necessary to affirm restitution as the country's ultimate goal, had had no intention of starting a war for the lost provinces. The more discreet Republican policy started from the assumption that while this remained the ultimate goal it was better not to talk too much about it, and that in the immediate future a modest diplomatic activity of an innocuous type should be followed in order to reaccustom Europe to France's participation in public affairs. The powerful inspiration of Gambetta, President of the Chamber of Deputies, but the real leader of the Opportunist Republicans, did much to shape this policy into a Franco-German *rapprochement*; Saint-Vallier at Berlin, although he always reserved the question of Alsace-Lorraine, helped to foster in Bismarck's mind the belief that the encouragement of these satisfactions of French *amour propre* might in time solve the issue of the provinces by turning indefinite postponement into final, if tacit, acceptance. Bismarck's decidedly more genial attitude since Saint-Vallier's appointment in February 1878[59] had expressed itself in a repeated advocacy of the Anglo-French *entente cordiale*; he had professed to believe, as Saint-Vallier reported later, that they would so complement, reassure, and moderate each other when united that their agreement would preserve them from any policy of adventures, to the benefit of the security of other states. This view Bismarck had repeated to Beaconsfield, Salisbury, and Waddington at the Congress of Berlin, and to Saint-Vallier on various occasions during 1879; his agreement to French control of Tunis had only been given after Salisbury had first shown his willingness to accept it. It seemed, therefore, that whether France wanted merely passive security or a modest phase of expansion she would be wise to square the British before seeking German support: but what would happen if there were a British government that Bismarck disliked?

No one, of course, quite trusted him in Paris. The normal assumption among the Monarchists and Radical Republicans was that safety lay in simply rejecting his advances on principle. If the Moderate Republicans were prepared to trust their judgment and their ability to exploit his pleasantries, they also suspected traps; they knew—it was indeed obvious enough— that his calculated friendliness had no necessary permanence, and was subject to the abrupt manœuvres of his unpredictable schemes. Nevertheless there were on the face of it obvious advantages for Germany in Bismarck's present policy and some grounds therefore for hope that he could genuinely intend to continue it; that, in short, it contained no pitfalls. The policy of

[59] Bismarck called him, in November 1880, 'notre drapeau de paix et d'entente' (*D.D.F.*, iii, no. 307).

reserve had saved France from injudicious interference in the Eastern crisis in 1876 and 1877, and at the Congress in 1878 she had stipulated that Western Mediterranean questions should not be raised; thereafter she had quietly supported the majority, while taking some personal interest in the claims of the Rumanians and Greeks. This policy, although ostensibly non-committal, meant in fact passive support of the Anglo-Austrian position, and when the Russo-German quarrel rose to great heights in 1879 the French government had reason to congratulate itself on having chosen the right side. Gambetta had distressed Madame Adam in October 1877 by telling her roundly that France had nothing to gain by associating with Russia. 'Beaten or victorious, only defeat awaits her', he said. 'Gorchakov is too old, Alexander II too hesitant. As Germany rises, Russia declines. And so, as Germany becomes stronger, it is necessary to add to her strength by our submission to her plans.'[60] And, two years later, on 19 September 1879, Waddington's exposition of French policy to Salisbury at Puys had revealed complete acceptance of, and confidence in, German and British policy. He agreed that the situation created in Turkey-in-Europe by the treaty of 1878 must be maintained and that the consolidation of the entente between Austria and Germany was a guarantee of peace; France wished to maintain close understanding with England and good neighbourly relations with Germany; she desired peace, and neither the people nor those who directed French policy contemplated a policy of compensations or of adventures abroad. The moderate Republican press, particularly the *Journal des Débats*, was lukewarm or unsympathetic towards Russia's Balkan claims in 1878 and 1879.[61]

It is not surprising in these circumstances that de Freycinet was friendly, but a little wary, in his reception of the Gladstone

---

[60] Madame Juliette Adam, *Après l'abandon de la revanche* (1910), pp. 73, 74. On taking office, de Freycinet was told by Waddington, 'La Russie est disposée, je crois, à un rapprochement, mais nous sommes épiés par le prince de Bismarck'. C. de Freycinet, *Souvenirs, 1878–1893*, p. 110.

[61] Waddington's visit to Puys: *D.D.F.*, ii, no. 470, and n.; *Salisbury*, ii, 364. Bismarck's discussions with Saint-Vallier: *D.D.F.*, ii, particularly nos. 408–9, 440, 448, 473, 476, 477; cf. Nolde, pp. 81–4; E. M. Carroll, *French Public Opinion and Foreign Affairs* (1931), p. 77.

government's programme.[62] Saint-Vallier reported on 31
March a long conversation in which Bismarck had said that the
Manchester School, if it returned to power with 'l'illuminé
Gladstone' and the feeble Hartington, would seek to set Europe
by the ears in order to extinguish competition and extend 'le
commerce de John Bull'.[63] A week later Saint-Vallier warned
Freycinet that the Liberal victory would have detrimental
effects on Anglo-German relations.[64] This situation would not
necessarily be to France's disadvantage, but her existing standing in European affairs depended mainly on Anglo-German
friendship and accordingly de Freycinet, a sensible, level-
headed, calculating, but not imaginative or over-bold politician, decided to watch and wait a little longer. There was a
further reason for caution. A forward policy in Tunis or Egypt
could be greatly eased by Turkish acquiescence, and it had yet
to be seen whether it would be better to buy the support of
England by vigorously pressing the Porte in the Montenegrin
and Greek questions, or to buy Turkish goodwill by doing
nothing of the sort.

So the Concert was established; Russia, Austria, Germany,
Italy, and France were each prepared to support the first steps
of the new British government, but with the conviction in each
case that national interests would be jeopardized if the coercion
of the Turks were allowed to proceed too far.

[62] Shortly after taking office, de Freycinet was asked by Prince Orlov about his
intentions towards Russia. 'Cultiver avec soin, répondis-je, toutes les occasions qui
peuvent développer les sympathies entre les deux gouvernements. Ne le crions pas
sur les toits, car il faut marcher prudemment; nous sommes entourés de mauvaises
volontés qui pourraient amener l'échec de nos tentatives.' Freycinet, ibid., p. 110.
The Hartmann episode shortly afterwards strained Franco-Russian relations for
some time.

[63] D.D.F., iii, no. 81.

[64] Ibid., iii, no. 83, 7 April 1880.

CHAPTER III

Montenegro and Greece:
The Goschen Mission

THE Sultan, Layard tells us, had a kind of horror of Mr. Gladstone. But the Sultan, according to Professor Vambéry, had no regard for Layard. 'I have torn him out of my heart, for he has shamefully abused my confidence.' By the spring of 1880 a not unjustified complacency was beginning to cushion the nerves of Abdul Hamid against the blows of fortune and of Europe. For three and a half years he had, with obstinacy and some courage, resisted demands and threats, surrendering only when some new disaster to the Empire seemed imminent; in this way he had learned that a patient procrastination, an ability to weary, confuse, and occasionally out-talk the powers, could be relied on to frustrate, or at any rate greatly attenuate many of their demands. These were familiar 'oriental' tactics which are the tactics of all weak powers with an inherited knack of survival. Gladstone's personal invective against the Turks and his plans for united pressure were certainly alarming, but it remained to be seen whether the powers could really unite, and whether Turkish diplomacy might not discover and exploit an absence of genuine resolution.

Although he still seems to have believed that Great Britain of all the powers had the greatest interest in the maintenance of Turkish independence and territorial integrity, he brooded over her strange behaviour. She had not offered the expected military help in the Russo-Turkish war; she had refused a loan in his desperate financial plight during the winter of 1878–9; her two ambassadors, Sir Henry Elliot the supporter of Midhat Pasha, and Layard the fierce advocate of internal reforms, had seemed bent on challenging the authority of the Sultan himself. He felt similar exasperation against Austria, and by the spring of 1880, as the Russian embassy at Constantinople understood well enough, it had become correspondingly difficult for him to resist Russian demands. During the winter of 1879–80 there had, indeed, been several broad hints (to which the Russians had not responded) that the Sultan would welcome a Russo-Turkish alliance. He had hopes of winning some support from Germany, some perhaps from France. He was already master of the situation in Constantinople. He believed that the bigoted old soldier, Osman Pasha, commanded the loyalty of the army, and allowed him to draw extravagant pay, at a time when most of the army had received no pay for three years. Osman Pasha was also Marshal of the Palace. Layard's correspondence bewailed the corruption of the so-called palace party, and the ascendancy over the Sultan of Hafiz Pasha, the Minister of Police, who had earned his influence by his zealous detection of conspiracies, imagined or real. Both Salisbury and Layard were convinced that disaster was imminent. 'It would be of no little advantage to defer the fall of Turkey till our railway has been made to Candahar', Salisbury wrote to Layard on 19 February 1880. 'It would be a great success to defer it till the revolution in Russia has taken place.'[1]

The Greek and Montenegrin frontier questions which faced Turkey and the powers in the spring of 1880 arose out of various clauses of the Treaty of Berlin of 1878. Greece had intervened tardily and ignominiously in the Russo-Turkish war in January 1878 and had been forced by the powers to withdraw her troops from Thessaly on 11 February 1878. In Article XXIV of the treaty the powers had merely promised to offer mediation if Greece and Turkey were unable to agree on the rectification of the Greco-Turkish frontier indicated in the thirteenth protocol of the Congress. Montenegro by comparison had received much more favourable treatment. Her picturesque mountaineers in their almost impregnable fastnesses had been at war with Turkey from 1 July 1876 until the preliminary peace of San Stefano of 3 March 1878, and had won the special

---

[1] The most graphic account of early Hamidian government is in Layard's unpublished memoirs of his embassy (B.M. Add. MSS. 38935–38938). See also Arminius Vambéry, *The Story of My Struggles* (1905), p. 365, and ch. xi. Also Medlicott, chs. viii and ix, for details of the situation in the winter of 1879–80.

affection of Russian panslavists; at San Stefano Montenegro secured independence, access to the sea, and the tripling of her existing territories, although her troops were in occupation of only about one-quarter of the territory that she had thus acquired. At the Congress her gains were much reduced. On her north-eastern frontier the greater part of the sanjak of Novi-pazar was restored to Turkey; on the north-western frontier a smaller area was restored to the Hercegovina, shortly to pass under Austrian rule. On her south-eastern frontier a considerable area was also restored to Turkey, but even so Montenegro was given territory which she had not conquered, and which was in some cases inhabited by fighting Mussulmans who seemed determined to remain under Turkish rule, even if it proved necessary to fight the Turkish army to do so. On the coast Montenegro was allowed to retain the port of Antivari, but had to hand over Spizza to Dalmatia and return Dulcigno to the Turks. North of the lake of Scutari she received the district of Gusinje-Plava, where on 27 August 1878 local Albanian tribesmen promptly murdered Mehemed Ali Pasha, who had been sent by the Porte to persuade them to obey the treaty. This was followed by hard fighting in which the attempts of the Montenegrins to occupy Gusinje and Plava were defeated.

The Albanian nationalist movement was too new to have received the recognition of the powers, who were convinced that the Turkish government was well able to force its Albanian subjects to respect the Berlin treaty if it wished to do so. The reluctance of the Albanians in the north and south to be transferred to Montenegrin or Greek rule (as the case might be) nevertheless gave the Porte an excellent excuse for delay. The Sultan disliked being compelled to cede territory: he disliked even more the stigma of having transferred his Moslem subjects to Christian rulers. But he disliked above all, perhaps, the challenge of the new Albanian nationalism to his own autocratic authority.

Early in June 1878, just before the Congress of Berlin, a group of prominent Albanians had formed at Prizren, in the vilayet of Kossovo, the so-called League of Prizren, whose full title was the 'Albanian League for the Defence of the Rights of the Albanian Nation'. The League had acted quickly, with considerable help at this stage from the Turks. A resolution was addressed to the Congress on 15 June 1878, although its only direct result was to draw from Bismarck the depressing comment, 'there is no Albanian nationality'. The murder of Mehemed Ali Pasha opened the violent phase of the League's activities, and from the heavy and successful fighting against the Montenegrins the Albanian commander, Ali of Gusinje, emerged as the first hero of the movement. Others in the north were Prenk Bib Doda, head of the Roman Catholic Mirdites, and Hodo Pasha of Scutari (Shkodra); the president of the Prizren organization was Ilijas Pasha of Dibra. A southern branch was formed at Argyrokastro (Gjinokastër), and although circumstances gave it a less active rôle than that in the north its leader, Abdul Frashëri, has been called the 'soul of the whole movement' in its first generation. The League's representatives in Elbasan, in central Albania, provided a link between north and south, and in a later generation the town was to become in some degree the cultural and educational headquarters of Albanian nationalism. But there was no effective central direction of the League at this stage.

In resisting the attempt to transfer Albanian territory to Greek or Montenegrin rule the Sultan and the League saw eye to eye. But as the beginning of a movement towards cultural and political autonomy the League was a challenge which the Sultan felt bound to meet. It would appear that the formation of the League represented the genuine beginnings of the nationalist movement; earlier risings against the government, although they had not been infrequent, had been in opposition to new taxes or to other specific acts of interference by the central authorities. The administrative reforms resulting from the Tanzimat of Gülhanè of 1856 had produced a number of these revolts, and they had also provided the basis of a cultural programme, for it was found that whereas almost every nationality throughout the Empire had been given its own schools, the Albanian population had to be content with instruction in either Turkish or Greek. But in 1878 the Albanian tribes were moved by an immediate apprehension that in the collapse of the Turkish Empire, which seemed quite a possibility, they

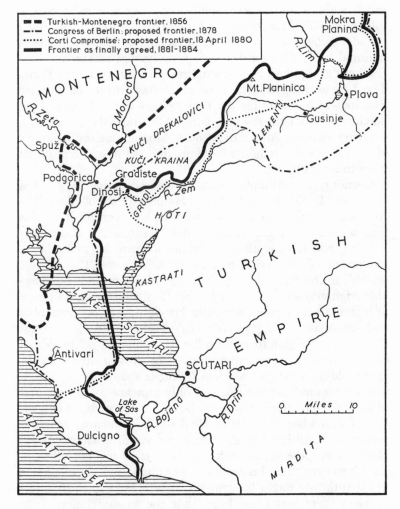

The Albanian-Montenegrin Frontier, 1878–84

Legend (within map):
- Turkish-Montenegro frontier, 1856
- Congress of Berlin: proposed frontier, 1878
- 'Corti Compromise': proposed frontier, 18 April 1880
- Frontier as finally agreed, 1881–1884

might be annexed by, and dispersed among, hated and despised neighbours. By the beginning of 1880 two tendencies had emerged within the movement, for while the fierce and strongly conservative tribesmen in the north saw the struggle, both against the Montenegrins and the Turks, as primarily a defence of their traditional territories and isolation, the southern movement, which from its geographical situation was more accessible to both Turkish control and non-Turkish ideas, produced a broader programme, of self-government on something like a national scale. This southern programme was accepted by the northern group, and viewed with great uneasiness by the Porte. The League was, in fact, prepared to stay within the Turkish Empire—at any rate for the time being—but it wanted local officials of Albanian stock, a single Albanian vilayet, a representative council, Albanian schools, Albanian as the language of administration, religious freedom, and the devotion of direct taxes to local objects.

Certainly the Albanian League was becoming as great a threat as Mr. Gladstone to Abdul Hamid's peace of mind. The Albanian problem has a wider interest, however, for it was his first serious encounter with Moslem nationalism within the Empire, and he was already seeking to turn the pan-Islamic movement of the period to political advantage. The Islamic revival, in the form given to it by the eloquent and indefatigable Afghan teacher, Sayyad Jamaluddin, who became a figure of international importance after his eight years of preaching and propaganda in Egypt (1871–9), sought essentially to adapt the Moslem religion to modern life. It involved a political, and even a revolutionary, programme, for it was necessary in Jamaluddin's view that Moslem countries should be freed from foreign domination; but this was only a means to an end, and to an end which might not easily be reconciled with the exigencies of Hamidian despotism. He looked forward to religious reform and political free thought in a revitalized Islam. Abdul Hamid's purpose on the other hand was to use the office of Caliph to strengthen his authority as Sultan, and the challenge to his authority might be domestic as well as foreign. In Tunis in 1880 there was some hope that the great religious confraternities of Islam could be mobilized against the French; in

Albania however it was only too probable that resistance to foreign pressure would develop into resistance to the Sultan-Caliph. At what point would it be advisable to give the powers the frontier rectification that they demanded in order to be able to repress the nationalist movement? Would the suppression of the movement damage the Sultan's prestige in the Moslem world, while strengthening his direct authority? The Porte seems to have been more ready for action against the Albanian tribes than the Palace, and although the two were agreed in their suspicion of the Albanian movement there were reservations and hesitations on the Sultan's side which the Porte did not seem quite to grasp. The Sultan might have been even more alarmed had he known that Gladstone, who had been studying Hahn's *Albanesische Studien* assiduously during the summer, felt that Albania had a 'special title to have its case put forward' in return for good behaviour.[2]

Greek and Turkish frontier commissioners had met at Preveza early in 1879, but most of the meetings had been taken up with discussion of the validity of the Congress protocol. The Albanian League carried on propaganda against the Greek proposal to annex Janina, Arta, and Preveza, and in the meantime, under the leadership of Abdul Frashëri, a strong force of 30,000 Albanians was kept under arms to resist a Greek advance. The Turkish commissioners finally offered 'a narrow strip of country parallel with the existing Greek frontier, and which starting from the Gulf of Volo, took in Domoko, and ended at a river called Aspropotamo'. The Greeks rejected this and the negotiations were broken off on 18 March 1879. They were resumed on 23 August 1879 under the mediation of the ambassadors of the powers; but the Turks again wasted a lot of time in trying to convince the other delegates and themselves that the Berlin protocol was not obligatory. The Greeks were

---

[2] J. G. von Hahn, *Albanesische Studien* (1854). For good recent accounts of the early Albanian movement: Stavro Skendi, 'Beginnings of the Albanian Nationalist and Autonomous Trends, The Albanian League, 1878–1881' (*The American Slavic and East European Review*, vol. xii), and 'Beginnings of Albanian Nationalist Trends in Culture and Education, 1878–1912' (*Journal of Central European Affairs*, January 1953); Th. Ippen, 'Beiträge zur inneren Geschichte Albaniens im XIX Jahrhundert' in *Illyrisch-Albanische Forschungen* (1916), i, 370; J. Swire, *Albania, the Rise of a Kingdom* (1929), pp. 1–60.

finally able to table their demands only on 17 November. They proposed a frontier line following the extreme northern watershed of the valleys of the Kalamas and Salambria (Peneios), which would have given them Janina and Metzovo; the Turks offered an alternative line running much to the south of the two towns; and after various adjournments had made it evident that agreement could not be reached the Greek commissioners were instructed, on 2 January 1880, to propose that the question should be referred to the arbitration of the powers. As it happened, Salisbury and Waddington both disliked the Greek line, although they could not agree on an alternative. Waddington thought that the line should follow in Epirus the southern limit of the basin of the Kalamas, and in Thessaly the northern limit of the valley of the Peneios. Salisbury objected to the French line because it gave Greece considerably more than the area suggested at Berlin, and 'did not entirely escape from the Albanian difficulty'; to the Greek line because by giving Metzovo to the Greeks it would deprive Turkey of her means of communication with the portions of Epirus left to her; and to the Berlin line because it neglected the aspirations of the Albanian nationality. He proposed therefore that an international commission of representatives of the mediating powers should examine the frontier on the spot, and de Freycinet, who had succeeded Waddington in January 1880, agreed; the other powers accepted the proposal but the Porte opposed it strongly. There was no doubt some justification for its concern at the possibility of demonstrations by the local population for and against annexation by Greece.[3]

There was a similar deadlock over the disputed Montenegrin frontier. The Porte had suggested to Count Corti in January 1880 that in order to avoid trouble the part of Gusinje inhabited by Christians should go to Montenegro, together with the district of Kuči-Kraina north of lake Scutari; other areas

[3] For the Greek question during this period there is ample material in the blue books, A. & P. *Greece No. 1 (1879)*, *Greece No. 1 (1880)* (c.2330; c.2474); *L.J.*, *Négociations relatives à la rectification des frontières de la Grèce, 1879*; *ibid., 1880*; *D.D.F.*, vols. ii, iii. M. Lhéritier's careful and detailed study, *Histoire diplomatique de la Grèce* (iv, chs. 1–3), appeared before the publication of the *D.D.F.* and the opening of the British F.O. archives after 1878. See also S. T. Lascaris, *La politique extérieure de la Grèce avant et après le Congrès de Berlin* (1924), pp. 151–73. See map, p. 234.

inhabited by Moslems would remain under Turkish rule. Hay-merle did not like the plan, for it involved a modification of the Berlin treaty; but ultimately all the powers agreed, and an arrangement on these lines was signed at Constantinople on 18 April 1880. Albanian opposition once more made a settle-ment impossible. The Roman Catholic tribes which were to be transferred made it known that they would resist and would be supported by the Mirdites, who had given solemn engagements to withstand their hereditary Orthodox foes, the Montenegrins. On 23 April Prince Nicholas announced that in violation of an agreement between himself and the Porte the Turkish authori-ties omitted to give twenty-four hours' notice of the evacuation of the positions in ceded districts held by Turkish troops; when the Montenegrins advanced they found that the positions had been occupied by Albanians. Sawas Pasha, the Turkish foreign minister, admitted that not more than eight hours' notice was given to the Montenegrin commander. On 27 April the Albanian League closed the river Boyana against Montenegrin commerce.[4]

It was in these circumstances that Granville made his first move to bring the Concert into being. On 4 May he proposed in a circular despatch that the powers should address a note to the Porte, requiring it to fulfil forthwith its obligations under the treaty with regard to Greece, Montenegro, and Armenia. He was, however, forestalled by Giers, who in a circular tele-gram on the same day proposed that the powers should threaten 'effective measures' for the protection of Montenegro unless the convention (of 18 April) were loyally carried out without fur-ther loss of time.[5] Haymerle did not like the Russian proposal. As it happened the ambassadors at Constantinople had asked the Porte on 3 May if it were prepared to reoccupy the positions in dispute and to hand them over to the Montenegrins, and as the Porte's reply was not yet known the other Powers agreed that the Russian proposal was premature. Austria's real objec-tion was probably the threat of coercion. Haymerle told the

[4] Layard to Granville, 29 April, F.O. 78/3085, no. 473. A. & P. *Turkey No. 22* (*1880*), nos. 31, 79, 122, 152, 153, 155; *L.J.*, *Affaires du Monténégro*, no. 1 (1880); also the Austrian red book, *Actenstücke . . . über orientalische Angelegenheiten* (1880).

[5] Circular to H.M. RR, 4 May, F.O. 76/1076, no. 176, etc. Cf. no. 173, 1 May; Granville to Layard, 8 May, F.O. 78/3073, no. 305.

Russian ambassador that he would like particulars of the proposed measures before deciding, and that under the Russian proposal the powers would assume a responsibility that properly belonged to the Porte.[6]

As the British circular merely proposed that Turkey should be called on to fulfil her obligations it met Haymerle's immediate objections.[7] But coercion, or the threat of coercion, was implicit in the Gladstonian programme, and Haymerle's hesitations were alarming. As early as 3 May he made it clear to Elliot that if the Porte were unwilling or unable to reoccupy the positions in dispute, 'it would not suit Austria either to make an active intervention in Albania herself or to see it attempted by any other power'.[8] This attitude was elaborated in a despatch to Károlyi, which the ambassador discussed with Granville on the 10th. Granville admitted that the use of force to compel unwilling populations to submit would be distasteful to the British government, but he argued that if the Turks were unable, or refused, to fulfil their treaty obligations in this respect, Montenegro had a right to look to Europe for the fulfilment of the treaty. He suggested three possible solutions. (1) The Greek frontier might be settled, and then the Greeks, Montenegrins, and Albanians might be left to fight it out among themselves. This was undesirable. (2) A compromise might possibly be made with the Albanians by which they might be induced to cede the district in question without bloodshed. (3) A compromise might be made with Montenegro which would give to

---

[6] Layard to Granville, 4 May, F.O. 78/3085, no. 487. In his acceptance of Granville's proposal Giers referred to the consideration of 'ulterior steps' if a collective European protest failed. The French and other governments took exception to this; he then explained that his allusion did not necessarily imply a resort to physical force. Dufferin to Granville, 18 May, F.O. 65/1080, no. 219. Elliot to Granville, 5 May, F.O. 7/990, no. 206. Haymerle, circular tel., W.S.A., 5 May; Haymerle to Kálnoky, 8 May. Odo Russell to Granville, 12 May, F.O. 64/960, no. 204.

[7] In the middle of May a rumour appeared in the press in Berlin and London that Russia would propose an Italian occupation of Albania. Wimpffen (Rome) to Haymerle, 14 May, W.S.A., tel. no. 60.

[8] Elliot to Granville, 3 May, F.O. 7/990, no. 201. He also told Elliot that 9,000 rations of bread were taken daily to the Albanian camps from Scutari, and argued that the Turks could easily end the Albanian resistance without bloodshed by stopping these supplies. 4 May, no. 204, conf. Suspicion at the Porte of Austrian policy in Montenegro continued to be fostered, after Fournier's departure, by the Sultan's French favourite, Dreyssé. Dubsky to Haymerle, 4 May, W.S.A., no. 36B.

that country an accession of territory in a quarter where the inhabitants would be willing to live under her rule. Károlyi promised that if force were not resorted to, Austria would be ready to concert with her allies for any practical compromise, of the nature suggested.[9]

Haymerle maintained this attitude for the next three months[10] although it appeared increasingly unlikely that Turkey would give way without a threat of force backed up by some tangible evidence that the threat was meant to be taken seriously. Moreover, Granville soon found that it was useless to hope that the other governments would be able to put Austria into a more bellicose frame of mind. The French were, if anything, more opposed to the use of force than Austria, and appeared determined to avoid any pronouncement whatsoever on the Montenegrin question; Bismarck might grumble to Saburov about the timidity of Austrian statesmen, but he had not the faintest intention of urging Haymerle to take any course which was distasteful to the Austrian government.[11] The Russian government was certainly prepared to act, but Haymerle was not likely to listen to suggestions from that quarter. He left the British government in no doubt that he still distrusted Russia, and preferred to find a solution of the outstanding difficulties by direct agreement with England; Giers understood the situation well enough to know that any attempt on his part to galvanize the Austrians would defeat its own end. He suggested to Dufferin that Austria might give up to the Montenegrins, as an equivalent to what they were entitled in the south, a corner of the Hercegovina where there was a cognate and sympathetic population; but when Dufferin asked if the suggestion had been made to the Austrian ambassador he replied, 'God forbid that I should do so'.[12] Granville, however, hinted at such a solution

[9] Granville to Elliot, 10 May, F.O. 7/985, no. 221. On 6th he urged the Porte to prevent any Albanian aggression. Haymerle to Dubsky, 6 May, W.S.A., tel. no. 76; Dubsky to Haymerle, 7 May, tel. no. 70.

[10] After an attempt by Dubsky to suggest, 'unofficially', to the Porte a compromise on the Montenegrin question (Dubsky to Haymerle, 11 May, W.S.A., 38A–F), Haymerle gave him specific instructions to act only in conformity with Hatzfeldt and Onou. Haymerle to Dubsky, 22 May, tel no. 96.

[11] Odo Russell to Granville, 12 May, F.O. 64/960, no. 200. Przibram, ii, 114; *Granville*, ii, 202.

[12] Dufferin to Granville, 8 May, F.O. 65/1080, no. 203.

in the third alternative outlined to Károlyi on the 10th, and told the French ambassador that he took Károlyi's reply to mean that the Austrian government had not finally given up the idea of compensating Montenegro in the Hercegovina.[13] Elliot had already on his own initiative hinted to Haymerle that some such cession was desirable; Haymerle's answer that it would not have suited the Imperial government to allow a further extension of Montenegro towards the north satisfied Elliot that if that was the feeling before the occupation it was not likely to be modified now, and Granville made no attempt to press the suggestion.[14] Károlyi, however, referred on the 11th to Granville's third alternative, and said that on examining the map he had been able to see no way in which the idea could be carried out without a curtailment of the rights with which Austria had been entrusted. As the Austrian government was so deeply affected by all changes in that quarter he hoped that Granville would confidentially explain to them his idea of compensation before discussing it with other powers.[15]

This invitation was repeated by Haymerle on the 14th. He told Elliot that he entirely agreed with Granville as to the importance of a concert of the powers in dealing with the affairs of Turkey; Granville would, however, agree that there were questions respecting which it would be desirable to have a confidential interchange of views between the governments more especially interested in them, previous to their being submitted to the discussion of the others who were more remotely, or hardly at all, affected by them. Austria, for example, had no direct interest in Armenia, and it was natural that on this question the British government should concert with Russia, and

[13] *D.D.F.*, iii, no. 113.

[14] He was also opposed to an extension of Montenegrin territory in the direction of Novipazar. Granville to Dufferin, 9 June, F.O. 65/1076, no. 243. Elliot to Granville, 11 May, F.O. 7/990, no. 223. The idea was also put forward by Moukhtar Pasha, in Constantinople. On 17 May Haymerle told Dubsky, 'Die Pforte möge sich nicht durch solche Projecte beirren lassen, denn wir werden nicht zugeben, dass ihre Fehler auf Kosten unserer Rechte gut gemacht werden'. Haymerle to Dubsky, 17 May, W.S.A., tel no. 91, Dubsky to Haymerle, 18 May, no. 40B.

[15] Haymerle to Károlyi, 10 May, W.S.A., tel. Granville to Elliot, 11 May, F.O. 7/985, no. 221A. On 15th Haymerle telegraphed to Thömmel (Cettinje), mentioning the forms of compensation suggested, and asking whether he could suggest any alternative scheme, not at Austria's expense.

that they should exchange views with France concerning Syria. 'In the same way', wrote Elliot, 'in matters relating to the Balkan peninsula, which touch the vital interests of Austria so much more closely than those of any other Power, he hopes that Your Lordship will not be unwilling to enter into an unreserved exchange of views before communicating the opinion of Her Majesty's Government upon them to all the other cabinets.'[16] A despatch to Károlyi on 18 May, in the form of a reply to the assurances of friendship given by Granville on 30 April, expressed in more general terms the desire for an intimate understanding and co-operation between the two powers on all Balkan questions, and at the same time accepted Gladstone's explanation of the 'misunderstanding' in a few brief and tactful phrases.[17] Two days later, in reply to Haymerle's suggestion of the 14th, Granville telegraphed that the British government would be ready to enter into an unreserved exchange of views with the Austrian government on matters relating to the Balkan peninsula.[18]

The discussions on the Montenegrin frontier between the powers during May had thus done little more than place the British government in friendly communication with Vienna and St. Petersburg, and had shown that unless the Sultan's resistance could be overcome by diplomatic pressure the Austrian attempt to veto direct action might force the powers into a deadlock. Granville hoped that the sending of Mr. G. J. Goschen as a special ambassador to Constantinople might avoid this calamity, and in the meantime turned his attention to the Greek frontier question, which seemed more amenable to treatment. On 28 April Freycinet had suggested to Lyons the advisability of avoiding Turkish obstruction by assembling the commission in a non-Turkish town, and after further pressure by M. Léon Say, the new French ambassador in London, Granville proposed to the powers on 11 May that if the Turkish government were unwilling that a boundary commission on the Greek frontier should meet, or if it were unable to guarantee its safety, a conference should be assembled at Berlin or Paris to

[16] Elliot to Granville, 14 May, F.O. 7/990, no. 236.
[17] Haymerle to Károlyi, W.S.A., 18 May.
[18] Elliot to Granville, 20 May, F.O. 7/990, no. 244.

consider and decide by a majority upon the proper line of rectification of frontier to be adopted.[19] Haymerle again seemed
reluctant to adopt any new procedure, but Freycinet continued
to urge the advantages of a meeting outside Turkey, pointing
out that if the choice was left to the Porte it would inevitably
choose the course which wasted most time. On 22 May Granville sought the opinion of the powers on this point, and found
within the next few days a general disposition to proceed with
the conference irrespective of the Sultan's wishes. Berlin, Paris,
and even Berne had been mentioned in London as possible
meeting places; but it seems that although Freycinet and Gambetta would have been pleased at the choice of Paris, their
hands were somewhat forced by Saint-Vallier. He told Freycinet on 12 May that Granville had, through Münster, proposed Berlin, and that Bismarck had accepted; actually it
appears that Saint-Vallier had taken upon himself to urge the
choice of Berlin in the name of the French government, and
Bismarck had accepted before Hohenlohe had had time to
report Freycinet's wishes. Freycinet showed in private some
annoyance at Saint-Vallier's conduct, but agreed to the choice
of Berlin. There seems no doubt that the British, Russian,
Austrian, and Italian governments regarded Berlin as the most
suitable centre.[20]

With the Montenegrin and Greek questions at this stage of
development, Goschen left London for Constantinople, arriving
at Therapia on 28 May. Goschen was the son of an able German business-man of Lutheran descent who had settled in
London in 1814; the family had kept up its German connexions, and George Joachim had spent some years at school in
Saxe-Meiningen before proceeding by way of Rugby and
Oxford into the English business world and then into politics.
He held office in Gladstone's first administration; supported
him in his Turkish policy in the late 'seventies, and reported on
Egyptian finances in the autumn of 1876 as the representative
of Egyptian bondholders in London. He was elected M.P. for
Ripon in March 1880, after declaring his unflinching support
of the British Empire, his equally unflinching opposition to

Home Rule, his condemnation of Lord Salisbury's un-English devices and surprises as Foreign Secretary, his frank pleasure that Constantinople had been kept out of Russian hands, and his deep regret that the rising nationalities of the East had not been taught to look to England as one of their staunchest friends. This good Englishman so far forgot his German connexions as to omit to visit Bismarck a few weeks later, an omission which reflects the curious, and largely unconscious, tendency of the Liberal leaders to avoid contact with the German Chancellor at this time. Goschen was a serious-minded, able, rather irritable man, with a long, severe upper lip, formidable side-whiskers, and extremely short sight. He had debarred himself from membership of the new Cabinet through his opposition to the extension of the county franchise, and for personal and political reasons he did not wish to accept the Viceroyalty of India which was offered him; nor did he wish to leave politics by entering the diplomatic service. But he agreed to undertake a special and temporary mission to Constantinople, and as the appointment was unpaid he did not have to vacate his seat at Ripon. [21]

It was arranged that he should travel to Constantinople by way of Paris and Vienna, and this was no doubt a meritorious attempt to improve the understanding of British policy in both capitals; but it was a bad blunder to omit a visit to Berlin. Bismarck was sensitive to such apparent rebuffs, and quite ready to suspect machinations against himself; and as he had in any case no desire to forward Gladstone's anti-Turkish policy he had already something of a guilty conscience on this score.

Freycinet had not been pleased at the abrupt dropping of Paris as the seat of the conference, and he was also surprised at what seemed to be an unnecessary delay by the British government in communicating to him the circular of 4 May. But on the 17th he accepted the British proposal; on the 19th he gave an interview to Goschen and Lyons, but seemed mainly anxious to be reassured that the British government entertained no special intentions concerning Turkish finance. He showed some interest in the Greek frontier, but none in the

---

[21] *Goschen*, vol. i; ch. vii, dealing with the Constantinople mission, is based on Goschen's own account.

problems of Montenegro or Armenia. In discussion he drew a
distinction between the Montenegrin frontier, where the Turks
were asked to reoccupy positions and if necessary fire on their
own subjects, and the Greek, where all they would be asked to
do was to withdraw. But when Goschen pointed out that if
Albanian populations were transferred to Greece there would
be the same difficulties as on the Montenegrin frontier, Freycinet could only say rather vaguely that care would have to be
taken to avoid this contingency. In any case his idea was
apparently that in the last resort the parties concerned would
have to fight it out among themselves. Goschen wrote privately
to Granville that Freycinet 'gave me distinctly the impression
that he had not mastered the Eastern question at all, and had
no policy except to draw a new frontier line and to be very
cordial to the English'. Goschen appears to have made a good
impression.[22]

Two days later Goschen, accompanied by Elliot, visited Haymerle, and found him equally anxious to emphasize his desire
for co-operation with England, but even more opposed than
Freycinet to any use of force against the Turks. It was impossible to disguise the fact that the two powers were still far from
agreement on the Greek and Montenegrin questions. Haymerle
admitted that he preferred Salisbury's proposal for a commission to examine the Greek frontier on the spot; the only
reason for this that Goschen could discover was Haymerle's
apprehension lest the opportunity should be taken to introduce
at the conference further questions connected with the East. In
the end he promised to support any step by the British government to do justice to Greece, but he also made it clear that 'the
Austrian government would be most reluctant that any material
pressure should be used', and appeared unwilling to face or
discuss the possibility. After speaking at great length and with
great earnestness on the Montenegrin difficulty Haymerle
announced that he could not take any military steps and was
quite determined that no other individual power should do so,

[22] *Goschen*, i, 198; *D.D.F.*, iii, no. 124; cf. no. 127. Goschen to Granville, 19
May, G.D., 29/188 (Granville Papers); 19 May, F.O. 78/3086, no. 1. The French
government, as a sign of its desire to act in harmony with England, withdrew its
ambassador at Constantinople, M. Fournier, who had quarrelled persistently with
Layard. His successor was M. Tissot. *Lyons*, ii, 210.

and he declined very emphatically to agree with Granville's confidential suggestion concerning the cession to Montenegro of a piece of territory now in the occupation of Austria. He promised, however, 'not only formal but cordial co-operation' in the Asiatic reform programme. The German ambassador to Vienna, Prince Reuss, made it clear to Goschen that Germany was also not prepared for material pressure.[23]

Yet Haymerle was anxious for close relations with the Gladstone government; it was obvious enough that his desire to prevent any weakening of the Ottoman empire was governed by fear of Russian machinations, and for this reason he dreaded any changes or negotiations at all concerning the Balkans. He admitted that Russia 'not from any real interest but on sentimental grounds' was the power most concerned after Austria with the Montenegrin question, but in reply to Goschen's inquiry as to whether Austria and Russia could not come to some preliminary arrangement he answered quickly that 'that was quite impossible'. No government, he said, had had more experience than his own of the inconstancy and petty trickery of the Porte; but the Congress had not aimed at stripping the Sultan of all his political authority, and the limitation of his power had been intended at the same time as a means of strengthening it, for the time had not arrived for the local population to demand, or for Europe to agree upon, a new political organization. The more one believed in the maintenance of the European Concert, the more necessary it appeared to him to exercise foresight in the choice of the means whereby a better order of things in the Near East was achieved: the maintenance of world peace was more important than the details of the Eastern question.[24]

Thus the interview had hardly brought the two governments nearer to solutions of the outstanding questions. It had, however, done something to reassure them as to each other's peaceful intentions. Haymerle decided that Goschen, in spite of his strong belief in the success of his mission, was a moderate man, who did not entirely accept the Gladstonian theories. Goschen's

[23] Goschen to Granville, 23 May, G.D. 29/188 (Granville Papers).
[24] Haymerle to Károlyi, W.S.A., 30 May. Goschen to Granville, 22 May, F.O. 78/3086, very conf.

opinion of Haymerle's peaceful intentions was confirmed after
an audience with the Emperor on the 22nd, and his reports
may have finally dispelled any lingering suspicions in the
British cabinet as to Austria's real intentions. He noted that an
uneasiness as to Russia was evident in many of the Emperor's
phrases, and concluded that the Emperor 'seemed most
desirous to act in harmony with England, and his general
attitude seemed rather one of great political timidity and embarrassment than one of far-seeing design'.[25]

By the time that Goschen reached Constantinople all the
powers had concurred in the British proposal for an identic and
simultaneous note calling on the Porte to fulfil forthwith its
treaty obligations in respect of Greece, Montenegro, and
Armenia. They had also agreed that the delay of the Porte in
replying to Salisbury's proposal of a Greek frontier commission
must be regarded as a refusal, and that in the interest of a
speedy issue the mediating powers should meet in Berlin to
determine by majority the proper line of frontier.[26] But there
was as yet no sign in Constantinople that the Porte and the Sultan had any intention of accepting these or any other recommendations. On 17 May the Porte, in reply to the collective
note of the 3rd, proposed an inquiry on the spot into the events
accompanying the evacuation of 24 April.[27] This was regarded
as a mere attempt to waste time, and no serious attention was
given to it. The next move was therefore the drafting and presentation of a further collective note to the Porte in accordance
with the British circular of 4 May, and this task Goschen found
awaiting him on his arrival.[28] Throughout June Goschen and
the other ambassadors were left to do what they could to bully or
cajole the Porte into surrender, and the powers endeavoured to

[25] Goschen to Granville, 23 May, F.O. 78/3086, no. 4, secret. Note by Tenterden: 'The expression "political timidity" exactly expresses the drifting policy
which the Austrian Govt. has pursued and which has brought them into Bosnia
notwithstanding Ct. Andrássy's repeated protestations. T.'

[26] Granville to Goschen, 27 May, F.O. 78/3074, no. 17.

[27] Dubsky to Goschen, 7 May, W.S.A., tel. no. 70; tel. no. 71; 11 May, no.
38A–F. Layard to Granville, 17 May, F.O. 78/3086, no. 515. Granville to Goschen,
27 May, F.O. 78/3074, no. 14.

[28] Elliot to Granville, 14 May, F.O. 7/990, no. 234; Granville to Elliot, 15 May,
F.O. 7/985, no. 231. Dufferin to Granville, 18 May, F.O. 65/1080, no. 217. Odo
Russell to Granville, 21 May, F.O. 64/960.

concoct compromises on which they themselves at least could agree.

The Sultan had shown some alarm at the Liberal victory in England and at Goschen's appointment, but he appears to have got over the worst of his fears quickly enough, and was evidently determined by the end of May not to be bullied or bluffed into unnecessary activity. Musurus Pasha, the Turkish ambassador in London, arrived in Constantinople about the same time; he was believed to be particularly successful in negotiating with Englishmen. The Sultan's genuine and somewhat wearisome sense of personal dignity had been profoundly disturbed by the sharp words and offhand manners of the new government, and the soothing of the ruffled little tyrant had the double effect of wasting more time and of robbing Goschen's arrival of its more dramatic qualities. [29]

Difficulties even arose out of the announcement of Goschen's appointment. On 7 May a telegram reached Layard from Granville instructing him to inform the Porte of Goschen's appointment as special ambassador to relieve him from his duties on quitting Constantinople on leave of absence. [30] Owing to the Muhammedan holiday Layard was unable to communicate this message to the Foreign Minister until the morning of the 8th. Sawas Pasha at once objected that the procedure was unusual; it was the invariable custom to ask the sovereign for his agreement before making such appointments, and consequently he would not venture to submit the communication officially to the Sultan. Instead he requested Sir Alfred Sandison to see Munir Bey, who as the Grand Master of the Ceremonies was considered the highest authority on such matters. The latter was no doubt acting on instructions when he told Sandison that he was of opinion that the Sultan would be much offended, and begged that he might not be charged with communicating Goschen's appointment officially to His Majesty. Layard accordingly telegraphed to Granville suggesting that the course usually followed on the appointment of an ambassador should be observed. [31]

[29] Cf. Dubsky's account, to Haymerle, 1 June, W.S.A., no. 44A–F. Also, concerning Musurus, no. 45A–H, 8 June.

[30] Granville to Layard, 6 May, F.O. 78/3073, no. 302A.

[31] Layard to Granville, 11 May, F.O. 78/3086, no. 499. Memoirs: Add. MSS. 38938, ff. 228–30.

It seems very unlikely that the British government intended to treat the Porte in any cavalier fashion; in the despatch which followed the telegram Layard was instructed to express the hope that the choice of Goschen as temporary ambassador at Constantinople would be agreeable to the Sultan, and in the drafting of the despatch care had been taken that the same wording should be used as on the occasion of Layard's appointment as special ambassador in 1877. Layard himself, who received that first intimation of his recall from the newspapers, could have felt little enthusiasm in fighting the diplomatic battles of the new administration. It was in this connexion that he remarked later, perhaps not altogether without sympathy, on the Sultan's 'kind of horror of Mr. Gladstone'.[32] Layard was faithful to the letter of his instructions in his announcement to Sawas, but it is difficult to believe that he failed to realize the probable consequences of an attempt to dispense with the Sultan's agreement at this stage, or that the possibility of his having misinterpreted Granville's intentions did not occur to him. The Muhammedan holiday on the 7th would have allowed him to telegraph a query on the point without delaying the announcement unduly. On the 11th he received a further telegram informing him that the omission to ask whether the appointment would be agreeable was quite unintentional, and instructing him to make the inquiry in the manner he might think best.

It was believed that the Sultan might refuse to receive Goschen; he had been induced to believe that Goschen's mission to Egypt in 1876 had led to the deposition of the Khedive in 1879, and that he was being sent to Turkey to bring about a similar result. Layard warned the Sultan of the serious consequences of such a refusal, and after the communication of Granville's second message the Sultan gave his agreement

[32] Granville to Layard, 6 May, F.O. 78/3073, no. 302A. Cf. Add. MSS. 38938, last pp. 'I see that Gladstone has written another violent article on the subject [of Greece] in one of the periodicals. However, little justice or fairness, or patriotism can be expected from him.' Add. MSS. 38961, Layard to Hammond, 7 June 1879. 'You know my sentiments too well to imagine that I felt any regret, either on public or private grounds, at the fall of Mr. Gladstone's Ministry. I believe that it attained to power on false pretences and grave misrepresentations . . .' etc. Add. MSS. 38939, Layard to Lord Duncannon, 5 July 1885.

promptly enough. Munir Bey in a private letter said that if the Sultan had hesitated for a moment in giving his agreement it was mainly with the aim of maintaining Layard in the post which he had occupied with so much distinction; and in a farewell interview at Yildiz Kiosk on the 29th Abdul Hamid expressed anew his regret at Layard's departure. 'It was principally owing to me, His Majesty said, that he was now on the throne.'[33]

There was further trouble on Goschen's arrival. He paid a formal call on Sawas Pasha on 29 May and was led to expect that his formal audience with the Sultan to present his credentials would take place on the 1st or 2nd June. Layard, dining with the Sultan on 31 May, was told that Goschen's application for an audience had not yet been brought before the Sultan.[34] In the end the audience was arranged for 3 June. The delay was due to objections raised by Sawas to the short address delivered by ambassadors on these occasions. A copy of this had been given to Sawas on 29 May, and three days later he pointed out to Sandison that the precedents were in favour of neutral speeches, but that Goschen's contained phrases which might make it necessary for the Sultan either to make a more or less political reply at the public audience or simply refer the matter to his Minister. The Sultan, according to Layard, had declared his willingness to listen to friendly advice in private audience, but not to be addressed in public in language offensive to his dignity. The terms of the speech had been agreed on by Goschen and Granville, and Goschen recognized that it was not altogether 'in the traditional style'. He said that he thought the speech contained nothing that was not perfectly suitable, but had decided that controversy and the consequent delay would be unwise, and accordingly he would cut out the offending passages, on condition that he should be granted a private audience immediately after the public reception.[35] When the incident became known in England it damaged the government considerably. As one versifier put it:

[33] Layard to Granville, 13 May, F.O. 78/3086, no. 508; 29 May, no. 556. Add. MSS. 38938, ff. 236-7.

[34] Goschen to Granville, 1 June, F.O. 78/3087, no. 8.

[35] Goschen to Granville, 2 June, G.D. 29/188 (Granville Papers), tel., personal and private.

Then Goschen set out as Morality's Saviour,
To trounce old Mahound into better behaviour;
But the first dose he gave him caused such a vagary,
That the Turk kicked the speeches right o'er to Scutari,
While he swore this new Doctor should have a good flooring—
And the Russ stood by smiling and softly 'Encore'-ing;
For the patience of Job, were he Jew, Turk, or German,
Could not stand the full blast of a Gladstonian Sermon. [36]

Nevertheless when the private audience at last took place Goschen did succeed in alarming the Sultan considerably.

He found that Granville's language to Musurus Bey on 30 April had not been passed on, and decided that he could not do better than communicate Granville's language textually. He said that his government desired to see the Sultan's supremacy maintained, but if their requests were disregarded 'it would be painful to Her Majesty's Government to think that it was the Sultan who had not been willing to agree to proposals which had been made in the most friendly spirit as regards the welfare of the Ottoman Empire'. The Sultan seemed greatly alarmed at this language, but made no comment and finally requested Goschen to put the substance of his remarks in writing. Later conversations with the Turkish ministers convinced Goschen that his references to the Sultan's responsibility had done more to alarm the timid autocrat than any other step. Musurus Pasha told him that the Sultan never acted except on the advice of his ministers or his council; that he was not a despotic or absolute sovereign; that a constitution existed and that it was impossible for the British government to place such responsibility on him as was suggested by the language which had been used. Goschen replied bluntly that the Sultan kept a ministry in power who were defeating all reforms and defying all good influences. If he did so the responsibility was his. [37]

There was a ministerial crisis during the week following Goschen's audience; its origins are somewhat obscure but the composition of the new ministry announced on 10 June made it clear that the Sultan's absolutism and his resistance to the

[36] 'Goschen's Potion', June 1880. *The Gladstone Rule*, by an Outsider, pp. 25, 26.
[37] Granville to Goschen, 18 May, F.O. 78/3074, no. 1 (Goschen's instructions), Goschen to Granville, 7 June, F.O. 78/3087, no. 17.

powers were to be continued. The retiring prime minister, Saïd Pasha, was believed to have acquired a 'Satanic' power over the Sultan, which meant that he had used his enormous influence to encourage the Sultan in resisting every movement tending to check the exercise of constant absolute power. Sawas Pasha, however, told Sandison in confidence that a day or two before Goschen's arrival the prime minister had laid before his colleagues a programme of reforms of which he made them feel the extreme importance at that particular juncture. The Sultan heard of this and sent for Saïd on the night/of 2 June, and a very warm discussion followed during which Saïd firmly maintained his views and finally left his master in a state of irritation and displeasure. Goschen's strong words on the following day convinced the Sultan that Saïd and Sawas had recommended the use of this language to the English ambassador, and he seemed unconvinced by Sawas's denials. The two then paid a courtesy visit to Goschen at the British embassy, and, departing from the usual custom of purely formal conversations, said that they would be glad of an exchange of ideas. After listening to Goschen's statement of the British policy Saïd, in a 'somewhat mysterious manner', told him that 'public opinion was shaping itself in the direction of a revival of the Constitution'. Goschen asked bluntly, 'but what does the Turkish Government say?' and Saïd replied, after a pause: 'The Government associates itself with the opinion of the Public'. He then hinted that difficulties lay not with the ministry, but 'elsewhere'.

The coincidence of Saïd's sudden interest in reform with Goschen's arrival is too close to be accidental, and was apparently due to his desire to frustrate intrigues by the British and other ambassadors for his removal, and even perhaps to increase his own power by forcing on the Sultan a modification of the absolutism. If so, he over-reached himself, and Sawas confessed to Sandison on 4 June that he and Saïd were in a great state of anxiety about their personal safety. Sandison said that Goschen's language at the private audience might be the means of saving the Empire, whereupon Sawas went on somewhat abjectly to say that should Goschen and the British government 'be prepared to save him and the Prime Minister from exile into some unhealthy part of the country, you will

have no reason to complain of them with regard to the introduction of the reforms which they feel are so greatly needed for
the safety and general amelioration of the present condition of
the Empire'.[38] The Sultan pressed the premiership in vain on
Mahmoud Nedim, who was at the palace for thirty-six hours;
he was said to have stated without reserve that he would not
undertake the responsibilities of the post without the power.
Nedim appears to have convinced himself by this stage that reforms alone could save the Turkish empire, and he still enjoyed
the confidence of the Turkish population, which Khair-ed-
Din, a more clever and up-to-date politician, lacked. Safvet
Pasha, a third possible prime minister, was generally believed
to be 'used up', and unequal to a crisis of such magnitude. In
the end, on 10 June, Kadri Pasha was appointed Prime Minister
and Abeddin Pasha Foreign Minister. Nedim was obviously the
strongest man in the new government, and in Goschen's
opinion was 'very anxious to be backed, and to be forced to
take the Premiership'.[39] Kadri had been Governor-General of
Baghdad, and was known as an active and intelligent official,
but he was believed to be almost fanatically opposed to all
reform measures based on European notions and experience.
Abeddin was an Albanian of Greek speech and education,
whose appointment was ascribed (at least by himself) to the
Sultan's desire to conciliate the British. He had held a number
of minor posts since the Congress; as vali of Sivas he had given
general satisfaction, and had been praised by Col. Wilson; as
vali of Salonica for a short period he had been equally popular.
But his career had been too brief and essentially undistinguished
for him to exercise any real influence, and although he might
be regarded as a friend of reform his Albanian birth was hardly
likely to predispose him to favour the idea of territorial cessions
to Montenegro and Greece.[40]

The new ministry was immediately presented with a fresh
identic note dated 11 June, in accordance with Granville's
circular of 4 May. In the end the note followed Granville's

[38] Goschen to Granville, 7 June, F.O. 78/3087, no. 17
[39] Goschen to Granville, 15 June, F.O. 78/3087, no. 48.
[40] Goschen to Granville, 11 June, F.O. 78/3087, no. 29; 25 June, G.D. 29/188
(Granville Papers), quite personal.

wording very closely. Giers on 19 May had asked Granville that a more accentuated phrase concerning Montenegro should be added, but Granville and Haymerle had persuaded him to agree that further details should be avoided, as Montenegro and Greece were already being dealt with.[41] The drafting of the note was left to the ambassadors at Constantinople. The Russian ambassador did succeed in carrying a few 'accentuated phrases concerning Montenegro', but these appeared quite within the general sense of the circular. Great cordiality prevailed among the representatives of the powers, and the absence of friction was the best proof of the innocuous character of the document. It was presented on 12 June, and received by the Porte with complete unconcern.[42]

The Porte had in fact already decided to stick to its earlier policy of more or less politely evading compliance with the decisions of the powers until convinced that serious military measures would follow the evasion. Abeddin told Sandison that the Porte was prepared to make certain territorial cessions to Greece, but declared that these were the only possible bases on which the Porte could come to an arrangement. His proposal reduced drastically the cessions recommended by the Congress. He said that the peace and safety of Albania could only be preserved by excluding from the cessions which the Porte must make certain districts in Epirus, as well as the town of Larissa in Thessaly, with a sufficient 'rayon' of territory for its existence. He demanded therefore that the port of Prevesa and if possible the town of Arta should remain to Turkey. As the Congress had recommended the river Kalamas as the new Greek frontier Abeddin's proposal implied that Turkey would get back practically the whole of Epirus. The counter-concessions in Thessaly that he proposed to offer to the Greeks were slight.

The significant part of this pronouncement was Abeddin's defiant statement that his government was determined to resist everything except genuine military measures by the powers. He said that neither the presence of combined European naval forces in Turkish waters, nor even perhaps stronger measures,

[41] Granville to Elliot, 25 May, F.O. 7/985, no. 252; to Dufferin, 26 May, F.O. 65/1076, no. 207.
[42] Goschen to Granville, 15 June, F.O. 78/3087, no. 45.

would induce the Sultan's government to give anything more than he had indicated. Such a refusal might be followed by the invasion of bordering Turkish provinces by Greek bands and forces, but this the government and the Albanian population were sufficiently prepared to meet. 'What the Porte considers as really serious', he went on to say, 'would be an armed European intervention, in which case Turkey would of course have to yield and accept what was imposed upon her by force of arms, but that it remained to be seen how far the powers would all agree upon a similar course and whether it could be adopted without placing them to considerable inconvenience and expense.'[43] Abeddin's confidence in the ability of the Turkish forces to resist the Greeks was fully confirmed by Captain Swaine, the British military attaché, who was sent shortly after Goschen's arrival to examine the military situation on the Greek frontier. He reported on 18 June that the Turks had already 25,000 troops on the frontiers in Thessaly and Epirus, under an able Albanian commander, Hidayeh Pasha, and that in a fortnight this force could be increased to 60,000, not counting Albanians. He was convinced that the Greeks were no match for them, and that under a leader of Baker Pasha's capacity they could be at the gates of Athens in a fortnight.[44]

So far, then, the Concert had failed to overawe the Turks: but the Sultan was not persuaded as yet that the Concert existed. Could the powers now agree on a plan of campaign? And could they agree to put the plan into action? The Sultan was still content to wait and see.

[43] Goschen to Granville, 15 June, F.O. 78/3087, no. 48. Abeddin used similar language to Dubsky. Dubsky to Haymerle, 18 June, W.S.A., no. 48c.
[44] Goschen to Granville, 18 June, F.O. 78/3088, no. 53. L. V. Swaine, *Camp and Chancery in a Soldier's Life* (1926), pp. 111–13.

CHAPTER IV

The Berlin Conference

THE conference of ambassadors met at Berlin during the last two weeks of June. It came to a unanimous decision about the Greek frontier; but there was a certain air of unreality in the proceedings, as though the powers were more interested in the establishment of good relations with one another than in the elimination of bad relations between Turkey and her neighbours. The harmony of the discussions was greatly helped by Haymerle's suggestion, which the others accepted, that Turkey and Greece should not send delegates: he argued that it was hardly fair to expect Turkey to defend herself in such circumstances. It was also helped by the decision to discuss only the Greek frontier question. Russia had indeed proposed on 19 May the consideration of all outstanding points, but the other powers had agreed with Freycinet's view that the conference should deal first with the Greek frontier, enlarging the reference later if that problem were successfully treated. Giers gave way on the point, although he grumbled to Lobanov on 4 June that Greece might obtain favours at the expense of Montenegro, mainly because of the passive resistance of Vienna and Constantinople to the claims of the latter.[1]

Giers also said that Haymerle had a 'certain indifference' to the Montenegrin claims, but this was far from being the case; he had every desire to settle the matter expeditiously, though on his own terms. He had begun to discuss fresh proposals with Granville immediately after Goschen's visit to Vienna. The

[1] Dufferin to Granville, 19 May, F.O. 65/1080, no. 224; 2 June, no. 341. Elliot to Granville, 19 May, F.O. 7/990, no. 266. Giers to Lobanov, R.E., 23 May/4 June. Prince Nicholas asked the agents of the powers to give Montenegro priority in the next phase of collective action. Thömmel to Haymerle, 2 June, W.S.A., tel. no. 222; Haymerle to Thömmel, 9 June, W.S.A., tel.

failure of this further attempt to find a basis of compromise came just before the Berlin conference, and showed that the awkward Montenegrin problem might very well have produced a dead-lock there. The new plan originated in discussions between the British consul-general and the Austrian consul at Scutari, and was intended to provide a line of frontier which the Porte would have the power to cede peacefully, and which Montenegro would gladly accept. The proposal in general terms involved the cession to Montenegro of territory to the west of the lake of Scutari, so as to include in Montenegrin territory, Dulcigno and the sea coast as far as the mouth of the Boyana. Granville recommended the plan to Haymerle at the end of May; the Austrian government concurred; on 3 June it was proposed to France, Russia, Italy, and Germany, and they had accepted it in principle by the 8th. This Anglo-Austrian *démarche*, showing the satisfactory resumption of co-operation between the two powers in the Balkans, was warmly praised by the Emperor Franz Joseph on 16 June.[2]

Giers was, as it happened, far from satisfied with this plan. Haymerle stipulated on 7 June that the rules contained in Article XXIX of the Berlin treaty should be applied to the additional coast line which Montenegro would gain.[3] Granville had already included this in his proposal of the 3rd. Giers told Kálnoky that the Russian government would remain true to the principle of not objecting to any arrangement that Monte-negro might accept, but his language seemed to show a hope that Montenegro would not do so. As the success of the plan depended largely on secrecy, its publication in the St. Peters-burg newspapers caused little surprise, and the inaccuracy of certain parts of the publication provoked some comments in the Vienna press on the supposedly unfriendly disposition of the British government towards Austria and Haymerle.[4]

[2] Granville to Elliot, 30 May, F.O. 7/985, no. 263; Granville's circular, 3 June; Granville to Dufferin, 9 June, F.O. 65/1076, no. 243; Elliot to Granville, F.O. 7/991, no. 319. The A.-H. government also proposed the plan to Russia. Giers to Lobanov, R.E., 23 May/4 June; 2/14 June.

[3] Placing the Montenegrin coast under Austro-Hungarian customs control, banning fortifications and Montenegrin ships of war, etc. Haymerle to Kálnoky, 8 June, W.S.A., tel. no. 64; Haymerle to Dubsky, 8 June, W.S.A., tel. no. 112.

[4] Granville to Elliot, 8 June, F.O. 7/985, no. 291; Elliot to Granville, 9 June, F.O. 7/991, no. 299.

But with the Montenegrin question put on one side for the moment the conference could meet in an atmosphere of cautious affability which brought the Gladstonian Concert to full flower. The British may have had a single-minded interest in the proceedings, but the continental powers had more complex preoccupations. Russia, Austria, and France were each anxious to secure British support for their immediate plans in the Balkans or the Mediterranean, as the case might be; each was watching the situation warily in order to avoid being pushed by British zeal into an embarrassing quarrel with the Porte, but each could conceal its reservations during the academic discussions on Greek and Albanian geography. Russia at this stage of her history had a far greater interest in the Montenegrins than in the Greeks, and there was uneasiness in St. Petersburg as to where a policy of coercion might lead the Concert; no one wished to see a British fleet in the Straits, even under a Gladstone government. Austria's attitude was even more negative. Haymerle wanted the aggrandizement in the Balkans of the power of neither the Russians nor the Montenegrins, he did not want to antagonize the Porte, he did not want to abandon the Anglo-Austrian friendship as it had functioned under Salisbury. Bismarck was now talking less about the revolutionary menace of Gladstonian radicalism, for he had come to the conclusion that Gladstone's anti-Turkish policy would be a much more likely cause of alarm to the Austrians. He believed that Haymerle would soon be forced to decide that an agreement with Russia to maintain the *status quo* in the Balkans would be preferable to an agreement with England which would produce constant crisis and so play into Russia's hands. Haymerle was clearly not unaware that this alternative was before him, but he still seems to have hoped, during June and July, that with British support he could patch up some settlement of the Montenegrin frontier which would satisfy Austrian aims with the minimum of trouble, and that thereafter the new British initiative would be exhausted, and the anti-Russian front restored.

Giers in his instructions warned Saburov of the danger that an unduly favourable settlement of the Greek claims might injure the position of the Slavs in the peninsula, but he seems otherwise to have left Saburov a free hand as to tactics.[5] The attempt of the Russian ambassador to reconcile all the interests involved was to lead to some strange results. Bismarck took advantage of the conference to continue his courting of France. After securing the consent of Granville and Haymerle, Hohenlohe, who was still acting as Secretary of State for foreign affairs, told Saint-Vallier that the German, Austrian, and British governments were anxious to see France take the initiative at the conference. On the 11th Bismarck gave his views to Saint-Vallier in writing; he promised to support whatever line France proposed, and said he had advised Russia to do the same; but he warned the ambassador that Freycinet, in drawing the line so far north of the bed of the Peneios (Salambria) as he proposed to do, was running the risk of arousing Austrian opposition.[6] The British government had decided, even before Bismarck's suggestion, that it preferred to leave the initiative to France, who in turn wished to come to an understanding with the British before approaching the other powers. Sir Lintorn Simmons was accordingly sent to Paris to arrange matters with Freycinet. The French proposal had been communicated to the British government on 4 June, and had indicated a line of frontier which was considered to depart somewhat from the Congress recommendations, particularly near the Aegean, where the line, in following what was supposed to be the watershed north of the Salambria, had been extended to include the whole of Mount Olympus in Greek territory. Simmons soon found that Freycinet had no strong views on the subject and was principally concerned to find the boundary which was most easily defined and at the same time least likely to generate disputes. It was agreed therefore that the basins of the Kalamas and Salambria should be proposed, as the 13th protocol had reocmmended, and the line north of, and enclosing, Mount Olympus, was abandoned. Freycinet showed throughout great anxiety to come to complete agreement with Granville on the frontier question, and to ensure that the ambassadors

[5] Kálnoky to Haymerle, 2/14 June, W.S.A., no. 388; Giers to Lobanov, R.E., 18/30 June.

[6] Haymerle, circular despatch, W.S.A., 5 June. Odo Russell to Granville, 9 June, F.O. 64/960, no. 256; 11 June, no. 263, secret. D.D.F., iii, no. 164. Cf. Hohenlohe to Radowitz, 17 June, Radowitz, ii, 144.

of the two countries received identical instructions on the point.[7]

At the first meeting of the conference on the 16th, after Hohenlohe had been elected president, the French ambassador presented a declaration setting out in detail the line agreed on by Simmons and Freycinet. Count Launay, the Italian ambassador, then announced that Italy joined with France in bringing this proposal forward. It was generally known that Italy had had no share in the authorship, but it was apparently considered wise to secure her support by associating her so prominently with the new scheme. The British ambassador also gave his support; the Austrian, stating that he had no precise instructions, accepted the proposals 'ad referendum'.[8] Saburov, while expressing general approval of the principles enunciated, did likewise. At the same time he made some apparently indiscreet remarks which formed the only surprise of the sitting. He said that although the proposal went further than what had been indicated by the treaty of Berlin he accepted it because it would give Greece a boundary approaching more nearly her natural frontiers, and because a departure in this instance from the strict provisions of the treaty would make it easier to admit other changes which might be desirable.[9] Hohenlohe reserved the German decision, but said he had no objections to express. Proposals received from the Turkish and Greek governments were submitted to the technical commission for report. In general terms the Turkish line followed the proposal made by Abeddin Pasha to Sandison on the 12th. It offered a frontier running from Kheramidi on the Aegean coast, to the town of Arta, giving Greece the whole of the Gulf of Volo but leaving Larissa to the Turks. The Greek line on the other hand was drawn from the coast opposite the northern extremity of Corfu and included the northern slopes of Mount Olympus.[10]

[7] Granville to Odo Russell, 9 June, F.O. 78/3182, no. 2; 12 June, no. 6. Simmons to Granville, criticisms of French proposal, 10 June, F.O. 78/3184; 15 June, D.D.F., iii, no. 161.

[8] L. Raschdau (ed.): 'Die Durchführung der Berliner Kongressakte (1880–81), aus dem literarischen Nachlass des Unterstaatssekretärs Dr. Busch', *Deutsche Rundschau*, May, 1911 (cited as *Busch*), p. 229. D.D.F., iii, no. 108.

[9] Széchényi to Haymerle, 16 June, W.S.A. tel. no. 65. Odo Russell to Granville, 16 June, F.O. 78/3183, no. 8, secret. Elliot to Granville, 18 June, F.O. 7/991, no. 332. [10] Lascaris, *La politique extérieure de la Grèce*, pp. 182–4.

Saburov's remarks caused considerable surprise, and Haymerle told Elliot on the 18th that if Széchényi's written report of the sitting confirmed his telegraphic summary he would be instructed to declare emphatically that if the Austrian government had believed that the French proposal went further than had been intended in 1878 it would not have given its approval. Granville sent Dufferin and Odo Russell similar instructions.[11] Saburov's language was found to be much less accentuated in the protocol, and in the end Granville and Haymerle refrained from taking formal notice of it, although Saburov admitted to Széchényi some days later that it was by the express instructions of Giers that he had stated to the conference that the French proposal gave more to Greece than was intended by the Berlin treaty.[12]

The technical commission met on the 19th and the French proposal secured general approval. But the Russian military delegate, General Bobrikov, announced that he was instructed to reserve his opinion, and at the next meeting of the conference in the afternoon Saburov moved an amendment to the French proposal, which gave the conference its second surprise. Before the sitting he told Busch that things had hitherto gone somewhat too smoothly and he must bring some life and variety into the discussions. He now announced that his government had rejected the Turkish proposition as insufficient, and had come to the conclusion that the French proposition might be completed by the Greek, without departing from the 13th protocol. He accordingly proposed 'to adopt the principle of the crest of the mountains for the western part of the delineation, in the same way as that proposed for the eastern', the line to run from a point on the coast of Epirus to the north of Lake Butrinto, to the point where the Greek line rejoined the French in

[11] Széchényi to Haymerle, 17 June, W.S.A., tel. no. 66. The despatch (no. 46, 17 June) fully confirmed the telegram. Elliot to Granville, 18 June, F.O. 7/991, no. 332, secret; 19 June, Granville to Odo Russell (no. 7), Dufferin (no. 194), F.O. 78/3182.

[12] Széchényi to Haymerle, 18 June, tel. no. 68; Haymerle to Széchényi, 18 June, tel no. 72. Elliot to Granville, 21 June, F.O. 7/991, no. 333; 25 June, no. 339. Giers, however, told Kálnoky on the 17th that Russia would not take the initiative and would support the Anglo-French line. Kálnoky to Haymerle, 17 June, W.S.A., tel. no. 68. Széchényi was Austro-Hungarian ambassador at Berlin.

the neighbourhood and to the south-east of Paraplana. In defending his proposals Saburov described the affinities of the southern Albanians as being thoroughly Hellenic, and insisted more especially on the importance of giving to Greece the territory in Epirus opposite Corfu. The speech was made in light, and at times even merry, tones, and the fact that he proposed at the sitting to give Mount Olympus to Greece, and then omitted this from the written statement circulated in the evening, gave the impression that the proposal was not being taken very seriously by the Russians. Saburov's flippant manner did not make a good impression, and the British, Austrian, and Italian ambassadors all gravely affirmed that they had supported the French proposal because it appeared strictly to adhere to the 13th protocol. In the end the Russian proposal was referred to the technical commission.[13]

The objection to the Greek line, and therefore, of course, to the Russian amendment, was not merely that it went beyond the 13th protocol throughout the greater part of its course. In Epirus it would have given Greece complete command of the narrow channel (one and a half miles wide) between the northern end of Corfu and the mainland near Butrinto, and thus with the narrows at the south end of the island only five miles wide, all this part of the Ionian sea would have become Greek waters and a *mare clausum*. Simmons believed that the probable object of the Greeks in trying to obtain the district north of the basin of the Kalamas was to secure the valuable fisheries of Lake Butrinto. It was, however, longer and less easily guarded than the French line, and enclosed a considerable population hostile to Greece. The French line, on the other hand, followed the Kalamas throughout a great part of its course, and presented a natural and impassable barrier between the two countries, and one, therefore, which could be easily observed by both. Farther inland the Greek line went north of the valley of the Voidomati, and thereby cut off a considerable number of villages of the Zagoris from their neighbours. From there to the Aegean coast it was frequently beyond the limits of the 13th protocol, and was considered longer and more difficult of

---

[13] Odo Russell to Granville, 19 June, F.O. 78/3183, no. 26, conf.; *Busch*, p. 230. Széchényi to Haymerle, 20 June, W.S.A., 49A–C, 49B.

observation than the watershed which followed the rugged summits of Mount Olympus.[14]

At the third meeting on the 21st the Greek and Turkish proposals were unanimously rejected. Széchényi, however, asked for an adjournment of the discussion on the Russian amendment, on the ground that he was not yet in possession of the opinion of his technical advisers. The technical commission met the same evening: the Austrian, French, German, Italian, and British representatives all voted to reject the Russian and accept the French line, and as the Russian representatives abstained from voting on both proposals any formal disagreement was avoided. On the same evening Saburov suggested a compromise and asked Hohenlohe to propose it in his own name to the other delegates.[15] During the next few days Hohenlohe did make some attempts behind the scenes to secure a unanimous vote based on Saburov's suggestion of the adoption of a portion of the Russian amendment as a compromise. Odo Russell and Saint-Vallier, however, declined to depart from the Freycinet-Simmons line and reports from St. Petersburg showed that the Russians had no objection to the French proposal. At the fourth meeting on the 25th Saburov, after a voluble defence of his amendment, withdrew it in the interest of a unanimous vote. The French tracing was then brought forward and duly voted unanimously.[16] A further Turkish proposal, which still provided for the retention by Turkey of the four towns of Preveza, Janina, Metzovo, and Larissa, had been rejected at the beginning of the sitting, but the unanimity of the powers enabled Hohenlohe to declare that the final act was the solemn manifestation of the will of Europe. The remaining business was rapidly disposed of, after Hohenlohe had announced on the 28th that the Porte declined in anticipation to accept the conference's decisions.[17]

The new line of frontier for Greece was communicated to the

[14] Odo Russell to Granville, 17 June, F.O. 78/3183, no. 11, conf.; 22 June, no. 35, conf.

[15] Széchényi to Haymerle, 23 June, W.S.A., 51A–C. Odo Russell to Granville, 21 June, F.O. 78/3183, no. 32, conf., secret. *Busch*, p. 231.

[16] Odo Russell to Granville, 23 June, F.O. 78/3183, no. 38, conf.; 25 June, no. 45, conf. *D.D.F.*, iii, no.180. *Busch*, p. 231; C. de Moüy, *Souvenirs et causeries d'un diplomate* (1909), p. 163.

[17] Odo Russell to Granville, 23 June, *ibid.*, no. 41, conf.; Granville to Odo Russell, 23 June, F.O. 78/3182, no. 15, conf.

Greek and Turkish governments in collective notes of 15 July, and although it agreed neither with the Turkish proposal nor with the Greek, it was sufficiently close to the latter for the Greeks to accept it without delay.[18] The Turks rejected it almost as promptly. The Porte's reply on the 26th said that in signing the treaty of Berlin it had not expected the powers to interpret a wish for the rectification of the Greek frontier in Epirus and Thessaly as including the cession of territory in Albania and the cession of the whole of Thessaly; the powers had instructed their plenipotentiaries at the Berlin conference to fix a solid defensive frontier between Greece and Turkey, whereas the frontier now proposed would expose the Turkish frontier provinces to attack against which the Porte would find itself defenceless. Furthermore it could never consent to the cession of Janina, which the Albanians had always regarded as their capital. The powers were perhaps wise in answering this able note with a plain statement that the question could not be reconsidered.[19]

But they were now forced to consider seriously the question of coercion; and throughout July plans for a naval demonstration in the Adriatic were discussed without enthusiasm. In the circumstances it was to be expected that they would deal first with the Montenegrin-Albanian frontier, where blood was being shed and the Turkish obligation under the Berlin treaty was clearer than in the south. It was not until the end of the year that the final stage in the Greek dispute began.

The Montenegrin crisis, which was to reach its height in September, will be examined in Chapter VI. We can conclude the present chapter by noting the position of the powers immediately after the conference. The Concert had held together during June, although Saburov's wayward course had caused speculation and some alarm. Haymerle thought that the most probable explanation was the desire of the Russian government to make certain the Porte's rejection of the decisions of the conference.[20] The King of Greece suspected that the Russian aim

<hr>

[18] Goschen to Granville, 14 July, F.O. 78/3090, no. 117; 15 July, no. 121; 16 July, no. 145; 20 July, nos. 165, 168.

[19] Abeddin to Musurus, 27 July (communicated to Granville, 29 July). Goschen to Granville, 27 July, F.O. 78/3090, no. 183.

[20] Elliot to Granville, 25 June, F.O. 7/991, no. 339.

was to induce the powers to depart from the strict maintenance of the decisions of the Congress of Berlin, in order to justify other encroachments later.[21] Odo Russell believed that the Russian government intended to take up the Greek question as a national one and make a weapon of it against the Turks.[22] However, Schweinitz was able to tell Bismarck that Giers had not authorized Saburov's action, and it appears that the proposal had been made by Saburov on his own initiative. He was a sanguine, ambitious man, excited by his new, prominent rôle in the higher diplomacy, eager to bring off some clever *coup*. The incident shook the confidence of both Giers and Bismarck in his judgment. Giers remarked on 22 June that in spite of his abilities he had 'also certain things in common with Ignatyev; my maxim, "plus être que paraître" he has not made his own'.[23] Bismarck's hitherto favourable opinion of Saburov was also shaken, and this distrust was to grow during the following years. The incident is also, perhaps, evidence that Giers' position was too weak for him to control very rigidly a favoured ambassador. Giers' main concern before the conference was, as we have seen, to prevent the Greek settlement being given a form which would injure Montenegrin interests, and it was possibly significant that Saburov sought to advance the Greek frontier in the direction which was most likely to arouse Albanian resistance. He may have calculated that if the powers were pledged to force a decision on the Albanians in this area they would find it difficult to avoid doing so farther north. It was believed in some quarters that Russia desired a close understanding between Greece and Montenegro, but although some steps were taken in this direction by the Greek government in July they met with little success. The fact that the French proposal followed discussions between France, Italy, and England no doubt gave Saburov the impression that Russia was expected to play a passive rôle: the chorus of thanks and congratulations which greeted Saburov's final acquiescence sug-

[21] Windelband, p. 156.

[22] Odo Russell to Granville, 29 June, F.O. 78/3183, no. 62, conf. Before the conference the Russian government had assured Tricoupis of its special concern for Greek interests. Wacken (Athens) to Haymerle, 26 June, W.S.A., no. 27D.

[23] Schweinitz, *Denkwürdigkeiten*, ii, 118.

gests that the others may have felt a little guilty in this con-nexion.[24]

But in general there was nothing in Saburov's conduct that was uncharacteristic of his government's activity at this time. While the *Dreikaiserbund* negotiations were suspended it was willing to join Great Britain in chastising the recalcitrant Turk; it had shown more willingness than the other continental governments for forcible measures, and, on the other hand, no strong preference for any one mode of action. This lively, but somewhat haphazard, activity did not appear to be bringing the conclusion of the alliance any nearer; Haymerle's suspicions of Russia seemed stronger than ever during July. Bismarck was, nevertheless, confident that the development of events would bring Austria and Russia together. He told Saburov on 25 July that if, as seemed probable, Gladstone's actions were to lead to the coercion of Turkey by an Anglo-French expedition, 'Austria will throw herself into your arms however little you may be disposed for that, and it will be easy then for us to make her espouse your point of view about the Straits'. Under the pre-text of carrying out the treaty of Berlin Gladstone might well be led to demolish Turkey itself, and the Straits were the most vul-nerable spot. 'Austria will not wish this, and that will be the moment to dwell on this point in order to make her adopt our idea.' Saburov knew that his government intended to support the British in securing a satisfactory settlement of the Monte-negrin problem, but believed that after that it could place itself 'frankly on the side of the Powers that are guardians of Turkey'.[25]

This adroit use of the British initiative meant that England was to be used both to frighten the Turks into acquiescence over Montenegro, and to suggest a Mediterranean menace which would provide the basis of a *rapprochement* between Austria and Russia. Odo Russell probably had some inkling of these intentions; if we can believe Saburov he made several sug-gestions as to the development of the Anglo-Russian agreement.

[24] He said to Széchényi on the 18th: 'Nous avons aussi notre rôle à jouer en Grèce et nous ne voulons pas nous laisser prendre à la remorque par la France.' Széch-ényi to Haymerle, 18 June, W.S.A., no. 48. Cf. 28 June, no. 55B.

[25] *Saburov*, pp. 140–1.

Saburov considered these suggestions to be so indiscreet that he reported them to Giers in a private letter, in order that Odo Russell should not be compromised by references in official despatches. On more than one occasion Odo Russell was reported to have said that Gladstone would probably offer no resistance if the Bulgars made a movement in favour of union, and that there would be no difficulty on this question between Russia and England.[26] To the somewhat sceptical Hohenlohe Saburov asserted that Odo Russell had suggested that Russia, apparently in return for the recognition of the Bulgarian union, should not oppose the opening of the Straits, and that England should oppose the Austrian seizure of Salonica![27] In general, the Russian government appears to have been well satisfied with the course of the negotiations, and to have felt no embarrassment in its dual relationship with Austria and Great Britain. A letter to Lobanov of 13 August (read to Granville on the 23rd) attributed recent progress in the Near Eastern settlement to the prudent perseverance of the British government, and said that the Emperor had given instructions that all the British efforts should be supported; only in Bulgaria had the British government appeared to depart from its conciliatory programme. The Tsar had agreed to support the British line, but only in order not to reveal to the Turks a possible disagreement in the Concert.[28]

The British line, so puzzling to the continent, was consistent and fair in Gladstone's eyes. He felt that the union of Bulgaria and Eastern Rumelia, desirable in principle, was inexpedient at this time, and should be postponed; it appears from his correspondence with Granville in May that he was chiefly concerned about the embarrassing consequences of Turkish military action

[26] Saburov to Giers, R.E., 6/18 Aug. 1880.

[27] 4 Aug., G.P., iii, no. 519. Odo Russell had no authority to make these statements. Gladstone told Granville on 22 May that 'an attempt to precipitate the union . . . wd. in the present state of things be most dangerous'; he asked W. E. Forster to ask Dr. Washburn 'to use his influence to keep the Bulgarians and Roumelians quiet'. Gladstone Papers, Add. MSS. 44544.

[28] Giers to Lobanov, R.E., 1/13 August, lettre particulière; cf. Schweinitz's comments, ii, 122 (19 August). The general course of developments in Bulgaria and Eastern Rumelia is adequately described in Alois Hajek, Bulgariens Befreiung und staatliche Entwicklung unter seinem ersten Fürsten (1939), chs. iv–vii, and C. E. Black, The Establishment of Constitutional Government in Bulgaria (1943).

against a movement for unification, and would have viewed it with approval if the Sultan had acquiesced. Granville was quite sure that it would be 'very dangerous even to sound the Sultan' but he played for a moment with the idea that the abrogation of the Anglo-Turkish convention of 1878 might put the Porte into the necessary good humour. He shared Haymerle's uneasiness at the continued entry of Russian arms and officers into Bulgaria, and at the disorderly politics and revolutionary unrest of the new state. Finally he and Gladstone agreed in June that the Concert ought to investigate Turkish charges about the ill treatment of the Moslem minority in Eastern Rumelia and Bulgaria. Gladstone, after speaking on this question in the House of Commons, readily agreed on 10 June that there need not be a collective inquiry: 'I can conceive that such an inquiry might seem like the setting up of a separate authority and might shake a young and feeble government.' But he wanted fair play.

I wd do everything to spare the reputation of a local Govt. in the face of its subjects, but I think that as our friendship to the Sultan is conditional upon the relief of his subjects from misgovernment, so we ought to make known to the rulers of emancipated Provinces that our friendship and sympathy with them is contingent upon their making effective arrangements for defending the rights of minorities, and that the want of such arrangements may prove an insurmountable bar to the extension of Liberal institutions in Turkey.

It was decided therefore to conduct a separate British inquiry, under Colonel C. W. Wilson.[29]

But somehow, to both the Austrians and Russians, fair play did not seem explanation enough; there was the usual search for clever politics behind the ostensible altruism of British aims. Giers appeared convinced that an attempt to discredit and isolate Russia was involved; this was certainly Haymerle's aim, and Granville had associated himself with it in inquiring about arms and officers. The Austrian government protested again, politely but firmly, on this point early in August, and Granville continued to question Lobanov, and to show alarm, during the

[29] Gladstone to Granville, 22 May, 10 June, 19 June; Add. MSS. 44544. Granville to Gladstone, 22 May, Add. MSS. 44172.

summer and autumn.[30] It was to all these Bulgarian issues that
Giers was referring when he said that in Bulgaria Britain had
departed from her conciliatory programme. He admitted that
recent disorders at Aidos and Kirdjala, the blunders of the
authorities in Eastern Rumelia and Bulgaria, and the agitation
of hotheads on both sides of the Balkans, had supplied pretexts
for the Austro-British criticisms. Somewhat ingeniously he
attributed the agitation to both the Greeks and the Turks. The
Turkish aim was to alarm the cabinets as to the aspirations of
the Slavs, in order to turn aside the attention concentrated on
the Greek claims. Ottoman diplomacy had adroitly provoked
questions by the Turcophils in the British Parliament. But the
Greeks had also, it appeared, inspired the campaign against the
Bulgars, presumably to place themselves in a favourable light.
Granville, said Giers, had announced haughtily that he desired
an impartial balance between Christian and Mussulman, but
in the case of Greece he was displaying an obvious partiality for
the Hellenic cause.[31] So argued Giers in a long despatch, which
was perhaps as much an attempt to supply Lobanov with
debating points as a statement of strong conviction.

We must conclude that the Bulgarian problem helped in no
small measure to lessen the willingness of both Russia and
Austria for co-operation with England. It played a large part
in convincing the Austrians that they could not expect the unequivocal support against Russian aims that had been given by
the Conservative government. 'The Austrians are desperately
alarmed at the Russian proceedings in Eastern Rumelia but
Calice is always saying it is an English affair, and that they
won't pull the chestnuts out of the fire for us', wrote Goschen on
5 October. 'They could not make out what line we should take
if a critical moment arrived and further reflections on that head.
I think Austria would be much more cordial with us but for its
alarm, or rather its annoyance that we will not take up firm
ground as regards Russia in Bulgaria, but yet they are most
timid themselves.'[32] The Russians on the other hand saw in the

[30] Lobanov to Giers, 5/17 August, R.E., no. 66; 10/22 September, no. 77.
[31] Giers to Lobanov, R.E., 1/13 August; see n. 28 above.
[32] Goschen to Granville, 5 October, 1880, Constantinople, copy. Add. MSS.
44172. Calice was Austro-Hungarian ambassador at Constantinople.

British proceedings no very noticeable departure from Conservative policy.

These considerations no doubt reduced still further the attractiveness of Russo-British collaboration in any form which delayed the conclusion of the alliance negotiations. In response to Bismarck's remarks on 25 July Giers authorized Saburov to propose that if the British programme should lead to plans for sending the British fleet through the Straits the three empires should prevent this action by a joint declaration. When he received this proposal on 4 August Hohenlohe pointed out that as recently as 30 July Saburov had told him that if England adopted active measures to solve the Montenegrin frontier problem Russia would support her. Saburov replied hopefully that the Montenegrin question was now on its way to settlement. Hohenlohe had already told the Austrian *chargé* on 1 August that Saburov considered his government to be much less interested in Greece than in Montenegro.[33] It appeared, therefore, that the British government could still count on Russian support in Montenegro, but was less likely to receive it in Greece.

Haymerle had still to conquer his fear of an understanding that would make him the dupe of Russian diplomacy, but Gladstone's plans for action soon convinced him that there was greater danger in remaining the partner of the British. Giers and Saburov had to rely on Bismarck to bring Haymerle to their side, and at the beginning of September he gave some evidence of real interest in their plans.[34] Their continued dependence on Bismarck was shown in their willingness to encourage the sending of German officers to Turkey. The Sultan had, on the suggestion of his confidant, Colonel Dreyssé, asked for the assistance of German military advisers in May, believing that they were more efficient, and less likely to involve him in international complications, than the British or French. Haymerle made no objection, and accordingly Bismarck recommended the mission to the German Emperor on 1 July. Bismarck was

---

[33] *G.P.*, iii, no. 519. Pasetti to Haymerle, 1 August, W.S.A., tel. no. 76. Cf. Haymerle's summary of Russian policy (circular, except to Kálnoky), 6 August, W.S.A., tel.
[34] See Ch. VII below.

not without some doubts as to the wisdom of this course; he had no desire to use the influence which the mission might give in order to push commercial or political interests in the Near East, and he had to balance the advantages of some additional control of the European diplomatic system with the possibility of trouble with Turkey's enemies. In the end he decided that the risk was worth taking, particularly as both Saburov, on 19 July, and Giers on the 28th, made it clear that they would prefer that German officers and officials should replace those of England and France. But some years were to elapse before the German mission arrived in Constantinople.[35] It is a curious commentary on these proceedings that in September Gladstone was attracted for a time by a plan to coerce the Sultan by requiring all British subjects to quit the employment, military and naval, of Turkey.[36]

[35] H. Holborn, *Deutschland und die Türkei, 1878–1890* (1925), pp. 11–19; Lucius, p. 190 (26 July).

[36] Gladstone to Granville, 27 September 1880 (Hawarden); to Tenterden, 28 September, Add. MSS. 44544.

CHAPTER V

Tunis and Morocco :
the Madrid Conference

AT this point it will be convenient to examine the French
dilemma a little more closely. French politicians were
preparing to abandon the negations of the period of
recueillement of the later 'seventies and to undertake the more
dramatic rôle in international politics which would re-establish
their country's standing, if only in French eyes, as a great
power; although strategic interest and economic determinism
did much to define the direction of French policy during the
next few years the compelling interest was national prestige.
But Freycinet shrank from the embarrassments that the more
adventurous programme would entail. France, indeed, in her
modest support of the existing equilibrium and her eschewing
of 'selfish' ends had been for a few abnormal years a model
exponent of the Gladstonian type of Concert, and although the
more mystical standards of Liberal idealism made little appeal
to Freycinet he did not wish to lose the practical advantages of
this conciliatory rôle without an assured prospect of greater
benefits. In Egypt or Morocco a forward policy would antagonize the British, in Tunis the Italians, in the Balkans the Austrians and in some measure the Russians and Turks; and
if Bismarck remained friendly would not this be evidence that
he was profiting from France's entanglements? Freycinet was
also well aware that injudicious activity abroad might create
political difficulties at home, particularly from the Radicals and
Monarchists; he did not wish to be accused of a second Mexican
adventure.

Gambetta was now advocating, behind the scenes, the
robuster policy, but he was an embarrassing counsellor. Lord

Lyons, the British ambassador, who understood, without altogether sympathizing with, Freycinet's difficulties, remarked in
a letter to Lord Granville on 2 July, 'did the King of Greece
understand Gambetta to say that France, with or without the
co-operation of other powers, would support Greece with
troops? Freycinet will no doubt do whatever Gambetta tells
him, but one of the inconveniences of the power behind the
Government greater than the Government is that Gambetta
does not talk as cautiously as he would if he felt direct responsibility'.[1] Gambetta's speech at Cherbourg on 8 August 1880,
a brilliant assertion of France's recovered strength, caused
rumblings in the German press which Freycinet sought to
appease at Montaubon a few days later by affirmations of goodwill and of peaceful intention. Freycinet and Gambetta were
agreed as to the importance of French interests in Tunis,
although they were not yet ready to risk the complications that
would follow a forward policy. But the government were not
united even on this course; there were those, including the
President, Jules Grévy, who preferred to retain Italian friendship. Grévy in a celebrated *mot* told Cialdini, the Italian ambassador, that Tunis was not worth a cheap cigar. So Freycinet
followed a rather timid and indecisive course; his resignation in
September was due to domestic issues, but Gambetta appears to
have been annoyed by the Montaubon speech. In the Greek
and Montenegrin questions Freycinet showed great reluctance
to follow up his modest initiative at Berlin in the summer with
coercive measures.[2] In Morocco and Tunis, two states in which
governmental imbecility, formidable French agents, and the
constant threat of the French Algerian forces had weakened the
power of effective native resistance, he was content to perpetuate a state of affairs which his bolder successors would turn
to France's advantage. On the whole this suited Bismarck's
plans—the important thing was that France under this leadership could offer no threat to the alliance negotiations—but the
continued uncertainty as to her future course tried his nerves
and added a further complication to his schemes. Any attempt
to hurry the French into action in Tunis might easily over-

[1] *Lyons*, ii, 295; cf. Freycinet, *Souvenirs, 1878–1893*, pp. 116–19.
[2] See Ch. VI below.

reach itself and swing attention back to the Rhine frontier; a too obvious attempt to separate France and England might have the same effect. An uncharacteristic but not unstatesmanlike patience marked his handling of the diffident Frenchmen during the next twelve months.

Bismarck's policy of balanced tensions provided for a partition of Anglo-French interests in the Mediterranean, similar to his suggested partition of Austro-Russian interests in the Balkans. In neither case could he have been unaware that his proposals, if carried out, would perpetuate existing hostilities, and that none of the four powers would regard its own advancement as a reason for accepting with equanimity the strengthening of its neighbour. So much was this the case that Bismarck's hints and suggestions, which he had been making whenever occasion arose since January 1876, were always received with suspicion and reserve, although usually with expressions of gratitude: for few of his neighbours were prepared to imitate Gorchakov's boldness in 1876, and to say that he reminded them of the tempter on the mountain. Austria was certainly tempted by the prospect of an advance to Salonica, and a dominating position politically and economically in the western Balkans; but it was less certain that she would ever accept the full implications of Russian dominance in the eastern half of the peninsula, with the facility to move troops through Rumania, and to dominate Constantinople, which this would presumably imply. Russia for her part could not have abandoned many of her interests in the western Balkans, including her traditional patronage of Montenegro. In the same way Great Britain, even if she were tempted to follow Bismarck's hints and install herself in Egypt, would not acquiesce in a corresponding French predominance in Syria or in North-West Africa, for at this period the independence of Morocco was still one of the cardinal points in her policy. It was unlikely too that France, even with protectorates over Tunis and Morocco, would abandon her interest in Egypt. Bismarck knew all this. Why did he persist?

It must be remembered that these suggestions were made cautiously and tentatively, always with the assurance that Germany herself had no counterbalancing ambitions, and that her aim was peace; they were academic suggestions, binding on no one, and they enabled him to show goodwill and to put himself on a friendly footing with the other four powers. Friendship can hardly flourish on generalizations and negations; Bismarck needed something to talk about.

His proposals were made too frequently and consistently, however, for us to be able to dismiss them as mere gestures of amiability, to which he himself attached no great significance. The plan was clearly a statesmanlike one in his own eyes, and not merely because it would turn the attention of two awkward neighbours, Russia and France, away from possible quarrels with Germany over frontier questions in Europe. He did not believe that great powers could remain both quiescent and good-tempered—this was the Gladstonian illusion—and although, in the extension of control, Europe would exchange new animosities for old a balance of advantage, for Germany and perhaps for Europe, might remain. He may have believed that a genuine *détente* in European tensions could result. If England took Egypt she could protect the route to India without alarming herself over Russian control of the Straits; deprived of British support Austria might acquiesce in Russian control of the Straits, providing that she herself could control her economic outlets through Salonica and Scutari; France might forget the lost provinces in building an African Empire. His outlook was pessimistic; struggle and vigilance were eternal necessities; but there was at least a chance that if the four powers would deploy their forces as he suggested they would gain sufficiently in assurance and have sufficient to absorb their energies, to preserve peace—and to leave Germany at peace—for another generation.

What critics can regard as the more sinister or selfish side of the programme was clearly present. He was increasing or perpetuating existing rivalries in order to escape from the isolation of which he had been so painfully aware in 1875; his plans involved an invasion of the sovereignty or territory of other states (principally Turkey), and as they were a little too bold for the conscience (or imagination) of the other powers they did not remove suspicion as to his intentions. Where a genuine difference existed with another power, such as France, he was incapable of concession. Although he protested his goodwill and disinterestedness to all in 1880 and 1881 he was soon to show, in his colonial disputes with Britain in 1884–5, that he could not maintain this pose and remain the honest broker for very long.

Bismarck's constant praise of the Anglo-French understanding puzzled many Englishmen,[3] who were sure that what he really desired was France's isolation. There was one obvious reason, however, for this encouragement: the Beaconsfield government would do nothing to further a Franco-Russian alliance, and with the moral support of the British friendship France would be less tempted to seek allies elsewhere. During the period of Russo-German tension it was not to his interest therefore to destroy the Anglo-French entente. When the new Three Emperors' Alliance had been concluded he would be in a stronger position *vis-à-vis* the French, for it would be an indispensable condition of the alliance that neither Russia nor Austria should join hands with France; he might then wish to bring the Anglo-French friendship to an end. He certainly did not desire to secure successes for France in the colonial field which would ultimately produce a revival of self-confidence sufficient to sweep her into a war of revenge, and it was essential that any such increase in self-confidence should automatically reduce, rather than strengthen, her ability to embark on activity in Europe. France would be progressively checkmated if her increasing activities in North Africa aroused corresponding British, and, for what it was worth, Italian hostility. His encouragement of French designs in North Africa was in accordance with this programme. He knew that no British government would welcome these designs, and that if France or Britain sought exclusive control in either Egypt or Morocco the two powers would probably quarrel; but he did not wish them to quarrel until his hold on Russia was complete. The British agreement, reluctantly given, at the Congress of Berlin to French control of Tunis suited his plans; it distracted French attention from the lost provinces without destroying Anglo-

[3] After reading Odo Russell's despatch of 29 April 1880, in which Bismarck said that he looked on an Anglo-French alliance as the basis of peace and order in Europe, Dilke thought that Bismarck 'seemed to me to have been laughing at him'. S. L. Gwynn and G. M. Tuckwell, *The Life of Sir Charles W. Dilke*, 2 vols., (1917), i, 323.

French friendship. He continued during 1879 and the early
months of 1880 to reiterate his support in the Tunisian question, but as long as Beaconsfield remained in office he did
nothing to encourage an Anglo-French quarrel.

The chief danger of such a quarrel was in Egypt. Bismarck's
intention is clear. From the beginning of 1876 he had told the
British that he wished them to control Egypt. On 2 March 1879
he told Odo Russell that Germany would side with England in
the event of any difference between England and France
respecting Egypt, because 'it was in the interest of Germany
that English influence should be greater in Egypt than that of
France'.[4] The French government seems to have been unaware throughout of this secret encouragement to the British.
As Salisbury in 1879 and Granville in 1880 had no desire for
exclusive influence Bismarck had no reason to fear that either
country would be in any hurry to get ahead of the other; on
certain occasions it seemed more probable that British hesitations would allow the internal situation to get out of hand, and
that France would take the risk of a single-handed intervention,
or, more probably, that Europe would be faced with a general
crisis at an awkward moment for German policy. Salisbury, and
Granville after him, were very much more averse than the
French ministers to being made the instruments of the bondholders; it is clear that the French government was susceptible
to the pressure of the French investors, and in any case glad to
be supplied with opportunities for subsequent intervention. 'We
have no wish to part company with France; still less do we
mean that France should acquire in Egypt any special ascendancy; but, subject to these two conditions, I should be glad to
be free of the companionship of the bondholders', wrote Salisbury on 10 April 1879.[5] Bismarck had showed his hand in the
summer of 1879, when the Khedive Ismail challenged the
Anglo-French financial programme with a scheme of his own
less favourable to the bondholders; when the French and
British governments failed to agree on a course of action he took
the lead himself with a public condemnation on 18 May of

---

[4] Odo Russell to Salisbury, 2 March 1879, no. 137, F.O. 64/932. Cf. *G.P.*, iv,
nos. 728–30.
[5] Lady G. Cecil, *Life of Robert, Marquess of Salisbury*, 2 vols. (1921), ii, 352.

Ismail's conduct, and this led ultimately to the Khedive's deposition. This solution satisfied Salisbury, who desired an efficient government in the country, and it met for the time being the financial preoccupations of the French. Having turned this corner and postponed an Anglo-French crisis, Bismarck was quite prepared to leave Egyptian affairs again in the hands of the other two powers. Salisbury suspected that German bondholders, and particularly von Bleichröder, had influenced Bismarck's intervention, but this appears to have been at best a minor consideration. [6]

On this footing Anglo-French co-operation continued in the Egyptian question during 1880 and 1881; the growth of nationalist feeling and growing pressure on the ineffective Tewfik of the rebellious army leaders under Arabi Pasha finally led Gambetta in November 1881 to press the British for their co-operation in a fresh intervention, but by that stage the new Three Emperors' Alliance was in being, and Bismarck could contemplate Anglo-French discordance with equanimity. During the period covered by this volume, however, Egypt did not complicate his plans unduly.

It was the Tunisian pear which, as Bismarck told Saint-Vallier in picturesque terms in January 1879, seemed ripe for French picking. The decisive moment seemed to have come on 5 May 1880, when Freycinet sent instruction to the French chargé, M. Theodore Roustan, to present to the Bey of Tunis a convention in four articles placing Tunis under French protection. The situation seemed favourable for French success, or as favourable as it was ever likely to be. Bismarck was agreeable; Great Britain (or at any rate the Conservative government) had been prepared since the Congress to acquiesce; the Sultan of Turkey, the nominal suzerain, could be ignored. Italy would be angry, but could also, perhaps, be relied on to do nothing sensible or effective. Behind the ultimatum lay a long struggle between the French and Italian representatives for concessions and the influence which they were supposed to

---

[6] Cecil, *ibid.*, ii, 353; cf. W. L. Langer's comments, *European Alliances and Alignments* (1931), pp. 260–2. Salisbury told Lyons, 'I should be glad to see loans forbidden altogether. To an oriental ruler they are like firewater to the Red Indians'. *Lyons*, ii, 189.

bring, and it was from this struggle that Freycinet now derived his excuse for action. France's general ground for this was that her position in Algeria compelled her to veto the establishment of the authority of other European governments in Tunis, and that the Tunisian government was too weak and incompetent to be a good neighbour; since the 'sixties, moreover, Tunis had been heavily indebted to European financiers, mainly French. In Tunis as in Morocco the British had been the chief support of the independence of the Bey before 1870, but in the 'seventies the Italians had become the great opponents of the French, and competed vigorously with them for concessions for the development of public works, railway lines, and the like.[7] After the Congress of Berlin this struggle was intensified, and the resolute Roustan found himself opposed after December 1878 by an equally formidable and tireless Italian consul-general, Signor Maccio. The most dramatic among a number of incidents was the success of a Frenchman, M. Géry, representing the company of Bône-Guelma, in securing the purchase on 14 April 1880 of the British-owned railway from Tunis to Goletta at a moment when the Italian Rubattino company was negotiating for the purchase in London. The Italians were intensely annoyed, and took steps to fight the case in the High Court in London; in the meantime, according to a dramatic message from Roustan to de Courcel on 27 April, Italian pressure on the Bey and the prime minister had become so violent that it would not be possible much longer to resist it by ordinary means and by the mere force of French influence.[8]

Freycinet was in such haste that the text of the convention of 5 May was telegraphed, and Roustan was instructed to act without waiting for more detailed instructions; even the latter

---

[7] W. L. Langer, 'The European Powers and the French Occupation of Tunis' (*American Historical Review*, October 1925, January 1926) is still perhaps the best account of the battle for concessions. See also T. F. Power, *Jules Ferry and the Renaissance of French Imperialism* (New York, 1944), pp. 32–72; S. H. Roberts, *History of French Colonial Policy* (1929), i, 4–12; L. Chiala, *Pagine di storia contemporanea* (1892), ii, 67–171, and M. Rosi, *I. Cairoli*, ii, 27–90, deal fully with Tunisian developments in 1880, but largely ignore Morocco. The best account of Italian policy is by Alberto Giaccardi, *La conquista di Tunisi* (Milan, 1940), pp. 112–38. Cf. also the illuminating comments in Federico Chabod, *Storia della politica estera italiana dal 1870 al 1896* (Bari, 1951), i, 541–62.

[8] *D.D.F.*, iii, nos. 80, 89, 90, 91, 94, 100.

had been sent off so hurriedly on the 4th that they were un-signed, and a signed duplicate had to follow by the next courier. The procedure was that laid down by Waddington, who had sent an earlier version of the convention to Roustan on 11 February 1879. The protection of Tunis by France that was proposed represented an important innovation in French colonial history for it abandoned, for obvious tactical reasons, the traditional French policy of assimilation; Waddington supplied Roustan later with arguments designed to reassure the Bey on this point, and to overcome the religious scruples which the latter would experience at the prospect of intimate relations with a non-Moslem country. The object of the convention was, he explained, to exclude other foreign influences; the Sultan's conscience had not prevented him from placing his Moslem subjects under the administration of a Christian power in Cyprus, but the French were not proposing anything of this sort, as they did not wish to occupy, administer, or annex the Regency, but only to conclude a close and permanent alliance with the Bey. There was to be a customs union with Algeria which would greatly benefit the Regency. Waddington had not tried to force the convention on the Bey, and Freycinet's version of 5 May 1880 made two important changes in the draft. One was to offer protection to the Bey alone, instead of, as before, to the Bey and his dynasty; the second was to omit a specific pro-vision for the French occupation of certain points in the event of a threat to the security of the state. These changes did not make the scheme any more palatable. Roustan telegraphed on the evening of 8 May that he had met with an absolute refusal; fanaticism and *amour-propre* would not allow the Bey to accept the protection of an infidel power. If Freycinet wished to go further he would have to use menacing language supported by military preparations on the frontier.[9]

But Freycinet drew back. No doubt his hasty move had been due to fear of an Italian *coup d'état*, and to the hope that the Bey would feel in the circumstances that he had no choice but to accept French protection; it would clearly have been impos-sible to acquiesce in an Italian seizure of the Regency, and French governments had been waiting for the moment when

[9] *D.D.F.*, ii, nos. 381, 449; iii, 109, 110, and n. 3.

circumstances would allow their own plans to be carried out without arousing the active hostility of the Bey, the European powers, or French public opinion. The Bey's refusal prevented immediate action, for Freycinet had not made preparations for a military demonstration; Cairoli, the Italian prime minister, had already, on 1 May, disclaimed any knowledge of threatening moves by Maccio, or any intention to treat the Rubattino affair as other than a private business transaction, and a cabinet crisis in Rome during the succeeding weeks reduced further the possibility of any serious Italian action. Accordingly, as neither government was ready for an open breach, a temporary *détente* could be achieved. The French pressed the Italian government to persuade the Italian press to drop its attacks on French policy; the Italian government was not prepared to do so until French ironclads, sent to Tunisian waters during the Goletta crisis, were withdrawn. Agreement on these lines was arrived at in the early days of the Ferry ministry. The British had done their best to encourage this more circumspect turn in Italian policy.[10] Freycinet did not abandon his plans; but he proceeded with a degree of caution which in the end postponed decisive action until after his fall from office, and had a very damping effect on any ardour that he might otherwise have felt for the British programme in the Balkans.[11]

It is, however, the Moroccan question which illustrates most clearly the uneasy relationships between the western powers at this moment when the European Concert was apparently in fullest harmony. The conference of the powers which sat in Madrid from May to July of 1880 to deliberate on British plans for the internal reform of the state received little publicity, but its decisions throw considerable light on the dispositions of all the participants, and are worth examining in a little detail. The technicalities of the protégé system, which formed the ostensible basis of discussion, need not detain us; the reform of this system would, however, have reduced opportunities for foreign interference in the internal affairs of the state, and it was this threat

---

[10] The British representative in Rome, Macdonell, warned the Italian government of the 'risk Italy would incur in attempting to cope with France in North Africa' (Macdonell to Granville, 1 September 1880, F.O. 45/407, no. 402).

[11] *D.D.F.*, iii, no. 106.

to the *status quo* which gave the problem its international significance.[12]

As Tunisian independence was threatened by two neighbours, France and Italy, so Morocco was threatened by two neighbours, France and Spain. Great Britain's position at Gibraltar and her susceptibility to potential threats to the route to India (both the Cape and the Suez routes could be threatened from Moroccan bases), made her the strongest supporter of Moroccan independence, and Morocco took her place along with Turkey, Egypt, and Tunis as a corrupt and inefficient Moslem state in which British governments, for both liberal and strategical reasons, desired to introduce reforms. Diplomatic support had been formally promised by Lord Palmerston in a confidential communication of February 1841. The Morocco-Algerine frontier was delimited by the Franco-Moroccan treaty of 18 March 1845, but the Sultan was incapable of preventing tribal raids from Moroccan territory across the frontier into Algiers, and in the circumstances it was fortunate for Morocco that France under the Second Empire had relatively little interest in north-west African affairs apart from the pacification of Algeria. During the early 'seventies she was again in no position to give much attention to Morocco. What real threat there was to Moroccan independence came from Spain. Her possessions along the north coast of Morocco caused constant trouble, and after winning, with some difficulty, the war of 1860 she gained in 1861 a number of concessions including the unidentifiable site of a port on the coast of Sus. She continued to make the pace for the next fifteen years with frequent, rather arrogant demands on the apprehensive Moroccan rulers; the scanty respect for both the Spaniards and the government shown by many of the Sultan's turbulent subjects provided ample material for a spirited Spanish policy, and there was an exceptionally aggressive phase of Spanish activity in 1875 and 1876.[13]

[12] There are useful discussions of the system of protection in H. C. M. Wendel, 'The Protégé System in Morocco' (*Journal of Modern History*, ii, 55–8) and E. F. Cruickshank, *Morocco at the Parting of the Ways* (1935).

[13] For general developments before 1880, A. Bernard, *Les confins algéro-marocains* (1911), pp. 137–50, 391–5; C. de Chavrebière, *Histoire du Maroc* (1931), pp. 402–46; A. Bernard, *Le Maroc* (1931), pp. 301–12; J. Becker, *España y Marruecos* (1903), pp. 9–176. Hay to Derby, 27 March 1876, no. 26; 7 May, nos. 45, 46, 47 (F.O. 99/173); 23 November, no. 118 (F.O. 99/174).

Great Britain had been represented since 1845 by Sir John Drummond Hay,[14] an able proconsular figure of the Stratford Canning type, whose long residence, vast knowledge of the country, command of languages, and strong personality made him the acknowledged defender of Moroccan independence. The Spanish pressure in 1875–6 and the accession of a new Sultan, Mulay Hassan, with some understanding of the need for reform, enabled Drummond Hay to initiate and support a series of attempts to remove some of the conditions which made the state peculiarly vulnerable to foreign attack. Thus a start was made in 1877 with plans to give the state an efficient army of 10,000 men, and there were plans for economic development and administrative reform which were vigorously pushed by Hay, although with little genuine progress. The main attack was on the system of protection, which gave European merchants trading in Morocco the right to secure the virtual exemption of their native agents from arrest and taxation. The system was not of recent origin; it had its equivalent in Tunis and other Moslem countries, and was the almost inevitable result of the chronic misgovernment of the country. The position of the powers trading in Morocco was, moreover, amply guaranteed by treaty. The practice had grown up of granting protection to all and sundry, and there was a real danger that this increasing interference by foreign agents in the internal affairs of the state would gradually reduce the already backward and miserably misgoverned country to anarchy, and would in turn justify and incite foreign intervention. A demand for the reform of the system was put forward on behalf of the new Sultan in the autumn of 1876; a series of conferences followed at Tangier and continued without result until the summer of 1879. The Moroccan programme was then referred to a conference of the powers at Madrid in 1880.[15]

During these deliberations the international importance of the problem became clearer, and some notable changes of front

[14] Minister plenipotentiary, 1872–86. Sultan Cid Muhammed was said to have offered to place in his hands the entire control of the foreign affairs of Morocco. L. A. E. Brooks, *Sir John Drummond Hay*, pp. vii, viii, 307–64. Cf. Capt. P. D. Trotter, *Our Mission to the Court of Morocco in 1880* (1881).

[15] Drummond Hay's full reports on these discussions are mainly unpublished (F.O. 99/173–181).

followed. The most striking was that of Spain, whose territorial footholds and claims on the Moroccan coast gave her a position independent of the protective system, and one which would be relatively strengthened if internal reform could remove the excuse for French intervention. In November 1878 a new Spanish minister, Señor Diosdado, assured the Moroccan government that Spain was determined to co-operate with Great Britain and Morocco in maintaining Moroccan independence, and during the next two years he was Hay's closest supporter in the attack on the protective system.[16]

France on the other hand became its uncompromising defender. Under Decazes the French attitude had been cautious, and he had not appeared to be opposed to all reform; for a time Hay regarded the French minister, Vernouillet, as his chief ally. But Vernouillet always appeared to be without instructions, and it had become clear by the summer of 1878 that his masterful subordinate, Hecquard, the chief dragoman of the French legation, was the real director of French policy. A good Arabic scholar who had passed his life in the Levant, Hecquard was probably the most aggressive of all the foreign representatives in Morocco; Hay declared roundly in February 1879 that even during the short time that he had resided in the country he had made himself notorious for his total disregard for justice and propriety. His browbeating of the terrified authorities, who knew that behind the dragoman was a powerful army within a few days' march of the capital, served the double purpose of securing his government's demands and satisfying his personal interests. Although it was probable that some of his activities were unknown to the French government and even to Vernouillet there was no doubt that he had been deliberately chosen to push French influence to its limits. An ambitious French plan for a railway from Algeria to the Soudan also contained an obvious threat to Moroccan independence; between November 1879 and April 1880 French officers surveying the routes had brushes with Moroccan tribesmen, and in

[16] Hay to Salisbury, 26 October 1878, no. 90; 4 November, no. 92; 15 December, no. 105 (F.O. 99/182). As late as August 1877 Derby had remarked that 'Spain is the only country likely to attack Morocco' (F.O. 99/178, no. 66). On Spanish commercial claims, *Intereses de España en Marruecos* (Sociedad española de Africanistas y Colonistas, Madrid, 1884).

February 1880 Albert Grévy, the governor-general of Algeria, warned a Moroccan ambassador that if the depredations of Moorish tribes on French territory did not cease, a French army would march across the frontier to punish the marauders. France agreed to enter the proposed conference at Madrid, but made her attitude clear by reserving all the rights of the French protégés.[17]

Italy proved a great disappointment to the British: she also decided to oppose reform. Italian sources at present available throw little light on her Moroccan policy, and at first it is strange that at the height of her fruitless struggle with the French in Tunis she should do anything to further French interests elsewhere. In 1877 the Italian minister, Scovasso, had joined Hay in criticism of the protective system, and complained that foreign consular officers had dealt with protection as an article of trade, and sold it to the highest bidder. But after the summer of 1878 it was found that Scovasso, acting no doubt under instructions, had veered round and had become a critic of the reform programme. The fact is that the Italian government was repeating in Morocco the policy of indiscriminate and short-sighted activity which she had been following elsewhere since the Congress. There were, according to Hay, only five *bona fide* Italian merchants in Morocco, and without the maintenance of the existing confusion Italy would play little part in Moroccan affairs. Unlike Spain, she did not bother herself about the opening for ultimate French intervention which would result from the perpetuation of the existing chaos; on the other hand she does not appear to have made any attempt to barter her support for French concessions elsewhere. Her policy was simply to hang on to her immediate, though very limited, advantages, without thought for the future.[18]

In these circumstances, with the British and Spanish votes

[17] Hay to Salisbury, 3 February 1879, no. 14; 28 November, no. 92 (F.O. 99/186); 12 February 1880, no. 20 (F.O. 99/191); 24 February, no. 24 (F.O. 99/255). Freycinet to Jaurès, 21 February 1880. P. Leroy-Beaulieu, *Le Sahara, le Soudan, et les chemins de fer transsahariens* (1904), pp. 34–72, 88–133; *Documents relatifs à la mission dirigée au sud de l'Algérie par le lieutenant-colonel Flatters* (1884), pp. 1–73, 89.

[18] The British ambassador in Rome, Sir Augustus Paget, tried unsuccessfully to persuade Count Maffei, the Italian foreign minister, to support the reform programme, saying that Italian policy 'I presumed must be like that of Great Britain and the other Powers, to strengthen rather than undermine the already feeble

balanced by the Italian and French, the German government could play a decisive part. But this was clearly a situation which could prove highly embarrassing for Bismarck's plans in the winter of 1879–80. He wished at this period to avoid an Anglo-French quarrel. If it occurred, he would no doubt wish to keep in the background, and to avoid losing the friendship of either; he might adopt the plan which he had followed in the Balkan committees in the previous winter, and show his impartiality by giving the German vote to the majority. But this course had proved a conspicuous failure in the Balkans, for the Russians, who found themselves consistently outvoted, ignored the subtleties of Bismarck's position and indignantly denounced his support of their enemies; the same might very well happen with the cooler-headed but equally sceptical French and British ministers. Bismarck accordingly did not commit himself until the last minute, and gave some encouragement to both sides. During the various conferences and deliberations at Tangier the German minister Weber did not play a particularly prominent part, but Hay had been able to report in July 1879 that the German and Spanish ministers 'entertained identical opinions with my own regarding the acceptance of all the demands of the Moorish Government'. In October 1879 the Duke of Tetuan wished to include the German government in the preliminary agreement which he desired the British and Spanish governments to conclude, and evidently counted on German support.[19] A despatch from Weber on 27 March 1880, giving details of the French Trans-Sahara railway project, allowed Bismarck on 8 April to renew his assurances to the French government of willingness to support their African policy and to extend these assurances to cover the situation that was arising in Morocco. But on the following day Weber was instructed to avoid giving his exclusive support to either the British or the French.[20]

authority of the Moorish Government'. Paget to Salisbury, 7 November 1879, F.O. 99/255. Scovasso was raised to the rank of minister plenipotentiary, and received an ovation, on his return to Tangier in an Italian frigate on 28 March 1880, from a large number of protected Jews and Muhammedans, who clearly regarded him as the chief supporter of irregular protection.

[19] West to Salisbury, 21 October 1879, no. 189, F.O. 99/255.

[20] Weber to Bismarck, 27 March 1880, G.P., iii, p. 396, n. 1; Bismarck to Hohenlohe, 8 April, ibid., no. 662; Bismarck to Weber, 9 April, ibid., no. 663.

It was not until after the Liberal victory in England that Bismarck definitely committed himself. An explicit promise to support France at the forthcoming conference was finally made in very satisfactory terms by Hohenlohe on 23 April. He said that Bismarck considered that this question was covered by the promise made at the Congress of Berlin to support and second French policy whenever French and German interests were not in conflict, and especially in the Mediterranean basin; he claimed that the Chancellor had remained faithful to his promise and had supported France in both Egypt and Tunis, and he wished to act in the same way in Morocco, taking advantage of the fact that Germany had no vital interests in that area to give a fresh proof of his friendly disposition. Count Solms, the German minister at Madrid, would be instructed to conform his attitude, language, and votes to those of his French colleague. In reply, Freycinet on the 26th forwarded a résumé of the instructions which were to be sent to Juarès, the French ambassador at Madrid. In these, Juarès was instructed to maintain all the privileges accorded to France by the treaties, although at the same time he was to do his best to satisfy the demand for the removal of abuses. [21] On 5 May Hohenlohe told Saint-Vallier that the note would be made the basis of Count Solms' instructions, [22] and on the following day Solms was duly instructed to support the French minister, though he was to leave the initiative to him as much as possible. [23]

Bismarck's action must not be interpreted as an expression of hostility to the Gladstone government; he was not unwilling to display some coolness or reserve towards the new government's plans, but this was certainly not the time for a quarrel. A remark in his instructions to Weber, to the effect that he expected the new Gladstone government to be less resolute than its predecessors, [24] probably gives the clue to his attitude. If the British were less interested in the problem than the French it was clearly better to follow the line of least resistance and support

[21] Saint-Vallier to Freycinet, 23 April 1880; Freycinet to Saint-Vallier, 26 April; note communicated by Saint-Vallier to the German government; *D.D.F.*, iii, nos. 85, 97, 98.

[22] Saint-Vallier to Freycinet, 4 May, and postscript of 5 May, *ibid.*, no. 108.

[23] Hohenlohe to Solms-Sonnenwalde, 6 May 1880, *G.P.*, iii, no. 664.

[24] *G.P.*, iii, p. 397.

the latter. Bismarck's remark was, in fact, a shrewd piece of guesswork; there is no indication that it was more than that, but it soon became clear that the Liberal government regarded its predecessor's programme in this question with distrust, and intended to make no special effort to push it through. In this it was anticipating its abandonment, a year or two later, of Salisbury's reform programme in Asia Minor. It was, after all, the declared opponent of the policy of defending corrupt Moslem governments for political ends, and Gladstone had made no secret of his conviction that reform programmes advocated by Western governments were in these cases probably unsuitable and probably selfish.[25] Salisbury had taken a close interest in Hay's programme, and had been responsible for a major decision on tactics which proved unfortunate in view of Granville's inaction. In December 1879 there were rumours in the French press of a Franco-Moroccan *modus vivendi* which raised the possibility that the French might, as Hay wrote, try to 'introduce the discussion of other matter affecting this country' at the conference. This was considered by the British and Spanish to be undesirable because it might supply an opening for a general attack on the state, and also because it was extremely unlikely that Morocco would get the better of the bargaining. Cid Muhammed Bargash, the Moroccan Foreign Minister, who was to represent Morocco at the conference, was not in favour at court, and his instructions gave him no scope for bargaining; he was believed, moreover, to be 'very torpid' and no match for the Frenchmen. In consequence Salisbury insisted that no subjects should be brought under discussion other than those for which the conference had been convoked.[26]

We are concerned here only with the influence of North African developments on the general relations of the powers, and all that need be said of the proceedings of the Madrid conference is that the new British government appeared to take no interest at all in the proceedings. Sir Lionel Sackville-West, the British ambassador in Madrid, was the British representative; in Hay's view he was also, like Bargash, a 'torpid' diplomatist,

[25] See above, p. 32.
[26] Hay to H. C. Jervoise (private), 10 December 1879; Salisbury to Sackville-West, 1 March 1880, no. 47, F.O. 99/255.

but he was without special instructions, and the British government made no attempt to press the British-Spanish-Moroccan
programme in Paris.[27] The conference opened on 19 May; on
the 23rd Freycinet sent uncompromising instructions that no
diminution of French rights of protection could be accepted;
minor points were discussed during the following week, but by
1 June a deadlock had been reached, and the conference
adjourned until the 6th. While the British remained inactive the
French secured a reaffirmation of German and Italian promises
of support, and accordingly, on the 6th, Juarès was more uncompromising than ever in refusing concessions, and Bargash's
surrender followed a few days later. The French secured the
confirmation of all their treaty rights of protection; minor concessions could not disguise the virtually complete defeat of the
reform programme.[28]

'The French policy has been *je veux*, and the silly Italians,
who really have no trade or interest in Morocco except to maintain its independence, backed the French', wrote Drummond
Hay to his sister. 'Now my responsibility ceases, and when
affairs take a disastrous turn I shall say, "I told you so".'[29] But
there was—for the moment—no disastrous turn, and the significance of the Madrid conference was soon forgotten among
the more dramatic happenings in Tunis and the Balkans. The
North African developments show the Liberal government
without a policy, seeking uneasily to evade acceptance of the
need for a bargain or arrangement with the French, and
shocked at the revelation in Tunis and Morocco of the energy
and ruthlessness with which French agents were preparing the
ground for subsequent action by the hesitant government in
Paris. Salisbury had been obsessed by the conviction that the

[27] West appears to have failed to note the French reservations until after the
conference met, and to have misunderstood the religious position. He signed the
convention without formal authorization to do so. West to Granville, 18 May 1880,
no. 105; 31 May, no. 120; 2 June, no. 124; 3 July, no. 177.

[28] West to Granville, 19 May, no. 106, F.O. 99/256; nos. 109, 110, 118, 119, 130,
134, F.O. 72/1566. *D.D.F.*, iii, nos. 124, 132, 133, 135, 144, 155, 165, 169, 170, 189.
Livre jaune: Questions de la protection diplomatique et consulaire au Maroc (1880), nos. 33,
35, 37, 43, 44, 48, 53. The protocols are printed in the British bluebook, *Correspondence relative to the Conference held at Madrid in 1880* (c-2707). A detailed commentary appears in *U.S.A. Foreign Relations 1880*, pp. 897–917.

[29] L. A. E. Brooks, *Sir John Drummond Hay*, p. 323.

independence of the Moslem world, from Constantinople to Morocco, might crumble at any moment, and had been busy and varied in his efforts to preserve it; in Asiatic Turkey and Morocco by promoting internal reform with the encouragement of military and naval support from bases in Cyprus and Gibraltar, and in Egypt by a watchful co-operation with the French. He had been prepared to abandon the traditional British policy in Tunis in order to strengthen British influence elsewhere and to hold the French to the traditional Anglo-French entente. This policy can be criticized at certain points where he may have misread the terms of the problem, but it showed every willingness to accept and control realities. The Liberals, however, sought to tranquillize Europe by re-establishing a traditional, and largely mythical, state of quiescence in international affairs; Turkey as the obvious trouble-maker must be overawed, and then it was hoped that the European powers would settle down and refrain from fresh adventures. The policy of Beaconsfield and Salisbury was accordingly regarded by many Liberals, in addition to Gladstone, as the real cause of much of the tension in Europe, and this view was probably shared by many of the permanent officials of the Foreign Office. Lord Dufferin wrote from St. Petersburg to Lord Granville in August 1880, 'I really think that if the late government had remained in office another year, we should have been in dispute if not at war with all the world. There is a fine bit of party spirit for you, but I thoroughly believe it.'[30]

Nothing more clearly illustrates the tactical weaknesses of Granville's foreign policy than this reluctance to accept and manipulate the ambitions of others; while Bismarck and Salisbury were prepared to barter connivance for goodwill in the market-places of diplomacy, the English Liberal could not but deplore the sordid and demoralizing consequences of trade. And Morocco seemed a particularly clear example of the way in which Salisbury's adventurous policy had been pushing the country towards a major crisis. In a note commenting on Sackville-West's account of the eighth session of the Madrid conference, Lord Tenterden, the Permanent Under-Secretary, wrote, 'I cannot help thinking that it would be no loss if this

[30] *Granville*, ii, 194.

Conference did break up. It has opened up a dangerous question for Morocco', and a few days later, on 18 June, he remarked in a further minute,[31]

The grievance of the irregular grant of protections was a scandal no doubt, but the disgraceful state of Moorish misgovernment is a greater one. The questions opened by the conference go far beyond the protection question and unless we pull up we may find ourselves in a Morocco difficulty with reforms and identic notes and general break up opposite Gibraltar. It would be better to let the matter be fought out in the Conference or drop altogether.

Granville clearly shared this view, and he was equally unwilling to recognize the fact that a French seizure of Tunis was imminent, and that he was expected to acquiesce. In his conversations with the French ambassadors on the subject during the summer he showed obvious embarrassment and a reluctance to commit himself finally. He told Léon Say (who held the French embassy in London for only a few weeks) that his government was not at all jealous of French influence in Tunis; but on 12 July he told Challemel-Lacour, Say's successor, that he had examined the despatches of Salisbury and Waddington over the British promises at the Congress and observed that the former contained reservations which were not reproduced in the others. 'We cannot give what does not belong to us. Besides we are not in a position to have any views on the differences which have arisen between France and Italy in Tunis. We can do nothing about them; we can only hope that they will be smoothed out and that good relations will be established in Tunis between the agents of the two countries.'[32]

Granville, it appears, really had no policy on this question; he had not decided whether to agree or disagree; he hoped that the decision could, somehow or other, be rendered unnecessary. If Cyprus could be returned to Turkey the French claim on British support in Tunis could, however, be more easily ignored. During the election campaign the Cyprus Convention had been a special object of Liberal attack. Gladstone denounced it as 'insane', and Goschen deplored it as a 'shabby' transaction which had 'impaired the reputation of England as

[31] Note on Hay's no. 107 of 7 June, F.O. 72/1566.
[32] D.D.F., iii, nos. 150, 159, 209.

the most clean-handed member of the European family'.[33] But Gladstone had also undertaken not to repudiate specific engagements entered into by the Conservatives, and as Russia was in a conciliatory mood and British energies concentrated on the Greek and Montenegrin questions, the tendency in the cabinet was to postpone a serious decision about the future of the convention and the execution or abandonment of the Conservative programme in Asia Minor. Nevertheless the abandonment of the convention and the retrocession of Cyprus had its attractions, and these cannot but have been stimulated by desire to put the clock back in North-West Africa. After a fortnight at Constantinople Goschen wrote on 16 June that he was appalled at the magnitude of British commitments: 'At present we have apparently the whole of the Turkish Empire on our hands. We have been remonstrating about deeds in every Province. . . . Can this continue? I am aghast at it.'[34] During May Musurus Pasha hinted that the Sultan would welcome a more or less thoroughgoing revision of the convention, including the abandonment of the British right of local interference in Asiatic Turkey, and the cancellation by the Sultan of his claim on British support in defending the Asiatic provinces against Russia. In a summary of the government's objections to the convention in a despatch to Goschen on 10 June Granville remarked that 'the acquisition of Cyprus is in their view of no advantage to the Country either in a military or political sense', a remark which drew from the Queen the marginal comment, 'I do not the least agree in this'.[35] The Turkish government did not follow up Musurus's hints, and many considerations—a genuine sense of responsibility for the Asiatic populations, fear of Russian encroachments in Armenia, and public opinion in England—decided the government against abrogation. But it was not until 1881 that it seems finally to have made this decision, and in the meantime Granville could allow his mind to remain open, and postpone any more precise discussions with the French.[36]

[33] W. E. Gladstone, *Political Speeches*, ii, 358; *Goschen*, i, 195.

[34] Goschen to Granville, secret, 16 June 1880, G.D. 29/188.

[35] Granville to Goschen, very confidential, 10 June 1880, F.O. 78/3074, no. 71.

[36] Further details are given in my article, 'The Gladstone Government and the Cyprus Convention, 1880–85' (*Journal of Modern History*, June 1940).

The result was a growing reserve on the French side towards the main British programme. France could not afford a breach with England, but she could also not afford to act as the pacemaker in the harrying of the Turks. Bismarck was making it abundantly clear that he wished to damp down the coercive programme of the Concert; a serious quarrel with Turkey was undesirable; French public opinion was averse to any policy of risks. In any case, if France had to choose between Germany and Britain it was now only too likely that Germany would prove the more active, as she was certainly the more weighty, of the two.

CHAPTER VI

The Concert in Action :
Dulcigno and Smyrna

THE action of the Porte during June and July made one thing clear: the Sultan was quite unmoved by the united voice of Europe. Turkish replies to the united voice, as it had spoken in the identic note of 11 June, were condemned by all the powers as unsatisfactory.

What was to be done next? During July coercion was discussed; and in these discussions Great Britain took the lead, with a reasonable degree of encouragement by Russia. But no one approaches a sanctions crisis with any zest, and the circumspect advance to the point of action was sufficiently leisurely to provide the Sultan with ample time for retreat had he desired it. The discussions over the Montenegrin frontier in July show that he was practising his tactics of calculated procrastination with studied patience, and with as yet no sign of nervous collapse.

In view of the imminence of the Berlin conference the Porte had replied promptly (on 14 June) to the section of the identic note dealing with the Greek frontier; the reply to the section on Montenegro was made on 24 June. It offered out of deference to the powers to carry out the measures laid down in the April memorandum, but only on condition that necessary time be given to the Turkish authorities.[1] The ambassadors had decided not to present the alternative proposal concerning Dulcigno (see p. 98 above) until the reply had been received. The Dulcigno arrangements, although accepted by all the powers, had not been received without some hesitation by Prince Nicholas. He wished to attach to his acceptance certain conditions; a

---

[1] Granville to Dufferin, etc., 17 June, F.O. 65/1076, no. 259. Goschen to Granville, 29 June, F.O. 78/3088, no. 97.

pecuniary indemnity from the Porte, the razing of a Turkish fort between Zem and the lake of Scutari, the prohibition of the erection by the Turks of any forts on the territory left to them between the lake and the sea, various conditions respecting the cession of Dulcigno, and the support if necessary of naval contingents of the powers. On some points Kirby Green's understanding of the prince's demands differed from those of the Austrian minister, Colonel Thömmel. Nicholas also mentioned his requirements to the Russian minister, and in this case asked for an assurance that the surrender would be peacefully and regularly affected. He objected to the constitution of Albania as an autonomous province. Haymerle considered it best not to attach too much importance to these conditions, and only to tell the prince that in determining the details of the arrangements there would be every disposition to attend to his interests. Nicholas was apparently quite satisfied with this, and accepted on the 18th, it being clearly understood that if the Porte failed to accept the new plan the scheme of 18 April would automatically be reverted to.[2]

The Dulcigno arrangement was proposed to the Porte in an identic note dated 26 June. Last-minute hesitation by Novikov, the Russian ambassador, delayed matters; in the end he would agree to the proposal only if it were made in sufficiently general terms to include whatever modifications Prince Nicholas might propose.[3] When Dufferin on the 28th expressed surprise that Novikov had not received instructions to support his colleagues, Giers replied somewhat evasively that Novikov was too timid and over-scrupulous in the exercise of his own discretion, and that immediately on receiving his telegram the Russian government had desired him to concur in the identic note. As Giers earlier in the month had shown that he would not be sorry to see the proposal defeated it is probable that Novikov's conduct was not due merely to timidity. There was, in any case, little hope that the Turks would consider the Dulcigno plan preferable to the Corti arrangement. They would have to surrender

[2] Thömmel to Haymerle, 11 June, W.S.A., tel. no. 240; 13 June, no. 244; 15 June, no. 248; 16 June, no. 250. Haymerle to Thömmel, 12 June, tel.; Károlyi to Haymerle, 13 June, tels. nos. 46, 62.

[3] Dubsky to Haymerle, 27 June, W.S.A., tel. no. 92. Dufferin to Granville, 29 June, F.O. 65/1080, no. 277.

Mussulman Albanians instead of Roman Catholics; they would lose what they called the port of Albania, and they considered that strategically Scutari would be threatened. For all these reasons they regarded the cession of the Hoti and Clementi clans as less objectionable. Goschen received one or two hints that the Porte would be prepared to bargain with the powers, offering a speedy settlement of the Montenegrin difficulty in return for concessions on the Greek frontier. But he ignored these approaches, and was then assured by Abeddin that the Porte really intended to execute the April memorandum, but could not attempt force at this stage.[4]

The Porte continued to make difficulties throughout July. The opposition to concession was led in the council by Osman Pasha, with the obvious approval of the Sultan. Abeddin sounded Goschen secretly as to the possibility of a Turkish cession of an island and of extra territory in Thessaly in return for the right to keep Preveza and Janina, but Granville's reply was unfavourable, and the matter was dropped.[5] On 30 June Abeddin told the Montenegrin *chargé* that the Porte declined the Dulcigno proposal, and had made the offer of a pecuniary indemnity to Montenegro; on 2 July he told Goschen that the Porte would make an effort to execute the April arrangement and would send some money and 6,000 men; a few days later the Montenegrin government was assured that the Porte would deliver up immediately the territory indicated in the April arrangement. But on top of this there came news that on 12 July in the same area, near Gulubovce, the Albanians had attacked the Montenegrin outposts; ten Montenegrins had been beheaded and six had escaped wounded. Both Turkish and Montenegrin accounts admitted that the Albanian losses were much less. It seemed evident that the Turkish military authorities knew of the preparations for the attack, and could easily have prevented it; and it had to be assumed that the Turkish governor-general was doing all in his power to frustrate the April arrangement. Abeddin made a brave attempt on 14

[4] Thömmel to Haymerle, 1 July, W.S.A., tel.

[5] Dubsky to Haymerle, 2 July, W.S.A., 53A–E. Goschen to Granville, G.D. 29/188 (Granville Papers), 3 July, 4 July. The Albanian League displayed great hostility to the consuls of the powers. Waldhart (Prizren) to Haymerle, 30 June, W.S.A., no. 57.

July to draw capital from the incident by accusing the Montenegrins of aggression: did not the smallness of the Albanian losses prove that they were behind entrenchments and therefore the defending party? But there is no doubt that the Albanians were the aggressors.[6] When the Porte replied on the 15th to the last proposal of the powers its offer looked so much like an attempt to haggle over details that the powers were probably right to give it no serious attention. The gist of it was that the Porte felt it could now peaceably surrender two-thirds of the area proposed under the Corti arrangement, and was prepared to give compensation for the remaining third in the direction of Dulcigno, but wished to retain the town itself, because it was inhabited by Mussulmans. Abeddin explained to Goschen that it was possible that Dulcigno might be occupied without resistance if there were a naval demonstration, but in that case the Albanians would undoubtedly attack Montenegro elsewhere.[7]

So the powers were forced to examine plans for some demonstration of force which would be taken, they hoped, more seriously by the Sultan than they were able to take it themselves. In England Gladstone showed remarkable firmness in the pursuit of this policy; from June until October he was the real driving force in British policy, although his partnership with Granville was one of perfect harmony and courtesy on both sides. It fell to Granville to restrain the impetuosity of the prime minister at some points, and the detailed pursuit of the common end was his, but it was Gladstone who insisted throughout on the impossibility of surrender.[8] As early as 19 June he asked Granville whether it was not time to consider 'the best and most available means of compulsion, actual or indicative, in case Turkey is recalcitrant'; ten days later he was calling for

---

[6] Dubsky to Haymerle, 15 July, W.S.A., tel. no. 104; Kosjek to Haymerle, 17 July, tel. no. 108.

[7] Haymerle to Dubsky, 3 July, W.S.A., tel. no. 138; Dubsky to Haymerle, 3 July, tel. no. 95; Haymerle to Kosjek, 22 July. Abeddin Pasha to Musurus Bey, 14, 15 July (comm. to Granville, 15 July). Goschen to Granville, 15 July, F.O. 78/3109, no. 120. Elliot to Granville, 19 July, F.O. 7/992, no. 404.

[8] This in spite of his illness in the summer, followed by a cruise around the British Isles in the *Grantully Castle* in late August and early September; he did not return to Parliament until 4 September, when he spoke forcefully on the Eastern question (*Gladstone*, iii, 8).

action. 'The Sultan is using both fraud and underhand force against us at every point and we have nothing to expect but from his fears.' Dilke on the previous evening had suggested that the British government's separate and long-standing differences with Turkey over commercial rights in Smyrna should be driven to an issue, and 'might do something to convince the Sultan'. Granville, however, was not prepared at this stage to follow a course which would mean separating from the Concert, nor to act as a mandatory of the powers if the Concert broke up. If that happened, he wrote on 30 June, 'I presume we shall not consent to act as a policeman to enforce general European objects, and we might then attend with all our firmness to our own special interests'. Subsequent events show that this escapism was not to Gladstone's liking, although he appears to have made no comment at this stage. On the same day he made another suggestion: that Granville should send Goschen 'a stout telegram' to let the Porte know that 'we have our eyes upon the desires of Albania for self-government, which are so strong that they have even found expression to us in unusual forms'. Granville again deprecated individual menaces. 'The other powers will be too happy to throw upon us the burden, which they feel weighs on us all.'[9]

Russia, however, could not fairly be accused of reluctance; on 21 June Lobanov had read to Granville a private letter in which Giers affirmed his belief in the need for a real and ostensible Concert, and for practical measures to prove to the Porte that the powers meant business. He promised to support any arrangements that Granville might think necessary to this end. Lobanov then went on, after carefully pointing out that he was speaking only for himself, to discuss ways and means; there followed an injudicious proposal which was soon to cause general embarrassment. 'In his opinion a naval demonstration would not be sufficient without troops on board the ships which might be landed as in the case of Syria in 1860. He believed that the Russian government might be induced to lend troops for this purpose, who might be embarked on British ships.' He suggested a force of 20,000 troops. Granville replied that he could

[9] Quotations from Gladstone papers: Gladstone to Granville, 19, 29, 30 June (Add. MSS. 44544); Granville to Gladstone, 29, 30 June (Add. MSS. 44172).

not give an opinion offhand, but it appeared to him impossible
that after taking all the steps they had agreed to take the powers
should allow their decisions to be disregarded.[10]

Lobanov's suggestion, which very soon leaked out, produced
a small panic on the continent. Granville mentioned it to
Münster on the 27th, and it appears to have reached the other
governments through this channel. The story became garbled
in repetition, and it was generally assumed that the Russian
government itself had offered 20,000 troops to England for the
purpose of constraining the cession of the Dulcigno district.
Hohenlohe succeeded in alarming the Turkish ambassador by
warning him that if Russia sent that number others would
probably do the same; but he could only promise Odo Russell
on 1 July that Germany, faithful to her declared policy, would
give her moral support to the concerted and unanimous action
of the powers, although if a naval demonstration alone were
resolved upon, Germany might, in certain circumstances, consent to 'shew the German Flag' in Eastern waters.[11] Busch remarked that Lobanov's suggestion showed what people dared
to offer this English Cabinet and its novices.[12] Within the next
few days Giers received telegraphic inquiries from almost every
court in Europe. He at once asked Lobanov for explanations,
and Lobanov in reply emphasized the fact that he had spoken
to Granville privately, and without authority.[13] Granville's
report of the interview, which Giers was allowed to see, confirmed this.[14] Giers accordingly proceeded, hurriedly and emphatically, to disavow Lobanov, who was himself informed that
the idea was quite contrary to the Emperor's ideas and policy
since the Congress. D'Oubril was instructed to assure Haymerle
that Lobanov had spoken entirely for himself and without

[10] Granville to Dufferin, 21 June, F.O. 65/1076, no. 272.

[11] Granville to Odo Russell, 28 June, F.O. 78/3182, no. 21, conf. Odo Russell to
Granville, 1 July, F.O. 78/3183, no. 70, conf. Hohenlohe, ii, 266. D.D.F., iii, no.
183. Granville told Széchényi of Lobanov's suggestion on 28th. Károlyi to Haymerle, 28 June, W.S.A., tel. no. 51; conf. despatch of same date. Odo Russell told
Széchényi on the 30th. Széchényi to Haymerle, 30 June, tel. no. 83; 1 July, no.
58A–B.

[12] Busch, p. 233. K. A. Busch was under-secretary to the German Foreign Office.

[13] Lobanov to Giers, R.E., 22 June/4 July; Giers to Lobanov, 2/14 July.

[14] Granville to Dufferin, 2 July, F.O. 65/1076, no. 285; Dufferin to Granville,
15 July, F.O. 65/1080, no. 293.

authority, but this communication appeared to make very little impression on the Austrian minister, who had long since persuaded himself that the Russian government was seeking to bring about a European intervention in Turkey.[15] The unfortunate aspect of the incident was that the Turks could not have remained unaware that the powers were unlikely to land troops. Goschen telegraphed on 1 July that the Porte would not accept the Berlin line unless active measures were taken, and on the following day the first concrete proposal for concise measures appears to have been made by Granville to Károlyi. The Porte was apparently withdrawing its regular troops from the Dulcigno district and pouring in Albanian volunteers, and as the Prince of Montenegro was able but unwilling to seize the district Granville proposed that the Prince should be asked whether he were willing to do so with the naval assistance of Austria, Great Britain, and any other of the powers who were willing to send ships and marines. He added optimistically that this action would prove to the Turks that the powers were in earnest, would settle the Montenegrin question, and would have an advantageous effect upon the fulfilment of the other conditions of the Treaty of Berlin.[16]

The proposal had evidently been carefully planned, and appeared to contain the two necessary conditions of a display of force which might overawe the Albanians and the Porte, and a limitation of the sphere of operations sufficient to prevent the dangers of military operations on land which Haymerle dreaded. To strengthen his case Granville suggested that each power should pledge itself not to take any selfish advantage. On the 5th he added the further proposal that the Porte should be informed that the powers strongly recommended the Dulcigno cession, but that if the Porte preferred the April arrangement it must carry this out within three weeks, otherwise it would be

[15] Elliot to Granville, 7 July, F.O. 7/992, no. 377. *Schweinitz*, ii, 121–2.

[16] Granville to Elliot, 3 July, F.O. 7/995, no. 362, secret. Goschen to Granville, 1 July, G.D. 29/188 (Granville Papers), secret and personal; 2 July, F.O. 78/3089, no. 99. On 30 June Haymerle told Elliot that if a naval demonstration on the coast of Albania or Epirus became necessary he hoped Britain would support the interests of Austria, and said he would wish it to be confined to British and Austrian vessels. 30 June, F.O. 7/991, no. 362. Cf. Haymerle to Károlyi, 2 July, W.S.A., extract from private letter.

expected to join England and Austria and other powers in
assisting the Prince of Montenegro to take possession by force
of the Dulcigno district. Károlyi was able to tell Granville that
his government would probably agree, and Granville accordingly proposed his plan to the powers on the 6th.[17]

Haymerle was in favour of giving the Porte a short period in
which to make up its mind, and was prepared after that to
proceed to a naval demonstration in accordance with the
British proposal. But he proposed to limit the active measures
very severely. No power was to furnish more than two vessels.
The idea of the entrance of gunboats into the Boyana, and their
eventual advance into the Lake of Scutari, ought to be put
aside, on account of the difficulties of navigation. No landing of
troops should be contemplated, because if it were attempted at
all it would have to be effected with considerable forces, great
difficulties would arise from such questions as the composition
of the troops, their commandment, etc., and the proportions of
the whole undertaking might grow into war against Turkey.[18]
Russia was the only power to show anything approaching an
unqualified approval of the British proposal, although even
Giers, after expressing himself perfectly satisfied with Granville's note and with his use of the word 'force', added that after
Russia's recent exertions she preferred following in the wake of
the other powers to taking the initiative.[19] The Russian government had, however, taken a more active interest in the matter
than this remark suggested. D'Oubril made every effort to persuade Haymerle to agree to more extensive measures; he argued
that the landing of 500 men from the allied squadrons before
Dulcigno would settle the question of the frontier at once without difficulty. Haymerle replied that d'Oubril might quite
possibly turn out to be mistaken; the Albanians might combine
in a resistance to, or even in an attack on, the Montenegrins,
and then either an Austrian army, or one belonging to some
other nation whose troops it would not suit Austria to see in

[17] Granville, circular: to Goschen, 6 July, F.O. 78/3075, no. 208, conf.
[18] Telegram to embassies (except Paris), 8 July, F.O. 7/995, no. 293 to Elliot.
Cf. Károlyi's conversation with Gladstone, Károlyi to Haymerle, 9 July, W.S.A.
57A–F, *sehr vertraulich*.
[19] Dufferin to Granville, 15 July, F.O. 65/1080, no. 295. Haymerle, circular
telegram, 5 July, W.S.A., no. 90.

those regions, would be involved. It was not even certain that a disembarkation of troops might not lead to hostilities with Turkey, and he could not therefore acquiesce in any scheme in which such a step was included. D'Oubril reproached him with being 'too particular and minute', and continued to ask what would be the practical effect of a naval demonstration on the coast of Albania if it were determined beforehand that not a man from the allied ships was to be landed. Haymerle at length seemed prepared to abandon his attempt to limit the number of ships, but would not agree to any possible operations on shore.[20]

Even greater reluctance to agree to effective measures of coercion was shown by the French government. Without actually rejecting Granville's proposal, Freycinet in his reply on 11 July showed great unwillingness to agree to any allusion to coercive measures until all the powers were prepared to participate, or to agree to a naval demonstration in the Adriatic, especially if the object of the demonstration were confined to Montenegrin affairs. For some days he continued to argue that it would be better for the powers not to make any definite threat in the proposed identic note, but merely to say that at the end of three weeks they would resume full liberty of action as to the measures to be taken by them. In the end, however, he promised on the 15th to agree to Granville's proposal provided that all powers participated in the naval demonstration, and that the same measures would, in case of need, be taken in support of Greece. He spoke the truth, but not perhaps the whole truth, about France's attitude when he said that it was especially with a view to Germany that he was so very susceptible with regard to the employment of any French force abroad. In the face of this public feeling, he could not, he said, venture to send a naval force to the Adriatic unless Germany sent an equal force. 'We cannot', he added, 'come out of our house unless Germany also comes out of hers!'[21] The other powers accepted the two

[20] Trauttenberg to Haymerle, 12 July, W.S.A., tel. no. 75; 2/14 July, no. 44c.; Oubril to Haymerle, 23 July. Elliot to Granville, 17 July, F.O. 7/992, no. 394; 10 July, no. 385. Haymerle was careful to tell the Turkish ambassador that there was no difference between the powers concerning the Greek and Montenegrin questions. Haymerle to Dubsky, 1 July, W.S.A., tel. no. 134.

[21] Lyons to Granville, 15 July, F.O. 27/2432, no. 610; no. 611, secret. Cf. Pasetti to Haymerle, 22 July, W.S.A., tel. no. 69.

French proposals without much hesitation, which meant that Germany, after first of all declining to take part in the naval demonstration, agreed to show her flag in order to secure a general participation.[22]

A collective note embodying the new proposals was placed in the hands of the Porte on 3 August. The possibility of a naval demonstration had already leaked out, and before the delivery of the note the Turks were preparing plans to meet the new situation. They still felt confident that the Albanian problem would baffle the powers. Abdul Hamid asked Hobart Pasha whether any ships had been designed that could ascend mountains, as such ships alone would avail against the Albanians. Abeddin Pasha asked the ambassadors whether the powers would be satisfied with the 'cession' of Dulcigno. This apparently meant that the Porte would leave Montenegro to expel the Albanians. Abeddin tried to argue that no more could be expected of the Porte than conditions similar to those accepted in the April Convention, but Goschen answered that the Porte would be held responsible for the action of the Albanians both at Dulcigno and on other parts of the Montenegrin frontier. The collective note stated that the powers strongly urged the Porte to agree to the Dulcigno proposal, but if the Porte nevertheless preferred the arrangement of 18 April and had not after three weeks carried it out the powers would expect the Porte to join them in carrying out the transfer of the Dulcigno district to the Prince of Montenegro.[23]

'The crawling offer of Abeddin Pasha is absolutely defective!' exclaimed Gladstone. But there can be no doubt that the Turks were employing the right tactics, for the idea of a naval demonstration became more and more distasteful to certain governments as the weeks went by, and it was difficult to see how the Concert could be maintained, if Turkish resistance went so far

[22] Széchényi to Haymerle, 1 July, W.S.A., tel. no. 84; Pasetti to Haymerle, 9 July, tel. no. 90; 12 July, tel. no. 92; 13 July, tel no. 94. Odo Russell to Granville, 23 July, F.O. 64/961, no. 322, enclosing Hohenlohe to Odo Russell, 22 July; Elliot to Granville, 23 July, F.O. 7/992, no. 414. Cf. Hatzfeldt's comments, Kosjek to Haymerle, W.S.A., 23 July.

[23] Haymerle to Kosjek, W.S.A., 29 July; Kuefstein to Haymerle, 2 August, tel. no. 81; Kálnoky to Haymerle, 5 August, tel no. 83. Goschen to Granville, 3 August, F.O. 78/3091, no. 209. Lippich (Scutari) to Haymerle, 21 July, W.S.A., tel.

as to necessitate the use, rather than the threat, of force. By the end of July Austrian newspapers of every shade of political opinion were criticizing British policy as a danger to the peace of Europe; the defeat of General Burrows at Maiwand in June was greeted with unexpected satisfaction on the ground that 'Afghanistan might yet save us from another Navarino'.[24]

The Porte raised a fresh objection to the demands of the powers almost immediately after the presentation of the collective note on 3 August. Novikov happened to be with Abeddin when the frontier-line proposals were presented to the Porte, and on Abeddin's request he indicated the line of the new frontier on a map. When Abeddin heard that the line left Dinozi to the Montenegrins he made an exclamation, and expressed astonishment at this concession to the east of the Lake of Scutari. Goschen saw him next day, and admitted afterwards to Granville that the rather vague wording of the original proposal gave some excuse for this surprise.[25] The Porte during the next week made continued objections to the cession of Dinozi and Gruda; the council of ministers apparently believed that as these places were occupied by Albanians they would incur almost the same difficulty as in carrying out the April arrangement. In these circumstances the Porte decided that the sole attraction of the Dulcigno arrangement—namely its practicability—had disappeared; it reverted suddenly to the April plan, and it was announced that the minister of war himself, with a body of troops, would be sent to execute it. On the 10th it was decided to send not the minister of war, but another pasha; on the 12th Abeddin was sent round to the ambassadors to announce that the Porte would after all accept the Dulcigno proposal, but only on condition that Dinozi and Gruda should be excluded, and that a further delay should be granted for the execution of the cession.[26]

Giers and Granville obviously viewed any concessions to

[24] Gladstone to Granville, 29 July (Add. MSS. 44544); Elliot to Granville, 2 August, F.O. 7/993, no. 443.
[25] Calice to Haymerle, 6 August, W.S.A., tel. no. 121; Goschen to Granville, 6 August, F.O. 78/3091, no. 216.
[26] Calice to Haymerle, 10 August, W.S.A., tel. no. 124; no. 65B; 12 August, tel. no. 127. Goschen to Granville, 17 August, F.O. 78/3092, no. 258.

the Turks as an error in tactics. But Goschen noted a change of tone among many of his colleagues, and was convinced that the Porte was resisting in the belief 'that the Powers are at sixes and sevens, if not with themselves, yet with public opinion'.[27] The French were determined to seek every possible means of compromise, and, as a preliminary, approached the Italian government with a proposal that the Porte should be called upon to execute the Dulcigno arrangement, and should be granted a further delay of a few weeks for this purpose; when the cession was completed the question of Dinozi and Gruda could be a matter for further negotiations. After the Italians had accepted this suggestion it was discovered that the Austrian government was willing to go even further and to abandon the demand for Dinozi and Gruda if this would facilitate a quick and final settlement.[28] On the 18th the Porte sent its written answer to the collective note of 3 August; it agreed in general with Abeddin's verbal communication, but in the meantime the Franco-Italian proposal had become known in Constantinople, and a more determined tone was consequently adopted. The note demanded an extension by several weeks of the three-week period originally allotted; insisted on the retention of Dinozi and Gruda, and announced that if these demands were refused the Porte would be unable to associate itself in any way with any action which might be taken by the powers to assist the Prince of Montenegro to occupy the ceded territory by force.[29] Further notes from Abeddin repeated the Porte's refusal. On the 23rd he announced that while adhering to the cession of Dulcigno and its environs the Porte was compelled to reserve the cession of Gruda and Dinozi, and a further note on 2 September declared that the consent of the Albanians to the cession

[27] Kálnoky to Haymerle, 16 August, W.S.A., tel. no. 88. Goschen to Granville, 10 August, G.D. 29/188 (Granville Papers). Hohenlohe told Pasetti that, if the Porte wished for a prolongation of the period of three weeks, the powers would be wise to concede it. W.S.A., 6 August, no. 77B.

[28] Wrede to Haymerle, 12 August, W.S.A., tel. no. 92; 15 August, tel. no. 93; Calice to Haymerle, 13 August, tel. no. 129; Elliot to Granville, 17 August, F.O. 7/993, no. 485. Memorandum by Hengelmüller, 19 August, F.O. 7/995, no. 546.

[29] Goschen to Granville, 20 August, F.O. 78/3092, no. 261. Gladstone to Granville (17 August): '. . . it seems to me we cannot have a stronger ground for a kind of united *sommation* to Turkey than she is now supplying for her impudent bad faith and interminable delays' (Add. MSS. 44544).

of Dulcigno could not be obtained unless the *status quo* were agreed to for the definition of the frontier east of the lake.[30]

With memories of the Sultan's rejection of even the innocuous London Protocol of March 1877 the powers could never entirely free themselves from the fear that some fanatical act of defiance would again plunge him into war with one or more of them. After the disasters of the last war, however, it seemed unlikely on the whole that he would take this plunge, and it was the probable effect on their own relations, rather than the apprehension of any serious military resistance on his part, that caused alarm. Preparations for the naval demonstration continued; there was, nevertheless, every wish to eliminate from the final demands of the powers any points which, in view of local or religious or other susceptibilities, he would find it genuinely difficult to concede. This explains the rather slow course of the discussions between the powers during the second half of August and first half of September; the fact that Gladstone, Haymerle, and Bismarck were holiday-making in August, and the Tsar in September, was less of an obstacle to progress than might at first appear.

The British government, as the leading advocate of strong action, had therefore to decide whether to try to hold the powers to the terms of the collective note of 3 August, or to agree to the modifications suggested by the Franco-Italian proposals, and so clearly welcomed by Haymerle. The pros and cons of these important decisions were discussed in a Cabinet meeting on 18 August, and in Gladstone's absence there was unanimous approval of compromise. Granville's account of the discussions, in a private letter to Gladstone, is worth quoting in full.[31]

The persons who composed the Cabinet yesterday in the Chancellor's room were Selborne, Argyle, Kimberley, Northbrook, Hartington, Chamberlain and Bright (Harcourt subsequently agreeing). I put before them clearly the disadvantage of separating at all from the Collective Note—which chiefly consisted in our giving a false key note to subsequent negotiations and encouraging the Turks to believe that they can succeed by dilatory negotiation.

[30] Goschen to Granville, 24 August, F.O. 78/3092, nos. 286, 288; 3 September, no. 321. Calice to Haymerle, 27 August, W.S.A., tel. no. 144; 2 September, tel. no. 148.

[31] Granville to Gladstone, 19 August (Add. MSS. 44172).

The chief arguments on the other side, are the rather shaky state of the Concert of Europe at this moment; the evident wish of Italy, France and Austria (though she has not given an official answer) to settle the Montenegrin question in the sort of way proposed by France. The strong opinion of Northbrook that the Naval demonstration should be reserved for the Greek Frontier question, when he believes it may be of real use—The false position of the fleet on the Coast, after that portion of the territory which alone they can command, has been agreed to be ceded, while the village which they cannot reach is the sole cause of quarrel—and the great advantage of a speedy settlement by the Concert of Europe of one of the questions in dispute—

The Cabinet were unanimous in favour of the compromise, if it were clearly defined, promptly carried into execution, and of a definite character. They thought the Austrian proposal to have a complete closing of the matter, much preferable to leaving an open sore. It appears that one of the villages named was never included in the proposed cession—the other is commanded by the Montenegrins, and is in ruins. It was occupied by Mussulmans who are now at Scutari. . . .

Gladstone, who was staying with Lord Granville's brother at Dorking, received this account by messenger, and replied the same day: he concurred, although not without some trace of uneasiness. 'The necessity of keeping the team together is a prime element in the case.' British acceptance of the Austrian solution enabled Haymerle to put proposals to the powers in a circular telegram of 24 August, which suggested that the territory of Dinozi might be left to Turkey without inconvenience, as Montenegro, being in possession of the Kuči-Kraina, would be able to command Dinozi and to defend Podgorica from more elevated positions.[32] This would have the advantage of maintaining the decision of the majority of the boundary commissioners in the Gruda district. The proposal was accepted promptly by all the other powers, but the Russian government worried poor Haymerle by subsequently qualifying its consent. Jomini on 28 August had expressed satisfaction and exclaimed that on this basis a definitive settlement would easily be reached. He also promised that his government would advise Prince Nicholas to

[32] Haymerle, circular tel., 24 August, W.S.A. (no. 198 to Calice). Circular despatch, 26 August.

agree. On 3 September Haymerle had accordingly announced that his government had had favourable replies from all the other cabinets, and was not prepared to accept the Turkish counter-demands unless all the other powers wished to do so. But on the following day Jomini told Kálnoky that Prince Nicholas was unwilling to surrender his claim to Dinozi, and accordingly proposed that the powers should revert to the original English plan. Pressure on Russia by the other powers followed, and on the 8th Jomini told Kálnoky that his government had once more changed its mind, and was now after all prepared to accept the Austrian proposal.[33] Then d'Oubril omitted for some days to communicate this agreement to the Austrian government, and when he did so on 13 September it was with the reservation that if the Porte failed to carry out the Dulcigno arrangement promptly the Dinozi compromise would be annulled.[34] The Austrian proposal with this reservation was presented to the Porte on the 16th, with the warning that the cession of the rest of the frontier east of the Lake of Scutari, together with the other territorial demands of the note of 3 August, must be carried out immediately and pacifically.[35]

In the meantime the powers had completed their arrangements for the naval demonstration, and the allied fleets assembled at Gravosa (Ragusa) on 14 September, two days before the presentation of the Allied note. If the Sultan had hoped that the powers would never come to the point of assembling their fleet he was disappointed, but subsequent events showed that he had convinced himself that the mere presence of ships need not, in itself, cause him any more concern than the bombardment of notepaper which had preceded it. The instructions to the officers in charge of the various

[33] Haymerle, circular telegrams, W.S.A., 30 August, 3 September; Pasetti (Berlin) to Haymerle, 30 August, tel. no. 129; 31 August, tel. no. 130; 9 September, tel. no. 136; Jomini to Kálnoky, 4 September; Kálnoky to Haymerle, 5 September, tel. no. 99; 8 September, no. 53; Calice to Haymerle, 6 September, tel. no. 154.

[34] Haymerle to Kálnoky, 9 September, W.S.A., tel no. 128; Kálnoky to H., 12 September, W.S.A., tel. no. 100; Haymerle, circular tel., 13 September. The Russian communications were probably confused by the fact that the Tsar and Giers were in the Crimea, leaving Jomini in charge of the Foreign Office in St. Petersburg.

[35] Goschen to Granville, 17 September, F.O. 78/3094, no. 362. Calice to Haymerle, 15 September, W.S.A., tel. no. 167.

was Montenegrin concession.[44] It really seemed as if a phase of resolute and decisive action was at last about to commence, and the admirals got so far as to depart from Gravosa and to invite Prince Nicholas by telegram to march troops into the district. Then once more a gesture of defiance from the Turks brought everything to a standstill. On the 26th, in reply to Seymour's telegram, Nicholas replied that a serious new development had occurred. Riza Pasha had announced that if the Montenegrin troops entered Dulcigno he would attack them. Nicholas pointed out that this would involve overcoming the formal resistance of the Ottoman troops, and not merely of Albanian bands; and he was not prepared to enter on what was really a war with Turkey without a promise from the great powers of political and military support more efficacious than a naval demonstration.[45] The promise was clearly one that the allied commanders could not give, and they decided that they must suspend further action pending instructions from their governments.[46]

Riza Pasha's message had the effect of moving the discussions back to Constantinople. Giers at once proposed that the powers should make a unanimous protest and should cast on the Porte all responsibility for the consequence of Riza Pasha's action, but Granville and Haymerle both felt that the last collective note, which had just been presented on the 27th, really covered the same ground, and the suggestion was dropped.[47] The powers in fact were really quite at a loss to know what to do next, when the Sultan supplied a further excuse for delay by announcing

[44] But on 9 October Granville instructed Goschen to make it known that the allied commanders had no intention of bombarding the town, or injuring the peaceful inhabitants. Fire was to be directed on the defensive positions outside the town. Granville to Goschen, 9 October, F.O. 78/3077, no. 581. Secretary to the Admiralty to Tenterden, 25 September, enclosing B. Seymour to Admiralty, 25 September; 29 September, enclosing further correspondence A. & P., *ibid.*, nos. 100, 129. Haymerle nevertheless instructed the Austrian commander that if he received orders to return the fire of a Turkish ship of war he was to refuse, on the ground that he must consult his government before involving it in war with Turkey. Haymerle, an den Kommandanten der K. K. Escadre, 29 September (rcd. 30th). W.S.A., tel.

[45] Thömmel to Haymerle, 29 September, W.S.A., no. 431; 30 September, tel.

[46] Sec. to Admiralty to Tenterden, 28 September (Seymour to Adm., 27 September). A. & P., *op. cit.*, no. 124.

[47] Giers to Haymerle, 14/26 September, W.S.A., tel. Haymerle: circular tel., 27 September.

that by 3 October a settlement satisfactory to all the powers of
all pending questions relating to the treaty of Berlin would be
made. The powers once more agreed to wait, although the
ambassadors could see nothing to indicate any prospect of surrender. The Sultan had now taken the whole management of
the negotiations into his own hands to a degree unparalleled
even in his own reign; the foreign minister was so obviously a
puppet that it was useless to speak to him on business, and even
Saïd had adopted so enigmatical an attitude that it was considered to be of little avail to communicate with him personally. The Sultan was reported to be extremely irritable, and it
appeared that some of the ministers only signed the final
minute under his direct command.[48] When the promised note
was presented (on 4 October) it simply repeated the demands
already made to the powers in connexion with the Montenegrin
question, and actually increased very considerably the demand
for territory allotted by the powers to Greece. It ended with an
ominous hint that Turkey might see fit to press her claims concerning the occupation of the Balkans and the demolition of the
Danubian fortresses. The Armenian reforms, the organic
statute for the European provinces, and the public debt were
also discussed, but the variety of the topics did not in any way
disguise the fact that the reply was deliberately uncompromising and that in the Montenegrin question the powers had now
no escape from the alternatives of surrender or more active
coercion.[49]

The strain was too great for the Concert, which virtually
went to pieces within the next few days. The Sultan's surrender
disguised this fact, and Europe was spared a public demonstration of the inability of the six powers to agree on methods of
force; but the diplomatic conversations during the first fortnight of October reveal only too clearly the prospect of a veto
on intervention which would, in all probability, have proved as

[48] Goschen to Granville, 28 September, F.O. 78/3095, no. 408; 5 October, no.
432. Calice to Haymerle, 30 September, W.S.A., tel. no. 184; Pasetti to Haymerle,
30 September, tel. no. 143.

[49] Goschen to Granville, 5 October, F.O. 78/3095, no. 423 (text of Turkish note,
dated 3 October). Art. XI of the treaty of Berlin of 1878 stipulated that all the
former Turkish fortresses in Bulgaria should be razed in twelve months at the
expense of the Principality. Art. XV allowed the Porte to defend and fortify the
frontiers of Eastern Rumelia.

to abandon the naval demonstration they would tie their hands
in relation to any further difficulties that the Porte might make
over the Montenegrin frontier. This was no doubt exactly what
the Porte intended. The self-denying protocol, by which the six
powers pledged themselves to seek, from the concerted action
concerning Greece and Montenegro, no exclusive influence,
augmentation of territory, or exclusive commercial advantage
was signed at Constantinople on 21 September;[38] on the following day, in the Porte's reply to the collective note of the 16th,
the three demands were repeated in even more uncompromising terms. In return for the evacuation of Dulcigno the powers
were to abandon all idea of a naval demonstration, in connexion with this or any other project, now and in the future;
the rights and possessions of the populations of the ceded districts were to be guaranteed; and any further claims by the
powers on behalf of Montenegro were to be abandoned.[39] One
curious incident in connexion with the note showed the close
personal share that Abdul Hamid was taking in the proceedings. When the ambassadors pointed out that one passage was
quite meaningless the Turkish under-secretary for foreign
affairs, Artin Effendi, looked embarrassed and finally replied
that he could not ask for authority to give an explanation as it
would be 'peu délicat' to suggest that anything written by the
Sultan himself was unintelligible. A personal telegram from
Abdul Hamid to the German Emperor appealing to him to
instruct Bismarck to endeavour to obtain the consent of the
other powers to the three conditions, was a further proof of the
Sultan's direct intervention. The Emperor in his reply on 24
September declined the proposed initiative and the acceptance
of the Turkish terms which it would have implied.[40] The powers

[38] Sir E. Hertslet, *The Map of Europe by Treaty* (1891), iv, 2994. The discussions
concerning the protocol proceeded quite rapidly in July, and then were rather lost
sight of for a time. Pasetti to Haymerle, 23 July, W.S.A., tel. no. 103; 1 August,
tel. no. 113; Haymerle to Hengelmüller, 24 July, tel no. 98; Kuefstein to Haymerle,
5 August, no. 49A–G; 10 August, F.O. 7/993, no. 466; Granville to Goschen, 1
September, F.O. 78/3076, no. 424; Goschen to Granville, 6 September, F.O.
78/3093, no. 328.

[39] Goschen to Granville, 24 September, F.O. 78/3094, no. 390.

[40] Abdul Hamid to Emperor, 22 September; Emperor to Abdul Hamid, 24 September. (Limburg-Stirum to Reuss, A.A. no. 749, 25 September; copies in W.S.A.).
Windelband, pp. 177–9.

were able on the 27th to reply that they had already agreed to
a stipulation in accordance with the second Turkish demand,
but otherwise they were not prepared to give any further consideration to the Turkish proposals.[41]

In the circumstances it was scarcely possible for the admirals
to succeed where the ambassadors had failed, and a very few
days were sufficient to reveal the ineffectiveness of the naval
demonstration. On the 17th Admiral Seymour sent Lord Kerr,
his Flag-Captain, to Scutari by way of Cettinjé to summon the
Governor to hand over Dulcigno. He also brought instructions
from the admirals to Kirby Green, the doyen of the consular
body, directing him to take steps for the removal of their
families to a place of safety. Kerr found little to justify Kirby
Green's alarm over the safety of the consular corps, but otherwise the situation appeared serious.[42] Riza Pasha, the Turkish
Commander, declined to hold any official communication with
the admiral until he had received orders to do so, and also
announced that as he did not possess copies of the protocol or
convention signed by the powers and the Porte clearly defining
the territory to be given up, he could not proceed to surrender
the town. On the 23rd Seymour himself visited Cettinjé, and
secured an emphatic promise from Prince Nicholas that on
receiving Seymour's official invitation to act he would advance
to occupy the position, even if he were opposed by Turkish
regulars; and on the 25th, after a conference with the other
commanders, Seymour announced his plan for compelling the
surrender.[43] The fleet would leave Gravosa on the 27th and
would take action on the 28th, after an official demand to the
Prince to occupy the district; although every care would be
taken to avoid any possibility of injuring the town, the positions
on the heights of Mazura and above Dulcigno, held by the
Albanians and probably by Turkish regulars, would be fired on.
He was quite prepared, he said, to assume the responsibility in
accordance with his instructions, and the only thing he feared

[41] Calice to Haymerle, 25 September, W.S.A., tel. no. 178; 27 September, tels.
nos. 179, 181. Granville to Goschen, 26 September, F.O. 78/3076, no. 517A;
Goschen to Granville, 27 September, F.O. 78/3095, no. 402.

[42] Thömmel to Haymerle, 24 September, W.S.A., tel. no. 42.

[43] Captain Sale (Cettinjé) to Granville, 23 September, A. & P. *Turkey No. 2*
(*1881*), no. 88. Lippich to Haymerle, 27 September, W.S.A., tel.

contingents had involved, as was natural, some delicate problems, which were a further symptom of the uneasy attitude of the powers towards the whole policy of sanctions. However, these had been more or less successfully solved by 14 September. In a circular to the powers on 13 August enclosing his first draft of instructions to the admiral in command of the Mediterranean station, Granville had raised the question of the command of the allied fleet, pointing out that decisions could be decided by a majority of the commanders, or the senior officer in rank among the admirals could undertake the command of the united squadrons. The nearest Turkish authorities were to be invited to join the powers in assisting Prince Nicholas to take possession of the Dulcigno district; if necessary, a meeting was to be arranged with the leaders of the Albanian clans in order to persuade them to abandon their resistance. If the Turkish authorities refused to co-operate, the allied commanders were to decide what action was to be taken to carry out the collective note of 3 August. The Austrian government suggested a few additional points, the most important of which was that the expedition, as far as all military matters were concerned, should be under the command of a British admiral; and the instructions, with the Austrian modifications, proved acceptable to all the other governments except the French. [36]

And now at last the Sultan was faced with a definite issue, a choice between surrender and defiance. He decided to resist. The powers had still not convinced him that they would use force, or that their ships could climb mountains; the coercion of the Albanians on the other hand would be an unpleasant and even dangerous task which could hardly be accomplished by mere haughty gestures from Constantinople. The Sultan had still some grounds for hoping that if the naval demonstration failed the powers would be unable to agree on more violent measures. If they did he still had time to give way. There can be no doubt that for a time the Sultan played with skill his peculiar game of courteous and calculated procrastination, and his grasp of the realities of the situation is shown by his refusal

[36] Elliot to Granville, 21 August, F.O. 7/494, no. 506; 27 August, no. 513. Calice to Haymerle, W.S.A., 27 August, no. 71B. Pasetti to Haymerle, 7 September, W.S.A., tel. no. 135.

to be overawed by the allied fleet in the Adriatic; in the end, however, his nerve failed, and his surrender when more serious measures were hinted at three weeks later probably saved the Concert of Europe from a somewhat ludicrous catastrophe.

This short phase of open defiance was inaugurated by a change of ministry on 12 September, when Saïd was appointed Prime Minister in place of Kadri, and Assim succeeded Abeddin as Foreign Minister. The immediate cause of the change appears to have been the refusal of Kadri and Abeddin to sign a protest against the naval demonstration and other proceedings of the signatory powers, expressed in language which they considered so violent as to be inadmissible and dangerous. Kadri gave the unusual spectacle of a Turkish minister more willing to defy the Sultan than the powers, and sent in his resignation, although in the imperial Hatt announcing the choice of his successor the Sultan spoke of his dismissal. Assim Pasha had been president of the East Roumelian Commission, and had the reputation of being honest and truthful; but he was exceedingly slow and heavy, difficult to convey ideas to, and quite ignorant of current affairs. With Assim merely a respectable figurehead Saïd would, it was thought, have no difficulty in keeping foreign affairs practically in his own hands.[37]

When the collective note of the powers was presented on the 16th it was found that the Porte already had in preparation a circular note of its own on the same subject. This was in fact despatched to the governments of the powers on the same day, and copies were in the hands of the ambassadors on the 17th. It stated that the prompt execution of the instructions received by the Turkish commander for the surrender of Dulcigno depended on the receipt of assurances by the Porte that the powers would abandon the naval demonstration in case of the surrender of the town; that the religion, life, and property of the towns ceded should be respected; and that the line of frontier 'previously traced' on the side of Pedorica for the surrender of Dulcigno should be accepted by the powers. One obvious objection to these proposals was that if the governments agreed

[37] Goschen to Granville, 14 September, F.O. 78/3094, nos. 355, 356; 14 September, G.D. 29/188 (Granville Papers); 18 September, telegram.

paralysing as the more famous deadlock created by the Armenian question fifteen years later.

Gladstone throughout was the champion of intervention,
refusing to listen to the waverers; things had reached a stage at
which, in his view, the immediate issue must be settled with a
high hand. His principal and most violent critic was, as usual,
Bismarck, although, as usual, the violence was concealed.

Recovered from his illness, although still not quite sure of his
capacity 'for a long and hard day's head work' as he told Lord
Acton, Gladstone found his indignation at the Sultan's tergiver-
sations mounting during September. He appears to have had
less confidence than Granville in the success of the naval
demonstration. 'I am afraid we are in danger of new mockeries
worse than before' he wrote on 11 September. On the 13th he
was, he said, profoundly impressed with the 'Protean shiftings
and shufflings of the Sultan, his bottomless fraud, and his im-
measurable lying'. He was surprised at the importance which
Goschen seemed to attach to the Turkish change of ministry on
12 September, saying (quite rightly) that in his view it was
'only one in the long series of blinds and frauds used with ingenious variation of form by the Sultan to evade the fulfilment
of his engagements', and he showed during the next few days
that he was not prepared to acquiesce in a retreat even if the
other powers held back.

This was a point on which the cabinet had not yet agreed,
and on which the Queen had strong views. She sent a cypher
telegram to Granville from Balmoral on 14 September. 'I am
anxious about naval demonstration. If the others hesitate we
must not act alone with Russia. I do not like proceedings which
may lead to war against Turkey.' Granville replied that he
entirely agreed about acting alone with Russia, but that he
hoped that Turkey 'will not attempt to treat England and
Europe with contempt'. Further telegrams and letters followed, and he remarked with resignation to Gladstone on the
18th, 'it would be more logical, if she were to object before the
thing is done, but it would be more inconvenient to us, and
would deprive her of the proud position of "I told you so" if
things go wrong'. Later he was summoned to Balmoral, and
Gladstone praised his firmness and tact. 'I have never read in

my life a better letter than the one you have last sent to Balmoral', he wrote on the 19th. 'We must not falter, nor hesitate even as to a Cabinet if needful.' The Queen could not maintain her objections beyond a certain point, and her intervention was not a major obstacle in Gladstone's path. But the correspondence had by no means represented Gladstone's latest views; he remarked to Granville on the 19th that he had never said a word, 'in 1876 or now', for dual action with Russia or any other power, but 'it would not be warrantable to ask any abstract pledge of us on the subject', and other references in his private correspondence show that he was already prepared for whatever measures would be necessary if the Concert broke up. 'The mind of the Sultan, who *is* the Turkish Government, is a bottomless pit of fraud and falsehood', he told Lord Acton on the same day, 'and he will fulfil *nothing* except under force or the proximate fear of force.'

The issue was too important to be decided by Gladstone and Granville alone, and after the failure of the naval demonstration a cabinet meeting was summoned for 30 September. The possibility of British action against some Turkish town or port had been in Gladstone's mind since Dilke's suggestion about Smyrna at the end of June. He had reverted to the idea from time to time; on 23 July for example he had asked Granville to seek military information as to how far Prevesa, Salonica, and Smyrna were open to a *coup de main*. He decided on 27 September that the cabinet must meet, 'for the measures that suggest themselves to me are beyond any other competency'. He thought that Riza Pasha might be about to attack the Montenegrins, in which case military action in their defence would be justified, including the sinking of the two Turkish ships of war, 'of course after warning Englishmen and others on board'. A telegram to Granville suggested the withdrawal of British subjects, and added:

Many other things suggest themselves as proper for consultation with the powers, e.g.

1. If a Turkish soldier cross the Montenegrin frontier, it is a casus belli.

2. Or if a subject of any of the Powers (or of Montenegro query?) be injured in giving effect to the Treaty of Berlin by the occupation of Dulcigno and its district.

Can it be doubted that if the Sultan had kept up the struggle he would have triumphed? A French veto would probably have made even the Smyrna demonstration impossible, and it is difficult to believe that Austria and France would have allowed the Russian and Italian fleets to enter the Sea of Marmora, even if they could have persuaded themselves of England's disinterestedness. In view of the rivalry of the two powers in Egypt France would probably have objected strongly to any such strengthening of England's influence at Constantinople. Yet if the Sultan had remained adamant these issues would have had to be faced, and proposals for a move to Constantinople would probably have been put forward by the British. On 9 October, after Austria's 'shabby answer' had been received in London, Granville inclined to what he called 'the rash or timid extreme'; he thought that 'Smyrna à trois would certainly not make the Turk yield'. This meant either 'washing our hands of the whole thing, as Europe wont do what we propose' or doing 'what is indefensible, but may be a great success, viz. go to Constantinople at once'. Jomini on the 5th had tried to persuade Plunkett that the move to Smyrna would have no effect until the powers made it clear that they were prepared to go to Constantinople, and 'sacrifice an iron-clad or two' if necessary. Odo Russell and Goschen gave the same advice.[58] Gladstone was not yet ready for either of Granville's courses. He proposed to try to secure an invitation to those powers who were willing to act as mandatories of Europe, Austria being approached for her agreement in the first instance (although her reply had given little encouragement for such an approach). How far Gladstone would have been prepared to go in face of further Turkish resistance, and a flat refusal of mandatory authority, cannot be said; he had simply not made up his mind (as far as the evidence goes). However, the resolution of the powers was not put to this final test. On the evening of the 9th came the first genuine sign of Turkish surrender.

The news of the British government's proposal to occupy

[58] For these and other British opinions, see *Goschen*, i, 201; *Granville*, ii, 218; Harcourt, i, 378; J. L. Garvin, *Life of Joseph Chamberlain* (1932), i, 315; *The Diaries of John Bright* (1931), pp. 447, 449. Cf. *The Letters of Queen Victoria*, iii, 141, 146. Jomini's comment: Plunkett to Granville, 5 October, F.O. 65/1082, no. 451.

Smyrna reached the Porte on 8 October or early on the 9th. The *Pall Mall Gazette* had published the news as early as the 6th. Granville told his wife on the 7th that he was very angry with Gladstone who had let the *Pall Mall* let the cat out of the bag; Gladstone, however, told Granville on the same day that he had no idea how the newspaper secured the news.[59] Yet if ever a leakage was tactically justified it was on this occasion: it would be satisfying to know that Gladstone had decided that indiscretion was the better part of valour.

At the same time the French and German ambassadors were said to have used strong language which was believed to be the immediate cause of the Sultan's collapse. The initiative in this case had been taken by Bismarck. He told the French government that Hatzfeldt had been instructed to use every means possible in order to persuade the Porte to give the powers some satisfaction before the deplorable note of 3 October led to measures of rigorous coercion. Tissot was instructed on 7 October to associate himself with Hatzfeldt.[60]

So followed the final moves: late on the evening of the 9th Assim Pasha went round to the ambassadors and stated that the government was determined to cede Dulcigno at once, and would inform the powers of this resolution in a note which would be delivered on the following morning. To the question which all the ambassadors naturally put to him he said that his government meant a cession, and not merely an evacuation. Subsequent events seem to show that the Sultan really had at last decided to give up the point, although his attempt to haggle even now over the details of the settlement kept the matter open until the end of the month, and created further suspicion as to his intention. The promised note, for example,

[59] *Granville*, ii, 222. Gladstone to Granville: 'I have not an idea how PMG got hold of Smyrna, but the thing had been talked of at the War Office before the Cabinet. I hope *nobody* told' (Gladstone Papers, Add. MSS. 44544). Cf. T. Bassett, *Letters of Gladstone to his Wife*, p. 231 (8 October).

[60] *D.D.F.*, iii, no. 2, instructions to Tissot. There is no evidence in *D.D.F.* that Tissot acted, or had time to act, on these instructions. Windelband (p. 186) refers in general terms to Hatzfeldt's instructions, but gives no particulars. There is nothing in *G.P.* There are references in *Saburov*, pp. 158–61; *Busch*, p. 241; and see Bismarck's remarks to Cohen, 15 October (B.B.M., p. 315). Gladstone's comments to his wife and others show that he attributed the Sultan's agreement entirely to the Smyrna proposal (cf. Bassett, pp. 231–4), and below, p. 165, n. 63.

be a somewhat dispassionate approval of the British policy, and on 9 October Odo Russell, who was evidently completely at sea, reported that Bismarck 'marvels that we do not go at once to the Bosphorus wh: wld: save time & settle the question once for all'.[53]

It is difficult to imagine anything more completely opposed to the explosive condemnations of even the Smyrna proposal in which Bismarck was indulging behind the scenes at this moment. Bismarck's attitude was compounded of a number of violently-expressed objections, and it is as usual difficult to be quite sure whether they expressed his own genuine convictions or were devised to sway susceptible hearers. He started on 29 September with an exaggerated estimate of the possibilities of war, and a disclaimer of all responsibility. 'That Europe cannot give way is a proposition that I cannot accept, for I do not admit the conception of "Europe" as a joint liability. The five powers have agreed on precise measures whose possible inadequacy we recognized from the very beginning.' He could not recommend the landing of troops, or any risk to the lives of German soldiers in an entirely foreign cause. The aims of English policy were unknown: but it was essentially unfriendly towards Austria. 'We cannot allow ourselves to be dragged by English policy towards unknown ends.' Among numerous other comments there was an elaboration of the same ideas on 2 October, which Windelband rightly characterizes as one of the sharpest of his many attacks on Gladstone. Haymerle could not be expected, *pour les beaux yeux de Mr Gladstone*, to pull the chestnuts out of the fire for such a notorious enemy of Austria.

I do not believe that the direction of English policy has ever been in such incompetent hands since the American War of Independence. To associate with such politicians would not be without danger for us as well, and the danger of associating with incompetent politicians is all the greater if this incompetence is combined with the sense of infallibility of a doctrinaire.

When the Smyrna proposal was officially presented on 4 October he at once said that the Sultan would probably not dare to

[53] Gladstone to Granville, G.D. 29/123 (Granville Papers), 1 October; *Granville*, ii, 217; Knaplund, pp. 161–2.

give way, and would rather lose Smyrna than his throne and his head.

We cannot embark under Gladstone's captaincy on adventures and complications in the unknown. No one knows what Gladstone finally desires; he doesn't know himself. His conduct is unacceptably antimonarchical, revolutionary, unpeaceful.

But still, after all this, he saw no point in protest or counter argument; if Russia and England wished to act alone, nothing need be done to hinder them.[54]

Much of this agitation was due to the favourable turn which the alliance negotiations had taken in September; further progress was not possible until the present phase of the eastern negotiations was concluded, and would be indefinitely postponed, or ruined altogether, if England and Russia drifted into some miserable war or long-drawn-out political struggle with Turkey. The progress of the alliance discussions will be examined in the next chapter. We need only note here that this was a turning point at which Bismarck's tactics called for a supreme effort to discredit Gladstone, and to persuade Russia and Austria to refuse his lead in future. How far he really believed that Gladstone was a mad professor is difficult to say;[55] that he felt this to be an effective line of criticism is, however, undeniable. There is no doubt also some truth in the view that he believed that Gladstone, lacking support, might be forced by the Sultan's defiance to a humiliating diplomatic defeat which would drive him from office.[56] But when all due allowance is made for these tactical moves there seems to remain some genuine consternation at the prospect of a Turkish defiance—proof that he read the situation far less accurately than Gladstone. And it would have taken more than this crisis to drive the Liberals from office. All that Granville anticipated as a result of a victory for the Sultan was that 'we shall be much chaffed in the papers and Parliament'.[57]

[54] Windelband, pp. 177–86, gives lengthy extracts from these minutes, which were all confined to the secret files of the German Foreign Office.

[55] He said to Dr. E. Cohen (25 September) 'Dulcigno sei ein Unsinn . . . Gladstone sei ein verrückter Professor, seine Bulgaren-schwärmerei reiner Blödsinn' (B.B.M., p. 313).

[56] Windelband, p. 183.

[57] *Granville*, ii, 223; *Gladstone*, iii, 9.

3. To reinforce the armament or move a force to the East of the Mediterranean.

4. In the last resort to offer Albania to the Kalamas (where the country inhabited by Greeks begins) its formal or practical independence. I wait anxiously your reply to my telegram.

A further telegram on the following day to Granville (who had taken to his bed) referred to the possibility of a seizure of the Dardanelles ('rather a big job'), and again insisted that if Montenegro were not given prompt support 'there is an end to all beneficial action of Europe and the Eastern Question will be left to pass into chaos and unlimited bloodshed'.[50]

The Sultan's promise of a settlement by 3 October slightly eased the tension, and the Cabinet (which also discussed Ireland and Afghanistan) agreed on 30 September that, if the Sultan did not surrender, the occupation of Smyrna should be proposed to the powers. When it dispersed it left the prime minister and foreign secretary full discretion, and endorsed their replies to the Queen. But the final and most difficult problem—whether to go forward alone if the Concert broke up—had still not been solved. On 4 October, as soon as the substance of the Sultan's circular had been received in London, Granville proposed to the other five powers 'that the allied fleets should proceed from the Adriatic to Smyrna, and that that port should be held as a material guarantee'.

The Italian government fully accepted the proposal on the 5th, subject to the adhesion of the powers; and the Tsar, who was particularly annoyed by the Porte's reference to the occupation of the Balkans, accepted without even this qualification on the 6th.[51] But on the 7th Odo Russell was told that Germany's decision would depend on that of Austria and Austria on the 8th said no. Already on the 6th, in rejecting Granville's suggestion that Austrian troops should guarantee the Monte-

[50] Gladstone Papers: letters to Granville (11, 13, 16, 19, 20, 27, 28 September); to Acton (19 September); to Lord Reay (16 September); Granville to Gladstone (11, 16, 18, 19, 28 September); Queen Victoria to Granville (copy of tel., 14 September); Gladstone: memorandum on foreign policy for talks with G[ranville], 23 September (Add. MSS. 44764).

[51] 'He had noticed especially, with dismay, the demands put forward by the Sultan for the re-establishment of Turkish garrisons in the Balkans.' Plunkett to Granville, 6 October, F.O. 65/1082, no. 455. Giers to Lobanov, R.E., 27 September/9 October.

negrin frontier in the event of a Turkish attack, Haymerle had said that it was impossible for him to recommend to the Emperor the sacrifice of a single Austrian or Hungarian soldier for the sake of Montenegro, and he again argued that any form of coercion might lead to disaster. 'If a demonstration before Constantinople did not make the Sultan give way, what would be the position of the Powers? The Sultan might retire from his capital, or insurrectionary movements might break out, unsettling everything, and leaving us in a worse state than before.' All he would offer on the 8th was to 'admit the demonstration' under the conditions of the self-denying protocol. His government must avoid any measures that might ultimately constitute an act of war, and accordingly declined to send its ships to Smyrna. The new French government, after learning of the Austrian reply, also declined to participate, explaining that 'they could not act with less than all' the powers. The real reason, as the new Foreign Minister, Barthélemy Saint-Hilaire, at once explained to Challemel-Lacour, was the opposition of French public opinion to this or any similar warlike demonstration; a subordinate but weighty consideration was that French contractors who had constructed the port of Smyrna were allowed to remunerate themselves by collecting certain dues which the Turks were only too likely to withhold, whether or not the French took part in the naval demonstration.[52]

The French and Austrian replies caused little surprise in London; Bismarck's was regretted, but not understood. 'Misericordia! Patience is a great virtue, but really the heavy-going Teuton is too slow' was Gladstone's rather puzzled comment on 1 October. Odo Russell's reports were misleading; he could get only the baldest statements from German officials, and Bismarck was said to be engrossed with questions of home and commercial policy. The ambassador heard, however, on 'reliable authority' that Bismarck did not apprehend war, so long as the European Concert lasted, and thought that its duration depended on the initiative of England, without which it would cease from want of a disinterested leader. This seemed to

[52] Elliot to Granville, 4 October, no. 616; 8 October, no. 629; F.O. 7/995 D.D.F., iii, nos. 271, 281. Lyons to Granville, 9 October, F.O. 27/2436, no. 964. Cf. *Lyons*, ii, 230.

did not appear until the 12th; it was stated in several quarters that the Porte had repented of the step taken on the 9th, and in conversation with Hatzfeldt the prime minister hinted that the mission of Assim Pasha had not been 'thoroughly official'. On receipt of the news Gladstone was 'simply furious, suggesting all sorts of fanciful messages'; these did not materialize, but the British government now proposed that those powers which did not wish to co-operate actively in the Smyrna demonstration should give a mandate to the others.[61] The Porte's hesitation on the 10th and 11th was naturally attributed by the British to the fact that news of the refusal of Austria, Germany, and France to accept the British proposal concerning Smyrna had leaked out at Paris and had quickly reached Constantinople. But the presentation of the Porte's note (dated 11 October) on the 12th at last made it reasonably certain that a genuine solution was in view. A Havas telegram, dated from Paris, was published in Constantinople on the afternoon of the 11th, and stated that Austria, Germany, and France had accepted the British proposals, and this may, as Goschen suspected, have once more alarmed the Sultan and his advisers. The note stated that the Porte would immediately give the local authorities categorical instructions for the peaceful cession of Dulcigno to the Montenegrins, and the only possible opening for further delay was the stipulation that a convention must be signed to regulate the conditions of cession.[62]

There seems no reason to doubt that the news of the Smyrna proposal explains the Sultan's surrender. It was of little advantage to the Porte to know that the powers were divided, if three of the powers were prepared nevertheless to go ahead with the demonstration. There is no evidence to suggest that Austria, France, or Germany gave, or desired to give, any hint that they might prevent the other three from acting alone. The semi-official *Norddeutsche Allgemeine Zeitung* said on the 5th that 'now, as formerly, the Porte is confronted with the united will

[61] Gladstone to Granville, G.D. 29/123 (Granville Papers), 11, 12 October. *D.D.F.*, iii, no. 274. Granville to Goschen, 11 October, F.O. 78/3077, no. 583 (extends no. 668).

[62] Goschen to Granville, 12 October, F.O. 78/3096, no. 461 (encloses copy of Note, 11 October); Goschen to Granville, G.D. 29/188 (Granville Papers), 12, 14 October.

of the Continent' and it continued to announce the solidarity of the powers. The *Journal des Débats* remarked, 'Germany has shown the same firmness as the other Powers; Germany's attitude involves that of Austria; and as for France, she will not be wanting in the general concert'. On the other hand the assumption that Abdul Hamid's decision on the 9th was due merely to the Franco-German representations is not convincing. It does not explain why the representations which the two powers had been making, or should have been making, since June, had not previously produced results. Gladstone, who was evidently nettled by a suggestion in *The Times* that the result had been due to diplomatic pressure on the Sultan, wrote to John Morley on the 12th: 'There *may* have been such pressure then, as there had been before. One thing and one only was new on Saturday in the situation at Constantinople. On that day he learned that the English government had proposed to the powers the occupation of Smyrna, and on that night he sent his solemn promise to *hand over* Dulcigno.'[63] The most one can say is that representations by the two ambassadors may have satisfied Abdul Hamid that Germany and France were not proposing to save him from the intervention of the three powers. But this points to the conclusion that their negative and enigmatic attitude may have created false hopes at the Palace during the preceding months.

Certainly Goschen's reports since August suggest that the ambassadors of the other five powers had failed to persuade the Porte that the powers were united or serious. 'Corti goes about very cynically and gives people the impression that the Powers can't agree' he wrote on 10 August, 'though he denies ever having said so. Tissot is very serious, and is changing his tone somewhat, though I won't say much. Calice is very frightened at the state of things. As to Novikoff, it is difficult to say what he is at . . . my colleagues think it odd that Russia always makes the very most of every difficulty, and some suspect Russia is not so loyal in trying to settle things as she might be.'[64]

---

[63] Gladstone Papers, Add. MSS. 44544. Windelband writes: 'Für Gesamteuropa hat sich die inoffizielle deutsch-französische Kooperation in Konstantinopel alsbald überaus nützlich erwiesen. Was niemand zu hoffen gewagt hatte, wurde unter dem sanften Druck der beiden Botschafter zur Wirklichkeit . . .' (p. 188).

[64] Goschen to Granville, 10 August, G.D. 29/188 (Granville Papers). Similar comments on Novikov by Calice: 27 August, W.S.A., no. 71T.

When Goschen decided to send Captain Swaine to Gallipoli to report on the feasibility of a Greek force being landed on the Aegean side of the peninsula he instructed the attaché to keep the mission a secret from the other embassies. [65] Abdul Hamid's appeal to the German Emperor in September is proof in itself of the hopes which had been raised by the non-committal attitude of Hatzfeldt, the doyen of the diplomatic corps at Constantinople; in this attitude Hatzfeldt was instructed to continue as late as 29 September. [66] The situation on the eve of the final crisis is described by Goschen with evident exasperation in a private letter of 5 October.

The Austrian Ambassador here seems the counterpart of his Govt. I must say, only that he has been almost ridiculous, and we have had to do our utmost to avoid incurring ridicule ourselves. During the last few days he would have liked us to go one by one or together to the Porte with an entreaty that they should be good boys and consent to give up Dulcigno. And we were to be conciliatory! we were to be 'encouraging' to the Porte. . . . The next week will be an intensely exciting period. Tissot has been more satisfactory since the new Govt. came into office. Corti entirely agrees in proposed measures for coercing Turkey into submission. Hatzfeldt is not absurd like Calice in what he proposes, but he is of no use, or only of little use in influencing Calice whom I presume he is bound to back. Hatzfeldt declares that he has been 'black' from the first—that he has foreseen all the troubles and taken the gloomiest view as to what would happen . . . [67]

The long and the short of it is that the Smyrna proposal had frightened the powers almost more than it frightened the Sultan, and in telling the Porte on the 9th that the British plans must be taken seriously they were themselves taking the Concert seriously for the first time.

The final stages can be summarized. All the powers agreed without hesitation to keep the allied fleets together in the Adriatic, and they appeared only too ready to take whatever steps were still necessary to expedite the final settlement and to keep the Porte to the point. A Russian proposal that the

[65] Swaine, *op. cit.*, pp. 117–20.
[66] Windelband, p. 179.
[67] Goschen to Granville, 5 October, Constantinople, personal (copy in Gladstone Papers, Add. MSS. 44172).

convention should deal not merely with Dulcigno but with the whole of the disputed frontier was dropped, and Prince Nicholas was warned not to make difficulties over the conditions of the convention.[68]

When Turkish and Montenegrin officers met at Rejka, 'a place between Cettinjé and Scutari, on the morning of 17 October, it was found that Turkey still intended to make a few difficulties. The Turkish draft convention was presented to the Montenegrin delegate and was found to contain seven proposals, five of which dealt with such matters as the protection of the lives and property of the ceded population, and the recognition of the Porte's property rights and previous acts; these the Montenegrin government accepted, but they felt compelled to reject the other two, the first and fifth. The first demanded that the *status quo* frontier to the north of Lake Scutari should be recognized, and the fifth provided that vessels belonging to inhabitants of Dulcigno who did not quit the principality should be entitled to fly the Ottoman flag for a further three years. The news that the Turks were once more raising the *status quo* proposal which the powers had emphatically rejected long before produced strong protests at Constantinople; Assim Pasha replied that Riza Pasha had received no instructions to raise the matter. On the 19th Assim Pasha announced that instructions had been sent to Riza Pasha not to raise the question; otherwise, however, negotiations were left in his hands for several days longer, on the excuse that thunderstorms had prevented telegraphic communications between Scutari and the capital.[69] During this period the negotiations made little progress. Riza Pasha and his agents continued to evade the Montenegrin demand for a guarantee that the cession would be carried out peacefully, and instead insisted that the Montenegrin troops should enter the district by a road past the Mazura heights, which were fortified, and probably occupied by Albanians. Assim Pasha in Constantinople continued to assure the ambassadors that the cession would be

[68] Granville to Elliot, 12 October, F.O. 7/987, no. 678. Giers to Lobanov, R.E., 1/13 October (comm. to Granville, 14 October).

[69] Granville to Goschen, 17 October, F.O. 78/3077, no. 605; 20 October, no. 619 (extends no. 708A); Goschen to Granville, 19 October, F.O. 78/3096, no. 480. *Busch*, p. 241.

carried out, and that instructions were prevented only by the weather. A more tangible proof of sincerity, however, was the despatch of Dervish Dorgut Pasha with four battalions to 'reinforce' Riza Pasha. Dervish arrived at Scutari on 2 November, took over command of the troops from Riza Pasha, and announced to the merchants of Scutari and the chiefs of the mountain tribes that Dulcigno must absolutely be given up. Further meetings with the Albanian chiefs took place during the following fortnight; evasive replies and requests for delays suggested that the Albanians were now endeavouring to postpone surrender indefinitely by using the Porte's own tactics; and for some days consular reports spoke pessimistically of the situation.[70] But the regular troops under Dervish Pasha's command had now increased to 10,000; and at length he advanced by the Scutari road to occupy Dulcigno, if necessary by force. On the morning of 22 November the Albanians opened fire on the Turkish troops in the neighbourhood of Lake Sas, at a point where the road skirted the foot of the Mazura range. The Turks at first fired high, but, after several Turks had been shot, fired on the Albanians, who were soon in flight. Dervish at once advanced to Dulcigno; negotiations for a convention commenced at Kunia late on the 20th and were completed by the following evening; the Montenegrin troops, which had been largely disbanded, were hastily got together, and the whole of the district of Dulcigno, with the exception of one point which was settled later, was in the possession of the Montenegrins by the 28th. The Turks carried out their side of the transaction satisfactorily, and the Albanian movement appeared to have collapsed completely, as far as the immediate problem of resistance to Montenegro was concerned.[71]

Of the Albanian movement for self-government there was also little information in western Europe. But when the decision to surrender Dulcigno had ended the usefulness of the League as an excuse for the Porte's inaction there was no further reason

[70] *Busch*, pp. 241–2.

[71] At this point the Montenegrin question ceased, abruptly and completely, to be a matter of public concern to Europe. Nevertheless, the frontier continued under discussion between the two governments concerned for many years. See the various agreements of August–September, 1883 (Hertslet, *op. cit.*, iv, no. 6030), December, 1884 (iv, no. 605), and July, 1887 (iv, no. 621).

why the League should be tolerated, and its suppression followed. Dervish Dorgut Pasha was an uncompromising supporter of the centralizing policy of the Porte. Before the end of 1880 he had exiled a number of leaders, including Hodo Pasha, Muderis Daud, and Prenk Bib Doda. This followed the demand in October 1880 for the creation of an autonomous province, and the exchange of visits between delegates from north and south Albania. Large-scale military resistance to the Turkish army began in January 1881 in Prizren; forces of the League quickly occupied Skoplje (Üsküb) and Prishtina, and the surrounding districts. Soon Dibra, farther south, was similarly taken over by forces under the direction of Abdul Frashëri. The Turkish counter offensive began on a big scale under Dervish Pasha in April 1881; but it was only after strenuous fighting that the Turkish forces, well equipped with mountain artillery, were victorious. After the collapse of the movement the Turkish commander handled the situation cautiously; reprisals were avoided, and although Abdul Frashëri, the apostle of union, was arrested and imprisoned in Constantinople, the remainder were exhorted to return to their former allegiance. In the south, however, the remaining leaders were arrested in May 1881 by the Governor-General of Janina, who could not afford trouble during the final stages of the Greek frontier negotiations. [72]

[72] Stavro Skendi, 'Beginnings of Albanian Nationalist and Autonomous Trends, The Albanian League, 1878–1881' (*The American Slavic and East European Review*, vol. xii).

CHAPTER VII

Friedrichsruh

IN the last chapter we saw that the reluctance of Austria, Germany, and France to take part in active measures of coercion against Turkey had seriously weakened the effectiveness of the Concert in the Montenegrin affair, and had done much to justify the Sultan's belief that he could defy the powers with impunity. The British hints about Smyrna showed that the threat of force even by one power might produce more speedy results than all the half-hearted attempts at joint action, and meant that Gladstone himself had led the retreat from the Concert system. A much more serious defection was in the meantime being prepared by the three empires, who commenced in September serious negotiations for a revival of the *Dreikaiserbündnis*.

This development was made possible by Haymerle's agreement, at long last, to discuss with Bismarck the conditions of an Austro-Russian understanding, and an occasion was offered by a meeting of the two at Friedrichsruh. Although Haymerle suggested the meeting (at the end of July), he entered upon the discussion of concessions and counter-concessions with every appearance of reluctance and even of trepidation. In the spring, as we have seen, he had declined to negotiate with Bismarck and Saburov, hoping to keep Russia isolated and to retain British support against any future Russian aggression in the Balkans. By the end of July he had been forced to realize that the friendly relations of Russia with both Germany and England made it possible that Austria-Hungary herself might soon be the isolated power. Effective joint action by England and Russia in the Greek and Montenegrin questions might bring about the collapse of the Turkish government; even if it failed to do this, the opportunity to move naval and military forces into the Straits or the eastern Mediterranean might be utilized by Russia for all sorts of vague and nefarious ends.

It was, moreover, now evident that Bismarck had quite made up his quarrel with the Russian government. On 22 May 1880, Széchényi, the Austro-Hungarian ambassador in Berlin, wrote in a private letter to Haymerle that Prince Orlov, during his passage through Berlin, 15–17 May, had brought from St. Petersburg 'a full load of assurances of goodwill and friendship'; he had dined with the Emperor and Bismarck, although he had had no special conversation with the latter. Széchényi added that it was 'scarcely possible for the Russians to exert themselves more than they are doing at the moment to stand well with Germany'.[1] Gorchakov himself passed through Berlin a few days later and after a visit from Bismarck said that 'he had been able to convince himself that the ill-humour of Bismarck towards Russia was past, and that he was happy to have found the Chancellor again the friend of old'.[2] The German Crown Prince, Frederick William, visited St. Petersburg in June for the funeral of the Czarina, and had conversations with the Tsar, the heir apparent (Prince Alexander), and leading Russian statesmen, including Miljutin. He was able to persuade Prince Alexander that Bismarck had no desire to seize the Baltic provinces. The visit was a success, although Bismarck refused to be convinced by Miljutin's protestations of friendship.[3] Saburov's cordial relations with his German colleagues were also obvious, and Bismarck missed no opportunity of calling the attention of both the Austrian and Russian ambassadors to the value of an understanding between their two countries. At his dinner on 16 June to the delegates to the Berlin conference, Bismarck, after discussing the Anglo-French programme, remarked to Széchényi, 'the essential point is always that between Russia and England no agreement or *rapprochement* exists; I cannot emphasize too strongly how necessary it is to avoid everything that can facilitate this'.[4] Haymerle

---

[1] Széchényi to Haymerle, 22 May 1880, W.S.A. (Varia Prusse, iii, 121). *D.D.F.*, iii, no. 125. [2] Széchényi to Haymerle, 5 June, W.S.A., *ibid.*

[3] Windelband, p. 165; Schweinitz, ii, pp. 116–18. 'Er (Miljutin) hat so ruhig, überzeugend und versöhnlich gesprochen, dass der Prinz mich später fragte, was ihm denn eigentlich vorzuwerfen sei' (p. 118).

[4] Széchényi to Haymerle, 18 June, W.S.A., no. 48.

therefore had his own desire to prevent an Anglo-Russian agreement strongly reinforced by the fact that Bismarck was continuing to throw his weight into the scale in favour of an Austro-Russian reconciliation.

The Austrian government could not afford to endanger the alliance with Germany by excessive resistance to her wishes. Bismarck was aware of this, and was careful not to trade on it, but clearly his advocacy of the *Dreikaiserbündnis* was an important factor in itself in the making up of Haymerle's cautious mind. It was probably not the determining factor. The Austrian minister had not been too timid to say no to Bismarck's approaches earlier in the year, and the Chancellor had not yet begun to hint that his patience was exhausted. Haymerle therefore, we must conclude, was genuinely apprehensive as to the consequences of the British government's burst of activity over Dulcigno, innocent though it was of ulterior ends. As we saw in Chapter IV, Bismarck had prophesied to Saburov as early as 25 July that Austria's fears of Anglo-French coercive measures against Turkey would lead Austria to throw herself into Russia's arms. Bismarck, who was about to depart to Kissingen, appears on this occasion to have kept the conversation on the Straits question, and to have greatly exaggerated the possibility of a British attack. An agreement would, he said, in that case 'acquire the character of a preservative measure, for the absolute closing of the Straits will be the most efficacious means of maintaining the Sultan in Constantinople, and preventing a catastrophe which neither you nor Austria desire at this moment'. Saburov was pleased to find that Russia's ideas had 'taken such good root in the mind of the German Chancellor', and although he apparently did not anticipate any early change in Austria's attitude, he secured Bismarck's agreement to his speaking in full confidence concerning the confidential pourparlers to Hohenlohe, should the occasion arise.[5] The Tsar was pleased at Saburov's success in restoring good relations between St. Petersburg and Berlin, and he did not at any stage abandon his willingness to commence discussions with Austria. On 30 June Giers made a direct approach to

[5] Saburov, pp. 140–2; cf. Lucius, p. 190, who shows that Bismarck left for Kissingen on 26 July.

Haymerle through d'Oubril, and expressed regret that doubts had appeared in Vienna as to Russia's loyalty to the *Dreikaiserbund*, and his determination to maintain the Berlin settlement. Nevertheless Schweinitz noted in his diary on 19 August that the Russian government appeared more inclined than ever to follow the English lead.[6]

There seems little doubt that the development of the Dulcigno crisis gave Bismarck's meeting with Haymerle at Friedrichsruh more importance than either had originally intended. We have seen that by the end of July the Austrian press was already openly hostile to the British plans for coercing the Turks, but it was the Turkish refusal during August to be overawed by the collective note of 3 August that raised the possibility of a really alarming crisis, and of a Turkish collapse following Turkish intransigence. So while Haymerle's suggestion at the end of July that he should visit Bismarck may have been originally intended to lead to little more than a courtesy visit, it provided an opportunity five weeks later for much more fundamental decisions. This seems to be confirmed by the discussions between the governments during August, as far as we know them. That Haymerle was contemplating no early change of policy is shown by his reply to Bismarck's invitation, which reached him on 2 August. Bismarck proposed that as Haymerle was spending a holiday in Norderney he should either stop, on his way there, at Kissingen, where Bismarck was staying until 25 August, or at Friedrichsruh on his return journey. That Haymerle was in no hurry to see the Chancellor is shown by the fact that he chose the latest date that the invitation allowed.[7] And Bismarck, who was suffering from facial neuralgia which he attributed to nervous irritability,[8] appears to have transacted as little business as possible during his cure at Kissingen, and to have made no special preparations for the conversations until the end of August, when Hohenlohe came to see him at Friedrichsruh. It was, in

[6] Schweinitz, pp. ii, 118, 119, 122; cf. the references to the Bulgarian inquiry in August, pp. 108–10 above.

[7] Kállay to Haymerle, 2 August 1880, tel. (unnumbered), W.S.A., Geheim Liasse III.

[8] Bismarck intended to consult Dr. Struck, and remarked, 'Wenn der nichts wisse, wünsche er ihm seine Schmerzen und sich seine Dummheit'. Lucius, p. 190.

fact, Hohenlohe, in conversation with Saburov, and with some encouraging news from Reuss as to the Emperor Franz Joseph's views, who had given the requisite impetus to the negotiations for the new alliance.

On 4 August Saburov had reported to Hohenlohe the Russian proposal that if, after the settlement of the Montenegrin crisis, the British fleet should make plans to pass the Dardanelles, the three imperial governments should prevent it by means of a common declaration.[9] Hohenlohe saw Saburov again on 18 August, and said that he had thought a great deal about all that Saburov had said 'last week'. He greatly desired a general agreement between Russia and Austria. The absence of it affected the whole situation in the Near East. 'If there were agreement on certain *eventualities* the day-to-day difficulties would solve themselves; for it is precisely the *eventualities* that alarm Austria and make her distrustful.' After Saburov had replied that Russia would like nothing better, Hohenlohe, asked to indicate the 'eventualities', gave the union of the two Bulgarias as an example. With further encouragement from Saburov he mentioned the possibility of a meeting between Haymerle and Bismarck and asked for information on two points. (1) If an *entente à trois* were seriously discussed, would the plan of the previous spring still be valid? (2) What compensation could Russia suggest to Austria for the union of the two Bulgarias? 'What do you think of the idea of offering him the permanent possession of Bosnia and the Hercegovina?' In reporting this conversation to Giers Saburov remarked, somewhat apprehensively it would appear, that the Bismarck-Haymerle interview would enable them to judge Bismarck's sincerity. If he (Saburov) were not invited, it would be merely a second edition of the Vienna meeting; if he were, it would prove that the situation was not the same as last year, and that the desire for an *entente à trois* was not a mere phrase.[10] Another meeting with Hohenlohe on 23 August carried matters a little further. Following a letter from Giers of 20 August,

---

[9] See above, p. 111, and Bismarck's comment: Windelband, p. 166. Windelband's chronology is confused through his failure to remember that all dates in Saburov's correspondence are in Old Style, unless otherwise indicated.

[10] Saburov to Giers, R.E., 11/23 August 1880, letter (secret).

Saburov said that Russia had no desire to accelerate the issue in Bulgaria, but she desired above all that if the union took place independently of her wishes, the matter should not become a source of discord between her and Austria. He also suggested, in passing, and on his own initiative, an Austrian 'prise de possession définitive' of Bosnia-Hercegovina as compensation for the union. He did this, he says, in case Bismarck had the idea of proposing something more substantial.[11] Hohenlohe for his part had reported the conversation of the 18th to Bismarck, who entirely approved, and promised to take advantage of his meeting with Haymerle to sound him and to work for an agreement.[12]

The immediate preparations for the Friedrichsruh meeting were, however, unnecessarily hurried and a little confused. Bismarck came there from Kissingen on 25 August; he saw Hohenlohe, and Saburov noted on the 28th that it was now Bismarck's idea that Turkey should be enticed into association with the triple agreement. Hohenlohe sent off a long despatch to Schweinitz on 28 August, setting out Bismarck's views as to the possible bases of an agreement, and instructing him to make the necessary communication to the Tsar and Giers. Unfortunately they had already departed (on the 28th) for the Crimea; not only was Schweinitz unable to hold the delicate and important conversations that Bismarck had hoped for, but there even seemed some doubt as to whether any reply could be secured before Haymerle's arrival. Schweinitz saw Jomini early on 1 September, and a telegram was sent to Giers saying that Bismarck would be glad to explain Russia's views to Haymerle, and suggesting that to save time instructions should be sent direct to Saburov.[13] Giers had already, however, on 27 August, written to Saburov giving the Tsar's reply to Hohen-

[11] Saburov to Giers, R.E., 11/23 August, letter (secret).

[12] 'Bismarck partage entièrement ce point de vue et profitera de son entrevue avec Haymerle pour le sonder et travailler à une entente' (*ibid.*).

[13] Bismarck's despatch reached Schweinitz on 30 August; Schweinitz's tel. is printed (in French) in his *Denkwürdigkeiten*, ii, 123. Windelband prints the substance of the despatch, and says that Schweinitz was instructed to talk personally to the Tsar and Giers. Bismarck was taken aback to find that they had left St. Petersburg, and instructed Schweinitz to telegraph to Giers in order to avoid dependence on Jomini, who was in charge of the Foreign Office in St. Petersburg in Giers' absence (pp. 167–70).

lohe's two questions of 18 August. This reply Saburov, on 1 September, passed on to Hohenlohe, who telegraphed it at once to Bismarck.[14]

Bismarck was still complaining of ill-health, and showing some irritability and impatience. As the invitation to Haymerle had been sent at the beginning of August there seems no reason to have left the sounding of the Russian government until the eve of Haymerle's visit, and the explanation is probably the obvious one that Bismarck did not want to be bothered with it before his return from Kissingen. The point is one of some general importance, for the Friedrichsruh meeting was the prelude to eight months of difficult negotiation in which Bismarck found himself continuously at cross purposes with Haymerle; subsequent misunderstandings on both sides must be attributed in part to some lack of concentration on his part during these vital preliminary discussions. For this his own ill-health and Haymerle's meticulous exposition of qualms and qualifications during the meeting were, perhaps, equally responsible. Bored with Haymerle, he perhaps listened imperfectly; but he was certainly not well briefed by the Russians.

Saburov, who had decided that those who talked least would go furthest in negotiation with Bismarck, contributed to these misunderstandings by withholding a portion of his instructions. In passing on to Hohenlohe on 1 September the contents of his instructions from Giers, he said that they did not mention Russia's conditions for entering an eventual understanding with Austria; they said only that the Tsar did not wish to accelerate events in Bulgaria. He added, however, that he knew they were ready in St. Petersburg to agree to the annexation of Bosnia and the Hercegovina, and perhaps also, although this was less certain, the annexation of the sanjak of Novipazar.[15] He had, in

---

[14] Giers to Saburov, R.E., 15/27 August 1880, *lettre très secrète*.

[15] The text of Hohenlohe's telegram was given to Haymerle, and is as follows. 'Der russische Botschafter theilt eine Depesche des Herrn von Giers mit, worin auf die Frage, welche Saburoff an Giers gerichtet hatte, "ob der Kaiser noch an den Grundlagen der Entente à trois festhalte", mit "Ja" geantwortet wird. Was die Frage einer eventuellen Verständigung mit Oesterreich betrifft, so sagt die Depesche nur, dass der Kaiser nicht wünsche d'accélérer les événements en Bulgarie. Das Land sei noch nicht stark genug um seine Vereinigung mit Ostrumelien *allein* gegen die Türkei durchzuführen. Der Versuch würde also Russland zur Theilnahme nöthigen. Und ein Krieg gegen die Türkei sei jetzt nicht genehm.

fact, received specific conditions for an agreement; but he did not communicate these to Bismarck, although he was authorized by Giers to do so. As it happened Jomini had shown Schweinitz the text of Giers' instructions, and Schweinitz had telegraphed particulars to Bismarck on 4 September. They showed that Russia would agree only to the annexation of Bosnia and the Hercegovina, and would reserve Novipazar for the future; she would demand a guarantee that Turkey would not occupy the Balkan mountains and would not make use of the military road through Eastern Rumelia.[16] Why did Saburov withhold these further details? Perhaps his main reason was, at this stage, to avoid frightening Haymerle with too long and precise a list of Russian requirements.[17] But later, in order that Bismarck should be left as long as possible to struggle with Haymerle's problems, he continued to conceal the refusal of his government to agree to any change in the status of the sanjak. Bismarck (and also Haymerle perhaps) lost sight throughout the winter of Russian reservations on this important point.

For the moment, however, the Russian messages probably gave Bismarck all he needed, for Haymerle was evidently not prepared to commit himself to anything very definite at this

Aber man sei in Petersburg bereit, über die Grundlagen der Verständigung zu verhandeln, damit man, wenn der Moment eintrete, schon vollkommen einig sei. Herr von Saburoff sagt, in der Depesche stehe Nichts über die Bedingungen, auf welche Russland eingehen wolle. Er wisse aber, dass man in Petersburg bereit sei, die Annexion Bosniens und der Herzegowina zuzugeben. Vielleicht auch, doch sei diess weniger sicher, die Annexion des Sandjak von Novibazar. Zusicherungen, dass Bulgarien sich nicht gegen Macedonien hin vergrössern werde, würde die russische Regierung auch geben.' (Telegramm Hohenlohe's durch Fürst Bismarck mitgetheilt in Friedrichsruhe, am 4 September 1880. W.S.A., G. III.)

[16] The statement that Saburov had received the private letter from Giers was made by Bismarck to Haymerle on 4 September, and presumably is derived from Schweinitz's message from St. Petersburg. Windelband (p. 169) says that Jomini showed Schweinitz the text of the despatch.

[17] If so, Bismarck did not appreciate this cautiousness: he gave Haymerle the contents of Schweinitz's telegram at once. Haymerle to Sectionschef Kállay, Heidelberg, 8 September 1880, tel., Geheim, W.S.A., G.III. Saburov may have been hoping to receive an invitation to Friedrichsruh himself: this was Bismarck's explanation. A third reason is suggested by some remarks to Hohenlohe, reported in his letter of 23 August. 'J'insistai toute-fois pour prier Hohenlohe de transmettre au Pce de Bismarck mon désir de ne pas laisser Haymerle sous l'impression qu'il le sonde *à notre demande*, et que nous voudrions, par là, soulever la question Bulgare . . .'

stage. He did not appear to have gained greatly in self-confidence since his unhappy rôle at the Congress of Berlin, but we have little more than Bismarck's comments to go upon, and they do not quite square with the picture of Haymerle that emerges from the negotiations. Bismarck told Saburov in November that he did not 'consider Haymerle dishonest; but he is timid; he is not accustomed to high politics; he fears responsibilities'. At Friedrichsruh he 'seemed like a school-boy impatient to get out of school, and thinking of nothing but how to extricate himself as well as possible, without losing too many feathers'.[18] Bismarck in his anxiety to bring about the triple agreement would tend to ascribe Austrian hesitations to some such cause as Haymerle's timidity rather than to more fundamental differences; and it must be said that Haymerle, in struggling so pertinaciously during the next eight months with so mighty a figure as Bismarck, showed stubbornness and some courage rather than a yielding disposition. In any case his government had not yet formally decided to commence the negotiations, although he had been assured by Kálnoky on 28 August that the Tsar warmly supported Saburov's efforts to bring about closer agreement between the three empires.[19] Bismarck's main purpose was therefore to secure Haymerle's provisional approval of the pourparlers; to persuade him that it was wise to enter on negotiations with Russia at all.[20] His general plan was to combat Haymerle's suspicions of Russia (which he could not wholly condemn) by attacks on Gladstone.

The conversations filled several hours on the 4 and 5 September. Virtually the only topic that Bismarck would discuss during these two days was the desire of the Emperor Alexander

[18] *Saburov*, pp. 172–3. Bismarck told Rantzau that Haymerle was 'ein bodenscheues Pferd'. Windelband, p. 73.

[19] Kálnoky to Kállay, 28 August, tel. no. 94, W.S.A., G.III.

[20] Haymerle's account of the interview (which I have followed here) is given in two despatches, Haymerle to the Emperor, dd. Stift Neuberg, 9 September 1880 (W.S.A., G.III). A tel. to Kállay on 8 September (*ibid.*) gives a summary of the conversations, with some additional points. The full text of Haymerle's two despatches is printed in my article in the *Berliner Monatshefte*, 'Bismarck und Haymerle: Ein Gespräch über Russland' (November 1940, pp. 719–29). This was accepted for publication by the editors of this journal before the outbreak of war in September 1939, and then published anonymously in 1940. A shorter account of the conversations, dictated by Bismarck to Rantzau on 8 September 1880, is printed by Windelband, pp. 195–7.

that the *entente à trois* should be maintained, and his own desire
for a better understanding between Austria and Russia. After
giving Haymerle an account of the various messages he had
received through Hohenlohe and Schweinitz during the previous few days he mentioned the letter that Saburov was known
to have received from Giers, and suggested that the Russian
ambassador was expecting an invitation to appear at Friedrichsruh during Haymerle's visit. He recommended the invitation on the ground that this suggestion of an *accord à trois*
would arouse a wholesome alarm in England. This rather
transparent attempt to hurry on the alliance discussions met
with an immediate rebuff: Haymerle said that before receiving
the permission of the Emperor he could very well have confidential conversations with Bismarck, but could not enter into
discussions and binding explanations with the very imaginative
(*sehr phantasie-reichen*) Russian ambassador. Saburov's communications would have to be submitted to him in an authentic
form, and he would need time for their consideration.[21]

Bismarck did not press his suggestion, and he assured Haymerle that he understood his mistrust of Russia; he had himself
agreed to the wishes of the military authorities that the re-
organized German army formations should be placed, not in
the west but on the eastern frontier, since Russia was not prepared to modify her own dispositions of troops in Poland. But
one should not show this mistrust, as this would not improve
the position and would only tend to bring Russia and England
together.

Republicanism, he went on, was making undeniable progress
in Western Europe, not only in France but even more in
England, thanks to the foolish behaviour of Gladstone. The ties
that bound the three empires in the interest of the monarchical
principle should therefore be strengthened and not weakened.
Alarm in England at the revival of the alliance of the emperors
was the only means of awakening her to a consciousness of her
true interests and of overthrowing Gladstone, which he regarded as one of his most important aims. Bismarck then argued

[21] This attempt at triple discussions is not mentioned in Bismarck's account, and
was apparently unknown to Saburov. Rantzau mentioned it to Herbert Bismarck
on 7 September (Windelband, p. 173).

that the union of the two Bulgarias could not be prevented if Austria were not prepared to fight: all she could do was to make conditions which would safeguard her interests in the event of a *fait accompli*. He was anxious to know what these conditions would be in the event of Austria being willing to embark on negotiations; for he would not do anything that was unacceptable to her.

Haymerle was prepared to give his personal agreement to the commencement of alliance negotiations, but before doing so he stressed all his apprehensions about Russian machinations in the Balkans. He said that the problem was not only that of Bulgarian designs on Eastern Rumelia, but also on Macedonia, and he proceeded to read to Bismarck numerous reports on these activities. No assurance could be more binding than the Berlin treaty!—to which Bismarck replied that the treaty had been forced on Russia, but she would now give her assurance voluntarily. Turkey, moreover, had the right to quell a rising in Macedonia, and was on more favourable ground there than in Eastern Rumelia; it would suit Austria to see her resume her right of action. Active intervention in the peninsula would involve Russia in loss of manpower and money, and if Russia should hasten to the support of a rising, Austria could threaten her flank.

Haymerle's reply was that Austria did not wish to be put in the position of having to attack the Russian flank. Russia had recently given emphatic assurances that she would maintain the Berlin treaty, and that she had given up the idea of realizing the union in the immediate future: events nevertheless continued to develop rapidly in Bulgaria and Eastern Rumelia under the influence of Russian elements, and today she was even pressing Bismarck to ask for Austrian agreement to the union. But Haymerle then proceeded to give his carefully qualified agreement to further negotiations.

I could not conceal the fact that the observance of the [Berlin] treaty appeared to me to be the first postulate of a conservative policy, and that a direct move against one of the treaty provisions was not possible for us. But I recognize the advantage of standing well with Russia, particularly since England is so actively trying to undermine Turkey, and can no longer be counted on. I know the position too well, I continued, not to realize that the unfortunate creation of Shuvalov and Salisbury could not in the long run be maintained, and that the union was only a question of time; I recognize also the importance of the argument that we are still in a position to lay down conditions in a peaceful fashion. I am therefore ready to enter into a discussion of our probable conditions subject to the above-mentioned reservation of the Emperor's orders, and to a more careful consideration of Saburov's communications. I note with satisfaction and complete confidence the assurances communicated through Count Kálnoky, and now repeated by Saburov, that Russia does not wish to hasten matters. . . .

It is unlikely that the ultra-cautious Haymerle would have committed himself thus far without securing the Emperor's agreement to preliminary discussions with Bismarck; his criticisms of Russia were no doubt intended to strengthen his hand in any subsequent bargaining.

That Bismarck understood Haymerle's position is shown from his own remarks later in the conversations, which Haymerle reports as follows.

He would put together those of my statements which he thought could be communicated to the Russians, and would send this memorandum to me in Vienna before entering into further details with Saburov; merely saying provisionally to the latter that he had found me disposed to enter on pourparlers with Russia when I had heard the commands of the Emperor and the opinion of my colleagues.

Bismarck found it necessary, when reporting later to Saburov, to censor Haymerle's statements because of the ambitious character of the Austrian counter-demands on both Russia and Germany.

The discussion of the Austrian requirements occupied most of the latter part of the conversations. The points that directly concerned Russia may be summarized as follows. Haymerle was particularly insistent that Bulgarian unification should not take place before the settlement of the Greek question; the Turks, driven to desperation by the double danger, might throw themselves on the nearest opponent, with results which would, though for different reasons, prove equally undesirable to both Russia and Austria. It was imperative that even after the union the new state should not be allowed to extend itself to south or west beyond the existing frontiers, and should leave the Vardar valley entirely free. He accepted the Russian promise to agree to the annexation of Bosnia and the Hercegovina, but pointed out that Russia had already agreed to this in the Budapest convention of 18 March 1877, and had also agreed, in the Berlin declaration of 13 July 1878,[22] to 'what is today to be reserved for the future' concerning Novipazar. Austria would be concerned lest the increased influence that would come to Russia as a result of the union should draw the neighbouring states into her orbit. Austria would want a free hand if Serbia's continued hostile attitude made it necessary to proceed against her with something more forceful than economic pressure. 'Our aim would not be conquest, but merely to turn a bad neighbour into a good one.'[23] Russia could easily avoid this eventuality if she would persuade Serbia to adopt a more friendly attitude. Austria would probably find it necessary to recommend a territorial compensation for Rumania, since the Bulgarian union would greatly upset the balance of power established among the Balkan states by the Berlin treaty.[24] He said also that Austrian acquiescence in Russian plans would be facilitated if the development of things in Bulgaria partook less of a Russian, and more of a national Bulgarian character, and that Austria was very much concerned to prevent Rumania becoming a passage way for Russian troops.

Haymerle was also very much concerned to prevent any weakening of the Austro-German alliance, and he questioned Bismarck very searchingly as to his intentions on this point. The Chancellor was careful to avoid any display of anxiety over

[22] Russia under this agreement agreed to raise no objection if, 'à la suite des inconvéniens pouvant résulter du maintien de l'administration ottomane dans le Sandjak de Novi Bazar, l'Autriche-Hongrie se voyait amenée à occuper définitivement ce territoire, comme le reste de la Bosnie et de l'Herzégovine'. Austria undertook to support Russia diplomatically in dealing with difficulties which might arise in execution of the Berlin treaty. The full text is printed in my *Congress of Berlin and After*, p. 404. Bismarck claimed to have heard of the agreement for the first time during the Friedrichsruh discussions (Windelband, pp. 197, 200–1), although Saburov states that he spoke of it to Bismarck in 1879 (*Saburov*, p. 149).

[23] Bismarck's account to Saburov omitted this reference to a possible attack on Serbia, and merely said that Austria would welcome Russian help in improving her relations with Serbia.

[24] Bismarck thought that Haymerle had in mind the cession of Silistria.

Franco-German relations, and referred to them only super-
ficially; Haymerle was, however, convinced that they formed
his constant preoccupation and explained the intensity with
which he had returned to the idea of a *rapprochement* with Russia.
Bismarck said that it was of the utmost importance to assure
Russia that she had no reason to fear attack by Austria or
Germany, and he therefore contemplated some form of treaty
whereby they should undertake not to take aggressive action
against each other. Haymerle objected that such a treaty
would alter the character of the Austro-German alliance, and
that it was impossible for the two powers to stand towards
Russia as they stood towards each other. He then read a report
of 30 May, in which he had set out Bismarck's earlier disclaimer of any intention to recommend an intimate or general
understanding with Russia. Although Bismarck replied that he
could still subscribe to all this, Haymerle felt that he was not
speaking with complete conviction. The Chancellor insisted,
however, 'in eloquent terms' on the identity of Austro-German
interests, and justified his Russian plans—which he claimed
had not yet assumed any precise form—on the ground that
reciprocal assurance against aggressive views, if they could be
arranged between all European states, would form one of the
greatest guarantees of peace.

Haymerle's reply was that this could hardly be done in a
form which would not weaken Austria's position. The conception of 'aggression' was already so elastic that the victim of
aggression was often branded as the aggressor. To attack Germany, Russia must straightway invade German territory, the
fact of aggression would then be clearly established, and the
casus foederis for Austria would apply. Russia could, however,
attack Austria not only in Galicia and in the Siebenbürgen but
also through her neighbours, and particularly Rumania.
Russia might even send troops through Rumania against
Turkey with Rumania's consent. Diplomatically speaking such
treatment of Rumania could not be regarded as 'aggression'
against Austria, since the attack would not be directly on her
territory. To Haymerle's inquiry whether Germany would consider the *casus foederis* under the October treaty to apply if
Russia attacked Austria in this 'indirect' fashion, and if Austria

were compelled to retaliate, Bismarck 'did not reply with the desired clarity'. He at first tried to reassure Haymerle by arguing that he could scarcely believe that any such breach of the peace was included in Russia's calculations, and that, if it were, Austria could easily take effective counter-measures, such as the immediate occupation of Serbia and Wallachia. In reply to Haymerle's direct question concerning the *casus foederis* Bismarck referred to Gorchakov's inquiry in 1876 concerning Germany's attitude towards a Russo-Austrian war; Bismarck had then said, 'You may fight a battle, but not win'. He would never allow Austria to be injured, 'whereupon I replied that we did not wish to be put in the position of having to guard ourselves against injury'. Bismarck repeatedly characterized a Russian march through Rumania as a blow to the European legal order, but one which must necessitate even German intervention. He was not, however, very willing to make himself the interpreter to Russia of the Austrian views concerning Rumania, and repeatedly asked Haymerle whether he really desired this: Haymerle replied emphatically in the affirmative. Bismarck thought in the end that he might be able to find a suitable formula, such as a statement to Russia that 'we take it for a matter of course that a war against Turkey would be conducted only in Asia or overseas'.

Haymerle suggested that the two powers might sign an agreement saying that in no circumstances would either invade Rumanian territory except with the agreement of the other; this would avoid a one-sided agreement, and give Russia a guarantee. Austria could also promise to accept Russia's proposed interpretation of the closing of the Straits.[25] But, whatever the form, Austria must have an assurance concerning Rumania to meet the eventuality of a Russo-Turkish war.

Haymerle told the Emperor Franz Joseph that during these long conversations Bismarck spoke with his usual freedom about the behaviour of other powers, and the state of international affairs in general; he showed extraordinary irritation

---

[25] Bismarck omitted all reference to this very important Austrian concession from his own report on the Friederichsruh interviews; when Reuss called attention to this omission on 3 October Bismarck confessed that his report had been faulty: '. . . ich war sehr elend damals'. Windelband, p. 199.

over Gladstone's policy, but would not agree with Haymerle's view that Russia had already certain engagements with England. Haymerle was evidently not entirely convinced by all this. Nevertheless he told the Emperor that the main ground for not simply refusing the understanding with Russia so warmly recommended by Bismarck certainly appeared to be the attitude of England, and the circumstance that there was no effective means at Austria's disposal of preventing the union, whether it was brought about by Russia or by a spontaneous movement of Bulgarian and Rumelian elements. Gladstone with his leaning to the southern Slavs would be more likely to forward than to hinder this process. Republican France and radical Italy would not oppose, except by paper protests, any consequence of the self-determination of nationalities. On the other hand, to leave the Turks in possession of Eastern Rumelia would possibly bring about another Russo-Turkish war, and this would conjure up for Austria the vital problem of the inviolability of Rumanian territory.

Haymerle's account of the Friedrichsruh conversations reveals so close a preoccupation with the details of an Austro-Russian agreement as to leave no doubt that he had already, in his own mind, accepted the need for it in principle. Three days after the meeting, on 8 September, Bismarck dictated to Rantzau a very incomplete account of the conversations which has been responsible for some misunderstanding of their significance. Bismarck commenced by saying that the discussions had had no very precise character owing to the failure of the Russians to state their views and wishes, and he went on to a bald summary of Haymerle's views about Bulgaria, Macedonia, Rumania, and Novipazar, as summarized above.[26] But this account omitted any mention of Bismarck's attempt to bring Saburov into the discussions or of his attacks on British policy, and it also omitted Haymerle's reference to a possible Austrian attack on Serbia, his offer to accept the Russian programme for the Straits, his questions about the *casus foederis* under the dual alliance, and most important of all, perhaps, his agreement to the commencement of discussions with Russia, subject to the Emperor's consent. Moreover an accompanying note by

[26] Windelband, pp. 171–3.

Rantzau, dated 9 September, said that Haymerle's views had
been so imprecise and undecided that it had been difficult for
Bismarck to grasp his main ideas.[27] This may mean that Bismarck had found Haymerle obscure and involved in speech,
and it is possible, as we have already noted, that Bismarck,
who was not feeling at his best, may have lost the thread of the
argument at times. The effort at recollection three days later
no doubt led to some exasperated asides to Rantzau. We must
conclude that Bismarck omitted some points from his account
through mere forgetfulness, some from discretion, and some
(particularly Haymerle's willingness to enter on negotiations)
because he was awaiting further authority from Vienna. The
essential point is, however, that Bismarck's piece of dictation
was made for a specific purpose. It formed the text of the
message which Limburg-Stirum (who had succeeded Hohenlohe
as interim head of the Foreign Office) gave to Saburov on
12 September, and it must be read only as a statement of
what Bismarck felt himself able to tell the Russian ambassador
at this point. In short, Haymerle's account of the conversations
disproves earlier views as to the absence of progress at Friedrichsruh; we must, indeed, now regard it as the decisive turn
in the negotiations. On the other hand it would scarcely be
safe to argue that Bismarck in any way dominated Haymerle
or captured his mind; on the contrary the Austrian Foreign
Minister seems to have known precisely how far he was, or
was not, prepared to go, and he showed himself on this and
later occasions to be singularly insusceptible to Bismarck's
charms and arguments.[28]

After receiving Limburg-Stirum's message on 12 September
Saburov suggested to Giers that it would be better at this stage
merely to round off the Friedrichsruh pourparlers by giving
them a form satisfying to everybody concerned, whilst preserving their strictly contingent character. By this he meant that the

---

[27] *G.P.*, iii, p. 149, n. 1. It was apparently because of this comment that the
editors of *G.P.* decided that Bismarck's account of the meeting was not worth
printing.

[28] Cf. the views of A. O. Meyer, *Bismarck* (1949), p. 564; Windelband, pp. 173–4;
Schunemann, 'Die Stellung Osterreich-Ungarns in Bismarcks Bündnispolitik'
(*Archiv für Politik und Geschichte*, June 1926); F. Rachfahl, *Deutschland und die welt-
politik* (1926), p. 356.

question of Novipazar, which 'contains the germ of a serious disagreement' should not be mentioned in the Russian reply.[29]

He had, however, indicated to Limburg-Stirum the probable line that Russia would take in objecting to any alteration of the status of the sanjak, and these views were evidently passed on to Haymerle by the Germans. Saburov could not very well deny that in the Austro-Russian declaration of 13 July 1878 it had been agreed that the Russian government should raise no objection if Austria should 'occupy the territory definitely, like the rest of Bosnia and the Hercegovina'. But he pointed out that Article XXV of the Berlin treaty gave Austria only very restricted rights in the sanjak, and left the civil administration in Turkish hands; 'there are indeed some stages to be traversed in order to compare the position of this sanjak with that of the two provinces bordering on Austria'. Austria had failed for the past two years to carry out the provisions in the agreement that she should give Russia diplomatic support in removing the difficulties which might arise in the execution of the decisions of the Congress; it was therefore 'better to speak of that agreement as little as possible'.[30]

Haymerle had naturally no intention of allowing the Russians to wave the agreement aside in this manner, and he indicated the obvious counter-arguments to Kálnoky in a private letter of 17 September. The text of the agreement clearly entitled Austria to ask for more than Russia was proposing to offer; moreover Austria had given diplomatic support to Russia in agreeing in 1879 to the postponement of the date of evacuation of Bulgaria, and in 1880 in the Montenegrin question, in the proposed British inquiry in Eastern Rumelia, and on other occasions. He referred also to the Austro-Turkish conven-

[29] *Saburov*, pp. 150–1. Kálnoky wrote on 17 September that Jomini had spoken of the very satisfactory news from Friedrichsruh, and said that the bases of an agreement had been found. Russia had succeeded for the moment in arresting in Bulgaria 'l'élan de ce mouvement unioniste par tous les moyens de pression morales possibles. Mais personne ne saurait douter, que le printemps prochain une explosion violante y est inévitable, et qu'alors la presqu'île entière des Balkans sera en feu, et toute la question orientale avec les dissensions, intrigues, massacres et conflits qu'elle porte dans son sein, serait réouverte . . .' Kálnoky to Haymerle, 5/17 September 1880, W.S.A., G.III, no. 54B.

[30] *Saburov*, pp. 148–9. Text of Austro-Russian declaration: Medlicott, p. 404.

tion,[31] and claimed that, as a result of the various documents, the question had been regulated as regards both Russia and Europe. Kálnoky was, however, warned that this statement of views had been sent so that he could be on his guard against false statements and insinuations, and he was merely to stress them, in the course of friendly conversations, in order to prevent any assumption on Giers' part that the Bulgarian union had been finally accepted. When the Russian government omitted any reference to Novipazar in its reply, Haymerle was content to leave the matter open for the time being.[32]

Saburov received a despatch from Giers, on the lines he had suggested, about 5 October, and communicated it at once to Limburg-Stirum; on the 7th d'Oubril read a copy to Haymerle. Giers said that the Tsar had gained the impression that the exchange of ideas which had resulted from the Friedrichsruh meeting 'could not but contribute to the entente between the three courts', and Bismarck was warmly thanked for his help. Russia would employ her best efforts to maintain the *status quo* in the two Bulgarias, but if circumstances in the future made the union inevitable it would be 'certainement précieux' to her to find that Austria did not oppose it. He gave the desired assurances concerning the boundaries of Rumelia and the restriction of Bulgarian propaganda in Macedonia; he also referred rather vaguely to Russian goodwill towards Vienna in the sphere of Austro-Serb relations. Novipazar was not mentioned.[33] On 10 October Haymerle was able to tell Bismarck that he had been formally authorized by the cabinet at Vienna to commence pourparlers, which could begin whenever the questions of the day, which were the objects of the European action in Turkey, should have been settled.[34] Bismarck's activity at Constantinople during the previous few days had, as we have

[31] On 13 July 1878 Andrássy had signed an agreement with the Turks stating that the occupation of Bosnia and the Hercegovina would be provisional, and would not impair any of the Sultan's rights. The reference in the text is to the convention of April 1879, which specifically maintained the Sultan's administrative, judicial, and financial rights in the sanjak. Medlicott, pp. 124–5, 407–8.

[32] Haymerle to Kálnoky, 27 September 1880, private, W.S.A., G.III.

[33] Giers to Saburov (copy communicated to Haymerle by Reuss), 13/25 September 1880, W.S.A., G.III (a despatch, identical except for unimportant verbal differences, was read by Oubril to Haymerle on 7 October). Cf. *Saburov*, p. 153.

[34] *Saburov*, p. 156.

seen, helped to bring about the final surrender of the Sultan on the Dulcigno question although this was not yet quite clear. The Greek frontiers had, however, still to be settled, and both Austria and Russia were content to make this a reason for not hurrying on the alliance discussions.

For Russia the advantages of this delay were twofold. Austria's growing fear that Gladstone's policy, if persisted in, would lead to the fall of Turkey meant that an Austro-Russian agreement must necessarily imply Russia's abandonment of the British programme; it was obviously wise not to throw Gladstone over before this programme had been fulfilled to Russia's satisfaction. Haymerle had, moreover, given evidence of much suspicion and stubbornness, and of an intention to fight desperately to secure his country's advantage in the alliance negotiations. Russia's continued co-operation with England, if not carried too far, would help to break down this resistance. Haymerle for his part seems to have desired delay in order to avoid being stampeded into unnecessary concessions, and in order perhaps to conquer his own aversion to any agreement with Russia, though Saburov was more inclined to suspect Haymerle of rapacity than of timidity. Certainly the two governments were deeply suspicious of each other's ambitions, and nothing had emerged from the preliminary discussions to suggest that they would be able to agree on the constructive policy of joint exploitation of the Balkans visualized by Bismarck. Saburov's comment on Haymerle's programme is significant. 'There are unavowed ambitions there which betray themselves in spite of themselves, and which are the more dangerous in that they can find friendly support in Germany. . . . It could be dangerous to-day to engage in that struggle with Austria for the East which a future generation will perhaps see, but which we can only pursue at present with any success on pacific lines, by being satisfied with the compromises which Germany offers to support, each time that the opportunity of doing so presents itself.'[35]

[35] *Saburov*, p. 152.

CHAPTER VIII

Greece and the Powers, 1880–1881

1. BARTHÉLEMY SAINT-HILAIRE OFFERS MEDIATION

THE Smyrna threat had solved the Montenegrin problem. But in preferring success to unanimity Gladstone himself had begun the retreat from the Concert system. He had been reluctant to accommodate the pace of British policy to that of the slower and more hesitant powers; during October he could speak of the Concert with little enthusiasm. 'It is I imagine our duty to say nothing of the recalcitrance of the three Powers: for out of the old jade "Concert" we must still get what good work we can.'[1] Germany, Austria, and France for their part now treated the more or less satisfactory settlement of the Montenegrin question as a sound reason, or at least a convenient opportunity, for abandoning the existing programme of threats altogether.

In the general review of the situation which followed the Turkish surrender it soon became evident that the British government had lost the initiative. It also received, somewhat illogically perhaps, most of the blame for the Porte's continued frustration of the efforts of the Concert. Undoubtedly the immediate responsibility lay with those powers which had, after accepting the British programme between May and July, assumed an air of detachment when visible proofs of unity were called for in the autumn. 'This impetuous statesman is compelled to go on', Saburov had written of Gladstone on 5 October, 'for, like a bicycle, if he stops he falls.'[2] The Liberal government, in spite of the pacific tendencies of some of its members, had been prepared to accept the consequences of its

---

[1] Gladstone to Granville, 14 October 1880, G.D. 29/123 (Granville Papers). Granville to Gladstone, 25 October. Cf. Crewe, *Lord Rosebery* (1931), pp. 142–3; J. L. Garvin, *Life of Joseph Chamberlain*, i, 315.

[2] *Saburov*, p. 155. Cf. Bismarck to Cohen, B.B.M., p. 315; *Hohenlohe*, ii, 271.

programme;[3] and the final surrender of the Sultan certainly strengthened its position at home, where Beaconsfield was said to have imagined that the crisis would force a dissolution of Parliament. On the continent, however, and particularly in France, the successful issue was regarded as the fortunate avoidance of a dangerous trap into which Gladstone was leading his unsuspecting friends.

But Europe could not ignore the Greeks. To have abandoned their cause would have been too ignominious a retreat from the position taken up with so much publicity in the previous summer. And if the three powers had disinterested themselves in the matter they might have left the way open for a yet more alarming plunge forward by the British-Russian-Italian group. Bismarck at this point could not afford such a calamity; he continued to grumble during October at Gladstone's lack of statesmanship, but, reversing his earlier tactics, left the British government in no doubt as to his wishes. We have seen that Odo Russell had been more than a little at sea about Bismarck's intentions earlier in the month.[4] Precise explanations were now given him.

Granville instructed Odo Russell on 13 October to 'fully talk out the situation with the Chancellor'. Bismarck had said more than once that the decisions of the Berlin Congress and Conference must be carried out, and the Concert maintained: 'how does he think this had best be done'.[5] Bismarck's answer, during a long talk with Odo Russell at Friedrichsruh on 18 October, was unequivocal: he was ready to act with the British government towards keeping the Concert together, but only by moral means and diplomatic pressure. He argued that the Dulcigno naval demonstration could be considered to be an attempt to assist Turkey in executing the treaty, but the proposed seizure of the port and custom house of Smyrna would be a 'de facto' declaration of war. He had been informed that the Sultan had already as Caliph written a secret paper or proclamation calling upon the Faithful to prepare for a Holy War. 'These were the considerations which led him to fear that the enforcement of the

[3] *Goschen*, i, 202.
[4] See above, p. 160.
[5] Granville to Odo Russell, 13 October, private: Knaplund, pp. 162–4.

Berlin Treaty by coercive measures was fraught with dangers, difficult if not impossible to avert or combat, and which might be followed by a general state of disorder, anarchy, and fanaticism in the East which might last for months and possibly for years.' He put his points politely. He was merely stating his private opinion, he told the ambassador; he offered no advice; he fully admitted that he might be mistaken. He would raise no objection if Great Britain, with or without other powers, resolved to carry out the Berlin treaty. He would not in any circumstances take Turkey's part. But as German Chancellor he could not risk war with Turkey. 'Personally therefore he was against the employment of force and in favour of continuous moral pressure.'

This was Bismarck's ostensible aim: to prevent war, open or veiled, in the Near East. But these exaggerated alarms do not carry much conviction, when we remember that, after indicating all the dire consequences of forcing the Turks to surrender a few miles of Albanian territory, he proceeded with complete equanimity to recommend a British annexation of Egypt. His real purpose was to prevent the Anglo-Russian co-operation that would accompany the Smyrna offensive. He did his best to persuade Odo Russell that Russia would gain all the advantages from the coercion of the Sultan: 'he could not but think that the great ends achieved by England would be purely moral and philanthropic, whilst all the material advantages would be reaped by her unscrupulous Ally Russia.' England had real material interests in Egypt, which she would be justified in annexing. He agreed that England was right to seek a friendly understanding with Russia, 'a far preferable policy to a permanent state of suspicion which could serve no practical purpose'. But Russia, under Miljutin's evil influence, was capable of any act of folly. He found it expedient to adhere to a uniformly friendly policy towards Russia, as Germany's most formidable neighbour; but 'if Russia attacked Austria he would turn against her without a moment's hesitation'.[6]

The frankest statement of his views at this time is, however, his instructions of 7 November to Radowitz, who had been

[6] Odo Russell to Granville, Friedrichsruhe, 18 October 1880, private, *ibid.*, pp. 164–9.

appointed German minister to Greece. The aim of Germany's policy in the East, he said, was the maintenance of peace, and in particular of peace between Austria and Russia, for a rupture between them would compel Germany, sooner or later, to choose between them, even if the *casus foederis* under the October treaty were not involved. Arising from these considerations there was a further general aim, which could not be openly displayed: to loosen or hinder the co-operation of Russia and England. This co-operation must lead inevitably to a regulation of Eastern affairs which would take no account of the interests of Austria, and would therefore involve the danger of a rupture between Austria and Russia, while on the other hand the continuation of the previous good relations between Austria and England would help to hinder a conflict between Austria and Russia. Owing to the incompatibility of their ultimate interests a war against Turkey undertaken by Russia and England, or by one of them, would probably destroy the momentary alliance between them, and it might, therefore, be argued that there was no need for Germany to hinder such collaboration. The danger was that in the face of events which appeared more decisive than they really were, Austria, whose policy was quick to take alarm, might interfere too soon. 'For this reason above all it is not advisable for us to favour joint Anglo-Russian action in the hope of ending the co-operation between these two powers, and we must do nothing to drive the powers into this course. Besides, recent events suggest that the Anglo-Russian intimacy with its threat to peace will dissolve of itself when the English politicians, although less astute than the Russian, at last come to realize that in hastening the fall of Turkey they are opening the way only for Russia, without advantage to England.'[7]

It followed that he was not prepared to promote the aggrandizement of Greece by any means which would involve war. But if it could be achieved without war he would welcome it as a counter-weight to Panslavism, which was a danger to Eastern Europe, not indeed because of the predominance of Russia which it would promote, but because of the revolutionary developments which might be set on foot among the uncontrollable Slav peoples even as far as Bohemia and Illyria.

[7] *G.P.*, iv, pp. 18–19.

Russian expansion at the expense of some Turkish province, and even the annexation of Constantinople, would not be dangerous to Germany, and perhaps not to Austria to the extent that was believed in Vienna; in any case, Russia would have to find satisfactory compensation for Austria. 'But Panslavism, with its revolutionary aims, is dangerous to both powers, to Austria even more than to us, and most of all to the Russian Empire itself and to its dynasty. Revolutionized Slavdom, with or without the Russian Emperor at the head, will ever be the ally of revolutionary elements not only in France, but also in Italy, in Spain, even perhaps in England. In England the beginnings, which lie in the Gladstonian doctrine, can already be seen.'[8]

No statement of policy by Bismarck can ever be accepted at quite its face value; each was, for all its customary air of rather impatient frankness, skilfully contrived to carry conviction in the affairs of the moment, and discrepancies between his recorded comments can usually be explained by reference to his audience. On this occasion he was writing in the first instance to convince the German Emperor, who expressed his entire agreement; on the main issues the two were, indeed, in close sympathy, so that the statement may come very near to Bismarck's innermost thoughts. For the Emperor's benefit, however, he had laid particular emphasis on the revolutionary menace of Panslavism, of which he said nothing (for obvious reasons) to Saburov, and little to Haymerle, who might all too readily consider it an added objection to alliance. While he told the German Emperor that good Anglo-Austrian relations would tend to hinder a conflict between Russia and Austria, he did his best to alarm Haymerle by pointing out the unpleasant consequences of an active British policy towards Turkey. He sought to damp the interventionist ardour of the British by reviving their hostility to Russian expansion, while at the same time turning their own thoughts towards Egypt. To the French at this time he advocated joint action by Germany, Austria, and France, on the ground that Russia, Italy, and England did not genuinely desire to maintain peace.[9] To Haymerle, Saburov,

[8] *Ibid.*, iv, p. 19.
[9] *D.D.F.*, ii, nos. 280, 294; cf. Windelband, p. 211.

and the Emperor he made Gladstone's anti-Turkish policy his chief argument in justification of the Three Emperors' Alliance, although he had already been working for the alliance in the previous winter, when the friendly Conservative government was still in office. He appears to have felt some measure of genuine uneasiness at the possible results of Gladstone's forward policy, but his real purpose, as in the spring, was to create or exaggerate alarm on this point in order to eliminate Great Britain as an obstacle to the alliance programme.

Everything was pointing towards a French initiative in the Greek question which French governments had made their special concern in the past. The British had no objection, and Russia, in spite of Bismarck's professions of alarm, was only too anxious to emphasize her accommodating attitude.[10] The co-operation of Hatzfeldt and Tissot in pressing the Porte to surrender Dulcigno led the inspired press in Germany on 13 October to praise Tissot and the French government, and it was Odo Russell himself who, after his conversations at Friedrichsruh, explained to the French that Bismarck had every hope that, with patience, the exercise of moral pressure on Turkey would achieve satisfactory results, and that he wished, therefore, to maintain the accord with France and Austria.[11]

An attempt by Bismarck to put the co-operation of the three powers on a more formal basis followed, but was evaded a little awkwardly by Saint-Hilaire. When Radowitz on 23 October proposed that the three governments should combine to bring pressure to bear directly on the Sultan, the foreign minister read the general instructions by which Tissot had already been directed to take energetic steps to secure the immediate cession of Dulcigno, and asked whether these were not sufficient for the purpose proposed by the German government. If Bismarck contemplated any special *démarche* not covered by Tissot's instructions the suggestion ought to be made to all the powers. He went on to say that England appeared likely to drop the Smyrna proposal and that in his opinion it was of supreme importance to maintain the European accord and to impress its durable character on the Porte.[12] This reply, delivered apparently in somewhat blunt language, probably reveals some

[10] See below, p. 244.   [11] *D.D.F.*, iii, no. 279.   [12] *Ibid.*, iii, no. 280.

uneasiness as to the effects on French opinion and France's bargaining powers of any exclusive reliance on German support; the immediate cause was, however, probably Saint-Hilaire's anxiety not to allow himself to be dragged into any threat of further coercive measures against Turkey. Bismarck, through Limburg-Stirum, expressed himself as entirely satisfied with the French reply, and protested that he had had no intention of substituting any separate action for the collective pressure of the powers.[13]

Bismarck had no reason to object to French caution, which was the best guarantee against French support for British plans of coercion. Germany, Austria, and France were completely in accord in refusing to continue the naval demonstration in the interest of the Greeks. At the end of October Granville suggested to the French that the formal and final separation of the allied fleets would have a bad political effect; he proposed that the admirals should be instructed to take separate cruises, with prearranged places of call. He pointed out that the separation of the fleets would not be in accordance with the assurance given by the powers to the French government in July, that they would be ready to act for the settlement of the Greek frontier question in the same manner as for Montenegro.[14] Barthélemy Saint-Hilaire objected at once to any delay in the final separation of the squadrons, and the Austrian and German governments also refused, promptly and decisively, to continue the demonstration after Dervish Dorgut Pasha's success. In order to prevent itself from being abandoned by one after another of its allies, the British government had to agree to withdraw the British ships too.[15]

In proposing the continuance of the naval demonstration the British government had treated France as the most likely supporter of the British plans for Greece.[16] The French govern-

---

[13] Ibid., iii, no. 283 (25 October).

[14] Granville to Lyons, 28 October 1880, F.O. 27/2424, no. 1423A, conf.

[15] Lyons to Granville, 8 November, F.O. 27/2437, nos. 1041, 1042. D.D.F., iii, nos. 294, 295, 299, 305. Busch, p. 342; Hohenlohe, ii, 272–3. Barthélemy Saint-Hilaire's defence of his own policy, Fragments pour l'histoire de la diplomatie française du 23 Septembre 1880 au 14 Novembre 1881 (Paris, 1882), p. 4. This consists largely of citations from speeches and documents, but is illuminating at times for both its admissions and its omissions.

[16] Lyons, ii, 230.

ment, without feeling much ardour for the Greek cause, was prepared to try its hand as conductor of the Concert, although circumstances compelled it to turn to Bismarck rather than to Granville in the search for a suitable programme.

This was a natural consequence of the successful opposition of the two powers in October to the Smyrna proposal, but it was influenced by other considerations, among which perhaps the most important was the possibility of a crisis at any early date over Tunis. We have seen that the accession to office of the Ferry ministry on 19 September had been followed by a temporary *détente* over Tunis between the French and Italian governments,[17] but the struggle for concessions was unchecked, and the French were fully persuaded that any relaxation of effort on their part would be immediately taken advantage of by their opponents.[18] Bismarck's assurances of support in this question continued; the use of force in Greece would mean separating French from German policy, and would probably produce an anti-expansionist scare, which would soon develop into an anti-German scare. In this way the support of both Bismarck and of French public opinion would be endangered, and the Porte, whose goodwill in Tunis was desirable, would be alienated. Perhaps, too, the new government would be in a better position to take the initiative in Tunis if it could demonstrate to the French people beforehand its ability to secure diplomatic success without war. But the government had no desire to break with England, and Saint-Hilaire replied very mildly to an outburst of criticism of Gladstone's intentions by Saint-Vallier on 22 November.[19]

With the Smyrna proposal and the naval demonstration out of the way the French government now made a complete volteface from its attitude in the previous summer, brought forward the admirable idea of submitting the Greek frontier question to arbitration, proceeded for the next two months to hector the Greek government upon the folly and imprudence of its conduct, and by implication at least blamed the Greeks for most of the difficulties which had arisen with Turkey since the Congress.

[17] *D.D.F.*, iii, nos. 258, 266, 287; see p. 122.
[18] Cf. *ibid.*, nos. 286, 292.
[19] *Ibid.*, nos. 299, 305.

Although the remaining powers had found it difficult to agree to coercive measures against the Turks, they had at least thoroughly accepted the view that the Porte was responsible for the delays in the treaty settlement. Even when the reasons behind the French initiative were understood, the means employed caused some amusement and some annoyance in various capitals. Lyons and others seemed disposed to regard Saint-Hilaire as an aged but still excitable amateur whose pronouncements were not to be taken altogether seriously, but the undiplomatic frankness of some of his phrases does not lessen the importance of the French initiative. Internal evidence seems to suggest that both in aim and composition they were more the work of Ferry than of the foreign minister, and the policy of restraining the Greeks was supported and approved by Bismarck himself.[20]

Freycinet had, moreover, repeatedly urged prudence on the Greek government; early in July he had, in conjunction with the British and German governments, pointed out that public and premature armaments would arouse Turkish *amour-propre* and offer a pretext for war; and although Greece had promptly accepted the conference decisions the preparations had continued.[21] Again on 3 September Freycinet had instructed the French *chargé* in Athens to warn the government that the Porte would make any acts of provocation by the Greeks an excuse for resisting the demands of Europe; he had, however, at the same time, admitted the right of the Greek government to prepare itself to meet every eventuality, and he had joined the other governments in condemning the various evasive replies of the Porte to the allied proposals concerning Greece. A collective note of 25 August, in reply to Abeddin's note of 26 July rejecting the conference line, had informed the Porte that the powers could not depart from the decision of the Conference,

[20] Lhéritier, iv, 97–8; *Lyons*, ii, 230. The government was attacked for its support of intervention in the Senate (30 November) and Chamber (2 December), B. St-H., pp. 17–47.

[21] Rangabé to Tricoupis, 6 July; Ypsilantis to Tricoupis, 10 July, cited by Lascaris, pp. 188–9; *D.D.F.*, iii, no. 195; Goschen to Granville, 17 August, F.O. 78/3092, no. 291. The Russian government had advised moderation at Athens, but had refused to join the other powers in advising against mobilization. Széchényi to Haymerle, 19 July, W.S.A., no. 67B; Wacken to Haymerle, 20 July, tel.

or enter into any discussion concerning it; nevertheless in the note of 3 October the Porte had once more refused to cede Janina, Tchamouri, Metzovo, and Larissa, and had indicated an alternative line which it was not prepared to cede until one hundred days after its acceptance by the powers.[22]

On 28 October Saint-Hilaire wrote to Challemel-Lacour, the French ambassador in London, that the French government did not wish to withdraw from the moral obligations which it had contracted, but it was certainly free to choose and to await a favourable opportunity for action, and was not obliged to follow Greece into an adventure. 'Un devoir supérieur envers la France nous interdit de compromettre d'une manière irréfléchie la conduite de notre politique nationale pour satisfaire les impatiences de la nation hellène, quelque légitimes que soient d'ailleurs ses réclamations après le verdict que nous avons provoqué en sa faveur à la Conférence de Berlin.'[23] This furnished the text for several subsequent sermons to the powers and the Greek government. On 10 November he repeated to Saint-Vallier that the powers had contracted a moral obligation towards Greece, but they, and not the Greek government, had to decide when a suitable time for action had arrived.[24] This line of argument was expanded for the benefit of the Greeks in the instructions to de Moüy, the protocolist of the Congress of 1878 and the Conference of 1880, who had just been appointed French minister at Athens.[25]

All this was in accordance with Bismarck's desire for a pacific solution, but he was more conscious than Saint-Hilaire of the tactical disadvantages of any programme which would lead to a relaxing of the pressure at Constantinople. For the time being, however, he was unable to persuade the French to apply equal pressure in the two capitals, although the two governments were able to work well enough together at Athens.[26] Radowitz, who had been sent back to his post there, was to remain for a time and use his influence to restrain the Greeks, after which he was

[22] Goschen to Granville, 27 August, F.O. 78/3092, no. 291; 3 October, F.O. 78/3095, no. 423; 5 October, no. 432.
[23] D.D.F., iii, no. 284.
[24] L.J., Affaires de Grèce en 1880, no. 115.
[25] C. de Moüy, Souvenirs et causeries d'un diplomate (1909), p. 166; B. St-H., p. 7.
[26] Cf. p. 195 above.

to go to Constantinople to replace Hatzfeldt.[27] This move was
not entirely governed by the exigencies of the Greek question,
for Bismarck appears to have suspected Radowitz of participation in intrigues, possibly for his (Bismarck's) removal
from office.[28] To justify this move Bismarck spoke to Radowitz
and the French government of his alarm at the character of the
Greek preparations, and may have found it expedient to be a
little more emphatic on the subject than the occasion appeared
to him to demand. Saint-Hilaire at any rate accepted gladly the
idea of joint pressure at Athens and Moüy's instructions were
shown to, and approved by, Bismarck; but on 16 November he
again showed reluctance to agree to a suggestion from Bismarck as to closer co-operation at Constantinople between
Hatzfeldt and Tissot, arguing that too apparent an agreement
might arouse the susceptibilities of the other powers.[29] It is
clear that Bismarck attached more importance to the negotiations at Constantinople, and less to those at Athens, than did
Saint-Hilaire. Bismarck wished the two envoys to exhort the
king and cabinet of Greece to be patient; but at the same time
they were to be assured that their interests would not be abandoned, and that the two powers were determined to secure the
execution of the decision of the conference of Berlin. Immediately after his arrival Radowitz 'privately and unofficially'
urged the Prime Minister, M. Coumoundouros, to await
patiently the course of events, and was told that Greece was
now too far committed to put a stop to the preparations she had
felt it her duty to adopt in order to take possession of the ceded
province.[30] Moüy arrived a few days later, and spoke much
more strongly, saying that the French government felt no
doubt that the new frontier awarded to Greece by Europe
would be eventually secured, but that, should Greece decide

---

[27] *G.P.*, iii, no. 285 (30 October).

[28] *Radowitz*, ii, 153–6; Lascaris, p. 193. M. Busch, *Bismarck, Some secret Pages from his History*, ii, 415–6, 425–9, 446–7. Holstein suspected that Radowitz had some secret information which forced Bismarck to show him deference. But as Radowitz was sent to Athens against his wishes (he hoped for an embassy) it is difficult to find justification for this view. N. Rich and M. H. Fisher, *The Holstein Memoirs*, pp. 96–7.

[29] *D.D.F.*, iii, no. 295; Lhéritier, iv, 94.

[30] *Radowitz*, ii, 161–2; *D.D.F.*, iii, no. 294; Corbett to Granville, 24 November, F.O. 32/520, no. 359.

upon a rash course of action in the matter, she need expect no moral support from France, or help in the event of an unsuccessful issue.[31] The difference of emphasis between the two ambassadors was further accentuated during December. Coumoundouros continued to reject all suggestions for a cessation of military preparations, and Moüy, acting on his instructions, continued to speak bluntly of the consequences.[32]

In the meantime no change had occurred at the Porte. Assim Pasha professed to take a serious view of the Greek preparations, and told Tissot on 22 November that his government would not commence hostilities but would resist energetically the invasion which was being prepared. He added that he had no fear of the result, and did not anticipate trouble in other parts of the empire; on the other hand, the attitude of the Albanians made it impossible for the Porte to make any concessions beyond those of 3 October.[33] The powers seem to have had little doubt that the Porte's confidence in its military strength was justified; its energetic measures during the last days of November to settle the Dulcigno question were also, no doubt, influenced by its desire to have its hands free for dealing with the Greeks. Saint-Hilaire was alarmed by a report that Greek bands had crossed the frontier, and that the Porte had made strong representations to Athens on the subject; on 27 November he sent telegraphic instructions to Tissot to urge the Turks to be patient, and he urged Bismarck to do the same. Hostilities did not break out; but the tension increased during the first half of December; on 14 December the Porte addressed a circular to the powers complaining of the Greek preparations, and asking the powers to urge the Greek government to open

[31] Corbett to Granville, 27 November, F.O. 32/520, no. 363, conf. Moüy to Saint-Hilaire, 30 November, *L.J.*, no. 119.

[32] *Moüy*, p. 166. *L.J.*, nos. 125, 127, 132, 134, 143, 146. Baron Erlanger asked in Constantinople, on his own responsibility, whether Turkey would settle the Greek question for £1,000,000 and £100,000 backsheesh. Gambetta favoured this suggestion. *Hohenlohe*, ii, 274.

[33] *D.D.F.*, iii, no. 300. British consular reports from Eastern Rumelia suggested that the Bulgarians would not move in the event of a Turco-Greek war. Cf. a long despatch by Stephen, who concluded that (a) little sympathy was felt among the Bulgarian population for the Greeks; (b) if the Porte made concessions, such as actually applying the Organic Laws prepared for Macedonia, the mass of the Bulgarians would probably remain quiet; (c) Russian influence was said to have declined of late. Stephen to Granville, 28 January 1881. F.O. 78/3311, no. 5.

direct negotiations with Constantinople.[34] As neither party was prepared to accept the other's programme, the French proposal that the dispute should be submitted to arbitration was an excellent one on the face of it.

Its weakness lay not in the method itself but in the fact that neither party was likely to accept it. Before making a general proposal Saint-Hilaire sounded Germany and Austria, and the idea appeared to have been first mentioned by Saint-Hilaire to Hohenlohe (who had returned to the Paris embassy) on 8 December. The proposal, as elaborated in a letter to Saint-Vallier on the 10th, was that the six great powers should agree to act as arbiters, that Greece and Turkey should then be persuaded to accept the principle of arbitration, and finally the powers should find a frontier line which would be a compromise between the existing Greek and Turkish demands. He even went so far as to suggest tentatively a frontier leaving Larissa and Janina to Turkey, and giving Greece compensation on the right bank of the Kalamas and north of the Peneios. His attempt to assess the practical difficulties of the proposal reveals a very imperfect grasp of the realities of the situation. He seems to have assumed that his arguments in favour of arbitration would persuade the two states to accept, and that the main difficulty would be to get them to keep their word after the decision was announced. On the other hand he overestimated the difficulty of persuading the great powers to act.[35] The powers would be certain to devise a compromise frontier less favourable than the ones that Turkey and Greece were each demanding; but as neither could maintain the existing armaments for long the arbitration proposal would at least provide a retreat without loss of face.

Among the powers the proposal was regarded with some suspicion, but although it involved the abandonment of the conference decision, all accepted it readily enough. Hatzfeldt had gained the impression that the Porte might be persuaded to modify its demands somewhat if the powers would support Turkey's interests at Athens, and he had recommended the

[34] Granville to St. John, 21 December, F.O. 78/3077, no. 770. *D.D.F.*, iii, no. 303. B. St-H., pp. 69–75.
[35] *Motiy*, p. 171.

German-Austrian-French combination for this purpose. When Paris and Vienna were approached they had agreed that Greece would be wise, without renouncing her ultimate claims, to take at once anything that Turkey offered; but Saint-Hilaire had then brought forward his arbitration scheme and this led Berlin to suspect that he was again alarmed at the idea of co-operating too closely with Germany and Austria. The fact that the proposal was immediately published in *The Times* (on 10 December) seemed to confirm this suspicion.[36] Nevertheless Saint-Vallier was able to telegraph on the 14th that Bismarck was inclined to accept, subject to certain conditions, one of which was that an agreement should be arrived at as to means of coercion in the event of the refusal of the parties to accept the decision. Haymerle had already indicated in his speech to the Delegations in November, and in conversation with the French ambassador, Duchâtel, that he did not regard the Conference decision as irrevocable, and he accepted the French proposal when he heard that Bismarck had done so.[37] Saint-Hilaire then proceeded to communicate the proposal to the ambassadors of the other powers, and in spite of the belief in Berlin that secret Anglo-French discussions were in progress the proposal was not made to Lyons until the 18th.

All the powers accepted during the next few days. In an attempt to remove Bismarck's doubts as to the responsibility of the powers in the event of a repudiation of the decision Saint-Hilaire quoted Vattel on the differences between mediation and arbitration; Bismarck was probably not very clear as to what their reference was supposed to prove, but he accepted on the 20th on condition that the two parties should formally and publicly agree beforehand to accept the decision, and that Germany should not be expected to take part in any forcible measures of execution. On the 21st Austria accepted on the same conditions; and Russia and Italy accepted without any reserves. Granville on the 22nd accepted on condition that Greece and Turkey also agreed and pledged themselves to abide by the award; he did not think that there was much

[36] *Busch*, pp. 242–3; cf. *D.D.F.*, iii, nos. 307 (p. 278), 312; Saint-Hilaire to Saint-Vallier, 11 December, *L.J.*, no. 128. *The Times*, 10 December, p. 5b.
[37] Duchâtel to Saint-Hilaire, 14 December, *L.J.*, no. 129.

likelihood that they would do anything of the sort. The same doubts were probably felt in other capitals, but the French proposal had at least the merit of offering a constructive solution.[38]

The correctness of Granville's forecast was shown as soon as the Turkish and Greek governments were approached. Already on 22 December the Greek prime minister had telegraphed to the Greek representatives abroad that his government would not accept arbitration if it were proposed; that they would refuse to renew direct negotiations with the Porte, and would, unless they could obtain it by pacific measures, attempt at all risk to take what they claimed by force.[39] In conversation with Moüy on the 24th Coumoundouros expressed his repugnance at the idea of arbitration and the abandonment of the Berlin line; and on the 31st he announced in the Chamber that the government would refuse arbitration if it were proposed. The Porte, on the other hand, used more diplomatic language, although Saïd Pasha's remarks to Tissot on the 27th left no doubt that both governments were in reality equally hostile to the proposal. Saint-Hilaire, the wish no doubt father to the thought, was confirmed in his view that the Greeks were the chief obstacle to a satisfactory solution,[40] and he proceeded in his three famous circulars to demonstrate his views for the benefit of the sceptical powers and the indignant Greeks.

The first circular, dated 24 December, was addressed to the French ambassadors, and pointed out that at the Congress of Berlin the powers had merely offered to mediate: the Porte had not agreed with the decision of the Berlin Conference of 1880, mediation had therefore failed, and Europe's responsibility was at an end. Greece was resolved to secure the contested territories by force; if war broke out the whole of the Balkans would, of course, be at once involved, gradually all the rest of the continent would be drawn in, ultimately all civilized

[38] Lyons to Granville, 22 December, F.O., 27/2425, no. 52. Gladstone to Granville, 19 December 1880, G.D. (Granville Papers); cf. Goschen's view in conversation with Granville, Granville to Gladstone, 19 December. Cf. *Schweinitz*, ii, 138.

[39] Corbett to Granville, 22 December, F.O. 32/520, no. 386; Lascaris, p. 196; *Moüy*, pp. 172–3; *Radowitz*, ii, 163–4. Cf. *L.J.*, no. 155.

[40] Corbett to Granville, 3 January, F.O. 32/528, nos. 3, 4, and 5, very conf. St. John to Granville, 3 January. Wrede to Haymerle, 2 January 1881, W.S.A., IA–D.

people and even those of Asia would feel the effects. It is clear
that he attached all the blame to the Greeks, and gave no consideration whatsoever to the view that although Greece would
be technically the aggressor, she could point to the action of
the powers in September as evidence that it was useless to
expect Turkey to yield to anything except force.[41] A long note
to Moüy on 28 December elaborated these arguments for the
benefit of the Greek government. To justify his view that the
conference of June 1880 had not conferred 'une sentence
exécutoire', and that Greece had no right to seize by force
territory which had not been ceded by its legitimate owner, he
quoted Vattel's definition of mediation, and went on to say
that the aggression which she was meditating would be 'une
atteinte toute gratuite au droit des gens'. He expressly approved
the correctness of Turkey's attitude, quoted Vattel once more
to show the difference between mediation and arbitration, and
in order to remove Greece's fears of the arbitral award, committed himself to the statement that after giving Greece 22,000
square kilometres in June 1880, the powers would not be likely
to reduce this by more than two or three thousand square kilometres! The second circular to the powers, dated 7 January,
emphasized again the precise and very limited meaning of the
13th Protocol of the Congress of Berlin.[42]

The success of Saint-Hilaire's proceedings was not assisted by
the fact that these despatches were published prematurely, as a
result of indiscretions, in London, and then in Germany. They
also appeared, much to his annoyance, in Vienna and Budapest.[43] They were translated from French into English, from
English into German, and then from German into French
again, and had finally appeared in the Paris newspapers with
all the alterations which these successive metamorphoses were
likely to produce. Later he attributed to this premature and
inaccurate publication much of the censure which he received,[44]
and defended himself from the charge of undiplomatic language
by arguing that they had been isolated from the context.

[41] *L.J.*, no. 158; B. St-H., pp. 96–102.
[42] *L.J.*, nos. 162, 175. B. St-H., pp. 103–15. Beust to Haymerle, 6 January,
W.S.A., no. 1B.
[43] Beust to Haymerle, 13 January 1881, W.S.A., tel. no. 5.
[44] B. St-H., p. 122, gives his defence of his action.

Actually the direct effect of the circulars was slight: no argument or absence of argument was likely to alter the resolution of Turkey and Greece to reject the arbitration procedure. His proceedings had, however, caused amusement and annoyance in many quarters where it was felt that his inexperience and excitability were likely to compromise a probably sound programme by faulty tactics. Bismarck was at pains to assure the Austrian government that press and public opinion were wrong in assuming that Germany had initiated the arbitration proposal, and protested that he had actually received the suggestion rather coolly. Gladstone on 6 January 1881 told the House of Commons that the French proposals were made with the perfect and absolute goodwill of the English cabinet, but the real feelings of the Foreign Office and diplomatic service were better represented by Goschen, who was indignant at the new policy and described it as being embodied in 'three state papers of portentous length, couched, for the most part, in almost hysterical rhetoric'.[45] On 12 January Lyons was instructed to point out to Saint-Hilaire that in his circular of 7 January he appeared to have adopted the Turkish arguments in opposition to those which had been used all along by the representatives of the powers at Constantinople; and in particular to remind him that in the collective note of 25 August the powers had refused to discuss any alternative to the conference frontier.[46]

The French government did not show any eagerness for collective representations at Athens and Constantinople, and it was only after suggestions from other powers that this was arranged. Tissot raised the question of arbitration in conversation with Saïd on 27 December, and made a more formal proposal on the 29th; the other representatives were left to act as they saw fit, which meant that the German and Austrian

---

[45] Kálnoky: Resumé einer Unterredung mit Prinzen Reuss u. Grafen Duchâtel, W.S.A., 11 January 1881; *L.J.*, no. 174; *The Times*, 7 January, 8c.; *Goschen*, i, 205. The following was attributed to Beust (*Hohenlohe*, ii, 277):

> Si pour éviter la guerre
> Il est utile de braire
> On doit prier M. St. Hilaire
> De faire une circulaire.

[46] Granville to Lyons, 12 January 1881, F.O. 27/2483, no. 35.

acted at once, and the Russian and Italian decided to wait until the British *chargé's* instructions arrived.[47] The Porte's replies, however, were, at the best, evasive; Tissot admitted that the Porte seemed to have gained the impression that the accord was not complete, and proposed a collective note, which, however, most of the others had no authority to support. Later when Tissot reproached his colleagues with having supported the arbitration plan very feebly, Novikov replied with a laugh, 'Come, you didn't overdo it in energy yourself'.[48] In the end it was decided that all the heads of missions should make the proposal in person.[49] Representations at Athens made equally little progress; Moüy passed on the arguments of the Russian, Italian, and British ministers as to the necessity of a collective step, and on 10 January Saint-Hilaire repeated Moüy's suggestion in a circular to the powers. The Italian government accepted at once,[50] but Haymerle did not appear willing to take part in a proceeding which had so little prospect of success, and Giers objected that an identic note could hardly be, as Saint-Hilaire proposed, officious.[51] Corbett was authorized to take part, but was to take care not to commit himself to any arguments which would lead Greece to suppose that her refusal of the proposal would entail the abandonment of her interests.[52] By the 12th, however, Saint-Hilaire had at last begun to realize that the attitude of the Porte was at least as important as that of the Greek government, and decided that it would be as well

[47] Granville to St. John and Corbett, 1 January, F.O. 78/3269, no. 1; *L.J.*, no. 161.

[48] He also described his task as a 'coup d'épée dans l'eau'. Calice to Haymerle, 11 January, W.S.A., no. 3A–F; 4 January, tel. no. 1B; 7 January, private, *L.J.*, no. 165 (2 January) Goschen to Granville, 17 February, G.D., 29/189 (Granville Papers).

[49] St. John to Granville, 3 January 1881, A. & P. no. 86; *L.J.*, no. 166 (3 January).

[50] Wimpffen to Haymerle, 8 January, W.S.A., no. 2; Haymerle to Széchényi, tel. no. 8; Széchényi to Haymerle, 12 January, tel. no. 6; 13 January, no. 7. Paget to Granville, 11 January, F.O. 45/426, no. 18; Corbett to Granville, 12 January, F.O., 32/528, no. 21. *Busch*, p. 243.

[51] Giers to Oubril, 2/14 January, W.S.A. (comm. to Haymerle, 15 January); Kálnoky to Haymerle, 3/15 January, W.S.A., no. 2A–B. Dufferin to Granville, 13 January, F.O. 65/1110, no. 12, conf.; Elliot to Granville, 12 January, F.O. 7/1013, no. 11, conf. *L.J.*, no. 179.

[52] Granville to Corbett, 10 January, F.O. 32/527, no. 4. Cf. Radowitz's comments on the British attitude, *Radowitz*, ii, 165.

to wait for the Turkish reply before proceeding with the local representations at Athens.[53] On the 14th a Turkish circular telegram complained of the 'legitimate anxiety' aroused by Greece's behaviour, and suggested that the most satisfactory mode of procedure for the rectification of the Greek frontiers would consist in negotiations between the Porte and the representatives of the great powers at Constantinople. Assim Pasha indicated on the 15th that this implied the rejection of the arbitration proposal, and this was notified explicitly to Tissot on the 17th. Saint-Hilaire accordingly gave up the struggle, and announced on the same day that his government had abandoned the arbitration scheme.[54]

II. BISMARCK OFFERS CRETE

When Challemel-Lacour announced his government's decision, Granville remarked that he did not think that they were premature in their action, and on the same day telegraphed an invitation to Bismarck to come forward with a proposal.[55] The Chancellor's reply was cautious, and apparently unhelpful: he knew of no effectual settlement that would not involve coercive measures, and could only suggest that the powers should accept the Turkish proposal to negotiate at Constantinople on the chance of its leading to a solution.

The British and French governments were both reluctant to allow the Porte this diplomatic triumph, which on the face of it meant that the decisions of the Conference of Berlin, and the last word of the powers on 25 August, were to be put aside. Granville had shown his annoyance at Turkish conduct by refusing to discuss the Greek frontier with old Musurus Pasha on 1 January, telling him that his recent presence at Constantinople 'had not been conducive to the favourable reception' of the proposals of the powers.[56] But this was about as far

[53] *L.J.*, nos. 124, 185. He concluded from his interviews with Essad Bey, that Turkey would agree to arbitration if sure of securing Janina and Metzovo. Beust to Haymerle, 12 January, W.S.A., tel. no. 4; Cf. Wimpffen to Haymerle, 13 January, tel. no. 3.

[54] Granville to St. John, 15 January, F.O. 78/3269, no. 29. Tissot to Saint-Hilaire, 17 January, *D.D.F.*, iii, no. 340; *Moüy*, pp. 174–5; B. St-H., p. 123.

[55] Granville to Lyons, 17 January 1881, F.O. 27/2483, no. 45.

[56] 'On this Musurus Pasha seemed much affected and said that if he had ceased to enjoy the confidence which had been placed in him for 30 years by successive

as Granville wished to go in association with France at the moment; he no doubt agreed with Odo Russell's comment on 15 January that the flagrant contradiction between the language and attitude of the French at Constantinople and Athens, 'now, and in August last, is calculated to increase the resistance of the Porte at Constantinople and the War fever of the deluded Greeks at Athens'.[57] Moreover, Bismarck was so ready to talk about the Greek frontier that he was obviously concerned with its outcome, and 'more likely than anyone else to pull the cart out of the slough'; the right course seemed therefore to be to find what was in his mind, and whether he could be induced to pull the cart or at least to push the carters on to firm ground.[58]

There was sufficient reason, unknown though it was to Granville, for Bismarck's interest. The *Dreikaiserbünd-nis* negotiations had begun seriously in December, with Haymerle still professing small confidence in the peaceful intentions of Russia; the Russo-German draft of the treaty was sent to Vienna on 16 January 1881 and while Haymerle was examining it with evident distaste it was imperative that nothing should happen in Constantinople or Athens to cause renewed friction between Austria and Russia.[59] Above all there must be no mad plunge by Gladstone into action, with all the embarrassments of another Anglo-Russian-Italian attempt to coerce the Sultan at this critical moment.[60] So Bismarck was willing enough to direct, if not to pull, the cart on to a safe track, and when Odo Russell sought an interview he responded at once. In their long conversation on 17 January he was clearly setting himself the

English governments, especially Liberal governments, it would be better that he should at once tender his resignation. I did not think it necessary to make any reply.' Granville to St. John (Constantinople), 1 January 1881, F.O. 78/3269, no. 2. Musurus had been Turkish minister in London, 1851–56, and was ambassador from then until 1885.

[57] Odo Russell to Granville, 15 January (private): Knaplund, p. 187.

[58] Granville to Odo Russell, 12 January (private), *ibid.*; Granville was also annoyed by French conduct in the Enfida case in Tunis during the next few weeks: see pp. 307–8 below.

[59] The negotiations are described in detail in Ch. IX.

[60] Windelband, pp. 209–10: but he also showed anxiety lest Gladstone should fall and be replaced by a Conservative government which would revive the Anglo-Austrian understanding and make Haymerle more difficult to deal with. *Saburov*, pp. 192, 202.

double task of persuading the British government against direct coercion and showing it that there was a path, if a somewhat devious one, to an ultimate solution even if the Greeks and Turks had to be left (in the last resort) to fight each other.

Odo Russell found the great man in an amiable mood in spite of the customary growls about his hard lot. 'After his usual complaints about the weary work imposed upon him by the obstinacy of his Imperial Master, the incapacity of his Colleagues, the ignorance of Parliament and the imbecility of mankind, he said that he was glad to rest his weary brain by talking over foreign affairs, which constituted the only recreation left him, in his overworked existence.' Odo Russell made flattering reference to his previous interview at Friedrichsruh in October,[61] and Granville's conviction that Bismarck could again pull the cart out of the slough; and to Bismarck's modest rejoinder that he was no *Hexenmeister*, to settle the Oriental question by a stroke of his wand, Odo Russell exclaimed that he had over and over again proved himself to be a magician, that at the present time he exercised a supernatural influence in Austria, France, and Italy, and that the other powers would gladly follow his lead if by a stroke of the wand he would point out the way to a pacific settlement of the Turco-Greek problem. These not insincere effusions led pleasantly on to some franker speaking. When Bismarck spoke disparagingly about France's recent policy, which he attributed to the government's discovery that the French people cared more for Turkish 'coupons' than for Greek aggrandizement, the ambassador asked: why then did he support her in a policy which would undo the unanimous Europe at Berlin? To flatter the vanity of the French and take their attention off the Rhine! was the reply. Bismarck's boldest comment was that Odo Russell overrated the danger to Europe of a conflict between Greece and Turkey: for his part he saw less danger in a Greco-Turkish conflict than in pressing too strongly on the Greek government to resist national aspirations. 'If the King of Greece and his Ministers yielded to the prudent advice of the Powers and knocked down to Turkey . . . they would lose all hold over the nation and be driven away. This would cause greater embarrassment to Europe than a

[61] See above, p. 191.

Turco-Greek war.' The Turks would have to be warned at the outset that Europe could not admit the destruction of Greece. If the Greeks were victorious they might make their own conditions; if, as appeared more probable, they were defeated, the Greeks would have to accept whatever conditions Europe might be able to obtain for them. For those portions of the Berlin award that the Sultan desired to retain owing to the strength of the Albanian influence at court, the Sultan would have to compensate Greece elsewhere; would Odo Russell be shocked if he suggested Crete as suitable compensation?[62]

Leaving the British to digest this programme he put the same arguments to Haymerle during the next fortnight. An agreement to localize the war, Limburg-Stirum told Széchényi on 21 January, would be a greater service to world peace than the everlasting squandering of time and trouble on sterile attempts to delay the outbreak of a war which in all probability could no longer be prevented.[63] The argument was elaborated in further talks during the next few days,[64] and in a note given by Reuss to Haymerle on the 29th. The powers could, without difficulty, prevent any danger from a Turco-Greek war to their own good relations; an outbreak in Macedonia or in the Bulgarian areas was not probable in the immediate future, the Slavonic elements in the peninsula would hardly be likely to take part in a Turco-Greek struggle without Russia's permission, and Russia had not, in his opinion, any intention of stirring up war in the Near East at this stage. If it were made clear to the Porte that the powers would accept the consequences of an unlikely Greek victory, but would not allow Turkey to derive any benefit from the more probable Turkish victory, the result would be to strengthen the reluctance of the Porte to resort to warlike measures. Finally if it became certain that no possible development of Turco-Greek affairs would be allowed to disturb the European Concert the powers could enter into negotiations with the Porte with more chance of success.[65]

Thus Bismarck, with memories of the Montenegrin crisis,

[62] Odo Russell to Granville, 17 January 1881 (Knaplund, pp. 188–91).
[63] Széchényi to Haymerle, 22 January, W.S.A., tel. no. 7, *vertraulich*.
[64] Széchényi to Haymerle, 25 January, W.S.A., private. Cf. Lhéritier, pp. 111–12.
[65] W.S.A., mitgeteilt durch den Kaiserlichen deutschen Botschafter, 29 January 1881.

sought to avoid international action that would produce mounting tensions during the next few vital weeks of the alliance negotiations; he was willing after that to accept the eventuality of a final breakdown. In the meantime the first step, the renewal of negotiations on the Turkish terms, was successfully achieved.[66] The British government did not at all like the idea of a localized war, which would mean the failure of the Concert even to defend Greece from attack at a time when no one doubted that Turkey would triumph. Valentine Chirol, who visited Thessaly just at this time, found that the Turks had 40,000 seasoned troops in the province, and every nerve was being strained to prepare for the threatened campaign.[67] Having asked Bismarck's advice, Granville was anxious to avoid running counter to it, but he felt that he must say on 20 January that the British government retained its liberty of action with regard to coercion, and was unwilling to abandon the decisions of the Congress and Conference of Berlin without seeing its way to a successful result. He asked whether Bismarck's willingness to accept the Turkish proposal (for discussions at Constantinople) meant that the Porte must first be willing to agree to the general opinion of the powers?[68] The French government, so recently rebuffed by the Porte, was also disinclined to accept the proposal unconditionally, and Saint-Hilaire told the Porte that its proposal would not be acceptable to the French government unless a satisfactory basis of discussion was reached. This was shown in subsequent communications to the other powers to mean that the Porte must show the extent of the sacrifice that it was prepared to make.[69]

The three empires could, however, see little practical advantage in delaying the opening of discussions at Constantinople with the difficult preliminary negotiations that the British and French programmes would have entailed. Giers said that he thought the French mode of procedure would be a mistake, and that the powers could be satisfied with an admission by Turkey that the October line was not a sufficient sacrifice.

[66] Károlyi to Haymerle, 18 January, W.S.A., tel. no. 7; Haymerle, 19 January, circular tel. *Moüy*, p. 175; *Radowitz*, ii, 165–6; *Busch*, p. 243.

[67] M. Valentine Chirol, '*Twixt Greek and Turk* (1881), p. 18.

[68] Cf. Windelband, pp. 210–11; Knaplund, p. 193.

[69] *D.D.F.*, iii, p. 336, n.1.

Haymerle proposed that the powers should merely announce that they had taken note of the conciliatory assurances given by the Porte, and would carefully examine any further proposals. He argued that in this way the Porte would gradually be brought to enlarge its concessions, but that it would be unlikely to do so if pressed to declare itself in the manner proposed by the French.[70] Bismarck also preferred an acceptance 'pur et simple', and thought that the simplest mode of procedure would be to ascertain what concessions the Sultan would be prepared to make beyond the insufficient and unacceptable line of 3 October.[71]

These replies seem to have suggested to the British and French governments that there was closer co-operation between the three empires than was actually the case. All three had arrived more or less independently at the conclusion that the resumption of negotiations at Constantinople, with as little fuss as possible, would be the least troublesome course for themselves; Austria and Russia were both as anxious as Bismarck to avoid at this point the embarrassment of a fresh crisis. But this was little more than an instinctive groping for the line of least resistance, and although Bismarck had thought out the possible future developments, there was no plan of action. Giers told the Turkish ambassador in St. Petersburg that Greece should certainly have a voice in the negotiations at Constantinople, and then on 20 January agreed to Haymerle's view that it would be wiser to keep Greece out of the discussions.[72] Odo Russell suspected that Austria, Germany, and Russia had agreed to oblige the Sultan by setting aside the Berlin award and leaving Janina and Metzovo to Turkey in exchange for Larissa and Crete for Greece, and that they would work out this idea in the proposed discussions at Constantinople.[73] Giers had indeed suggested an isolated intervention by the three powers at Constantinople, but Bismarck, who had no desire for any such

[70] Elliot to Granville, 20 January, F.O. 7/1013, no. 25; 23 January, no. 37, conf. Kálnoky to Haymerle, 20 January, W.S.A., tel. no. 3; Széchényi to Haymerle, 21 January, tel. no. 9.
[71] Odo Russell to Granville, 21 January, F.O. 64/979, no. 28, secret.
[72] Dufferin to Granville, 19 January, F.O. 65/1110, no. 20. Kálnoky to Haymerle, 20 January, W.S.A., tel. no. 3.
[73] Odo Russell to Granville, 21 January, F.O. 64/979, no. 28, secret.

assumption of responsibility, said that an isolated move by the three would lead the Sultan to suspect disagreement among the powers. It was Giers also who had first suggested the cession of Crete, and Bismarck had seen some advantages in the plan; but the German and Austrian governments were both suspicious. Busch remarked on 19 January that the proposal was in accordance with the Russian plan of turning the Greeks as far as possible into an island people, and therefore less dangerous to the Slavonic cause.[74] Gladstone, however, remained Bismarck's chief worry.

But the British proved unexpectedly accommodating and placed themselves of their own accord in his hands. On 28 January, after discovering that none of the powers was prepared to demand more of the Turks than a promise of concessions beyond the line of 3 October, Granville telegraphed to the powers his agreement to pourparlers at Constantinople on the same conditions.[75] He admitted to Károlyi during the course of the next few weeks that the British government, preoccupied with the Irish situation, the war in South Africa against the Basutos and Boers, the probability of another war on the Gold Coast against the Ashanti, and the question of the evacuation of Candahar, was intensely anxious for a peaceful solution of the Greek question. Károlyi felt justified in assuring Haymerle that there was nothing whatsoever to justify the belief that Gladstone was playing any kind of double game, and secretly encouraging the warlike tendencies of the Greeks.[76] The idea of a further approach to Bismarck originated from Odo Russell.[77] He and Bismarck welcomed the proposal that Goschen on his return to Constantinople should visit Berlin and invite Germany to take the lead.[78]

[74] Windelband, p. 210. Goschen to Granville, 8 February, G.D. 29/189. Lhéritier, pp. 108-9. Busch, p. 244.

[75] Calice wrote on 28th: '. . . les propositions anglaises rendraient maintenant toute médiation impossible. Déjà le langage du Palais devient de plus en plus belliqueux . . .' C. to Haymerle, 28 January, W.S.A., tel. no. 23. Granville to Elliot, 28 January, F.O. 7/1011, no. 31, etc.; to St. John, F.O. 78/3269, no. 53.

[76] Károlyi to Haymerle, 17 February, W.S.A., no. 19A-G.

[77] Odo Russell to Granville, 21 January, F.O. 64/979, no. 28, secret; Granville, ii, 225. Cf. Dilke, i, 341.

[78] Granville, ii, 225-6. Bismarck's distrust of Gladstone continued: he told Moritz Busch on 17 February: 'Professor Gladstone perpetrates one piece of stupidity after another'. M. Busch, Some Secret Pages of His History (1898), ii, 456.

Goschen had been in England for a short period of leave; he had a long conversation with the Chancellor on 5 February, and a provisional agreement was arrived at whereby Bismarck's ideas for the localization of the Turco-Greek differences were adapted and developed to suit British concern for the interest of the Greeks. Bismarck's earlier suggestions to Haymerle on the question of localization were known to the British government, and it is evident that he was prepared, in order to meet the British point of view, to show more consideration for the Greeks than he had originally intended. He was now, in fact, prepared to agree to the idea of military or naval support for Greece in the event of a Turkish attack. He agreed that the policy of scolding her into prudence should no longer be pursued, and on Goschen's suggestion that despair might lead her into dangerous courses, exclaimed, 'why not send your ships to the Piraeus?' Goschen replied cautiously that if the other powers agreed Britain would probably be quite ready to act. Bismarck offered the roguish formula, 'If moral support did not suffice, why they must have immoral support', and made various suggestions as to how the naval forces of the powers could be used to help the Greek operations. One suggestion was that if the powers could not land troops they could at least take Greek troops on board their ships, and land them at vulnerable points, such as the Dardanelles. At the second interview he repeated this suggestion, and spoke of forty thousand Greek troops being carried on foreign ships. The result of the interview was, therefore, a plan whereby the powers would agree on measures for defending Greece against Turkish invasion, and the possibility of such action was to be used to hold out some inducement to Greece if she were reasonable, and some threat to the Porte if it were not. Bismarck would not, however, promise German participation in any active measures, and in any case did not wish to make a final decision until he had had an opportunity for reflexion.[79]

[79] 'Conversation with Bismarck yesterday justifies hope that he may make satisfactory proposals in the sense of my plan grafted on to his own for what he calls localization, but what nearly resembles contingent coercion.' Goschen to Granville, 6 February, F.O. 78/3274, no. 1, conf. (recorder). Goschen's official account is in his despatch to Granville, 3 March, F.O. 78/3275, no. 155, conf. See also Goschen to Granville, 7 February, G.D. 29/189 (Granville Papers), *Goschen*, i, 211–12; *Radowitz*, ii, 166.

The discussions were continued on the following day when Bismarck entertained Goschen, Odo Russell, Hatzfeldt, Limburg-Stirum, and Busch to dinner.[80] At the close of the conversations Bismarck dictated a circular despatch embodying the agreement arrived at with Goschen, and this without substantial alterations was forwarded to the remaining four powers on the 8th. Goschen found that although the Chancellor still admitted the idea of other than moral support for the Greeks he was anxious that further discussion of this idea should be postponed until the need for it arose. Bismarck was, no doubt, thinking of the difficulties and suspicions which would inevitably follow any attempt to revive the type of naval action which had been practised and proposed in the Adriatic during the previous autumn, and the reluctance of Haymerle only a few days before to take up with any enthusiasm the idea of localization formed a further reason for cautious action. He commented ironically to Goschen on Haymerle's indecision, and remarked that Germany had only a 'dull card' to play in the next phase, but that as a politician, he would like 'to play the Austrian card', with which something could be done.[81]

The circular proposed that the six powers should agree on the proper degree of concession which would enable them to demand that Greece should renounce the idea of disturbing the peace. This decision could best be arrived at by the ambassadors at Constantinople; he believed it would be better to make the acceptance of the Greek government the second step, and that only after Greece's consent had been secured should negotiations be undertaken to secure the Porte's acceptance. With regard to the details of the territorial arrangements he proposed that in the interests of peace and of the healthy development of the Greek state it would be advisable to include as few Albanian elements as possible within the new frontiers; if, therefore, the conference line had to be modified as a result of refusal of the Porte to accept it the best course would be to separate some of the westerly districts from the area allotted to Greece. In return an attempt should be made to provide compensation, the exact value of which could not be calculated in

---

[80] *Busch*, p. 244; *Goschen*, i, 210.
[81] *Busch*, p. 245.

terms of the territory surrendered to Turkey. The island of Crete would fulfil these requirements in an eminent degree; it was not only practically equal in extent to the Albanian portion of Epirus, but offered in its overwhelmingly Greek population and its geographical position specific advantages which would not give scope for a comparison with the Albanian areas.[82]

Goschen found the Chancellor strong in his belief that no trouble was to be expected of Russia: she was in need of peace and money, and had no intention of provoking a Bulgarian movement at present. He revealed also considerable knowledge of the Albanian question, told Goschen that he had tried to persuade the Austrians to make friends with them, and 'appreciated them as the basis of a future settlement'.[83] But he made no attempt to conceal his lack of sympathy for the Greeks; he showed concern for the safety of the Greek sovereign, and was willing to work in the Greek interest in order to satisfy the other powers and to prevent any general disturbance of European peace, but if they lost the sympathy of the other powers he was quite willing to leave them to their fate. It was in this connexion that he made the celebrated remark, 'When I hear of the sufferings of a negro in China or in other remote part of the world, I may mention him in my prayer, but I cannot make him an object of German policy.'[84] Although Turkey's attitude was not stressed in the circular it is clear that the consequences of her refusal would be, in Bismarck's view, much more serious than that of Greece; and his proposals had not been made without evidence that there was a good chance of their acceptance at the Porte, and elsewhere. Russia was

[82] Bismarck to Münster, 8 February, *G.P.*, iv., no. 722. W.S.A. Notizen aus einer Depesche des Fürsten Bismarck vom 8. Februar 1881. Granville did not receive a copy. It is difficult to see the point of Lhéritier's comments (iv, 113, n. 1). Busch's account differs from those of Bismarck and Goschen on some points, but was merely a private record. In spite of Lhéritier it is clear that Bismarck and Goschen were agreed as to the desirability of Crete as compensation, and also that the Turkish government should not be consulted until the Greeks had accepted. These points were also made clear to Széchényi. '. . . Hierbei konnte nöthigenfalls auch die Frage der Compensation, wobei Candia ins Auge zu fassen wäre, erwogen werden. Dieses Tracé würde zuerst in Athen mitzutheilen und die Pression auf die Pforte erst nach Annahme durch Griechenland auszuüben sein.' Széchényi to Haymerle, 7 February, W.S.A., tel. no. 14.

[83] *Granville*, ii, 227.

[84] *Busch*, p. 245; *Hohenlohe*, ii, 275; cf. *Schweinitz*, ii, 158.

supposed to have originated the Cretan proposal, but Calice
heard, from what he believed to be a reliable source, that very
shortly after his audience on 30 December 1880 the Sultan
himself had formulated the idea of ceding the island, and had
sent a confidential hint on the subject to Berlin.[85] The Sultan
continued to look to Germany for favours, and had followed up
his request in the previous summer for German officers, and
his correspondence with the Emperor, by offering the Baghdad
railway concessions to the German entrepreneur, Dr. Strous-
berg, although the latter was not prepared to accept unless the
concession was accompanied by a grant of land and various
guarantees.[86] Bismarck's remarks probably betrayed a fear that
Austria rather than Turkey would provide the real obstacles
to a settlement.

At Vienna Goschen found Haymerle struggling dismally with
his doubts and reservations; strongly deprecating 'coercion' and
disapproving 'compensation', thinking only of what would content the Turks. Goschen 'could not quite extract from him
whether he would stand a Turkish Fleet in the Piraeus', but
felt it wiser to leave Bismarck to clear up the situation.[87] In the
end, however, Haymerle and the other powers accepted Bismarck's proposals readily enough. Granville admitted to
Goschen that he did not altogether like the Cretan proposal,
but Gladstone seemed satisfied with the arrangements, and
when Münster on 11 February indicated the terms of Bismarck's circular, Granville agreed that it was substantially the
same as the account received from Goschen, and that the
British government was prepared to accept the mode of proceeding so far as it had been defined.[88] The French and
Russian governments both accepted promptly, but Haymerle
delayed his acceptance until he had had prolonged conversations with Hatzfeldt, who stopped in Vienna from 12 to 14
February.[89] He told Elliot on the 12th that he was still of the

[85] Calice to Haymerle, 15 February, W.S.A., tel. On 28 January Assim Pasha
told the RR of the powers that a substantial extension of the line of 3 October
could be expected only in Thessaly. Calice to Haymerle, 1 February. no. 7A–G.

[86] Granville to Odo Russell, 22 December, 1880, F.O. 64/957, no. 792; Odo
Russell to Granville, 3 February, F.O. 64/979, no. 62. conf.

[87] Goschen to Granville, 8 February, G.D. 29/189 (Granville Papers); Goschen,
p. 217.   [88] Granville to Odo Russell, 11 February, F.O., 64/958.

[89] Kálnoky to Haymerle, 6/18 February, W.S.A., 6A–D. D.D.F., iii, no. 373.

opinion that it would be best to begin by inviting the Porte to state the concessions which it was prepared to make,[90] but after seeing Hatzfeldt he accepted the German programme. On the 15th he assured Elliot that his earnest wish was to extend the land frontiers of Greece as much as possible,[91] but his predominant sentiment seems to have been fear of what Russia's interest in Crete might signify, and, even more, fear of what Hungarian public opinion might think it signified; the almost ostentatiously pacific comments of Giers seem merely to have increased his suspicions. Giers told Kálnoky that 'in the Greek question we shall maintain the attitude that we have observed hitherto. Any combination which has the agreement of the majority of powers can count on Russian support, for we have neither preconceived ideas nor special wishes, and it will give us nothing but pleasure to see this struggle ended.' Although the news from Greece was alarming he was not inclined to take it too seriously; he believed that the Greek king and ministers were only waiting to be forced to give up their present awkward position. He did not believe that the Greeks seriously intended war; moreover, everything was now quiet in Macedonia and Rumelia, and it was to be hoped that it would remain so. These assurances were specific enough, but were not sufficient to remove all Haymerle's fears, and although he had not attempted to shipwreck the Bismarck-Goschen procedure, the alliance discussions did not advance.[92] The agreement of the powers was completed by the adhesion of Italy, who had indeed been favourable to Bismarck's proposal of Crete throughout, but had delayed in order to secure the opinion of other governments, and particularly of Great Britain.[93]

III. THE PORTE OFFERS RESISTANCE

Europe was now to witness the last and the most surprising incident in Bismarck's short phase of leadership: within a few days of the resumption of negotiations at Constantinople the

[90] Elliot to Granville, 11 February, F.O. 7/1013, no. 81; 12 February, nos. 82, 83.
[91] Elliot to Granville, 15 February, F.O. 7/1013, no. 90.
[92] *Schweinitz*, ii, 145. See p. 277 below.
[93] Wimpffen to Haymerle, 11 February, W.S.A., tel. no. 16; Kálnoky to Haymerle, 6/18 February, no. 6A–D.

Bismarck-Goschen programme had virtually been thrown aside. The ambassadors held their first meeting on 20 February at Hatzfeldt's invitation, and decided to hand to the Porte on the following day replies to the Turkish note of 14 January 1881. The notes of the various ambassadors were substantially identical in effect, and stated that the governments, in the expectation that the intention of the Porte was to make overtures going beyond those presented in the note of 3 October, were prepared to receive any proposals which the Porte might have to offer. The ambassadors added that note was taken of the promise of the Porte to abstain from all aggression. They advised their governments to notify to the Greek government without delay the opening of the negotiations, inviting it at the same time to abstain from all acts of hostility during the course of the ambassadors' labours. Thus the Porte was asked to state its terms, and when it resorted to its inevitable Fabian tactics, day after day went by without any attempt on the part of the ambassadors to draw up in secret a suitable territorial settlement, secure Greece's acceptance, and then press it on the Porte, as Bismarck had proposed.[94]

An explanation of this independent action must be sought in a variety of circumstances, among which personal motives played no small part. Bismarck in March remarked to Ampthill[95] that 'Constantinople was at all times a peculiar place, in which the Powers never seemed to have their Representatives in hand, as at other posts', and it would appear that Corti and Tissot at least were piqued by a programme being imposed on them from Berlin, and were ready to ignore it until the insistence of their respective governments became too strong. Calice, on the other hand, knew that Haymerle had not really given up his objections to Bismarck's plans, and Calice, most un-

[94] Goschen to Granville, 22 February, F.O. 78/3275, no. 135. Odo Russell stated that on 24 February Hatzfeldt read copious extracts from his instructions, which were 'to the effect that if the reply of the Porte is not satisfactory and prompt the Ambassadors should then be invited to recommend a line to the Governments themselves'. It is thus clear that Bismarck agreed to the presentation of notes; the object of this was, however, merely to link up the previous procedure with the new. Radowitz, who only learnt the details of the Bismarck-Goschen agreement from Corbett, considered it would be bad tactics to approach the Greeks first. *Radowitz*, ii, 167.

[95] Odo Russell was created Baron Ampthill on 12 March 1881.

expectedly, found an ally in Hatzfeldt. The attitude of the latter provides the real puzzle, and it is unfortunate that so little evidence as to his relations with Bismarck at this stage has come to light. Goschen wrote that 'Hatzfeldt supports his master's programme languidly', and it was believed in British diplomatic circles that he was irritated at the entire change in German policy, in which he had had little say. But Bismarck kept too tight a hold on his ambassadors for us to be able, without direct evidence on the point, to accept the view that Hatzfeldt was merely indulging a sense of grievance; and although Bismarck displayed annoyance at the turn of events he does not appear to have blamed his ambassador for it. Novikov was apparently without detailed instructions, and was willing for any settlement as long as peace was preserved; this and the state of Austro-Russian friendship naturally led him to support Calice and Hatzfeldt.[96]

The ambassadors were, moreover, with the exception of Goschen, Turcophil in the sense that they were dominated by the curious fear of, and respect for, the Sultan's feelings which appeared in other capitals to be so curiously disproportionate to the Sultan's real powers of unpleasantness or aggression. Abdul Hamid had indeed already established this strange ascendancy over most of the foreign missions, where it was firmly believed that his almost morbid susceptibility to polite speech and courteous circumlocution made any rough or hostile language both a serious error in tactics and a grave breach of good taste. 'It is all very well for you', said one ambassador to Goschen, 'who are going away afterwards, to stand out very strongly, but the case is very different with us.' The possibility that ruffled dignity might stampede him into an expensive, but by no means disastrous, war with Greece was probably the dominant consideration with the ambassadors at this moment. No observations were made to Goschen by any ambassador which would indicate the slightest intention on the part of any government to take steps to prevent such a result.[97] This attitude had already been indicated before Hatzfeldt's arrival

[96] *Goschen*, i, 224–5, 228–9; *Granville*, ii, 230; *Busch*, p. 246.
[97] Goschen to Granville, 15, 17 February, G.D. 29/189 (Granville Papers); *Goschen*, p. 218; Swaine, p. 115.

on the 18th; after his arrival he, too, to Goschen's surprise and annoyance, said nothing to indicate that Bismarck had accepted the view that concerted action by the powers to prevent a Turkish attack on Greece was desirable.[98] Bismarck had himself made it clear that he wished the idea of coercion to be kept in the background; Hatzfeldt interpreted whatever instructions he had on this point by concealing the Chancellor's views altogether.[99]

After the ambassadors on 21 February had requested the Porte's proposals there was a long delay before the Porte made any reply; the ambassadors continued to meet, and according to Bismarck's plan should presumably have busied themselves with the drawing up of a territorial settlement that the Greeks could accept. Attempts were indeed made to define the maximum and minimum concessions to be demanded of the Porte, and also to decide what should be done if the Porte should ask the powers to make proposals.[100] But Goschen found it impossible to make any headway against the depressing effects of his colleagues' conviction that they could do nothing but conform to the Turkish requirements; Hatzfeldt made no serious attempt to secure the acceptance of Bismarck's proposals concerning Epirus and Crete, and whispered to Goschen during one meeting, 'if we were to attempt to draw up a line at this moment it is questionable whether we should all agree'.[101] The result was that Goschen and Bismarck, the authors of the Berlin plan, both began to doubt the success of their efforts; Goschen on 25 February suggested to Granville the bold alternative of an evacuation of Cyprus, and on 2 March Bismarck, in the

[98] Goschen to Granville, 22 February, F.O. 78/3275, no. 137, secret. Goschen asked Granville for precise instructions; Granville waited for some days in the expectation of a statement through Münster of Bismarck's views; when this did not come he instructed Goschen on the 21st that the government 'desire to leave as much as possible to Y.E.'s discretion in regard to the conduct of the negotiations'. Granville to Goschen, F.O. 78/3269, 16 February, no. 97; 18 February, no. 115; 21 February, no. 118. Cf. *D.D.F.*, iii, no. 398, n. 2.

[99] Radowitz was apparently not informed that Bismarck had agreed to coercion. *Radowitz*, ii, 166.

[100] Calice to Haymerle, 1 March, W.S.A., no. 13B.

[101] *Goschen*, i, 223. Goschen to Granville, 25 February, 1 March, G.D. 29/189 (Granville Papers). Windelband (p. 216) refers briefly to Bismarck's annoyance at the attitude of the ambassadors, but does not explain why even Hatzfeldt failed to support the Chancellor's plan.

Norddeutsche Allgemeine Zeitung, indicated that owing to the procedure of the ambassadors he had abandoned the initiative. Goschen argued that the restoration of Cyprus to the Turks would be a gesture of renunciation which would raise British prestige at Constantinople and elsewhere, indemnify the Turks, secure an adequate settlement for the Greeks, and relieve the British taxpayer of an expensive and probably useless burden; but, although Granville was not altogether opposed, the cabinet, which was shaken on 28 February by the Majuba Hill disaster, decided that an evacuation policy was at the moment impossible.[102]

In the meantime it was understood that numerous meetings of the council were taking place, and various suggestions were advanced by the Sultan and his ministers to the ambassadors with the obvious aim of discovering the real intentions of the powers, and, if possible, of creating divisions between them. At length it was announced, late on the night of 3 March, that Server Pasha and Ali Nizami Pasha had been appointed to confer with the ambassadors. Tissot, who had become extremely suspicious of Hatzfeldt's activities, telegraphed to his government on the same evening that the Sultan, who had at first seemed disposed to cede the whole of Thessaly, was now prepared to offer only Crete and possibly one or two small islands, and had moreover maintained that Germany had suggested this solution.[103] Calice, in a private letter to Haymerle on the 4th, gave a fuller, and probably more accurate, version of the discussions at the Porte. According to his information the council was prepared to recommend the cession of the whole of Thessaly up to Mount Olympus; the Sultan, however, would agree only to the cession of Crete and some small islands, without any cession of territory on the mainland. The first of these solutions had been proposed to Calice by Assim Pasha on the 3rd. The idea of ceding Crete as compensation only for Epirus had definitely been excluded by all the Turks; they maintained

---

[102] Széchényi to Haymerle, 2 March, W.S.A., tel. no. 25; *D.D.F.*, iii, no. 398; *Busch*, p. 246; Lhéritier, p. 120; *Goschen*, i, 221–2. Lhéritier is clearly in error in stating that Goschen proposed that Cyprus should be given to Greece (iv, 121, n. 3).

[103] Goschen to Granville, 3 March, F.O. 78/3275, no. 156; *D.D.F.*, iii, no. 398, n. 2; cf. Haymerle's comments on Tissot, to Calice, 5 March, W.S.A., tel. no. 36.

that Crete would represent a greater extension of territory for Greece than the whole area proposed by the Berlin Conference. If Crete were ceded nothing further could be given except perhaps one or two of the smaller islands. Calice added that the Turks were determined that in no circumstances whatsoever should Prevesa be given up; Goschen himself, although the most determined defender of the Conference line, had admitted repeatedly that a great mistake had been made in giving Greece a portion of Albania. The Greek minister in Constantinople, M. Condouriotis, had admitted to Calice that a peaceful cession of that area by Turkey was out of the question, and in an attempt to persuade the Greeks to drop this point Calice had remarked to the Greek minister that an insistence on this area would prove that the Greeks really wanted war. Condouriotis had replied, 'it is necessary to put Turkey in the wrong'. Calice concluded that all the ambassadors had really given up Prevesa, and the whole of Epirus was regarded merely as something for which compensation must be given.[104]

The Porte's move on 3 March had the effect of forcing the ambassadors to evolve some definite plan of action. A telegram from Tissot on 8 March seems to indicate further discussions between them, ending in the acceptance by Hatzfeldt of the view, urged by Tissot, Calice, Corti, and Novikov, that the intentions of the Porte must be ascertained before the drawing up of a line which would be presented in turn to the powers, to Greece, and finally to Turkey.[105] It was agreed that Hatzfeldt, as doyen, should be the spokesman of the ambassadors, but Bismarck's procedure was definitely to be abandoned, and Goschen alone continued to recommend it. The understanding between the ambassadors was sufficiently close for them to present a united front to the Turks at the first meetings, but Calice's very clear summary of 4 March shows that as early as that date the differences of opinion which were to divide the ambassadors for the next few weeks were already clearly defined. Goschen understood his agreement with Bismarck to mean that Crete was to constitute compensation for Epirus;

[104] Calice to Haymerle, 4 March, W.S.A., private. *Radowitz*, ii, 167–8, 172–3.
[105] *D.D.F.*, iii, p. 380, n. 1.

Hatzfeldt on the other hand regarded it as compensation not for Epirus alone but for the whole difference between the Berlin Conference proposals and whatever was finally ceded on the mainland. Hatzfeldt believed that a peaceful solution could be secured with the cession either of Thessaly up to Mount Olympus without Crete, or Crete with the October line. Goschen replied that in such a case he would not make the choice but would like to combine the two alternatives into a demand for both Thessaly up to Mount Olympus, and Crete. A more fundamental difference existed between those who preferred the cession of Crete, and those who preferred the cession of Thessaly. Novikov was the protagonist of the first, Tissot of the second.[106]

After the usual delays the Turkish delegates met the ambassadors on 7 March. The two Turkish pashas were accompanied by the distinguished soldier, Ghazi Ahmed Moukhtar Pasha; he and Ali Nizami both spoke French, and made a favourable impression by their soldierly and businesslike manner. The Turks, without too much beating about the bush, proposed a line of frontier which followed the thalweg of the Salambria, giving Larissa to the Greeks and leaving Tricala to the Turks, passed south of Metzovo and finally followed the course of the Arta to its mouth, as in the proposal of 3 October. A long discussion followed, during which the Turks admitted that so shallow a river as the Salambria constituted a bad frontier; the two generals, however, contended that no good boundary could be found, and brought up various quite unanswerable objections to the Berlin Conference line, without, however, giving the impression that the Salambria proposal was necessarily their last word. They showed, however, uncompromising opposition to the cession of Metzovo, Janina, and Prevesa, bringing forward the familiar, but none the less weighty, arguments as to the difficulty of ceding the Albanian districts; Metzovo was essential as the only point through which Epirus could be reached; Prevesa was all important as a port, and for other reasons. Hatzfeldt, who had emphasized throughout that the starting-point of the ambassadors was the Berlin Conference line, then asked the Turks what compensation they

[106] Calice to Haymerle, 4 March, W.S.A., private.

could offer if they wished to refuse the conference line in Epirus; the Turks suggested the retention of the old frontier, 'as it was a very good frontier', and the substitution of some area elsewhere, and after this suggestion, which clearly foreshadowed the offer of Crete, had been rejected in decided language, the meeting broke up on the understanding that the powers must insist on a satisfactory rectification of frontier in Thessaly, and that the idea of compensation could only be entertained in reference to Epirus. The Turks did not appear to anticipate so much insistence on the Berlin line, and seemed also to be surprised at the united front presented to them.[107] The front was maintained at a further meeting on the 9th. The Turks asked for information as to the general nature of the compensation suggested, and were told that the ambassadors regarded Crete as a suitable compensation for territory deducted from the Conference line, but still maintained their reservations with regard to important points, especially Prevesa. The Turks in reply still maintained the idea of 'substitution': they would agree to cede territory either on the mainland or in the islands, but not to both at once. A long discussion followed as to the exact size of Crete, which the Turks claimed was 12,000 kilometres, whereas the British admiralty chart gave it as only 8,300; no progress, however, seemed likely on the main point, and the meeting was about to be adjourned when the Turks, after a private consultation, put two questions to the ambassadors. 'In the first place did we refuse the idea of Crete without territory on the mainland because it was too limited in extent? . . . In the next place, would we consent to throw back the frontier line they had offered in Thessaly southwards if they gave Crete?' Both questions were at once answered in the negative. An affirmative answer to the first would have allowed the Turks to keep their mainland areas and to settle the matter by ceding additional islands; the second would have involved the return to the Turks of Larissa as well as Epirus. The Turkish delegates then withdrew for further consultations with their colleagues.[108]

[107] Goschen to Granville, 8 March, F.O. 78/3275, no. 172, secret. Calice to Haymerle, 8 March, W.S.A., no. 15B.

[108] Goschen to Granville, 11 March, F.O. 78/3275, nos. 183, 184.

Although Goschen had fallen in with the wishes of the majority he was determined not to abandon his programme; having failed to convert his colleagues he sent vigorous messages to London, and in a letter of 8 March to Granville complained bluntly about the lack of information and support he was receiving from his government. 'Not a hint, or advice, or suggestion, or criticism, or sketch of politics. Nothing! The whole responsibility is to be thrown on me', he wrote to his wife. Granville made a good-tempered reply, and promised to do all in his power to bring the powers back to the Berlin programme; he was forced, however, to admit that he was no more able to fathom their policy than was Goschen or Bismarck.[109] Granville's pressure and Bismarck's grumbles did, however, produce some results. Saint-Vallier on 4 March had reported Bismarck's annoyance at the action of the ambassadors, and had remarked bluntly that he could well understand the Chancellor's discouragement at their deplorable conduct. A few days later Odo Russell and Saint-Vallier had again reported to their governments that if the ambassadors at Constantinople continued to follow their own courses Bismarck would retire from the leadership completely.[110] Széchényi in a lengthy telegram on the 9th gave further evidence as to Bismarck's view. The Chancellor did not experience any *amour-propre d'auteur*, and was quite prepared to acquiesce if others wished to follow new paths. It was not for him to propose to other governments that they should give their ambassadors stronger instructions. Tissot's attitude in particular caused surprise, as his government had accepted the German proposal warmly. After him Corti was criticized. Novikov's recent attitude had been satisfactory, and there was no real complaint against Goschen. Hatzfeldt had taken credit for securing the support of Calice. Launay at the same time informed the Italian government that Bismarck had

[109] *Goschen*, i, 225; Goschen to Granville, 8 March, G.D. 29/181 (Granville Papers). A telegram on 3 March had expressed entire approval of 'your proceedings in the difficult position in which Y.E. is placed'. Granville to Goschen, 3 March, F.O. 78/3269, no. 149 (extends tel. no. 154).

[110] *D.D.F.*, iii, no. 398. Széchényi to Haymerle, 8 March, W.S.A., tel. no. 27. On the 8th Münster informed Granville that Bismarck had repeated his instructions to Hatzfeldt to maintain with Goschen 'the most complete understanding in the Greek frontier negotiations'. Granville to Goschen, 8 March, F.O. 78/3269, no. 158.

particularly blamed Corti for having accepted the present programme.[111]

Bismarck knew perfectly well that the Austrian ambassador had been at least as indifferent to the Bismarck-Goschen scheme as his French and Italian colleagues. He could not, however, with far greater interests at stake, afford to grumble at Haymerle about the Greek question, and in any case Haymerle had made no pretence of accepting the programme very warmly. Bismarck's criticism of Tissot and Corti accordingly served the double purpose of giving a hint to Haymerle and of bringing pressure on the French and Italian governments, where results seemed possible. Both governments responded readily. Saint-Hilaire on 7 March instructed Tissot to support the view of the British and German ambassadors, and leave the responsibility of conducting the negotiations to them; on the 11th he repeated these instructions, mentioning also that Bismarck appeared not unfavourably impressed by the report of the second conference with the Turks; on the 13th he confirmed his instructions again, and equally categorically. He was striving at this moment to persuade the French Council of Ministers to seize Tunis; he needed Bismarck's support, and the minimum of friction with the Turks. 'I can only instruct you to give support pure and simple to the solution which Count Hatzfeldt and M. Goschen agree to recommend. This line of conduct appears to me sufficient to relieve us of responsibility in the event of the difference between Turkey and Greece ending in war.'[112] Similarly the Italian government was disturbed by the news that Berlin and London were annoyed at the failure of the ambassadors to support the Bismarck-Goschen programme, and telegraphed to Corti that if the ambassadors thought it desirable to return to that programme he was to regard his original instructions as being still in force.[113] Calice was not instructed

[111] Széchényi to Haymerle, 9 March, W.S.A., tel. no. 30; Haymerle to Calice, 10 March, tel. no. 39; to Calice and Széchényi, 11 March. Bismarck evidently was, in spite of Széchényi's statement, extremely annoyed at the failure to take his proposals seriously. Windelband, pp. 214-16.

[112] Saint-Hilaire to Tissot, *D.D.F.*, iii, no. 400, and n. 2, p. 380. On Tunisian developments, see pp. 306-10 below.

[113] Menabrea claimed that Corti had merely followed the lead of Hatzfeldt. Granville to Goschen (no. 163), Odo Russell (no. 117), F.O. 78/3269, 9 March. Haymerle to Calice, 11 March, W.S.A., tel. no. 37.

to change his attitude, but Haymerle warned him by telegraph on the 10th that complaints from Berlin against the ambassadors were concerned mainly with the lack of co-operation between them, and with the fact that they were wasting time in sterile discussions instead of proceeding to elaborate a new line in accordance with the Bismarckian plan.[114]

This pressure produced some results, and considerable annoyance. Corti and Tissot were particularly displeased, and Corti remarked to Goschen, 'I don't mind receiving my orders from Downing Street but I don't care to have them from the Wilhelm-strasse'.[115] An attempt was, however, made on the 11th to expedite matters and to bring the action of the ambassadors into line with the procedure of the Berlin plan. It was decided that if the Turks failed to attend the meeting on the following day, and gave no satisfactory assurances, the ambassadors should announce their intention of recommending a line to their governments. They then proceeded to discuss academically a suitable line, and after Tissot had made an ingenious and unconstructive attempt to bewilder his colleagues with an exposition of the many possible combinations before them, arrived without difficulty at a provisional agreement on all except one point. Thus it was generally held that a solution including Crete was, at the present stage of the proceedings, necessary; if Crete were demanded, Prevesa should be abandoned; but the cession to Greece of Punta, opposite Prevesa, and the razing of the fortresses at the entrance of the Gulf of Arta, would be a *sine qua non*. No agreement was, however, reached as to the frontier in Thessaly. Goschen agreed that the Salambria line and Crete were more in the spirit of the arrangement which had to be come to; but the others were all prepared to agree to the frontier of 3 October 1880. Hatzfeldt reserved his decision, explaining later to Goschen that he did not wish to leave him isolated; but he announced to the Turks on the following day that the ambassadors would proceed to draw up their own plan unless the Porte had communicated its proposals by the 17th.[116]

[114] Haymerle to Calice, 10 March, W.S.A., tel. no. 39.

[115] *Goschen*, i, 224; Goschen to Granville, 11 March, G.D. 29/129 (Granville Papers).

[116] Calice to Haymerle, 12 March, W.S.A., tel. no. 48. Goschen to Granville, 15 March, F.O. 78/3276, no. 195; 17 March, no. 211; *Moüy*, pp. 176–8.

The Porte did not take this warning very seriously: on the 14th it offered to cede Crete together with a strip of territory averaging four kilometres in width on the frontier in Thessaly; when the ambassadors promptly refused this the Turks offered Crete and 'a few little islands'. The ambassadors replied on the 15th by demanding large concessions on the mainland, and the Turks declined to make any substantial advance on their offers. On the 17th they promised to meet the ambassadors on the 19th, and the ambassadors, in spite of their threat to embark upon separate discussions, decided to wait for another two days. But on the 19th the Turks merely offered a small augmentation of the four kilometre strip;[117] after this was rejected they promised to make a final communication as to their last word on the 21st, and on the 21st merely asked for a few more days' delay. By this stage the separate discussions had already commenced, and the Turks were informed that any further communications from them would only be received as so much information.[118]

Unfortunately these discussions produced a deadlock almost immediately. It was stated, in some quarters, that Baron Testa, the first German dragoman, had told the Sultan that the ambassadors were disunited, and there seemed no doubt that the Porte had managed to discover the real state of opinion among them. At a meeting on Sunday, the 20th, Goschen proposed a cession in Thessaly up to the Salambria in addition to Crete, and received no support; Hatzfeldt and Calice objected on the ground that to insist on the Salambria might endanger peace, but no other proposal was forthcoming. This deadlock reproduced accurately enough the attitude of the powers.

The King of Greece continued to refuse agreement to any cession which excluded Prevesa, and Granville had been pressing the claims of the Greeks to the Salambria frontier for some days, without any success. On 13 March he had urged Bismarck to send instructions to Hatzfeldt in favour of this line, and although Bismarck did not apparently refuse he made it clear that he was prepared to accept any peaceful solution, and

[117] Goschen to Granville, 22 March, F.O. 78/3276, no. 212.
[118] Goschen to Granville, 22 March, F.O. 78/3276, no. 221. Calice to Haymerle, 20 March, W.S.A., tel. *Goschen*, i, 230.

regarded the October line and Crete as the best combination.[119] This was repeated to Vienna on the 19th, and Reuss at the same time explained to Haymerle that Hatzfeldt's reserve was probably due to the fact that he was in direct contact with the Sultan, and that although this might arouse the suspicion of some of his colleagues it was the only way to discover the real aims of the palace, and to influence them.[120] Haymerle continued to regard the situation unhappily, and spoke to Elliot of the necessity of doing everything that was humanly possible to avert a war; Granville replied to this in a lengthy despatch on the 21st in which he argued that peace did not depend entirely upon the Porte, but was equally likely to be endangered if the expectations of the Greek people were not duly considered.[121] The deadlock at the ambassadors' meeting on 20 March was thus due more to an absence of plans than to a conflict of policies. Before the meeting Hatzfeldt had sounded Calice and Novikov as to their willingness to accept the October line; they had not felt able to do so, although instructed to leave the initiative to him, and he had then apparently received instructions to agree with them, but also not to take the initiative. Corti and Tissot had been told to follow the lead of Goschen and Hatzfeldt; with the result, as Calice remarks, that Goschen alone was in a position to make a proposal.[122]

iv. Abdul Hamid offers Peace

The Porte virtually ended the crisis on 23 March with an entirely unexpected and, in the circumstances, not ungenerous proposal. This was for an exclusively continental solution, which would increase Greek territory by an addition of some 14,000 square kilometres in Thessaly, and would add an area of

---

[119] Granville to Goschen, 13 March, F.O. 78/3269, no. 188, secret; Goschen to Granville, 17 March, G.D. 29/189 (Granville Papers). Széchényi to Haymerle, 14 March, W.S.A., tel. no. 33; Haymerle circular tel., 17 March; Calice to Haymerle, 20 March; Beust to Haymerle, 21 March, tel. no. 33. *Granville*, ii, 231.

[120] Elliot to Granville, 18 March, F.O. 7/1014, no. 138. Haymerle to Calice, 22 March, W.S.A., tel.; cf. *D.D.F.*, iii, p. 387, n. 1.

[121] Granville to Elliot, 21 March, F.O. 7/1011.

[122] Calice to Haymerle, 22 March, W.S.A., private.

2,300 square kilometres beyond the Salambria line. The new
frontier was to follow a line of heights to the north of the
Salambria as far as Mount Kratchovo, and would then follow
the thalweg of the Arta to its mouth. The ambassadors accepted
this communication 'only as information', but it was at once
evident that no opposition was likely from any of the powers
except Great Britain and Germany.[123] Goschen, however, was
attracted from the start. On the same day he asked his colleagues whether they thought that the October line and Crete
would be ceded pacifically by the Porte, and they were unable
to say that it would. He then suggested that they should send an
identic telegram to their governments, asking whether they
were authorized to submit a line without Crete, and although
this proposal was rejected on Hatzfeldt's opposition, Goschen
telegraphed early in the morning of the 24th to Granville pointing out that a purely 'continental' solution was much more
likely to produce agreement than one involving Crete.[124] On
the 25th Granville agreed to accept the Turkish proposal if all
the powers agreed, and on the following day it became known
that Bismarck had instructed Hatzfeldt to accept any line upon
which his colleagues were agreed, but not to take the initiative.
The other four powers were surprised and relieved at the
prompt acceptance of the Turkish proposal by the British
government, and on the 26th the ambassadors agreed to recommend it to their governments. They made their recommendation subject to the condition that Punta should be ceded to
Greece; that fortifications on both the Prevesa and Punta sides
should be dismantled, and the free navigation of the gulf
secured. They appear to have arrived at these decisions with
remarkable ease. Goschen regretted that the Conference line
had not been secured, but agreed with the others that the
difference was not worth the risk of a further crisis; all were

[123] Goschen to Granville, 25 March, F.O. 78/3276, no. 235. Granville to Goschen,
19 March, F.O. 78/3269, no. 205. On 21 March the Porte had nominated a fourth
delegate, Artin Bey, and it had appeared that fresh delays would be created.
Calice to Haymerle, 22 March, W.S.A., no. 19A-C.
[124] Goschen to Granville, 24 March, tel. (2 a.m.); 29 March, F.O. 78/3276, no.
247. 'My taint of Jingoism is a guarantee to you that this suggestion does not come
from one who is usually addicted to giving up.' Ibid., 26 March, G.D. 29/189
(Granville Papers), personal tel. D.D.F., iii, 390, n. 1.

also agreed that the Turks were prepared to go to war to retain Prevesa, which must, therefore, be conceded.[125]

All the powers had been tired of the Greek question for months past, and most of them had given unmistakable signs of willingness to accept anything which would end the crisis without war. Haymerle made it clear to Elliot on the 24th, in reply to Granville's despatch of the 21st, that if he was in favour 'of our contenting ourselves with a smaller cession of territory from Turkey than Her Majesty's Government might wish to insist upon, it is not that he would not prefer the larger, but that he disbelieves the possibility of obtaining it from the Porte'. Bismarck told Ampthill that to avoid war 'the ambassadors must take, not what they wanted, but what they could get the Turks to give', and had no reason to object to the new plan, although he appears to have betrayed some sulkiness at having to drop his Cretan proposal.

Goschen's action in accepting the Turkish plan is also not really surprising, and was fairly summed up in his own comment that his whole attitude 'had been a continued and decided protest against the willingness of the other powers to accept too little and to shrink from real pressure on the Turks'.[126] His determination had faced Granville and the ambassadors at Constantinople with the prospect of an awkward deadlock, and he did not feel that either he or his government was sufficiently committed to the demand for Crete to be obliged to insist on it any longer. Turkey's decision appears, at first sight, more difficult to explain. But her various offers, however inadequate they may have seemed to the powers and to the Greeks, prove that she had long reconciled herself to the necessity for some cession of territory, and the very restricted offers made by her up to 19 March were probably advanced in a bargaining spirit, on the simple tactical plan of bringing the price down by

[125] Granville to Goschen, 24 March, F.O. 78/3269, no. 220; 25 March, no. 224. G.D., *ibid.*, 26 March. Haymerle to Calice, 25 March, W.S.A., tel. no. 47; Széchényi to Haymerle, 26 March, tel. no. 45; Haymerle to Széchényi, 28 March, Depesche; Károlyi to Haymerle, 30 March, no. 33A–C, vertraulich. *D.D.F.*, iii, nos. 410, 411, 414; Beust to Haymerle, 28 March, W.S.A., tel. no. 35.

[126] Goschen to Granville, 27 March, F.O. 78/3276, no. 247. Cf. Paget to Granville, 29 March, F.O. 45/427, no. 119; Elliot to Granville, 29 March, F.O. 7/1014, no. 164. *Goschen*, i, 232–3.

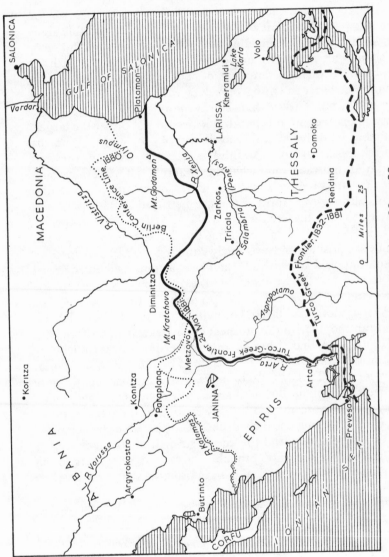

The Turco-Greek Frontier, 1880–1881

offering less than she was ultimately prepared to concede. Her offer of the 23rd, although an advance on those that had immediately preceded it, was still very far from meeting the proposals of the powers at Berlin in 1878 and 1880, and their prompt acceptance may merely prove that the Sultan had shown admirable judgment in choosing the right moment to impose his terms upon them. More probably, as such intelligent opportunism was foreign to the usual dogged or dilatory tactics of the Porte, we must look for the solution in some temporary panic; the Turkish delegates showed themselves decidedly uneasy at the determination of the ambassadors to draw up their own scheme, and the accession of the new Tsar, whose Panslavist sympathies caused alarm in other capitals than Constantinople, may have suggested that the moment was ill-suited for a voluntary acceptance of isolation.[127] An attempt to secure a promise of military support from the Khedive in the event of a Turco-Greek war had been met with an evasive reply from the Khedive's agent.[128]

The ambassadors' recommendations were accepted by all the powers during the next few days, and although the protests of the Greek government prevented much progress during April the question was at last satisfactorily disposed of, as far as the powers were concerned, in May. Immediately after receiving the news of the acceptance of the Turkish line by the ambassadors, the Greek government announced to several of the powers its inability to accept such a settlement; the replies were, however, uniformly firm and discouraging. Granville on 29 March left the Greek minister in no doubt that if the Greek government persisted they would have to fight the Turks single-handed;[129] Radowitz, on Bismarck's instructions, told the Greeks that the powers had considered it necessary to accept less than they had considered desirable, but the Greek government must not hope that any power could come to its assistance

[127] Elliot to Granville, 18 March, F.O. 7/1014, no. 138. Cf. Lhéritier, iv, 127. Windelband admits that in this case the Sultan's decision cannot be attributed to Bismarck's intervention: Hatzfeldt was as much in the dark as anyone (p. 216).
[128] Calice to Haymerle, 29 March, W.S.A., no. 21K.
[129] Granville to Corbett, 29 March, F.O. 32/527, no. 52. Cf. Granville to Gladstone, 29 March, G.D. 29/124 (Granville Papers); Gladstone to Granville, 28 March.

in the event of war. Giers sent similar instructions to Athens, and on 1 April, on hearing that the Greeks still believed that they could count on British assistance in the event of war, Granville instructed Corbett to make it clear not only to members of the ministerial party, but also to the opposition, that no such help could be expected.[130] The Greeks on the same day appealed to Rome to suspend all action at Athens until the Greek government had been able to pronounce upon the new line, but they were advised in reply to wait for the communication of the powers and to weigh very seriously the consequences of opposing reunited Europe. Nevertheless on 2 April a long memorandum was addressed to the powers setting out the objections of the Greek government to the new line.[131]

The powers now displayed almost excessive eagerness to secure the prompt agreement of the Greek government, feeling no doubt that if the latter were allowed to delay matters by negotiation the Turks would 'fly away from their present engagements'. Granville, however, failed to persuade Bismarck to take the lead; a request on 28 March for his opinion as to the best mode of procedure was meant as a hint that the Chancellor should take the initiative, but merely drew the reply that he preferred to receive first the suggestion of powers more directly interested, such as Great Britain herself. The refusal was taken in some quarters as evidence that the Chancellor was still annoyed at the departure from his original programme, and inclined in consequence to disbelieve in the success of the new course. He told a friend that the Turks would object to the Prevesa and Punta clause added by the ambassadors, and the Greeks would object altogether; the scheme could not be imposed on either country without coercive measures, and as the powers collectively had declined to resort to coercion, and singly would not break up the Concert, and as his advice in the matter had met with so little favour, he would merely give his moral support to what the powers most interested in Eastern

---

[130] Granville to Corbett, 1 April, F.O. 32/527, no. 57. Haymerle, circular tel., W.S.A., 31 March. Cf. Elliot to Haymerle, 27 March, W.S.A., private.

[131] Wimpffen to Haymerle, 1 April, W.S.A., tel. no. 28. The text of the Greek note is given by Lascaris, pp. 203–6. Cf. Wrede to Haymerle, 3 April, W.S.A., no. 14A–E.

affairs chose to do.[132] Saint-Hilaire suggested that as Bismarck was disposed to retire into the background, and France was at the moment *mal vu* and with little authority in Greece, it was desirable that England should take the lead. Granville, however, told Károlyi that it appeared better to apply united pressure, and all the powers then accepted Haymerle's proposal of 2 April that the ambassadors' line should be submitted in an identic note to the Greek government; they also accepted a further suggestion from Bismarck on the 4th that they should adopt the note which the ambassadors at Constantinople were drafting. As a result of this admirable display of promptitude the text of the note, together with authorization to sign and present it, had been received by all the representatives of the powers in Athens on 5 April.[133] They, however, took it upon themselves to place a quite unnecessary brake on this progress; after meeting under the chairmanship of Radowitz, as doyen, they despatched on the 6th an identic telegram to their governments proposing two or three slight verbal amendments, such as insertion of the word 'supreme' before 'decision of Europe'. The delay annoyed the powers, not merely because of the general desire for a speedy settlement, but because it had been considered advisable to have the note presented before the public excitement which the celebration of the declaration of independence on 6 April was expected to produce. Bismarck, in particular, was furious; after seeing his proposals abandoned first by the ambassadors at Constantinople and then by the powers, he was hardly in a mood to accept further checks from Athens. He described the identic telegram as mischievous and uncalled-for, and telegraphed to Radowitz ordering him to name at once the colleagues who had suggested the alterations; in reply Radowitz appears to have made the French and Russian ministers responsible. The national festival, however,

[132] Széchényi to Haymerle, 30 March, W.S.A., tel. no. 49; Károlyi to Haymerle, 2 April, W.S.A., tel. no. 21. Ampthill to Granville, 1 April, F.O. 64/981, no. 171, secret. *L.J.*, *Affaires de Grèce, 1880–1881*, no. 65.

[133] Károlyi to Haymerle, 2 April, W.S.A., tel. no. 21; Haymerle, 2 April, circular; Beust to Haymerle, 3 April, tel. no. 39; Kálnoky to Haymerle, 4 April, tel. no. 37; Széchényi to Haymerle, 4 April, tel. no. 50; Wimpffen to Haymerle, 4 April, tel. no. 30. In connexion with the latter cf. Granville to Gladstone, 3 April, G.D. 29/124 (Granville Papers). Oubril to Haymerle, 4 April, W.S.A., note. *Goschen*, i, 234–5.

went off quite quietly, and the note was presented on 7 April.[134]

The note placed the Greek premier in an extremely unhappy and difficult position. Active preparations for war were still being made; the fortification of the principal points likely to be attacked by land or sea was being hurried on, and additional troops were sent from Athens to the frontier.[135] Demands for a negative reply came not merely from the opposition, with Tricoupis at its head, but also from the prime minister's own followers; even inside the cabinet there was a natural reluctance to incur the odium of a full and unequivocal acceptance. The official representations of the agents of the powers were, however, reinforced by strong personal pressure on the King of Greece by the Tsar and the German Crown Prince, and Coumoundouros' reply to the identic note on 12 April was, in spite of careful vagueness, regarded as a surrender.[136] The reply emphasized the difference between the Berlin line and the new one, 'the points of which do not offer, generally, any security, and are wanting in all natural defensive capabilities'. Past experience would certainly not encourage the Greek government to believe that her acceptance would advance the question and ensure its full, sincere, and pacific solution. Greece desired peace; she would therefore hasten to enter into possession of the territories which had fallen to her, but she considered it neither dignified nor generous on her part to see her children who were left outside the new frontier, and whose rights Europe recognized solemnly at Berlin, abandoned to their present lot. She consequently hoped that the Great Powers would take into their serious consideration this appeal to their pity. Although the note allowed the government to argue that the new frontier had not been definitely accepted, and in any case was only to be accepted as an instalment, it

[134] Calice to Haymerle, 4 April, W.S.A., tel.; Széchényi to Haymerle, 7 April, tels. nos. 55, 67; Wrede to Haymerle, 7 April, tel. Ampthill to Granville, 7 April, F.O. 64/981, nos. 187, 188, secret. *Radowitz*, ii, 175–7. *L.J.*, nos. 93, 94.

[135] *Radowitz*, ii, 174–5, 178; cf. Gladstone to Granville, 5 April. G.D., 29/124 (Granville Papers).

[136] Ampthill to Granville, 10 April, F.O. 64/981, no. 195, secret. *Moüy*, pp. 179–80. Cf. Gladstone's comments to Granville, 15 April, G.D. 29/124 (Granville Papers).

produced a storm in the Athens press, and Coumoundouros explained to the agents of the powers that the government had found it difficult to give a more precise reply without endangering the dynasty and the internal tranquillity of Greece, and hoped that the powers would not demand a more specific answer.[137]

A little ingenuity on the part of the ambassadors at Constantinople, and considerable courage on the part of Coumoundouros, allowed a satisfactory settlement to be reached on this basis. The ambassadors drew up notes to the Greek and Turkish governments recommending the acceptance of the new frontier line, and decided, after considerable debate, that any statement pledging the powers to any action with regard to the 'children' beyond the new frontier would be either too vague or too dangerous and had better be omitted altogether. On the other hand the powers were pledged to make themselves responsible for the 'prompt and pacific' execution of the award. When the note was presented to Coumoundouros on 20 April he merely observed that it contained no reference to the Epirotes excluded by the new frontier line; this and the appointment of a new Greek *chargé d'affaires* at Constantinople appeared for a moment to foreshadow a demand by the Greeks for fresh concessions.[138] All the powers in the meantime had authorized their representatives at Athens to give a vague assurance that they would 'interest themselves' in the fate of the Christian population outside the new Greek frontier line; Radowitz as doyen was therefore able on the 27th to give this assurance to Coumoundouros, and to persuade the prime minister to abandon the idea of replying to the note of 19 April. This undertaking was given with reluctance, but as the note had assumed the acceptance by the Greek government of the new frontier his promise represented Greece's final agreement. The Turks had delayed their reply until the intentions of the Greeks had been made clear, but they too announced their final concurrence on 2 May.[139] The Greek minister, Con-

[137] Haymerle, W.S.A., circular tel., 13 April; Wrede to Haymerle, 17 April, no. 17A–C; *Radowitz*, ii, 179–80.

[138] *D.D.F.*, iii, nos. 463, 464, 466. Cf. Dilke's remarks, to Granville and Gladstone, 5 April, G.D. 29/124 (Granville Papers); *Goschen*, i, 238.

[139] *Radowitz*, ii, 171–2; *D.D.F.*, iii, 472–3, no. 496; *Goschen*, ii, 238–9.

douriotis, returned to his post at Constantinople on 4 May, and the details of the settlement were worked out there during May; the last of the Turks were evacuated in November.[140]

[140] Swaine, *op. cit.*, pp. 128–39. The work of the delimitation commission, and the situation in Greece immediately after the settlement, is discussed by Lhéritier, iv, 146–57.

CHAPTER IX

The Three Emperors' Alliance

1. THE RUSSO-GERMAN DRAFT

IN the last chapter we saw the extent of Bismarck's control of
the Concert in the Greek question: although the Constantinople ambassadors had proved annoyingly unresponsive in March 1881 he had been able by his exertions in
February to frustrate the development of a fresh coercion crisis
similar to the Dulcigno-Smyrna imbroglio. He was as conscious
as ever of Gladstone as the danger to his plans, and was paying
lip service to the Concert idea in order to render it innocuous.
By thus preventing another coercion problem he was making
possible the progress of the alliance discussions between the
three empires, which had been virtually at a standstill for three
months after the Friedrichsruh meeting in September 1880. We
can now follow the negotiations until the signing of the treaty
on 18 June 1881.

Haymerle's stipulation in October 1880 that the alliance discussions should not begin until the 'present phase' of European
action in Turkey had been concluded[1] had the effect of leaving
the drawing-up of the first draft of the treaty in the hands of
Bismarck and Saburov. In speaking of the present phase Haymerle was probably referring only to the Montenegrin discussions, but he made the meeting of the Delegations in November a further reason for delay. The Delegations dispersed,
however, without any embarrassing questions being put to the
minister, although in Budapest he would appear to have been
strengthened in his suspicions of Russia by Andrássy. He again
asked that the opening of negotiations should be postponed.[2]
Bismarck took him at his word, and in the middle of December

[1] See above, p. 188.
[2] Windelband, pp. 194–5; *G.P.*, iii, no. 520.

Haymerle began to show uneasiness over the schemes that the wily Saburov might be devising behind his back. He certainly had some reason for these qualms. Although the delay had given him time to accustom himself to the distasteful idea of agreement with Russia it also left him in the embarrassing position of having to wrestle with Bismarck in later efforts to modify clauses in which Russia appeared to be unduly favoured.

The Russians for their part were prepared to proceed with the negotiations, although considerable suspicion of Bismarck and the Austrians remained, and there was little disposition in St. Petersburg to follow Saburov in his almost lyrical acceptance of Bismarck's assurances. Saburov's optimism was strengthened by conversations with Radowitz during a short visit to Paris in the second half of October 1880, and by a further conversation with the German diplomat after the latter had seen Bismarck at Friedrichsruh on 8 November. Radowitz had told him (quite untruthfully) that he had 'found Bismarck completely won over again to his old sympathies for Russia'. Jomini continued gloomily to argue the case for isolation; Austria was spreading her net over Serbia and the Danube, Bismarck was the 'Minotaur', alliance must entrap Russia into some degree of acquiescence in the schemes of her disloyal and crafty neighbours. To this Saburov was able to reply that Austria's expansive policy was an evil which would correct itself, because of the hatred it would arouse in the Balkans; Russia was only asked at this stage not to adopt a hostile policy towards Austria in Serbia, and this fitted in with the government's desire to put an end for the time being to the contest with Austria. 'Since we are flanked by a great Germany, it is probable that we can only live beside her either as allies or as enemies', he wrote on 23 November. 'There is no middle course; or else it is a middle course in which one could only learn to maintain oneself by miracles of balancing, as on the blade of a knife.' Certainly isolation would be less dangerous while Gladstone's ministry lasted, but Gladstone was 'only a shining meteor—a meteor which will pass'. Saburov could afford to challenge Jomini's presentation of the now discredited Gorchakov policy of non-commitment, for Giers had, in two letters of 26 October, already enabled him to recommence the confidential discussions with Bismarck, on the basis of the treaty draft of the previous February. [3]

Bismarck's intervention at Constantinople early in October over the Montenegrin deadlock had perhaps been due to an exaggerated estimate of the readiness of the London and St. Petersburg cabinets for forcible measures of coercion, either in collaboration or alone. [4] He could see a change of front but little sign of a permanent change of heart in St. Petersburg, and he felt that Giers too was a meteor—if not a very shining one—which might soon pass. His pessimism as to the future arose from his innermost conviction that after the phase of quiescence which Russia now clearly desired she would resume an aggressive rôle, and that this would either lead to a quarrel with Germany (here Miljutin's army programme seemed ominous), or to renewed activity in the Danube Valley, the Balkans, the Straits, or Asiatic Turkey which could produce a breach with Austria unless he could perform the difficult feat of devising spheres of influence which would satisfy both. A despatch from Schweinitz on 5 December 1880 was reassuring on the immediate prospects, but Bismarck's marginal comments show his continued uneasiness as to the permanent trends of Russian policy. Giers had just returned (on 3 December) with the Emperor from Livadia, and on the 5th, in his first conversation with the German ambassador since August, spoke of the satisfactory results of the Friedrichsruh meeting between Haymerle and Bismarck, concluding with the perhaps not very tactful comment that Bismarck's mistrust towards Russian policy, 'which was so pronounced last year, appears to have vanished'. Schweinitz retorted that this was not the case; distrust was still strong and would last as long as the perpetual increases in the Russian army organization continued. Giers did not appear to take this amiss; he took advantage of the opening to speak fully about the policy which he was following with the full agreement of the Emperor and, he believed, the unreserved support of the Minister of War. 'Alliance with Germany was the only one possible; relations with Austria could be moderated (*temperirt*) only through us; an alliance with England was out of the

---

[3] *Saburov*, pp. 160–2, 165–7; see p. 38 above.
[4] See above, p. 163.

question; Russia to be sure wished to take advantage of the opportunities offered by her present relations with that country, but that was a transitory situation; the permanent consideration was the alliance with Germany.' Giers went on to say that Miljutin shared this conviction with him. 'Dies glaube ich nicht' was Bismarck's comment on the margin of the despatch. Giers said that everything that Miljutin had undertaken arose from his fear ('glaube ich auch nicht' commented Bismarck) that Russia would be lost if she were attacked by both Germany and Austria. Giers said that earlier, when Gorchakov still exercized influence over Russian foreign policy, there were sharp differences between the Chancellor and the Minister of War over the course of foreign affairs: 'wer von beiden war *für* uns? wohl beide nicht, aber G. noch eher, weil er klüger ist', was Bismarck's comment. He was presumably therefore not convinced by Giers' further assertion that he and Miljutin had reached complete agreement in the spring, and to Giers' statement that Miljutin had no thought of an understanding with France, commented: 'weil da nichts zu holen ist als Anarchie: sonst—'. To these assurances Schweinitz had simply remarked that Germany must base her judgment on the facts, which were that the War Minister was creating with heavy sacrifices an overmighty war machine, which in the wrong hands would be a menace to her neighbours.[5]

But even Schweinitz felt that Bismarck's apprehensions over Miljutin were exaggerated. At the end of November the Tsar had agreed to a cut of 40,000,000 roubles in the military budget on the proposal of the new Finance Minister, Abaza.[6] Giers told Werder that the solution of the Dulcigno question had been a matter of honour and sentiment for the Tsar, who in all the other outstanding questions in the Balkan peninsula would go along with the other powers.[7] On 5 December he told Schweinitz specifically that the maintenance of Turkey in its present strength was in accordance with the wishes and interests of Russia; in Bulgaria, Eastern Rumelia, and Macedonia, Russian

---

[5] Schweinitz to Bismarck, 5 December 1880 (Abschrift), no. 377, A. A. Russland, no. 61.

[6] Windelband, pp. 195–6.

[7] Von Werder to Emperor, 8 December 1880, no. 34, A. A. Russland, no. 61.

agents had been instructed accordingly; suspicion directed against these agents in Vienna could with greater justice be applied to the Austrian agents.[8] All this was reassuring, and although Bismarck's doubts were not removed he kept them to himself. He continued to grumble to Saburov and others about Gladstone, and the Russian ambassador echoed these criticisms, without quite realizing the extent to which they could be applied to his own country's conduct. The best exposition of Bismarck's point of view at this critical stage in the alliance negotiations is contained in his masterly instructions of 7 November to Radowitz, which have already been summarized in Chapter VIII.[9] This document showed exaggerated alarm at the possibilities of Panslavism with its revolutionary aims; less alarm at the prospect of Russian expansion at Turkey's expense; and a belief that the Anglo-Russian co-operation against Turkey would dissolve itself as a result of natural incompatibilities, but that it was nevertheless unwise, even for this reason, to favour it, owing to the probability that Austria would take alarm and interfere too soon. What is significant about this exposition is its automatic acceptance of responsibility for Austria's position, in spite of his pretence to Saburov of a mediatory position.

Giers set out Russia's requirements in two letters of 26 October,[10] and the substance of these was communicated by Saburov to Bismarck, apparently on 13 November. The ambassador explained to Limburg-Stirum that Russia's position in the East 'had more points of contact with Austria, since the last war, than was formerly the case', and that the difficulty of acting in concert with Austria was correspondingly increased; as Russia desired to go in agreement with Germany it was up to Bismarck to come to Russia's assistance in those matters which were at the moment threatening to cause disagreement. These matters were the treaty of commerce with Serbia; the Danube; the Bulgarian railways. Two days later Limburg-Stirum was

[8] Schweinitz to Bismarck, 5 December 1880, no. 377, *ibid.*
[9] See above, pp. 192–4.
[10] Referred to in Saburov's letter of 1/13 November as of '14 October' (i.e. O.S.), and as having been 'at last received'. There is a reference on p. 167 to 'your letter of 24th October'. This is apparently the same letter or letters from Giers (*Saburov*, pp. 163–7).

able to say that Bismarck had received the Russian communications in the most friendly spirit, and had promised to use every effort to remove the causes of friction in the East. He hinted that Russia might look for more far-reaching advantages although it would be necessary to take account of the interests of Austria, where those interests were just. This confirmed Saburov's most sanguine estimate of the situation: two days before he had told Giers that on two occasions Bismarck had said, 'I do not share the prejudices of the other Cabinets on the subject of the danger of giving up Constantinople to Russia', and that although the immediate purpose of the alliance would be to secure a breathing space, 'we know sufficient to be able to judge of the scope that the Triple Entente holds in store for us'.[11] Further confirmation appeared to come later in the month from Odo Russell, who had been assured by Bismarck that it was his desire to reconcile the interests of Russia and Austria, and to support very fully the interests that Russia possessed in the Eastern question.[12]

Saburov again received assurances of Bismarck's friendly intentions in conversations at Friedrichsruh on 9 and 10 December.[13] The Chancellor gave some additional details of his conversations with Haymerle in September, and in reply to a question gave his opinion that the latter was not trying to evade pourparlers, although he would never take the initiative in them. He was not dishonest, but 'he is timid; he is not accustomed to high politics; he fears responsibilities'. When Saburov, in the hope of securing more information about the Austro-German alliance, suggested that Haymerle's plan was perhaps to postpone negotiations indefinitely in the belief that the alliance protected Austria-Hungary adequately, Bismarck replied, 'with a certain animation', that Austria would be much

[11] *Saburov*, pp. 165–6. Cf. conversation with Odo Russell, p. 169.

[12] According to Saburov, Odo Russell said to him one day, 'The only man in the world who has inspired respect in Bismarck is the Emperor Alexander' (*ibid.*, p. 170). For Bismarck's real feelings towards the Tsar at this time see *Schweinitz*, ii, 135–7. Schweinitz recalls Bismarck's instructions 'den Kaiser Alexander wie einen älteren preussischen General oder wie eine nervöse Dame zu behandeln'.

[13] Windelband (p. 223) refers to these discussions as having taken place on 27, 28 November, the dates given by Saburov (*op. cit.*, p. 171). This is, however, the O.S. date: Saburov's own account (p. 167), shows that he was in Berlin on 28 November.

mistaken if she thought herself completely protected by Germany. 'Our interest orders us not to let Austria be *destroyed*, but she is not guaranteed against an attack.' Saburov did not succeed in extracting any more precise information, and could only guess that Germany was not unconditionally bound by an offensive and defensive alliance.[14] It is evident that he was content to accept Bismarck's willingness to enter a triple alliance as the best proof that the Austro-German alliance was not necessarily inimical to the interests of his country.

Saburov felt that the moment had come for further consideration of the text of the draft treaty which had received the favourable annotations of the Russian Emperor in the previous February.[15] Bismarck gave tactful signs of lively satisfaction at the sight of the Emperor's handwriting, and readily accepted the Russian amendments to the original draft; Saburov in turn accepted provisionally certain changes. The most important of these was an addition to the second article, designed to meet Haymerle's uneasiness at the prospect of a Russian invasion of Rumania. Saburov objected that Russia felt similar concern at the prospect of an Austrian invasion of Serbia, and a paragraph was drafted providing that none of the three powers should send troops into Rumania, Serbia, Montenegro, or Turkey-in-Europe without concerted agreement with the other two. In addition the whole emphasis of the proposed treaty was changed by the bringing forward of the third article, which had concerned the general relations of the powers, to the first place, and the addition to it of an opening paragraph providing for mediation by the third power if a difference should arise between the remaining two.

It was finally agreed that Saburov should take the draft to St. Petersburg for his government's decision, and that the Grand-Duke of Saxe-Weimar should be suggested to the Tsar as an intermediary between the German and Russian Emperors and the Austrian Emperor. To the latter suggestion the Tsar appears to have agreed without hesitation, although it was to cause difficulties in Vienna.[16] Saburov was back in Berlin at

[14] *Saburov*, p. 173.   [15] *G.P.*, iii, nos. 516, 517; p. 38 above.
[16] Saburov apparently left for St. Petersburg on 18 December (Széchényi to Haymerle, 16 December, Bericht no. 131, W.S.A., G.III). For the Tsar's comments on the Friedrichsruh discussions: *Schweinitz*, ii, 137–8.

the beginning of January 1881, but further discussions with Bismarck were necessary before the draft treaty was ready for presentation to the Austrians.

In the meantime the renewed Russo-German discussions, in which he had not yet been invited to share, were causing Haymerle some uneasiness. Reuss visited Friedrichsruh after Saburov's interviews with Bismarck on 9–10 December, and was shown the draft agreement, but was not allowed to speak of it to the rather apprehensive Austrians. It was apparently arranged at this time that he should go to Weimar to inform his father-in-law, the Grand-Duke of Saxe-Weimar, of the proposal that the latter should act as intermediary in the negotiations. He could only say to Széchényi, who managed to see him after his return from Friedrichsruh, that Bismarck continued to be taken up with the idea of an Austro-Russian understanding, and was seeking a formula which would make such an understanding possible without infringing Austrian interests. The Russians, said Reuss, 'desire nothing more ardently than an understanding with Austria-Hungary, and Saburov had recently expressed himself repeatedly in this sense at Friedrichsruh, but they can make no headway with you'. These platitudes gave little comfort. Széchényi retorted that Austria had had many experiences in recent years which accounted for the not inconsiderable distrust of Russia which she now felt, and Reuss replied with a smile that this could in the circumstances be understood. Széchényi was further tantalized by the fact that although he and Saburov exchanged calls without seeing each other, the Russian ambassador did not make any pretence of wishing to seek out his Austrian colleague. When they did meet Saburov would only say that Bismarck had expressed his desire to maintain the European Concert, but had said that if one or other of the powers was driven to coercive measures he would no longer co-operate. To this Saburov had replied that in no circumstances would this power be Russia.[17]

When Reuss returned to Vienna he was plied with questions by Haymerle and was very much embarrassed by his inability to give a plain answer. He seems, however, to have spoken more

[17] Széchényi to Haymerle, 15 December 1880, tel. no. 193; 16 December, Bericht no. 131, W.S.A., G.III.

openly than he admitted in his official reports, and he pointed out to Bismarck the extremely false position he would be in if the scheme for bringing the Grand Duke into the negotiations were carried out without Haymerle's knowledge.[18] On 18 December he tried to persuade Haymerle that the negotiations had been suspended only owing to the desire of the Vienna cabinet and that nothing had occurred in the meantime to draw new declarations from St. Petersburg, but that Bismarck was anxious now to take up the matter again and to know Haymerle's opinion.[19] The latter showed little satisfaction with this statement, but clearly found it difficult to frame an answer which would be sufficiently favourable to the alliance project to draw forth further information, and sufficiently non-committal to express his own genuine doubts and tactical reservations. He admitted that it was no doubt in the interests of Austria-Hungary to maintain good relations with Russia, and said that he did not wish to depart from the bases agreed on at Friedrichsruh in September. But he qualified this by saying that since the negotiations commenced Russia had not given evidence of any spirit of conciliation; Russian agents were opposing Austrian interests in every quarter.[20] As Reuss remarked to Bismarck, Haymerle feared any form of link with Russia, by whom he felt certain to be deceived; his confidence that Bismarck would not agree to anything hostile to Austrian interests alone reconciled him to the idea of alliance. Bismarck in reply elaborated the argument that Austria would have less to fear if the Russian government were bound by a treaty than she would if its hands were free, and he asked whether Russia on her side had not some justification for her suspicion of Austrian

[18] *Saburov*, p. 184.

[19] According to Haymerle's account of this conversation, Reuss went much further, and said that Saburov would use his visit to St. Petersburg, 'um sich über die Grundlagen einer solchen Entente eingehend zu informiren und deren Zustandekommen nach Möglichkeit zu fördern. . . . Nach der Rückkehr Saburov's aus Petersburg schiene es dem Fürsten an der Zeit, die Wiederaufnahme des pourparlers zu versuchen.' (W.S.A. Aufzeichnungen über eine Unterredung mit Prinz Reuss am 18 Dezember 1880.)

[20] Haymerle said, 'Die russischen Agenten aber scheinen durchwegs nach *Einer* Richtschnur zu handeln, "Tritt auf gegen Alles, was Oesterreich will, sei es begründet in dem Buchstaben des Gesetzes und des Traktats, in natürlichen Interessen oder in der politischen Lage".' *Ibid.*

policy in the Balkans. He was still unable to give Reuss permission to mention the Russian propositions.[21]

Haymerle had a far clearer idea as to what he wanted than the Germans appear to have thought;[22] he set out the Austrian programme in a memorandum drawn up primarily for Kálnoky's guidance in future conversations at St. Petersburg, and the document is of considerable importance, as a statement of Austria's maximum demands. It will be examined in the next section. Kálnoky took this memorandum with him to St. Petersburg on his return from leave, and had an interview with Giers on 29 December, but his government had still to wait for nearly another three weeks before the secret was revealed. Giers, however, did his best to prepare the ground by assurances of Russia's peaceful intentions; he said that she desired to see the *status quo* maintained as long as possible in the Balkans, where the new states had, on the whole, been given favourable conditions of existence by the Berlin treaty, and he went so far as to recognize that the maintenance of Turkish power on the Bosphorus for a longer period was very desirable. Russia also, he said, greatly desired peace owing to her internal situation. Kálnoky was satisfied that during his two-months' absence the peaceful and conciliatory tone in St. Petersburg had been maintained and seemed on all sides to be increasingly strongly expressed.[23] He also saw Saburov, who, over-acting as usual, tried to deny that his visit to Friedrichsruh had any special significance: he said that his position was the same as that of Odo Russell, who had sought an interview with Bismarck because he was ashamed to return to England on leave without having seen the leading statesman of the German Reich for six months.[24] Széchényi, who saw Saburov in Berlin on 11 January 1881, was likewise puzzled by the Russian ambassador's

[21] Bismarck to Reuss, 22 December 1880. *G.P.*, iii, no. 521. Bismarck's comments in this despatch on the working of the treaty system (p. 152) are worth noting.

[22] Reuss's remark on 25 December, that Haymerle's proposals 'sind genauer präzisiert als seine damaligen mündlichen Auslassungen' (*G.P.*, iii, p. 154) probably refers to Bismarck's report on the Friedrichsruh meeting in September, where, as suggested above, Haymerle's attitude was misunderstood by Bismarck.

[23] Kálnoky to Haymerle, 29 December/10 January, 1881, W.S.A., G.III, no. 1A–D.

[24] *Ibid.*, no. 1B, *Geheim*.

transparent and apparently unnecessary reticences.[25] A few days later, however, Russo-German agreement was reached and Haymerle could at last be brought into the discussions.

The modifications proposed by the Russian government had been mainly intended to increase its freedom of action in the Balkans, and Bismarck had therefore been concerned, not to defend German interests, but to decide how much he could persuade Austria to accept. One modification was, however, due directly to suspicion of Bismarck; Saburov was instructed by his government to ask that in the second paragraph of Article I the reference to war by any of the parties 'with a fourth power', should be altered to, 'with a fourth great power'. This was in order that Russia should not be bound to neutrality if Germany attacked a small state, such as Denmark or Holland. But in the discussions which now followed in Berlin Saburov decided to adhere to the original wording, for Bismarck proved willing to accept considerable alterations in the first article, and to apply its stipulations to the contingency of a Russo-Turkish war. Saburov argued that the provision whereby, if one of the signatories found itself at war with a fourth power, the other two should see to the localizing of the conflict, would work out unfairly for Russia if Turkey were not included among the possible fourth powers. It would mean that Russia would have to give material assistance if England or Italy supported France in the event of a Franco-German war, or if England or France supported Italy in an Austro-Italian war. Where was the advantage for Russia if a Russo-Turkish war were excluded from the provision? 'With England we can be at war only as a result of a conflict with Turkey. You will prevent France or Italy from joining England, well and good; but already we shall have two enemies on our hands.' Moreover according to Article II, Russia could enter the war only after a preliminary entente with Austria concerning the result of the war; accordingly 'we shall engage in battle with Turkey and with England while it is Austria who benefits with folded arms, and without risking anything if we are beaten!' Bismarck agreed that Russia could not be expected to be the only one to bear all the costs

[25] Széchényi to Haymerle, 15 January 1881, W.S.A., G.III, no. 5; also private letter of same date; Haymerle to Széchényi, *Privat-schreiben*, 19 January, *ibid.*

and sacrifices of a joint programme with Austria, and to Saburov's great satisfaction agreed to the inclusion of Turkey among the Powers envisaged by Article I.

Article II provided greater difficulties. Saburov had to tell Bismarck that it was repugnant to the Russian Emperor to contract an unconditional engagement as to non-intervention in Turkey, and that his government therefore proposed an addition allowing the armed intervention of one of the powers 'if the political *status quo* guaranteed to certain provinces of Turkey happened to be endangered'. Although Bismarck professed himself fully satisfied that Russia would regard this as merely a 'precaution for the future', he was compelled to insist that the addition would arouse insurmountable opposition and distrust in Vienna, and when Saburov in turn insisted that he could not give up the point, it was decided, on Bismarck's suggestion, to suppress altogether the amendment concerning the non-entry of troops into Rumania, Serbia, Montenegro, and Turkey-in-Europe. He accepted however an additional paragraph providing for the exchange of written communications on the points (such as the union of the two Bulgarias) which had already been established in principle.[26] On 13 January Saburov received a telegram from St. Petersburg announcing the Tsar's acceptance of the amended draft, and a few days later the project was forwarded to Vienna.[27]

RUSSO-GERMAN DRAFT[28]

I

Les trois Cours de Russie, d'Allemagne et d'Autriche-Hongrie se promettent que si un différend ou un grief venait à surgir entre deux d'entre Elles, ce différend serait déféré à la médiation de la troisième, pour être ensuite aplani par un accord à trois.

Dans le cas où l'une d'Elles se trouverait forcée d'être en guerre avec une quatrième Puissance, les deux autres maintiendront à son égard une neutralité bienveillante et veilleront à la localisation du conflit.

---

[26] *Saburov*, pp. 179–83.

[27] Saburov to Bismarck, 21 January 1881, A.A., Russland, no. 61.

[28] This is the text sent to Vienna; it is printed in *G.P.*, iii, pp. 163–5, with the alternative version of Article I discussed by Bismarck and Saburov. The Russian text given by Saburov (pp. 262–5) has some inessential differences: in particular, para. 3 of Article II appears in a slightly different form as paragraph 3 of Article I.

Pour le cas spécial où l'une d'Elles obtiendrait de l'un de ses deux Alliés un concours plus positif, la valeur obligatoire du présent article restera dans sa vigueur pour la troisième.

II

La Russie, d'accord avec l'Allemagne, déclare sa ferme résolution de respecter les intérêts qui découlent de la nouvelle position assurée à l'Autriche par le Traité de Berlin et définie en dernier lieu par sa convention avec la Turquie au sujet de l'occupation de certaines parties du territoire Ottoman.

Les trois Cours, désireuses d'éviter tout désaccord entre Elles, s'engagent à tenir compte de leurs intérêts respectifs dans la Péninsule des Balcans. Elles se promettent, de plus, que de nouvelles modifications dans le statu quo territorial de la Turquie d'Europe ne pourront s'accomplir qu'en vertu d'un commun accord entre Elles.

Si l'une des Puissances se croyait forcée de faire la guerre à la Turquie, Elle se concerterait préalablement avec les deux autres sur les résultats éventuels de cette guerre.

Afin de faciliter l'accord prévu par le présent article, accord dont il est impossible de prévoir d'avance toutes les modalités, les trois Cours constateront, dès à présent, dans des communications confidentielles entre Elles, les points sur lesquels une entente a déjà été établie en principe.

III

Les trois Cours reconnaissent le caractère européen et mutuellement obligatoire du principe de la fermeture des Détroits du Bosphore et des Dardanelles, fondé sur le Droit des Gens et confirmé par les Traités.

Elles veilleront en commun à ce que la Turquie ne fasse pas d'exception à cette règle en faveur des intérêts particuliers d'un Gouvernement quelconque, en prêtant à des opérations guerrières d'une Puissance belligérante la partie de son Empire que forment les Détroits.

En cas d'infraction, ou pour la prévenir si une pareille infraction était à prévoir, les trois Cours avertiront la Turquie qu'Elles la considéraient, le cas échéant, comme s'étant mise en état de guerre vis-à-vis de la Partie lésée, et comme s'étant privée dès lors des bénéfices de sécurité, assurés par le Traité de Berlin à son statu quo territorial.

II. The Unavowed Aims

It will be seen that while this draft satisfied Germany's major interests, it covered only the minimum Austrian and Russian requirements in the Balkans. It meant that Germany could fight, and, indeed, attack, France without interference from Russia. Russia could not attack Austria. Russia was only too glad to give Bismarck this assurance: it seemed that his strange behaviour towards her in the recent past had been due to apprehensions caused by her more or less frivolous gestures of friendship to France, and that he might be again the friend of old if these apprehensions were removed. There were advantages, too, apart from the appeasement of the German Chancellor, in patching up some temporary *modus vivendi* with Austria. Nevertheless, the Russians were bound to ask themselves whether they could secure greater advantages in the immediate negotiations, and also whether their hopes of gaining more in the future would be facilitated by the agreement. Austria too was bound to ask herself whether the agreement would open the way to future gains, and she had also to ask whether it would not be safer to refuse the agreement altogether.

Accordingly, while the Russian and Austrian governments were viewing each other's minimum requirements in the Balkans with apparent uneasiness they were both speculating about future possibilities, and we have sufficient documentary evidence to be able to define the more ambitious Austrian and Russian plans in some detail. It will be useful to examine them at this point before resuming the story of the negotiations.

Austria's problem was to hold and develop the advantages that she had gained in the Balkan peninsula since 1878, and it was by no means certain that any compromise plan, such as division of the peninsula into spheres of influence, would not involve greater concessions to Russia than she was prepared to contemplate. She had, as we have seen, [29] greatly extended her political, economic, and to some extent territorial control since 1878, and this influence could be threatened at numerous points by Russian official hostility backing an active Panslavist programme by local agents: Rumanian resistance over the Danube and other questions, Bulgarian resistance over the railways, Bulgarian acquisitions in Macedonia, Serbian resistance to Austrian commercial terms, and so on. With the October treaty protecting her against military attack, would she not gain more

[29] See above, pp. 46–9.

by openly challenging Russian influence than by a policy of bargaining which would involve reciprocal concessions?

Haymerle, in fact, had little to offer Russia. Everywhere, he asserted, the Russian agents were opposing Austrian plans and interests: would Russia show her peaceful intentions by reversing these activities? This was really a rather peevish demand for the concession of Austrian predominance in the peninsula. It was on these lines that he spoke at length to Reuss on 18 December. He need cite, he said, only the questions of the Bulgarian railways, the Danube, and the treaty of commerce with Serbia (where Russia was in his view responsible for Serbian procrastination). In the Montenegrin question Russia had not been far from wishing to compensate Montenegro at the expense of Austria.[30] That Russian influence was stronger in the Balkan peninsula than Austria's was regrettable, but unavoidable; Russia, however, should not use her influence solely to create difficulties for Austria. If Russia wanted a free hand in the north-east part of the peninsula she ought to leave freedom of action to Austria in the south-west, and moreover if territorial changes had to take place in the Balkans she should not take every means to ensure that Austria gained fresh enemies in the process.[31]

Bismarck called Saburov's attention to this passing reference to a division of spheres, but Haymerle was very far from being willing to give Russia a free hand even in the 'north-eastern' portion of the peninsula. His agreement to Bulgarian unification was very far from being a recognition of Russia's right to paramount influence there. This comes out clearly in the full statement of his requirements which he drew up for Kálnoky before the latter's return to St. Petersburg.[32] Austria, wrote Haymerle, would not oppose the union of Bulgaria and Eastern Rumelia, and would not encourage the Porte to exercise its right to occupy the Balkan mountains, provided that (1) the union should be accomplished without pressure or help from abroad, (2) it should not overstep the frontiers of Bulgaria and Eastern Rumelia, and in particular Macedonia and the

---

[30] This is apparently a reference to Giers' suggestion in May: see p. 81 above. Bismarck denied knowledge of this incident (*G.P.*, iii, no. 520, n. 3).

[31] *G.P.*, iii, p. 149.   [32] See above, p. 250.

Vardar valley should remain undisturbed, and (3) no positive act forwarding the union and no pronouncement weakening the Berlin treaty should be demanded of Austria. He then set out seven concrete stipulations. (1) The Russian government must delay the proclamation of the union as long as possible, and at least until the completion of the razing of the Danube fortresses. (2) In order to establish clearly the character of the movement as the product solely of local relations and to justify the passivity of the Austrian government before public opinion by reference to the 'force of events', but above all in order to achieve the essential aim of an understanding, namely the avoidance of war as a result of the Bulgarian question, the Russian government should undertake to refrain from any armed intervention in the event of Turkish opposition to the union. There must be no Turkish encroachment on Bulgaria, nor any alteration by Turkey of the Berlin Congress arrangements. (3) If the movement extended to Macedonia the Porte should exercise a free hand, and Austria-Hungary and Russia would agree not to intervene diplomatically against the Porte, and not to hinder it in the securing of its possessions. (4) The new Bulgaria should be given a new constitution, which would strengthen the power of the sovereign. The title of 'King' was to be regarded as excluded. (5) Frontier rectification in favour of Serbia and Rumania, to protect these states against the increased strength of the new formation, should be contemplated. (6) The execution of Austrian claims concerning the railways, as well as the maintenance of Austrian commercial interests, should be undertaken by the prince for the whole of the new Bulgaria. (7) Russia should renew her earlier promises not to oppose, either actively or diplomatically, an annexation of Bosnia and the Hercegovina and of the Sandjak, and should in general undertake not to oppose the influence of Austria-Hungary in the western half of the Balkan peninsula. A final paragraph stated that Austria-Hungary would be inclined, after the completed union, to recognize the independence of the united Bulgarian territories, if at the same time every special influence on these lands of another state were expressly and legally excluded.[33]

---

[33] *Zugeständnisse.* Gf. Kálnoky mitgegeben als vertrauliche Andeutungen. 26 December 1880. W.S.A., G.III.

There can be no mistaking the implication of these last three paragraphs: unchallenged influence for Austria in the 'western half' of the Balkan peninsula, and no special advantage, political or economic, for Russia even in the new Bulgaria. The programme does not reveal fear of Russian hostility so much as an intense preoccupation with the possibility of unexampled gain for Austria, to be secured by the full utilization of Bismarck's friendship. Saburov was not far wrong when he remarked at the end of September 1880, 'there are unavowed ambitions [in Vienna] which betray themselves in spite of themselves, and which are the more dangerous in that they can find friendly support in Germany'.[34] And Bismarck himself was driven to comment on Haymerle's persistent grumbling to Reuss about the hostility of Russian agents towards Austrian interests: 'is it not also vice versa?'[35]

The Russian government's desire for quiescence, a postponement of crises, in the Balkans, was genuine; in that sense it was undoubtedly in a more accommodating mood than the Austrian. The repeated and explicit denials by the Russian government of the hostility to Austria of its agents in the Balkans were met in Vienna by the stock retort that Russian agents spoke with two voices; and no doubt there were some who more or less indiscreetly voiced the now traditional animosity. But the Serbs had no doubt that they had been left in the lurch: when Mijatović paid his first visit to the Russian minister in Belgrade and ventured to suggest the hope that Russia would not henceforth be a mother to Bulgaria and stepmother to Serbia, Persiani laughed at the suggestion that Russia should change her Balkan policy merely because Mijatović had accepted the portfolio of foreign affairs.[36] And where the duality of voices existed it was due far more to indecision than to duplicity, indecision in the mind of the Tsar which fostered hesitations and some indiscipline in the conduct of foreign affairs.

The Tsar's agreement in the spring of 1880 to enter the Three Emperors' Alliance was in one sense a sign of this indecision; it was a postponement not only of action but of the mental effort

[34] *Saburov*, p. 152. [35] *G.P.*, iii, p. 151—'nicht auch vice versa?'
[36] C. Mijatovich, *The Memoirs of a Balkan Diplomatist*, p. 36.

required to define and plan new courses of action. But Saburov, who greatly exaggerated his influence over Bismarck, was hopeful throughout that with Germany's help much more could be achieved at an early date. Bismarck, in the conversations of 9 and 10 December 1880 with Saburov, had referred to the possibility of a demarcation line between the Austrian and Russian spheres in the peninsula, and he read to Saburov on 10 January 1881 portions of Reuss's despatch of 18 December, including Haymerle's reference to a line running from south-west to north-east. In reporting this to Giers on 10 January 1881 Saburov appears to have given it far more importance than it deserved, and to have represented it as a positive offer from Haymerle, which Bismarck supported.[37] As there was no response from Giers, Saburov returned to the charge on 4 February with a more explicit recommendation that his government should prepare for wider discussions. He wrote to Giers that, although elementary prudence forbade even the most tentative discussion of the broader aspects of the Near Eastern question before it was known whether Germany and Austria were prepared to talk on the subject, it nevertheless seemed expedient to him to make use of the negotiations that had already taken place 'pour faire un peu de lumière sur les dispositions éventuelles de l'Allemagne et de l'Autriche'. He had, he said, urged Bismarck to ask Haymerle to discuss these matters with Reuss, saying that every new point agreed would serve to perpetuate the alliance of the three emperors. Bismarck had given an encouraging reply, and promised to write to Reuss, advising him however not to mix the current negotiations with a discussion of the wider possibilities.[38]

---

[37] This is Skazkin's view; he quotes the relevant portion of Saburov's despatch (p. 150, n. 2). Haymerle's remark (see p. 255 above) far from being an offer of an amicable division of spheres was really a complaint that the Russians were not respecting Austria's position on the western side of the peninsula. Skazkin thinks that Saburov deliberately misrepresented Haymerle's statement in order to set on foot discussions about wider eventualities. Saburov's memoir (p. 187), also quotes a portion of Haymerle's statement as read by Bismarck from Reuss's despatch, but this differs from the version quoted by Skazkin from Saburov's despatch, and omits any suggestion that Haymerle favoured the allocation of spheres of influence. As this account was edited for publication it must be assumed that Saburov was concealing his attempt to urge the sphere-of-influence plan on his government.

[38] Skazkin, pp. 151–2.

Discussions about the adjustment of Austro-Russian interests in the Balkans could thus be conducted with three possible ends in view: either to agree on the minimum necessary to preserve the *status quo* for a few years, or to arrange for a division of interests in the peninsula in order to satisfy the broader interests of the two countries, or to plan a complete solution of the Near Eastern question, on the lines of the Reichstadt discussions of 1876 or the Tsar Nicholas's optimistic proposals about the Sick Man's heritage of 1853 and 1844. Bismarck, Giers, and Haymerle, each for his own reasons, saw only the first of these as within the range of practical politics, although the programme that Haymerle had elaborated for Kálnoky's instruction showed a desire to secure the advantages of the second, without compensating advantages for Russia. Haymerle shuddered away from the third.[39] Bismarck was certainly aware that nothing more than the first and most restricted programme had any chance of acceptance in Vienna, and there is no evidence in the German documents that he gave Saburov the encouraging reply that the latter claimed.[40] This must have been either an invention on Saburov's part, designed to push his government into further discussion, or a tactful remark by Bismarck, who would not wish to appear anything but receptive; it may be that he wished to see how far the Russians would go. He did not write to Reuss.

Saburov suggested to Giers in his letter of 4 February that a recent proposal by Miljutin would serve as a suitable basis for wider discussions with Haymerle. Miljutin's plan, set out in a note dated 5 November 1880, included the setting up of a Balkan confederation in which Austria-Hungary, by virtue of her connexion with Bosnia-Hercegovina, would participate. The plan, which had some mention in the Reichstadt discussions,[41] included a tariff union for the Balkan peninsula. It

[39] 'Wenn nun Österreich unter Voraussetzung einer solchen Umkehr bereit ist, in einen Meinungsaustausch mit Russland einzutreten, so glaubt der Minister, dass die Erörterung sich nicht auf die ganze Orientfrage, auf eine Regelung derselben für die ganze Zukunft, auf Spekulationen für einen Zusammenbruch der Türkei und eventuelle Teilungspläne zu erstrecken habe. In diesem Falle würden sich die Gegensätze so schroff zeigen, dass die Anbahnung eines guten Verhältnisses daran scheitern könnte.' Reuss to Bismarck, 25 December 1880, *G.P.*, iii, p. 154.

[40] Cf. Windelband, pp. 195–6.

[41] Cf. B. H. Sumner, *Russia and the Balkans, 1870–1880* (Oxford, 1937), p. 588.

was at first sight conciliatory to Austria and the confederation was not to include Russia. But Miljutin seems to have hoped that it would lead in due course to a strong Slav counter-balance to Austria and the ultimate loss of Bosnia and the Hercegovina, visualizing very much the course of events from 1912 onwards. Although he was strongly antagonistic to Austria he believed like Giers that an open struggle with her, and also the acquisition of the Straits, were outside the field of practical policies in the 1880's. Giers saw no need to hasten on a course which might very easily turn to Russia's disadvantage, and he saw indeed many objections to the plan. All this was unknown at this stage to Saburov, who took the copy of Miljutin's note, which had been sent to him, as evidence that his government was not unwilling to discuss the 'final' solution of the 'great question'. His proposal was a bold one. Austria should be offered participation in the Balkan confederation as proof of Russian goodwill, and should in return agree to Russian control of the Straits. He was almost certain of Bismarck's support, and of his help in persuading the Austrian government.[42]

Giers did not, as one might perhaps expect, instruct Saburov to abandon these dangerous speculations, although even Saburov had suggested that the agreement ought to be a verbal one, in order to reduce the danger that England would hear of it. Giers' position was too unsafe for him to reject out of hand a proposal that was so closely linked with Miljutin's plan, and that might well attract the Tsar. His reply to Saburov was cautious and non-committal: it would be difficult to embody such serious possibilities in a hypothetical form in an official agreement: Miljutin's note was not the only basis for an exchange of opinions, and was still under discussion: Miljutin's note was, however, based on the principles which underlay the Reichstadt agreement, and it was difficult to find any solution of the Eastern question that was so reasonable. He was opposed to a division of spheres in the peninsula, not through sympathy for Panslavism, 'dont les chimères ne se laissent pas analyser'

[42] Skazkin, p. 153. Schweinitz was convinced that Saburov had not thought out the implications of the Straits plan: he asked him whether he really thought that Austria would be willing to see Russian warships from Sebastopol in the 'harbour of Montenegro'. Saburov replied that he had certainly not thought of that (10 January 1881: *Schweinitz*, ii, 140).

but because of Austria's excessive demands. But he qualified
even this objection by allowing for a division of an informal
character, that would merely determine 'the frontiers within
which it would be possible to expand one's influence and work
for the furtherance of one's interests without having to encounter the distrust and opposition of others'. This cautious and
ambiguous letter was almost an invitation to Saburov to return
to the attack, which he did on 14 February, putting his plan
more explicitly and boldly than before. Saburov it is clear was
now prepared to sacrifice everything for the attainment of the
one great aim, Russian acquisition of the Straits; his advocacy
of the demarcation line was due to tactical considerations only,
and he was ready to hand over the Balkans to Austria (which
he assumed would be the result of Miljutin's proposal) if
Russia would secure in return 'the keys of her own house'. The
guarantees in clause III(i) of the Russo-German draft for the
closing of the Straits were excellent as far as they went, but
depended on the duration of the alliance; the only permanent
guarantee would be the actual control of the Straits. Constantinople should, according to Reichstadt, be a free city, but
this would not prevent Russia from securing possession of the
Bosphorus. He again advocated therefore the Balkan federation plan, with Austrian but without Russian participation, as
the bait to secure Austria's agreement to the Russian occupation of the Bosphorus. In a private letter to Giers on the same
day he advocated the creation of a secret committee to work
out plans for the seizure of the Straits.[43] The apparent strength
of Saburov's position is shown by the Tsar's comment on these
letters: 'je trouve ses idées très justes'.

This embarrassing situation brought Miljutin to Giers'
rescue. He sent a personal note to Giers recommending that not
even preliminary talks with Bismarck about the broader issues
should be commenced before the signature of the tripartite
agreement, and Giers drafted instructions to Saburov on this
basis. The Tsar, who can hardly have understood what all this
was about, annotated the draft of Giers' letter, 'C'est bien',

[43] He sometimes talks of the Bosphorus and sometimes of the Straits, but it is
clearly a military occupation of the Bosphorus that he hoped to secure with
Austrian and German support: *ibid.*, pp. 155–6.

thus unwittingly withdrawing his recent approval of Saburov's suggestions.[44]

Giers had thus prevented any broaching in Berlin of the sanguine, ambitious plans that he so distrusted. He did not believe that the schemes of Miljutin and Saburov would necessarily work out to Russia's advantage. His uneasiness at Saburov's restless spirit, so little suited to the task of cautious appeasement to which the Russian government had committed itself, was growing. He knew only too well how the other powers automatically took alarm at Russian attempts to discuss the demise of the Sick Man of Europe. But he was pessimistic because he was much more realistic than the other two. After further discussions in St. Petersburg a series of detailed recommendations were drawn up on 5 March to form the bases of a later agreement between Russia and Austria, and a copy of this document was sent to Saburov on 9 March, with a long personal letter with Giers' explanations.

The recommendations, which represent so clearly Giers' point of view, were under nine heads, and may be summarized as follows.[45] (1) The two powers consider the maintenance of the present *status quo* in the East to be necessary for as long a period as possible. (2) They will enter into an agreement to use all their influence to maintain this *status quo* against attempts from whatever quarter to break it. (3) As long as the *status quo* exists both powers will, by mutual agreement, endeavour to maintain the Christian peoples within the framework of the Berlin treaty and to guarantee the maintenance of this framework. (4) For that purpose both powers will advise their representatives and agents in the Balkan countries to avoid all personal competition, to co-ordinate their activities in all fields, and in case of disagreement to consult their governments before deciding action. (5) Both powers will agree that the growth of their trade interests and the resulting political influence over the neighbouring countries should not lead to mutual antagonism and to the deterioration of their understanding. For this purpose they will agree upon a rational frontier[46] beyond

[44] Giers to Saburov, 13/25 February 1881, *ibid.*, pp. 154, 156.
[45] 'Bases d'entente entre la Russie et l'Autriche, Petersb. 21/11–81': *ibid.*, pp. 161–3, gives the full text.   [46] 'limite rationelle': as Skazkin points out, any reference to a line of demarcation was avoided (*ibid.*, p. 162).

which each power will refrain from actions directed against the other. In cases where their interests inevitably clash they will attempt to find a solution acceptable to both sides. (6) If, notwithstanding all efforts to the contrary, the existing state of affairs is threatened by the unforeseen developments which may always arise in the East the two powers will immediately enter into consultations concerning the principles that are to govern their actions, as well as the areas within which each will act. (7) The principles affirmed during the Reichstadt agreement with regard to an eventual collapse of the Ottoman Empire shall apply to the following points: the creation of independent states in the Balkan Peninsula; their federation in their own interest; neutralization of Constantinople and the Straits; a European guarantee of these arrangements. (8) Having agreed not to accelerate this plan prematurely both powers will do their best to carry it out if the decisive crisis should take place before the plan had been given formal shape. (9) Should events, contrary to all expectations, take a different turn and call for different arrangements both powers will, before deciding on action, consult each other in order to find a solution best suited to their mutual interests.

This remarkable document was intended, it must be remembered, as a basis for discussion of the broader eventualities in the Near East only after the signing of the Three Emperors' Alliance and then only if relations with Berlin and Vienna were sufficiently cordial and auspicious. As it happened, they never were; but the programme is nevertheless of great importance as an indication of the ideas and influence of Giers. He had made short work of Saburov's plan. The acquisition of the Bosphorus was not even hinted at, and he was also not prepared to surrender the Balkans to Austria-Hungary as Saburov had so lightheartedly suggested. Giers pointed out to Miljutin, who entirely agreed, that the separation of the question of the Bosphorus from that of Constantinople was not covered by the Reichstadt agreement; it would create a new situation which would concern all the European powers, and it would radically alter the basis of the projected alliance, which was to guarantee the inviolability of the Straits. He could not, however, reject Miljutin's federation plan quite so boldly, although—and here he agreed with Saburov—it could only mean Russia's abdication of influence in the Balkans. Miljutin was opposed to the division of spheres because he saw in it the handing over of some of the Balkan Slavs to Austrian control; and he had hoped that the small Slav states in the federation would in combination be strong enough to resist Austrian influence. But Giers was well aware that Austria might dominate a Balkan federation as she had dominated the German Confederation before 1862, and that Miljutin's conception, which was purely political and even romantic, ignored the realities of Austria's growing economic pressure on all the Balkan states. He argued, therefore, that the immediate task before Russia, which must be tackled at once, was the development of commercial relations. As he put it in his letter to Saburov on 9 March: 'In all other countries it is possible to separate the economic and political aspects of unions. In the East it is impossible. Trade and transport are the conductors of political influence.' The sphere of influence which each government could legitimately regard as its own ought, therefore, to be defined, together with those in which it would have to make room for another government's predominance. This was, then, the sphere-of-influence plan in a new form: Giers went on to say that such spheres were clearly indicated—for Russia, Bulgaria; for Austria, Bosnia and the Hercegovina. Austria had, he added, also reserved the sanjak for herself at the Congress of Berlin, and at Friedrichsruh in September 1880, in agreeing to the union of the two Bulgarias, Haymerle had insisted on the exclusion of Macedonia: she was insisting that Russia should not interfere with Austria's trade agreement with Serbia, and in the case of Montenegro, she 'has taken into account the special sympathies of our August Emperor for that country, but has nevertheless safeguarded her trade and maritime interests which the port of Spizza and the control of the seacoast offer her'.[47]

It is this conviction that, if direct military occupation were ruled out, political influence in the Balkans would follow economic predominance that explains the fifth point of the Russian nine-point programme, and shows the pessimistic and self-defensive attitude of the Russian government at this stage.

[47] *Ibid.*, pp. 158–62.

Russian predominance in the eastern Balkans was essential for strategical reasons; it was necessary to be well placed in order to deal with a crisis in the Straits. But Giers felt that even in Bulgaria Russia was on the defensive against Austrian penetration, and could only hope that by the 'limite rationelle' her interests could be defended in this one field. It was a moderate, practical, self-defensive programme, with little in it to justify the real, or pretended, alarm of the statesmen in Vienna.

It will be seen that these two programmes, Austrian and Russian, were in remarkable agreement as to the situation in the peninsula; both saw the struggle for influence in economic terms, both saw that Austrian success was more likely than Russian in this struggle. Both governments felt it necessary to exclude at this stage the discussion of fundamental changes in the Near East, but they saw possibilities of early advantage for themselves beyond the narrower limits of the Three Emperors' Alliance which they were discussing. To the continuation of these negotiations after the presentation of the Russo-German draft to the Austrian government we must now turn.

III. AUSTRO-HUNGARIAN DRAFT

The procedure carefully worked out by Bismarck and Saburov[48] was followed by Reuss on 21 January 1881, when he informed Haymerle that he was commissioned to forward a letter from his sovereign to the Emperor Franz Joseph.[49] At this same time he explained the object of the letter. Bismarck hoped that in this way the interest of the Emperor in the success of the negotiations would be enlisted, and that Haymerle would also have no reason to suspect that he was himself being sidetracked. The Emperor 'anxious to keep correct as a constitutional sovereign' on the following day requested Reuss to send the imperial letter to him 'through the medium of the Minister of Foreign Affairs'.

On the 23rd Reuss handed over to Haymerle the text of the

[48] See above, p. 247.
[49] Kaiser Wilhelm an S. Maj. Franz Joseph, 16 January 1881. (Cf. *G.P.*, iii, p. 161). This and subsequent documents from the Vienna archives cited in this chapter are from the collection entitled: 'Geheim Liasse IV. Drei Kaiser Bündnis. Osterreich-Ungarn; Deutschland; Russland, 1881' (cited as 'W.S.A., G.IV').

draft agreement, together with an explanatory memorandum by Bismarck,[50] and was able to form some opinion as to the Austrian government's first impressions. Haymerle did not, however, commit himself very far; after mentioning the joy with which the Emperor had received the proposal for discussion, he was content to put forward some explanations as to why he had to have time for consideration. He remarked that the present scheme went beyond the ground of the Friedrichsruh discussions: Bismarck then had simply indicated tentatively that the three powers might be drawn together into a reciprocal assurance against aggression. Since then there had been merely discussion between Austria and Russia concerning the settlement of certain immediate Near Eastern problems. He must, therefore, consider the draft maturely, and learn, so to speak, to understand it, since the intellectual preparation which had gone to its composition was quite unknown to him. There would then be some questions concerning the meaning and implication of certain major points, and on the answer to these would depend his judgment of the proposed agreement. These questions referred particularly to the relation of the triple agreement to the Austro-German alliance of 1879, which his government was above all concerned to maintain. He found the provision for neutrality 'in the event of one of the three Powers being forced to go to war with a fourth Power', misleading and vague: it would require Austria to maintain a benevolent neutrality while Russia conquered Rumania! Reuss assured him that Bismarck was fully conscious of the necessity of maintaining intact the spirit and text of the dual alliance, but the arrangement with St. Petersburg had only been concluded after much toil, and Bismarck laid great value on the arrangement.[51] On 27 January the Emperor gave an audience to

[50] Bismarck to Reuss, 17 January 1881, no. 1, Geheim: W.S.A., G.IV. The sketch of the negotiations in Vienna, given at second hand in Saburov's account, must be used with caution; it is chiefly of interest as evidence of what Bismarck thought it useful to tell, or withhold from, the Russians. The chronology at this stage is also difficult to follow. Saburov's account (pp. 199–210) of Reuss's interview with Haymerle corresponds with Haymerle's account of the conversation of 23 January.

[51] Haymerle: Gespräch mit Pr. Reuss, am 23 Jänner 1881: W.S.A., G.IV. Haymerle's immediate reaction to the draft, in a series of rough notes, starts with the following significant comment. 'Der vorliegende Entwurf sichert Deutschland die

Reuss, and after expressing his lively satisfaction with the general tendency of the proposal, emphasized his concern that the 'Middle-European peace-grouping' should not be weakened.[52] Haymerle had, once again, managed to create the impression that his quite justifiable cautiousness was the product in the main of mere timidity; 'I only entreat you', he had said to Reuss, 'not to hurry me; to give me time to study it more in all its aspects. Don't be afraid of my analytical mind; your project will not suffer from it.' Bismarck thought that Reuss had been unwise to suggest that extensive amendments would be frowned on in Berlin. 'It does not do to frighten a timid man too much', he told Saburov. 'One must help him along by gentle dealing.'[53] He had telegraphed to Reuss on the 25th an amicable message that he was very ready to mediate over amendments and additions to the agreement; the only point which he had not anticipated was that Haymerle could have believed the October treaty to be prejudiced.[54]

On the 30th Haymerle, after again pointing out that the Russo-German draft went beyond his Friedrichsruh discussions with Bismarck, and that it was necessary for him to understand the *'geistige Arbeit'* which had led to the various details, gave Reuss a number of specific queries.[55] He said that in general Bismarck could rest assured that wherever an eminent

grössten Vortheile, allerdings erstreckt sich die Rückversicherung auch auf Oesterreich bez. Italien, doch hat Deutschld nur 2 gefährdete Grenzen—gegen Ost u West, Osterr ausser Betracht bleibt. Die Garantie aber dass unsere Interessen im Oriente gewahrt werden, hängt von der Meinung der dritten Macht ab, welche um Freundschaft mit Russland zu erhalten über eine die selbe weniger direkt berührende orientalische Frage, sich leicht nach Russld neigen, jedenfalls sich nicht in einen Krieg stürzen wird' (Bemerkungen zu dem Entwurfe. January 1881, *ibid.*).

[52] *Gedankengang der von S. Majestät an Prinz Reuss gemachten Ausserungen bei der Audienz am 27 Jänner 1881* (W.S.A., G.IV). Reuss reported on 29 January that 'to his greatest astonishment' the Emperor had repeated Haymerle's argument as to the necessity for maintaining the October treaty intact, and had also said that the position with regard to Rumania needed elucidating. Reuss to Bismarck, 29 January, Geheim no. 3 (A.A., Deutschland No. 129, Geheim).

[53] *Saburov*, pp. 198–202.

[54] Bismarck to Reuss, 25 January, tel. no. 7, A.A., *ibid.* Cf. Windelband, p. 201.

[55] The account of this conversation in this and the next paragraph is based on the two following, which closely agree: Reuss to Bismarck, 30 January, no. 4, Geheim (A.A., *ibid.*) and 'Notizen über ein Gespräch mit dem Prinzen Reuss am 30 Jänner' (W.S.A., G.IV).

German interest was concerned, Austria would take account of it. He did not fear for a moment that the agreement *à trois* was intended to modify, or was capable of modifying, the treaty of 1879. But then he noticed at once the provision for mediation—Was this of Russian origin? And what was behind it?[56] The occasion for mediation would occur, according to Article I, 'if a difference or grievance were to arise' between two of the signatories. He took it for granted that questions of internal government and legislation could not be regarded as subjects for mediation. Moreover, the terms *'griefs'* and *'différences'* extended much too widely the opportunity for mediation, and an expression should be chosen, such as 'qui pourraient troubler les relations', which would limit the mediation to the most recent issues. He would like the point which Bismarck had emphasized as the real aim of the agreement, namely the maintenance of peace, stated explicitly in the first Article. He also wanted to know Bismarck's opinion of the expressions in the first Article, 'forced to be at war'. Did it refer to the position of Germany and Austria-Hungary in relation to a threatened attack by France and Italy? If so, he had no objection. But if the phrase had been put into the draft by Russia, then the position was different: she might easily maintain that she had been compelled to fight by Turkey.[57] He considered that a reciprocal agreement was necessary between Austria and Germany providing that, in the event of unsuccessful mediation under Article I of the new treaty, the *casus foederis* stipulated in the Austro-German treaty of 1879 would be unaffected. At the end of the conversation he gave Reuss the draft terms of an Austro-German agreement on these lines: in this he made the *casus foederis* under the October treaty apply to a Russian attack on the *'Kriegsmacht'* of either power, instead of the *'Reich'*.

He also called attention to the provision in Article II of the treaty of 1879 for joint military action by Austria and Germany

[56] Bismarck's annotation of these two questions in Reuss's despatch was, 'Ja'; 'sehr klar! u. sehr günstig für Oest. auf Basis '79'. Saburov maintained later that the proposal for mediation was of German origin (see p. 270 below).

[57] Bismarck's annotations: 'Ornamental!'; 'russ. Ursprungs. die Russen haben ohne Zweifel Türkei im Auge...'; '"forcée" ist nicht wesentlich; nur factum entscheidet'.

to meet a Russian attack or military threat against one of the two powers. Bismarck knew how important Rumania's position would be in the circumstances, yet it was not mentioned in the draft. He did not know whether the phrase, 'points on which an entente has already been established in principle', referred to his discussions at Friedrichsruh with Bismarck or to earlier agreements, or to others yet to be arrived at. The reference in Article III to the closure of the Straits to ships of all powers represented a great concession to Russia; but no equivalent for Austria appeared. There was no mention in the draft of the duration of the treaty; the dual alliance must, he said, have in any case a longer duration than the agreement à trois. He evidently felt that this list of criticisms was quite long enough for the time being, but he promised Reuss that he would bring forward other amendments after hearing Bismarck's reply to these.

Haymerle embodied his suggested amendments in a memorandum[58] to which Bismarck replied immediately by telegraph. He assured Haymerle that the 1879 treaty would remain intact in all circumstances, and accepted all the points in the Austrian draft agreement, with the exception of the clause providing that if, after the failure of an attempt at mediation, Russia should proceed to an attack on the military power of Austria or Germany, the casus foederis of the 1879 treaty should come into operation. This would necessitate an enlargement of the terms of the 1879 treaty, for which he would have to secure the agreement of the German Emperor. He was, however, prepared to discuss in the negotiations à trois the Rumanian and other problems raised by Haymerle, and suggested that it might be possible to make any initiative by Austria and Russia with regard to Rumania dependent on the agreement of all three powers.[59] But Haymerle told Reuss that his government wished to fill the gap in the draft agreement concerning Rumania by an agreement with Germany alone: this was in fact the real purpose of the formula concerning an attack on the military

[58] The draft of Haymerle's memorandum is dated 'Jänner 1881'. Nolde (p. 255) is clearly in error in stating that Haymerle did not formulate written amendments until March.

[59] Bismarck to Reuss, 1 February, draft tel. in Bismarck's handwriting (A.A., ibid., see G.P., iii, no. 525).

power of the two states. He admitted that this went beyond the letter of the 1879 treaty, but if the spirit of that treaty were considered it seemed rather obvious that the protection against attack already provided by that treaty with regard to the two states should include their military forces, which were essential to their security. When Reuss suggested that Haymerle had previously appeared to desire a clarification of the position of Rumania by agreement between the three powers, the minister replied that Austria did not wish to enter into any more contracts with Russia than was necessary. Moreover an arrangement *à trois* over Rumania would lead in effect to a declaration of the neutralization of this principality, and such declarations 'make young states refractory'.[60] Bismarck appears to have given Saburov a reasonably full account of Reuss's discussions with Haymerle, but to have omitted the all-important discussions as to the *casus foederis* under the October treaty. The Russian ambassador noted with somewhat malicious satisfaction that the proposal for mediation was of German, and not Russian, origin, and that in attacking it so vigorously Haymerle 'was spending his ardour in contending with Bismarck himself!'[61]

It will be seen from these exchanges that Haymerle had, at this stage, two main aims: first, to ensure that the new treaty, by its provision for mediation or otherwise, did not alter adversely the existing relations between Austria and Germany; secondly, to secure from Germany a promise of military support if Russian troops entered Rumania. On neither point was he able to make satisfactory progress, and the negotiations made little headway during the greater part of February.

Bismarck wished to reassure Haymerle concerning the unaltered validity of the Austro-German alliance, but to resist its extension: and since the matter had been raised by Haymerle with particular reference to Rumania he was forced to re-examine the treaty draft with Saburov on this point. Fearing perhaps that the discussion would suggest to the Russians that

[60] Reuss to A.A., 3 February, tel. no. 19, A.A., *ibid.* Haymerle: 'Unterredung mit Pr. Reuss', 3 February, Geheim, W.S.A., G.IV.

[61] *Saburov*, p. 212. Bismarck, however (see fn. 56, above) thought that the mediation plan was of Russian origin.

the October treaty was an obstacle to the triple agreement he proceeded, if we can trust Saburov's narrative, to give the Russian ambassador a highly misleading picture of German obligations under that treaty. On 26 January, after explaining that Haymerle was pressing him to say whether the presence of Russia in the proposed triple entente would modify the arrangements concluded in Vienna, he told Saburov that he had said to Andrássy in Vienna in 1879 what he had said to d'Oubril in 1876, that, in the event of a war between Russia and Austria, 'Germany's interest indicates to us in a like circumstance a course from which we cannot deviate; we must see that neither of these two Powers is *completely defeated*'. This could only mean —and Saburov certainly interpreted it in this sense—that Germany had no automatic obligation to join Austria in a Russo-Austrian war, and indeed that she might intervene on the Russian side in the unlikely event that Austro-Hungarian forces were threatening Russia with complete defeat.[62] The terms of Article I of the October treaty were, however, unambiguous: Germany must support Austria with all her military strength in the event of a Russian attack on Austro-Hungarian territory, and must continue the war until both she and Austria were fully agreed on terms of peace. It was precisely the danger that Bismarck would wish to emasculate this all-important provision which disturbed the Austrians, and Bismarck had the delicate task during the next few weeks of reassuring Saburov in Berlin that he could at any moment without offence to Austria make a treaty with Russia exactly like the October treaty, and at the same time reassuring Haymerle that he had nothing to fear.[63]

Bismarck was, however, quite willing to discuss the Rumanian question with Saburov. They examined it on 26 January, on the strength of Haymerle's first objections to Reuss on the 23rd. Saburov in his over-clever way decided that Haymerle was skilfully exaggerating his fears about a possible Russian invasion of Rumania because he was alarmed, as Russia had

[62] *Ibid.*, p. 208.

[63] Haymerle reported Reuss as saying on 3 February 1881: 'Fürst Bismarck betont ausserdem, dass unser Bündnis vom J. 1879 nicht blos in d. Buchstaben d. Vertrages, sondern in d. Uberzeugung würzle, dass *wir einander nicht im Stich lassen können*.' (Haymerle: 'Unterredung mit Pr. Reuss', 3 February, W.S.A., G.IV.)

been, at the free hand which the wording of Article I ('compelled to go to war with a fourth power') allowed Germany in relations with such small states as Denmark, Belgium, and Holland. Saburov also concluded that as Haymerle had referred only to Rumania he was willing to acquiesce in the eventuality of a Russo-Turkish war. Feeling very pleased with himself for having manœuvred Haymerle into proposing what Russia herself desired he suggested that the variant reading of the essential words in Article I should be proposed to Haymerle—namely the substitution of 'fourth great power' for 'fourth power'. Bismarck pointed out that Haymerle was particularly sensitive as to the possibility of the passage of Russian troops through Rumania in the event of a Russo-Turkish war, which was not excluded by this variant reading. He suggested therefore that in place of 'fourth power' that words 'one of the other powers signatory to the Treaty of Berlin' should be used. Saburov was delighted with this: it included Turkey and excluded all the small states of Europe.[64] However, Haymerle's memorandum of 30 January seems to have convinced Bismarck that Haymerle must have some more explicit assurances about Rumania, and after a further discussion with Saburov on 4 February a new clause was drafted for inclusion in Article II.[65] This Saburov was able to tell him on 8 February had been approved in St. Petersburg. He explained that there seemed to be two Austrian preoccupations: first, that Rumania might be invaded as a result of exposing herself to an imprudent war, and secondly that she might become the victim of too close an intimacy with one of her neighbours, which might result in her occupation by foreign troops. The first eventuality was met by the proposed variant to Article I. The second could be met by a provision that none of the three powers should send troops into the territory of Turkey-in-Europe, Rumania, etc., without first discussing the situation with the other two. Russia, however, was particularly concerned with the maintenance of the *status quo* in Eastern Rumelia and Bulgaria against a possible Turkish intervention, and could only agree to limit her freedom of action in regard to Rumania as long as the *status quo* was

[64] *Saburov*, pp. 198–207.
[65] *Ibid.*, pp. 211–15.

maintained in all the countries concerned. The amendment that his government had authorized was therefore as follows:

Aucune des Puissances ne fera entrer des troupes sur le territoire de la Turquie d'Europe, de la Roumanie, de la Serbie ou du Monténégro, sans s'être concertée avec les deux autres. Cet engagement sera valable tant que durera le statu quo actuel des pays susindiqués.

This was to be inserted between paragraphs two and three of the existing draft of Article II.[66]

After these discussions Bismarck was able to send fresh proposals to Vienna on 8 February, and Reuss discussed them with Haymerle on the 11th, pointing out at the same time that Bismarck had once more accentuated most emphatically the spirit of the 1879 treaty, according to which Austria and Germany could not leave one another in the lurch. The despatch, however, contained a very positive rejection of Haymerle's plan for safeguards against a possible Russian attack on Austrian or German 'military power'. The protection of Austrian or German military forces lying outside the territory of the two states had not hitherto been within the terms of the *casus foederis* under the 1879 treaty; he could not see how, in the light of the hypotheses on which the treaty was based, a situation could arise in which the military power and territory of Austria-Hungary did not coincide. The extension of the 1879 treaty on the lines proposed would create difficulties similar to those which had had to be overcome a year and a half before; the amendment would, moreover, not be so readily understood by German public opinion as the existing purely defensive alliance with Austria had been. Bismarck then proceeded to argue at considerable length that the extension of the 1879 treaty in the manner proposed would be of no particular advantage to Austria. Haymerle had had in mind the possibility that a Russian entry into Moldavia would compel Austria to send troops into Wallachia. Such action would, said Bismarck, be quite natural in the circumstances, as would also the occupation of Serbia, but he could not see that Austria would need

[66] Saburov to Bismarck, 27 January/8 February 1881, A.A., *ibid.* The new clause restored the one which had been discussed by Saburov and Bismarck in December, and dropped (p. 252 above).

German support in maintaining such a position. An attack by Russia on Austria's military power in Wallachia alone would, in the circumstances, be unlikely, and, from a military point of view, without decisive result; if Russia attacked Austria elsewhere, as in the Cracow region, the *casus foederis* under the 1879 treaty would apply. Similarly, if the unlikely happened, and Austrian troops were driven back from Wallachia, then Germany would have to protect the Hungarian frontier.[67]

Bismarck went on to say that there was certainly a gap in the draft with regard to Rumania, but suggested that it could perhaps be filled more peacefully and securely by agreement between the three powers. The simplest means would perhaps be the following stipulation:

None of the three powers will send troops into the territories of Rumania, Serbia, Montenegro or Turkey-in-Europe without consulting the other two.

If this should be considered too extensive, the following might be added:

as long as the present *status quo* in the above-mentioned countries continues: as soon as it is altered the three powers will consult together.

The eventuality envisaged by Haymerle could be covered even more specifically by saying that if one of the two neighbouring powers should enter one of these territories, the other would acquire the right to take a corresponding pledge of security. Finally, all direct reference to the Rumanian question could be excluded from the treaty, and in Article I of the draft, after the words 'in the event of one of them finding itself compelled to be at war with a fourth power' could be inserted 'signatory to the treaty of Berlin of 13 July 1878'. The effect of this would be that Austria would not be pledged to remain neutral if Rumania were attacked by Russia: Bismarck would,

[67] 'Dazu kommt, dass wir, auch ohne *Vertrags*verpflichtung 'Oestreich nur dann ohne Unterstützung lassen könnten, wenn es allein stark genug bliebe. Sobald das zweifelhaft wäre, müssten wir doch eintreten, wenn nicht nach dem Buchstaben des Abkommens von 1879, so doch aus allgemeiner politischer Nothwendigkeit. . . .'

however, prefer one of the other alternatives because they were 'more peaceable'.[68]

These, then, were the new German proposals presented to Haymerle by Reuss on 11 February. Haymerle was disappointed, but not defeated. He professed himself to be greatly reassured by the Chancellor's interpretation of the character of the Austro-German alliance, and to meet Bismarck's objection that the Austrian proposal could not be reconciled with the defensive character of the October treaty he put forward an alternative wording:[69]

Should therefore mediation by Austria-Hungary between Germany and Russia, or by Germany between Austria-Hungary and Russia, remain for any reason unsuccessful, the mediating power will deliver to the other power, if threatened by a conflict with Russia, the declaration provided for in Article IV of the October treaty.

He claimed that this wording would cover the specific problem of Rumania, but would apply at the same time to Germany. The possibility of a failure of mediation provided a 'new link in the chain of eventualities' with which Austria and Germany were concerned under their treaty of alliance; the new clause was no more than a deduction from the general principles that the triple agreement should not affect the *casus foederis* under the October alliance. He told Reuss at the same time that he could never sign an article referring to Rumania, Serbia, and Montenegro on the lines suggested by Bismarck: it would completely bind the hands of the Austrian government in its relations with its small southern-Slav neighbours. He could well imagine that Russia would be well pleased to accept this proposal, for it would mean that if Montenegro should stir up

[68] Bismarck to Reuss, 8 February, Geheim, Wien, no. 2 (A.A., *ibid.*); the substance of this despatch was communicated to Haymerle, 'Auszug aus einer depesche des Fstn Bismarck übergeben vom deutschen Botschafter, 11 febr. 1881' (W.S.A., G.IV).

[69] i.e. for the proposed Austro-German declaration defining the terms of the October treaty. Art. IV of the latter expressed the hope that Russian military preparations would not prove threatening to either Austria or Germany '. . . sollte sich aber diese Hoffnung wider Erwarten als eine irrthümliche erweisen, so würden die beiden hohen Contrahenten es als eine Pflicht der Loyalität erkennen, den Kaiser Alexander mindestens vertraulich darüber zu verständigen, dass sie einen Angriff auf einen von ihnen als gegen beide gerichtet betrachtet müssten'.

trouble in the Hercegovina, or if Serbia should embark on activities in Bosnia or elsewhere which Austria would not tolerate, the Vienna government would nevertheless have to await or purchase Russia's permission before taking action. The case of Rumania was different, as this state was a neighbour of both Austria and Russia, and therefore a possible point of conflict between the direct interests of both. In general, he said that he did not wish to arrive at very specific agreements in the accord à *trois*: Austria was at a disadvantage in dealing on a footing of equality with a power like Russia, whose 'active political tendencies' tempted it to disturb the peace. He would greatly prefer that Germany and Austria could come to agreement on preliminary questions without discussions with Russia at all.[70]

But Haymerle had now taken a line which Bismarck was bound to resist. Haymerle cannot be blamed for fearing that the provision for mediation might allow Germany on some future occasion to take up an attitude of virtual neutrality in an Austro-Russian dispute, or even to give a decision in favour of Russia which would make it impossible for Austria to invoke the defensive clauses of the 1879 treaty: this was, indeed, precisely what Bismarck wished Saburov to believe. Bismarck's real view was doubtless that no fundamental incompatibility between the two treaties existed, for if the triple agreement had the effect desired it would bind Russia to peaceful courses and so remove the necessity for a German defence of Austrian territory. Moreover, provision to meet the possibility of a renewal of Russian aggression might tempt Austria into indiscretions, and also pledge Germany to support offensive action by Austria in the Balkans. An irritable despatch to Reuss on 10 February shows that he suspected Haymerle of a deliberate attempt to secure German armed support for Austria's forward policy in the peninsula, a policy which was rendered even less attractive by its failure to secure the goodwill of the small Balkan states.[71] It may be assumed that Haymerle was not blind to the possibility of enlisting Germany's support for some

---

[70] Haymerle: 'Gespräch mit Reuss.' 10 (? 11) February, W.S.A., G.IV.

[71] Bismarck to Reuss, 10 February, no. III, Geheim, A.A., *ibid*. Cf. Windelband, pp. 101–3.

future forward policy in the Balkan peninsula, but his immediate preoccupation appears to have been the securing of some form of written guarantee that the advantages secured to Austria under the 1879 treaty would not be lost. The history of Austro-German relations after 1881 was to show that Bismarck was sincere in his promise to maintain the 1879 treaty, and that his choice had been made for Austria and not Russia; but he was determined to avoid the necessity for admitting the existence of a choice, and had no intention of encouraging Austria to risk trouble with Russia in the peninsula. Haymerle had no great confidence, or any particular evidence, that Bismarck's word on this point could be trusted; Bismarck, as so often, was the victim of his own reputation. Haymerle was, however, well aware that in the last resort he would have to take the risk of accepting Bismarck's assurances.

In these circumstances the negotiations made little progress for some weeks.[72] Haymerle continued to bring forward counter-proposals which did not substantially modify his original demands. Reuss, without making any direct proposal, raised the Rumanian question in a conversation on 17 February, saying that, in view of the present disposition of the Emperor William, Bismarck found it very difficult to make any substantial modification in the draft treaty. Haymerle thereupon produced yet another draft clause:

The three powers promise not to infringe Rumanian territory either for preparations or operations of war against Turkey.

If this were not acceptable he would prefer to choose the third alternative mentioned by Reuss on the 11th, namely to omit all reference to Rumania, and so preserve freedom of decision. Reuss on this occasion also discussed the question of the

[72] Reuss to A.A., 15 February, tel. no. 24; A.A. to Reuss, 16 February, tel.; Reuss to Bismarck, 16 February, Geheim VI (A.A., *ibid.*). Kálnoky, in a private letter to Haymerle (6/18 February, W.S.A., G.IV), wrote: 'Euer Excellenz kennen meine Überzeugung, dass unser bisheriges Verhältnis zu Russland, welches ohne eigentliche Basis weder gut noch schlecht war, à la longue nicht haltbar sei. Wir können es einmal nicht ändern dieses colossale Reich an unseren Gränzen zu haben und es bleibt uns nur die Alternative, entweder uns mit ihm zu vertragen oder es nach Asien zurückzuwerfen. An letzteres jetzt oder in der nächsten Zukunft zu denken, müsste wohl jeder gewissenhafte Staatsmann als eine Unmöglichkeit für Österreich-Ungarn erklären . . .' Cf. the Tsar's comments, *Schweinitz*, ii, 145.

duration of the treaty, and said that Bismarck was firmly of the opinion that this should be less than that of the October treaty: he proposed a term of two or three years. Haymerle thought that Russia would not regard a two-year period as sufficiently binding, and would treat it as a mere armistice. He suggested three years, or termination on 1 January 1884, or perhaps, in order not to make the duration appear too short, the maintenance of the treaty 'for three years in the first instance'.[73]

Bismarck, his exasperation mounting, grumbled and made notes; he was not prepared to give way.[74] A telegram on 16 February told Reuss that the German Emperor declined to alter the 1879 treaty, and in view of the very accommodating policy of the Petersburg cabinet would not plan anything to Russia's detriment. Fresh arguments were sent to Reuss on the 26th. Haymerle was to be told that Bismarck did not feel able to persuade the Emperor to undertake further commitments and was to be asked to say whether Bismarck should advise the Russians to drop the proposal about mediation and whether, with or without this deletion, he would be interested in an agreement limited to three years.[75] Reuss had a conversation with the Emperor Franz Joseph at a ball on the same evening and, apparently acting under instructions from Bismarck, endeavoured to convince him of the inevitability of Bismarck's attitude; he explained the grounds on which it was impossible to alter the October treaty, and spoke of the unfortunate consequences of a failure to establish the *accord à trois*. The Emperor replied in the friendliest possible manner, and agreed that advantage must be taken of the peaceful inclinations of the Tsar; but he said also that he must be satisfied that the October treaty was in no way threatened, and his confidence in the peaceful and honourable outlook of the Tsar did not remove his profound distrust of Russian policy in general. In short, the Emperor was not prepared to overrule his foreign minister. An

[73] The conversation took place on Haymerle's request. It is reported in a 'Nachschrift' of 17 February to Reuss's despatch, no. IV, Geheim, of the 16th (A.A., *ibid.*). Haymerle's report: 'Notiz über eine Unterredung mit Pr. Reuss am 17 Februar' (W.S.A., G.IV).

[74] Cf. the memorandum dictated by Bismarck on 22 February, and Limburg-Stirum's letter to Reuss of 27 February, A.A., *ibid.*

[75] Bismarck to Reuss, 16 February, tel., and 26 February, Geheim, A.A., *ibid.*

attempt by Bismarck to bring the King of Saxony into the negotiations was without immediate result, although the King promised to use his personal influence later in the negotiations if the opportunity occurred.[76] Reuss had, accordingly, to make a fresh attempt to secure Haymerle's agreement. He did so on the evening of 1 March, elaborating Bismarck's message of 26 February. If Haymerle objected to the mediation proposal it could be given up, and the two essential points in the agreement would then be the benevolent neutrality of Russia in the event of an Italo-French attack on Austria or Germany, as against the regulation of the Dardanelles question on the lines that Russia desired. Reuss had then to repeat Bismarck's previous objections to Haymerle's plan for meeting an attack on the 'military power' of Austria, and to advance arguments against his more recent proposals on the same subject. But he repeated Bismarck's assurance that the October treaty should continue in force, during the existence of the triple agreement, and his proposal that the latter should be limited to a short period, perhaps of three years. Then he spoke bluntly of the consequences of an Austrian refusal. The immediate result of the failure of the negotiations would be renewed distrust of Austria in St. Petersburg; if it was also believed there that Germany did not desire the agreement the effect on Russian policy would be grave. The Tsar would again be brought to believe that Germany desired war, and the peaceful influences to which he was now accessible would be reversed. Bismarck could not take the responsibility for the rejection of the Russian proposal, and would have to tell Saburov the true facts.[77]

Bismarck's decisive language had the desired effect. Haymerle

---

[76] Reuss to Bismarck, 27 February, Geheim; 2 March, Geheim VII, A.A., *ibid.*; cf. *Saburov*, pp. 217–19.

[77] This account of the important meeting of 1 March is based on Haymerle's very lengthy minute: 'Notizen über Mittheilungen des deutschen Botschafters übergeben am 1 Marz 1881' (W.S.A., G.IV). There is a briefer reference in Reuss's despatch, Geheim VII, to Bismarck, 2 March; A.A., *ibid.* A day or two later Bismarck told Schweinitz: 'Haymerle machte Schwierigkeiten; kleinlich, ohne grosse Auffassung, in Angst vor der Presse, setze er den ganz verständigen Anerbietungen Russlands Hindernisse entgegen; ohne Kraft und ohne Mut erhebe Österreich Ansprüche, die es gar nicht ernst meinen könne; die Augen seien grösser als der Magen usw.' (3 March: *Schweinitz*, ii, 148.)

was silent for several days; on 4 March Reuss reported pessimistically to Berlin, and seemed to think that the Austrian objections could not be met. [78] But on the 5th came the Austrian reply, in the form of a redraft of the agreement in accordance with Bismarck's alternative suggestions; it went a considerable way towards acceptance of what appeared at the time to be the Russo-German viewpoint (although the Russians were to show themselves by no means satisfied with it). It omitted the mediation proposal from Article I, and after the provision binding each to benevolent neutrality in the event of war between one of the signatories and a fourth great power, defined more precisely the conditions under which this provision should apply in the event of a war between one of the signatories and Turkey. None of the three powers was to undertake a war of aggression against her, and the provision for benevolent mediation would apply only if a previous agreement had been reached between the two courts concerning the 'conditions' and the results of such a war. As an alternative to 'conditions' Haymerle suggested 'territorial limits'. This provision in its original form had been included in the second article of the first German draft, which otherwise remained substantially unaltered in Haymerle's version. He omitted altogether, however, the third paragraph of the third article of the German draft, which had made provision for a joint warning to Turkey by the three powers if she should allow the region of the Straits to be used for the military operations of a great power. A fourth article provided for a duration of three years, and a fifth for secrecy.

Austro-Hungarian Draft [79]

I

Préciser le but de cet arrangement qui est destiné à donner de nouvelles garanties à la paix au maintien de laquelle les trois Puissances sont résolues de vouer tous Leurs efforts.

Dans le cas où l'une d'Elles se trouverait forcée d'être en guerre avec une quatrième Grande Puissance les deux autres maintien-

---

[78] Reuss to Bismarck, 4 March, Geheim; Reuss to Limburg-Stirum, 4 March; A.A., *ibid.*

[79] The text is taken from a copy in the Austrian archives, with no heading except 'Pr. Reuss, übergeben 5 Marz 1881'.

dront à son égard une neutralité bienveillante et voueront Leurs soins à la localisation du conflit.

Aucune[80] des trois Puissances n'entreprendra une guerre agressive contre la Turquie. Si toutefois l'une d'Elles était forcée d'être en guerre avec cet Empire, la stipulation de l'alinéa précédent s'appliquera également à cette guerre, mais seulement dans le cas où un accord préalable aura été établi entre les trois Cours sur les modalités[81] et les résultats de cette guerre.

Pour le cas spécial où l'une d'Elles obtiendrait de l'un de ses alliés un concours plus positif, la valeur obligatoire de cet article restera dans toute sa vigueur pour la troisième.

II

La Russie d'accord avec l'Allemagne déclare Sa ferme résolution de respecter les intérêts qui découlent de la nouvelle position assurée à l'Autriche-Hongrie par le traité de Berlin.

Les trois Cours désireuses d'éviter tout désaccord entr'Elles s'engagent à tenir compte de Leurs intérêts respectifs dans la péninsule des Balcans. Elles se promettent de plus que de nouvelles modifications dans le statu quo territorial de la Turquie d'Europe ne pourront s'accomplir qu'en vertu d'un commun accord entr'Elles.

Afin de faciliter, le cas échéant, l'accord prévu par le présent article, accord dont il est impossible de prévoir d'avance toutes les modalités, les trois Cours constateront dans des communications confidentielles les points sur lesquels un échange d'idées antérieur a démontré un accord en principe.

III

Les trois Cours reconnaissent le caractère européen et mutuellement obligatoire du principe de la fermature des détroits du Bosphore et des Dardanelles fondé sur le droit des gens et confirmé par les traités de Paris, de Londres, et de Berlin.

En conséquence la Turquie ne pourra faire d'exception à cette règle en faveur des intérêts particuliers d'un Gouvernement quelconque en prêtant à des opérations guerrières d'une Puissance belligérante la partie de son Empire que forment les détroits.[82]

[80] The following 'Alternativ' is written in the margin of the copy opposite this paragraph: 'Cette stipulation s'appliquera également à une guerre entre l'une des trois Puissances et la Turquie, mais seulement dans le cas où un accord préalable aura été établi entre les trois Cours sur les modalités et les résultats de cette guerre'.

[81] Note in margin: 'ou au lieu de "modalités": sur les limites territoriales et les résultats de cette guerre'.

[82] Note in margin: 'Wenn nöthig, könnte noch beigefügt werden: sans se mettre en guerre vis-à-vis de la partie lésée'.

IV

Durée

provisoirement pour trois années.

V

Secret[83]

The receipt in Berlin of Haymerle's draft completed the second phase of the negotiations; it was now necessary for the Russian government to examine the Austrian proposals, and pronounce on them.[84] The assassination of the Tsar, which followed almost immediately, had, however, the effect of holding up further progress in the negotiations for some weeks.

In the meantime an opportune proposal by Bismarck on 5 March, which reached Reuss after Haymerle had given him the redrafted agreement, gave the Austrians some satisfaction with regard to the Austro-German alliance. The positive assurances given by Reuss on 3 and 11 February and 1 March 1881 that the triple agreement would not in any way alter the October treaty no doubt had their effect, and Bismarck now offered to exchange ministerial declarations which would meet the Emperor Franz Joseph's desire for explicit confirmation of this guarantee. Reuss was able to say that this proposal had been successful in persuading Haymerle to abandon his plan for a revision of the dual alliance.[85]

IV. HAYMERLE'S CAPITULATION

The Tsar was assassinated on 13 March. It seemed to Bismarck in the days of crisis that followed that many disasters were

[83] On a separate sheet attached to Haymerle's draft the following possible insertions were noted. 'Einschalten im Alinea I des Art. II nach "traité de Berlin": L'Autriche-Hongrie se réserve, si la défense de ces intérêts l'exigeait, de faire des changements dans la situation politique de la Bosnie, de l'Herzégovine, et du Sandjak de Novibazar.' And, 'oder Alinea 2 des Art. II formulieren wie nachstehend: Les trois Cours désireuses d'éviter tout désaccord entr'Elles s'engagent à tenir compte de Leurs intérêts respectifs dans la péninsule des Balcans; Elles se promettent de plus que de nouvelles modifications dans le statu quo territorial des provinces de la Turquie d'Europe actuellement soumises à l'autorité du Sultan ne pourront s'accomplir qu'en vertu d'un commun accord'.

[84] 'Entwurf eines Berichtes des Prinzen Reuss an Bismarck', 6 March, W.S.A., G.IV; *Saburov*, pp. 222–3.

[85] Bismarck to Reuss, 5 March, tel. no. 16; Reuss to A.A., 6 March, tel., A.A., *ibid.*

threatened: revolution in Russia, a pro-French and anti-Austrian turn in Russian external affairs. His immediate anxiety can be seen in a telegram to Schweinitz on 14 March instructing him to telegraph daily, morning and evening, until further notice: discontinuance of the telegrams would be taken to mean that the telegraph had ceased to function.[86] It soon became clear that there would be no revolution, and that the new Tsar welcomed his father's alliance policy and its promise of peace abroad in order to free his attention for the stern task of restoring discipline at home. Alexander III was the embodiment of the Russian autocracy, blunt, honourable, and a little stupid; a man of strong will and stronger physique, he knew his own mind, suspected brains, and was as incapable of surrendering to his Nihilist opponents as he was of understanding what they were driving at. He accepted the need for good relations with Bismarck; but he never trusted him.

The Russian negotiators made good use of the mood of uncertainty in Vienna and Berlin which followed the untoward event of 13 March; hints that the new Emperor, or his new advisers, might be of sterner stuff than their predecessors were frequent during the next few weeks. The first indications of outlook were, however, reassuring. On the day before his death Alexander II had agreed on the terms of Giers' instructions to Saburov, and on the 15th the new Emperor added a note to the draft saying that he accepted its contents and the matter to which it referred not only as a legacy but also as a statement of his own convictions.[87] Giers was accordingly able on 16 March to announce to Saburov that the new Emperor had confirmed his father's last instructions, and Bismarck received this welcome message from Saburov on the 19th. He recommended that for the time being Haymerle should be kept in the dark as to Alexander III's intentions: 'If Austria desires that there should be no change, it is necessary for her to deserve it'. Saburov did

---

[86] Bismarck to Schweinitz, 14 March, tel., A.A. Russland, no. 61; draft in Bismarck's handwriting.

[87] Schweinitz sent this information to Berlin in a telegram (no. 21) of 15 March, A.A., Deutschland no. 129, Geheim. A further tel. of 17 March from Schweinitz said that Giers had assured Kálnoky that Alexander III intended to continue his father's policy of peace: A.A. Russland, no. 61. On the confusions in the drafting of these instructions, which followed the discussions in February described in section II above, see Skazkin, pp. 164–5.

not, however, raise strong objections to any points in Haymerle's draft except the changes in Article III regarding the
Straits, and here Bismarck was inclined at first to put in a word
for Haymerle, arguing that Austria had conceded Russia's
right to declare war on Turkey if she opened the Straits to a
belligerent power. He did not press the matter, however, when
Saburov insisted that Russia's primary aim was to prevent such
an eventuality by means of the joint declaration of the three
courts which Haymerle had rejected. On 22 March the Russian
ambassador left for St. Petersburg to be present at the Emperor's funeral, and to take part in the discussion of the
Russian counter-proposals. Before his departure he had an
interview at his own request with the German Emperor.[88]

This was, therefore, a reasonably encouraging start—from
Bismarck's point of view—to the new reign. But so far the
Tsar's statements had been in very general terms: he had not
yet shown, by concrete decisions, what his precise intentions
were, and Bismarck was on his guard against surprises.[89] For
more than a month after the Tsar's accession there was no
reply to the Austrian treaty proposals, and while this might
very well be due to the pressure of internal policy it was not
reassuring. When the Tsar decided to abandon his father's
reform programme (signed only on 13 March), Loris-Melikov,
Minister of the Interior, Abaza, the Finance Minister, and Miljutin, the War Minister, all resigned; a great surprise was the
appointment of the famous Slavophil diplomatist, Count
Ignatyev, to succeed Loris-Melikov on 7 April. Did this foreshadow a bid for Panslavist support in the form of an energetic
Balkan policy? On this point there was some uneasiness in
Vienna,[90] and in St. Petersburg Kálnoky, the Austrian ambassador, also had reason for anxiety. He took the first opportunity to sound Giers concerning the reception of the Austrian
draft, and Giers appeared 'very satisfied and fully convinced

[88] *Saburov*, pp. 223–4; Bismarck to Emperor Wilhelm, 18 March 1881, A.A.
Russland, no. 61.

[89] Windelband argues that Bismarck took steps at this point to limit the Russian
government's opportunity to contract other alliances should the three-emperors'
negotiations fail. There is some evidence for this in Bismarck's contacts with Italy,
France, and England at this time (p. 265).

[90] Cf. the remarks of M. Duchâtel, French ambassador to Vienna, *D.D.F.*, iii,
no. 453, and Haymerle's speculations on the evening of 13 March (*G.P.*, iii, no. 527).

that it would give rise to no particular difficulties'. Giers, however, was known to have expressed a wish to retire, and Schweinitz impressed on Kálnoky the importance of a decision before this happened. He thought that Lobanov was more likely to be Giers' successor than Saburov, but believed that both were 'good-for-nothing'.[91] Moreover, after further contemplation of Haymerle's draft, Giers himself appears to have become indignant at the omissions of Russia's chief proposal about the Straits.[92] On 29 March Saburov professed himself to be somewhat discouraged at the state of the negotiations; he now said that they had been disappointed over the Austrian draft in St. Petersburg, for Bismarck had indeed spoken of amendments, but changes of such importance had never been anticipated. 'Moreover it must not be forgotten that with the new Emperor certain adjustments in this affair are necessary, which had not to be considered in the case of the Emperor Alexander II, who was the most ardent of all in favour of the re-establishment of a satisfactory agreement.' He evaded any discussion of details 'in deference to Berlin'.[93] Haymerle showed his uneasiness by telegraphing in reply a defence of Austria's conduct.[94] Saburov continued until his departure for Berlin to refrain from giving Kálnoky any chance to discuss the alliance plans; Giers told the Austrian ambassador on 5 April that the Austrian amendments were more important than his government had foreseen, and said that the Emperor was hesitating to agree to change what had been in effect his father's draft. Saburov was, perhaps, a little embarrassed by the thoroughness with which mere verbal emendations in the Austrian draft had been introduced at St. Petersburg. In a note to Bismarck on 25 April, after his return to Berlin, he remarked: 'toutes ces expressions donneraient lieu, je le crains, à des discussions nouvelles; car si à

---

[91] Kálnoky to Haymerle, 13/25 March, private letter, W.S.A., G.IV.

[92] Giers to Saburov, 25 March/6 April: Skazkin, pp. 170-1.

[93] Kálnoky to Haymerle, 18/30 March, tel. no. 33, Geheim, W.S.A., G.IV. Cf. Schweinitz's comments: Schweinitz, ii, 164-5.

[94] Kálnoky was to say to Saburov, if the occasion arose: 'Das Project ist ganz ohne unsere Mitwirkung redigirt worden; bei den besten Intentionen der Redacteure, die gerne anerkannt werden, konnten naturgemäss die Erfordernisse unserer Lage die nur jeder selbst genau kennen kann, nicht vollständig erwogen werden. Demnach haben wir wesentliche Änderungen nicht gemacht . . .' (tel. no. 40, April, W.S.A., G.IV).

Vienne il y a des amateurs d'argutie, il y en a malheureusement aussi à Petersbourg'.[95]

Nevertheless Kálnoky had satisfied himself by the time of Saburov's return to Berlin that the Russians were genuinely anxious to reach an agreement.[96] The Russian reply to the Austrian draft seemed on the whole to bear this out. Haymerle's proposals with regard to Article I were accepted, with the exception of paragraph 3 (concerning the terms on which a signatory could go to war with Turkey). The Russians preferred the original text. More substantial opposition was raised to the Austrian redrafting of Article II, which dealt with Austria's relations with Turkey. Two amendments designed by Haymerle to reserve Austria's right to make further changes in Bosnia, the Hercegovina, and Novipazar were rejected, together with his attempt to limit the provision for an immediate declaration by the three Courts of the points 'on which an understanding has already been established', to a rather vaguer declaration of the points on which 'a previous exchange of ideas has demonstrated an agreement in principle'. As there seemed considerable likelihood that Bismarck might support Austria on these points, Saburov said that his government would be satisfied to maintain the original wording, which could not cause misunderstanding. In Article III, on the other hand, where Haymerle had proposed to suppress the provision for wanting Turkey to maintain the neutrality of the Straits in time of war, Bismarck promised to support the Russians in insisting on the maintenance of the original wording. The Russians agreed, however, to the complete suppression of the provision for mediation in Article I, and to the limitation of the duration of the treaty to three years. In general their policy was to insist as far as possible on the original draft, which suited them well enough, and had been accepted by Bismarck: this had the double purpose of forcing Haymerle to struggle with Bismarck on some points and of abandoning others for fear of offending him.[97]

[95] Saburov to Bismarck, 'Jeudi soir' (Note by A.A.: 25/4, enclosing extracts from two letters from de Giers (A.A. Deutschland no. 129 (Geheim)).

[96] Kálnoky to Haymerle, 25 March/6 April, no. 4, Geheim, W.S.A., G.IV.

[97] Saburov, pp. 227–32; Bismarck to Reuss, 25 April, no. v, Geheim; letter from Bismarck to the King of Saxony, 27 April, on the state of the negotiation; A.A., *ibid.*

Bismarck's diplomacy during the next few weeks can lay little claim to fairness or finesse; his irritability was probably due in part to ill-health, in part to knowledge that he was pressing the Austrians unreasonably, but it resulted in some gestures of heavy-handed impatience, at a time when delicacy of touch and a note of Olympian understanding were more than ever necessary. He was not by nature a patient man. Combative and supremely dominating by temperament, he was the master of the sudden, powerful, well-judged blow, delivered to an opponent who had been manœuvred into the position of maximum vulnerability. All through the 'seventies the quest for German security had called for the winning of confidence by the avoidance of these methods; and Bismarck had had to learn, and had succeeded only partially in doing so, that it might be harder to drive a coy neighbour into friendship than an enemy into defeat. He could understand intellectually the need for a suavity that irked him temperamentally. Saburov's deference and urbanity in the earlier negotiations had pleased the great man, not because he really liked or trusted the Russian, but because in this particular problem of human contact he somewhat distrusted himself; he was gratified to have made so much progress with so little emotional wear and tear (a very unusual experience in his dealings with the Russians). Haymerle's manner and methods provoked him, and we have seen how consciously he had imposed standards of patience on Reuss and himself earlier in the year. Now in mid-April he found that the Austrian draft, which already represented substantial concessions on Haymerle's part, was being challenged by Russia, at a moment when he was supremely anxious to avoid her defection; policy demanded that Austria should be forced to give way, consideration for Austria's position that the matter should be presented to her in a sympathetic and even apologetic form.

Bismarck instead fired at Haymerle a powerful broadside of threats and recriminations, which repeated and accentuated the messages from Giers which he had recently received through Saburov. This assault was launched in a long despatch to Reuss on 25 April; the King of Saxony, who had been kept informed of the progress of the negotiations by Bismarck, sent a personal letter to the Emperor Franz Joseph on the 30th, supporting the early conclusion of the alliance negotiations.[98] Haymerle was told that Bismarck considered that the objections raised in Vienna went further than the situation warranted. In the last resort peace depended on the guarantees which the three Emperors were willing to give by their personal word; if good faith were lacking, no drafting would be adequate protection against threats or violence. The essential point was to secure the word of the Emperor of Russia that he would not ally himself against Austria with any other state. To secure this, Germany would willingly give her agreement to Article III of the draft, which did not go beyond the formality of a warning to Turkey. Bismarck could not let the opportunity of securing an understanding with Russia slip by; already, as a result of the difficulties raised by Austria, Russia was working for a separate agreement with Germany, and he believed that he could conclude such an agreement without infringing the letter or the spirit of the October treaty. In his view Austria should also take advantage of the opportunity to ensure that Russia did not join her enemies, even if Haymerle regarded Italy as being less important in this respect for Austria than France was for Germany. Bismarck believed that the Tsar, worried and inexperienced, would believe that he was sacrificing Russian interests if he went beyond the proposals agreed to by his father, and would retire from the discussions altogether if his undertaking to pledge his imperial word in favour of the peace policy found no echo in Austria. Ignatyev's appointment was a warning not to allow a chronic state of ill-humour to develop. Bismarck was forced in conclusion to fear that if the Russian proposals were not accepted in Vienna, his work, which he had anticipated would be easier than it had been, would be ruined.[99]

In thus throwing on Haymerle's shoulders the entire responsibility for the fate of the negotiations Bismarck had told the Austrian government plainly enough that he lacked the patience—or else the courage—to press the Russians to be a

[98] This letter is mentioned in the Emperor Franz Joseph's reply, a copy of which, undated, but annotated 'ende April 1881?' is in W.S.A., G.IV.

[99] Haymerle's notes of Bismarck's despatch of 25 April, read by Reuss on 29 April, W.S.A., G.IV.

little more accommodating. He had made no attempt to test the resolution of the Russian government, or to find out whether their amendments had been advanced for bargaining purposes or as a final, irrevocable demand.[100] The statement that the new Emperor regarded the maintenance of his father's draft as a pious duty had to be accepted with respect, but Saburov's account leaves no doubt that this move could have been merely tactical; in any case the new Emperor was showing no slavish adherence to his father's wishes in his domestic policy. It cannot even be said that Bismarck set so high a value on Russo-German friendship that he was determined to avoid any disagreement; he did, in fact, temporarily break off the discussions with Russia a month later. The plain fact is that Austrian feelings were expendable; the Russians were incalculable. He could rely on the acceptance in Vienna in the last instance of almost anything short of the revocation of the October treaty. He knew that on the immediate merits of the case he was not maintaining a fair balance between Russian and Austrian demands. He eased his conscience to some extent by renewed grumbling about Haymerle's meticulous draftsmanship. Mere impatience, the urge to carry things through with a high hand, probably played its part.

However that may be, Bismarck's ultimatum was successful: not because it had contained anything very new, but because it indicated with brutal frankness that Bismarck was not in a mood to fight Austria's battles or to continue the triple negotiations much longer. As a reminder and guarantee that Germany's friendship was valuable even without this support Bismarck sent with his instructions of 25 April the draft text of the ministerial declaration affirming the continued validity of the Austro-German treaty; this was promptly accepted by the Emperor and the Austro-Hungarian government, without argument.[101] After presenting Bismarck's demands on 29 April Reuss had to struggle for several days with Haymerle;[102] then

---

[100] It will be remembered that on the main point at issue, the future of Novipazar, Russian policy had been defined as far back as September 1880, although Saburov had kept quiet about it during the winter. See p. 176 above.

[101] Reuss to Bismarck, 2 May, no. xvi, Geheim, A.A., *ibid.*

[102] Haymerle told Reuss on 28 April that he could not conceal the fact that he had hoped that Bismarck would support Austria-Hungary's wishes more warmly: not

on 2 May he was able to report Haymerle's surrender; he was willing to accept the whole of the Russian draft, with the exception of the following addition to the first paragraph of Article II, without which the Emperor would not agree to sign the treaty.

L'Autriche-Hongrie se réserve de faire, si la défense de ses intérêts l'exigeait, des changements dans la situation politique de la Bosnie, de l'Herzégovine, et éventuellement du sandjak de Novi-pazar.

He asked Bismarck to recognize that after this it could not be said that he was subordinating European to Balkan interests, and appealed to him to support this single Austrian proposal with the same energy which he had displayed in pressing the Russian demands on Austria. Reuss, who admitted to Bismarck that he was taken aback by the extent of Haymerle's concessions, recommended the acceptance of the amendment and expressed the personal view that no valid Russian objection to it could be offered.[103]

It was an appeal that Bismarck could hardly ignore, whether on grounds of mere justice or because of the counter-ultimatum which it contained. He telegraphed to Reuss on 4 May his satisfaction with the Austrian reply, his agreement with the Austrian case over '*Bosnien u.s.w.*', and his willingness to put the Austrian case to Saburov. He did this on the 7th, reading to Saburov the relevant portions of Reuss's despatch. In supporting the Austrian proposal he told Saburov that Austria suspected that Russia wished to cancel what she had already granted. 'If you have no such intention, I think that in strict justice you cannot refuse to set Austria at rest on this subject.'[104]

Bismarck seems to have been unaware of the importance that the Russians attached to the prevention of an Austrian annexation of the sanjak; they had never abandoned their reluctance

merely juristic points, but very vital interests, were involved. 'Und nun sei ihm die Möglichkeit, diese Interessen mit dem Russischen Cabinet weiter zu diskutiren, so gut wie abgeschnitten.' Bismarck annotates: 'durchaus nicht'. Reuss to Bismarck, 28 April, no. xiii, Geheim. Cf. Bismarck's general comments in despatches no. vi, Geheim (2 May), and no. vii, Geheim (3 May): A.A., *ibid.*

[103] Reuss to Bismarck, 2 May, no. xiv, Geheim (recd. 10 May) and no. xv, Geheim (printed in *G.P.*, iii, nos. 528, 529).

[104] Bismarck to Reuss, two tels., 4 May, A.A., *ibid. Saburov*, p. 234.

to exclude finally the possibility of a union of Serbia and Montenegro. Bismarck's willingness to support the new Austrian draft of Article II does not mean, therefore, that he anticipated, or was prepared for, any serious struggle with the Russians. But Saburov tells us that he felt that the critical moment of the negotiations had come: for the first time Bismarck had set himself on the side of Austria against Russia. Novipazar was the real point of difficulty, for the Austro-Russian declaration of 13 July 1878 had provided only that the Russian government would raise no objection if Austria found it necessary to occupy the sanjak, like the rest of Bosnia and the Hercegovina. Neither on this nor any other occasion had Russia agreed to the annexation of the sanjak, although she had done so with regard to Bosnia and the Hercegovina.[105] The matter was not one on which Saburov could give a decision, and after protesting that his government had no intention of disputing things which had been granted he suggested that the point should be dealt with among the special questions, which in accordance with Article II were to be included in a protocol to the treaty. Bismarck readily agreed to it; Saburov thus secured time to consult his government. Bismarck was still unaware that he had arrived at the most serious crisis in the negotiations. In a despatch to Reuss on the same day (7 May) he remarked that he had found that Saburov and his government fully recognized Austria's claim that the Bosnian question and Novipazar should be mentioned in a form which took account of earlier negotiations; and he passed on the proposal that Haymerle should draw up the protocol in which the Bosnian and Novipazar questions were to be included. The tone of this despatch leaves no doubt that he assumed that the final phase of drafting would present little difficulty; in fact, speaking as if the negotiations were virtually complete, he proceeded to thank Reuss and Haymerle for their co-operation in the cause of peace. 'For the rest I believe the

---

[105] The Austro-Russian 'convention additionelle' (signed 18 March 1877) to the Budapest agreement of 15 January 1877, agreed to Franz Joseph's annexation of Bosnia and the Hercegovina, 'à l'exclusion de la partie comprise entre la Serbie et le Monténégro au sujet de laquelle les deux gouvernements se réservent de se mettre d'accord lorsque le moment d'en disposer serait venu'. There is a more ambiguous reference in the partly conflicting texts of the Reichstadt agreement of 8 July 1876. Cf. B. H. Sumner, *Russia and the Balkans*, pp. 585, 587, 600.

agreement of the three courts to be assured [by Haymerle's agreement] and I thank your Highness for your fruitful co-operation and request you at the same time to convey to Baron Haymerle the satisfaction that it will give the Emperor to know that the weighty guarantee of peace that we have striven for in this negotiation appears assured.'[106]

But the time had not yet come for the formalities of reciprocal congratulation. It will be remembered that paragraph 3 of Article II of the Russo-German draft of December 1880 had provided that the three courts should 'declare, immediately, the points on which an understanding has already been established in principle' with regard to 'the agreement envisaged by the present Article'. This paragraph had originally been brought forward by the Russians in order to secure Austria's written consent to the union of the two Bulgarias and to serve as a starting-point for a more general entente 'on the eventualities of the future in the East', and it was presumably linked with the second paragraph, in which the three courts undertook to take into account their respective interests in the Balkan Peninsula. The article meant, in short, that a protocol would be attached to the treaty defining the attitudes of the three governments towards the more specific problems of the Balkan peninsula, and on 7 May Saburov had rather ingeniously sidestepped discussion of the Austrian amendment by assuming that the third paragraph also covered the first, which contained the promise of Russia and Germany to respect the new position assured to Austria by the Treaty of Berlin. In the previous August 1880, at the beginning of the negotiations, the Russian government had made two demands of Austria-Hungary—Bulgarian unification and the closing of the Straits —and had been prepared to make two concessions—postponement of the unification of the Bulgarias, and recognition of the annexation of Bosnia and the Hercegovina. The curious course of the subsequent negotiations, which had given the Russians the initiative over the Austrians in drafting, had resulted by May 1881 in a text which fully catered for Russia's main specific interests, while it referred to the Austrian more sketchily:

[106] 'Abschrift eines geheimen Erlasses des Fürsten Bismarck an Prince Reuss, dd. Berlin, 7 Mai 1881' (W.S.A., G.IV); cf. Windelband, pp. 234-5; *Saburov*, p. 236.

that is to say, the Russian plans for the Straits were fully
defined in Article III, whereas Austria had only so far secured
the general assurance in Article II that her new position under
the Berlin treaty would be respected. It was natural, therefore,
for Haymerle to seek to elaborate this part of the treaty, and
also for him to wish to include the elaboration in the main text
of the treaty, where it would have equal weight with Russia's
gains. Saburov's proposal that the Austrian demand should be
dealt with in the protocol was due mainly to his desire to avoid
a head-on collision with Bismarck, but it was also a subtle
depreciation of the significance of the Austrian claims.

It is at first sight surprising that Bismarck, who had told
Saburov so often that he deplored Haymerle's hairsplitting
methods, and who on this occasion said plainly that he would
prefer Saburov to draft the protocol, should have had so little
inkling of Russian opposition to the Novipazar proposal.[107]
Saburov had been warned by Giers in September 1880 that
Russia would probably not agree to the annexation of Novipazar, but Saburov as we have seen had followed the policy of
remaining silent on this point in discussion with Bismarck.[108]
Bismarck, whose grasp of detail was often at fault during the
negotiations, seems to have failed to understand the significance
of Saburov's reticence on this point, and to have assumed that
Russia had acquiesced in Austria's plans for the sanjak—whatever they were. Nevertheless he should have been suspicious
of the ambassador's uncharacteristic readiness to give the
initiative to Haymerle. Haymerle himself seems to have felt
some uneasiness, although he agreed to the task, subject to the
Emperor's approval, which was given on 12 May.[109]

The draft protocol which Haymerle presented in response to
Bismarck's and Saburov's invitation was as follows:

Annexe au Traité secret (Article II alinéa 4) signé à . . . le . . .
entre l'Autriche-Hongrie, l'Allemagne et la Russie.

Les points sur lesquels une entente a déjà été établie en principe
sont les suivants:

[107] He showed some uneasiness on the point in a letter to the King of Saxony on
11 May, Windelband, p. 235.

[108] See above, p. 187.

[109] Bismarck to Reuss, 7 May 1881, no. VIII, Geheim (as in n. 106 above);
Reuss to Bismarck, 10 May, no. XVII, Geheim; 12 May, tel. no. 70 (A.A., ibid.).

1. Danger d'une occupation de la Roumélie Orientale et des Balcans par les troupes turques.

2. Admission éventuelle d'une union entre la Bulgarie et la Roumélie Orientale, si elle venait à se poser par la force des événements; les trois Gouvernements ne feront rien pour l'accelérer et employeront leurs meilleurs efforts pour maintenir le statu quo qu'ils trouvent désirable dans l'intérêt des populations et de la paix de l'Orient. Cette union ne pourra s'étendre au-delà des limites actuelles de la Bulgarie et de la Roumélie Orientale. Si la propagande bulgare prenait une extension menaçante, dirigée contre les autres provinces de l'Empire Ottoman, les trois Cours avertiront les Gouvernements de Bulgarie et de Roumélie Orientale qu'une attaque partant de leur territoire ne pourrait se faire qu'à leurs propres risques et périls et leur ferait perdre la protection des Puissances.

3. Annexion de la Bosnie, de l'Herzégovine et du Sandjak de Novibazar; l'Allemagne et la Russie y donneront leur adhésion si l'Autriche-Hongrie la trouvait nécessaire pour la sauvegarde de ses intérêts.

4. Instructions générales à adresser aux Agents des trois Cours en Orient en vue d'une attitude commune dans toutes les questions qui peuvent surgir.

Haymerle told Reuss, when he discussed the draft with him on 15 May, that he had based it on the Russian statement and synopsis sent by Giers to Saburov and d'Oubril on 13/25 September 1880.[110] Haymerle's first point was awkwardly worded, but was a considerable advantage to Russia: it meant Austria's agreement to the cancellation of the chief British gain under the treaty of Berlin. The second met both the Austrian and Russian wishes about Bulgaria; Giers' draft of September 1880 had however merely provided for the addressing of 'conseils de prudence' to the Bulgarians in the event of their propaganda in Macedonia taking a dangerous turn; Haymerle wished to substitute for this the more emphatic language contained in the third sentence of his second paragraph. He justified this change by arguing that the wording corresponded with that of the last paragraph of Article III, under which the Porte was to be warned against the consequences of allowing any belligerent power to occupy the region of the Straits; Austria had agreed

[110] See above, p. 188.

to this very unwillingly, and in order to meet Russian wishes; he asked the Russian government to meet his wishes in the same way. His third point now referred explicitly to the annexation of Bosnia, the Hercegovina, and the sanjak. Haymerle's proposals were accompanied by a note in which he pointed out that in agreeing at Friedrichsruh to the closing of the Straits and to the eventual union of Bulgaria and Eastern Rumelia he had put forward many counter-proposals (concerning Serbia, Rumania, etc.) in addition to the maintenance of earlier promises with regard to Bosnia, the Hercegovina, and Novipazar; after giving up these additional counter-proposals it was astonishing to find that the remaining Austrian claim concerning the transformation of the occupation of Bosnia, the Hercegovina, and eventually of Novipazar should also be deleted.[111]

Saburov in the meantime had drafted his own version of the appendix and had sent it to Giers for approval, at the same time giving a copy to Bismarck. There seems no doubt that Bismarck regarded Saburov as a better draftsman than Haymerle, and would in any case, in the interest of stylistic felicity, have preferred to leave the drawing-up of the protocol to him. When he saw Haymerle's draft (on the 16th or 17th) he found that it was awkwardly phrased; his apparent exasperation at Haymerle's clumsiness in this respect is, however, surely excessive, when we remember that he could himself have taken a pen and rephrased the whole document in a few minutes. On the 17th he sent Reuss an extremely bad-tempered despatch about Haymerle's odd and tactless communications on the subject of the Austro-German trade negotiation then in progress.[112] A comparison of the two drafts now revealed the fundamental difference over Novipazar, and he showed much irritability at this

---

[111] Reuss to Bismarck, 15 May, no. xviii, Geheim, A.A., *ibid.*: includes text of Haymerle's draft. Reuss reports Franz Joseph as saying to him, that he now regarded the *Dreikaiserbündnis* as assured. 'Er habe sich erfreut, dass Euere Durchlaucht den einzigen Wunsch, den Er gehabt habe, unterstützt hätten. . . .' Haymerle's note to Reuss, dated 'Mai 1881' (W.S.A., G.IV), starts with a reference to the Budapest convention of March 1877 and says that the annexation of Bosnia and the Hercegovina was accepted in the communication which Saburov made to Hohenlohe and which formed the basis of the Friedrichsruh discussions.

[112] Bismarck to Reuss, 17 May, Geheim (unnumbered): text in *G.P.*, iii, no. 530; Reuss's reply, 22 May, A.A., *ibid.*

new deadlock; his annoyance was genuine, but it became clear that he was feeling around, subconsciously perhaps, for an excuse to abandon Austrian interests once again. Saburov's account of the proceedings at this point is coloured by his somewhat artless admiration for his own cunning, but there seems to be some justification for his claim that by concentrating Bismarck's attention on the imperfections of Haymerle's drafting he evaded some of the consequences of the Russian refusal to agree to Bismarck's wishes on the Novipazar question. 'That one of the two who spoke and objected the most, was certain to get the worst of it', wrote Saburov. 'Therefore I adopted the tactics of saying as little as possible, and acting in such a way that the objections came from Vienna.'[113]

Bismarck saw Saburov on the 18th, gave him Haymerle's draft, and advised its acceptance by Russia, on the ground that by confessing in writing the intention to deviate from the treaty of Berlin Austria would be irrevocably compromised with regard to Turkey and England, and be unable to protest when Russia in due course found it necessary to deviate from the treaty. Bismarck hinted that if Russia did not accept the Austrian version Haymerle might end by getting out of the treaty. Saburov however held out no hope that his government would accept the Austrian draft.[114] A day or two later he received a letter from Giers of 17 May saying that the Emperor had agreed to his, Saburov's, draft of the appendix which excluded the annexation of Novipazar,[115] and there followed another of his curious manœuvres; without mentioning that he had received Giers' reply he told Limburg-Stirum that if the Chancellor wished to conclude the negotiations at once he could do so by accepting the Russian draft, which was 'almost certain' to be accepted in St. Petersburg, whereas some time might elapse before a reply was received to his despatch conveying Haymerle's draft there. In his memoir he explains that he wished to avoid a direct refusal of Bismarck's recommenda-

---

[113] *Saburov*, p. 240.

[114] *Ibid.*, pp. 238–40.

[115] Skazkin (p. 172), states that Giers was inclined at first to favour the recognition of Austria's right to annex the sanjak in exchange for Austrian agreement to Bulgarian unification, but that the Council, influenced by Miljutin, rejected this plan.

tion that the Austrian draft should be accepted, and he hoped that Bismarck, being anxious to get away to Kissingen, would send Saburov's draft to Vienna for Haymerle's consideration. If Haymerle then rejected the Russian draft Bismarck would, Saburov calculated, be annoyed for a third time with the Austrians and not the Russians.[116] If this was really Saburov's reading of the case at the time (and not a subsequent attempt to dignify his evasive conduct) then it is strange indeed that he can have imagined that Bismarck would fail to realize that behind all these shufflings was the desire to postpone a show-down on the Novipazar issue. Bismarck in fact was not deceived. He sent a despatch to Reuss on 24 May saying that he had just learnt to his regret that the Tsar's acceptance of Haymerle's draft, particularly with regard to Novipazar, could not be taken for granted, and asking Haymerle to consider the alternative draft that Saburov had drawn up.[117]

Reuss gave his message, and Haymerle replied promptly on the same day (the 26th): Reuss's despatch in reply reached Bismarck on the 27th.[118] Haymerle made little attempt to conceal his exasperation. He told Reuss that he would not indulge in recriminations, but he complained nevertheless that Russian diplomacy tended to repudiate things that had already been promised, and asked why, if Saburov already had in his hands a draft acceptable to the Tsar,[119] he had thrust on to the Austrian cabinet the task of defining the relevant points? He then criticized Saburov's draft, and maintained his own position; he summed the matter up by saying that the three principles on which Austria must insist were, (1) complete freedom of decision concerning Novipazar as well as Bosnia and the Hercegovina; (2) the unification of the two Bulgarias not to be hastened; (3) a guarantee that the Bulgarian movement should not extend to Macedonia. Here was a deadlock: would Bismarck seek to break it by insisting on the justice of Austria's case? Would his pride and his conscience allow him to follow

[116] The story has to be based on the somewhat sketchy narrative of Saburov at this point, as there appears to be no account of his talks with Bismarck (on the 18th) and Limburg-Stirum in A.A. The date of the latter is not given. *Ibid.*, p. 241.

[117] Bismarck to Reuss, 24 May, no. x, Geheim, A.A., *ibid.*

[118] Reuss to Bismarck, 26 May, no. xx, Geheim, A.A., *ibid.*

[119] Bismarck's annotation: 'hatte er nicht' (Reuss's no. xx, *ibid.*).

the more discreet course of surrendering to Russian intransigence? He decided to avoid both alternatives by retiring from the negotiations.

There is a graphic account of the next stage in the negotiations in a memorandum of Herbert Bismarck's. As soon as Reuss's despatch no. XX of 26 May had been received on the 27th he called on Saburov and told the ambassador that his father could no longer act as postman between Vienna and St. Petersburg; he must leave the two governments to reach a direct understanding about the remaining problems of phrasing and drafting. For his part he could only repeat the advice, which he had already given to Saburov, to accept the draft which Haymerle had undertaken at Russia's invitation. Herbert added that 'the Chancellor could not shut his eyes to the truth of Baron Haymerle's assertion that Russian diplomacy had repeatedly withdrawn promises it had already made, and the resulting fruitless labour was exhausting him too much'. Saburov, so Herbert tells us, listened to this remark in silence.[120]

Nevertheless, Saburov could not give way. He had just received further instructions from Giers, and had to tell Herbert that Haymerle might expect to secure Russia's agreement to all his amendments except that concerning Novipazar. He argued that his government had made a great concession in agreeing to the annexation of Bosnia and the Hercegovina, and a further concession was the express recognition of the agreement of 13 July 1878, which had allowed Austria the unquestioned occupation of Novipazar. But to agree to the *annexation* of Novipazar would be a new Russian concession, without counter-concession on Austria's side. Such a counter-concession might be the unification of the two Bulgarias; but the impression in St. Petersburg was that Haymerle would oppose the latter as soon as he had secured the annexation of the sanjak. He did not believe that this was really Haymerle's intention, and he was inclined to propose to his government that the unification should be accepted as compensation for the annexation of the sanjak. He wished above all that Giers would send him to Vienna to complete the final version of the draft treaty; he was

[120] Saburov's account (p. 242) omits all reference to this incident and suggests that Bismarck blamed only Haymerle for the deadlock.

sure that he could arrange everything with Haymerle in an hour.[121]

Saburov's voluble criticism of Haymerle was no doubt intended mainly to exonerate the Russian government from the accusation of unreasonableness that Herbert Bismarck had repeated so bluntly; but Saburov, an ambitious man, was evidently excited also by the vision of a final diplomatic *coup* in Vienna.[122] His government showed no interest whatsoever in his plans: the Tsar flatly rejected his proposal to treat the questions of Novipazar and Bulgarian unification simultaneously with one word—'*impossibilité*'. Saburov showed no particular concern at Bismarck's withdrawal, and continued his manœuvres; would Bismarck propose his going to Vienna, he could hardly propose himself?[123] Not for the first time he criticized his own government; according to Herbert Bismarck's report of 1 June he said that he could see no Russian interest that was served by the refusal of Austria's desire for Novipazar, but the Tsar, who lacked judgment and experience of foreign affairs, adhered stubbornly to the single principle of not going an inch beyond the concessions made by his father.[124] A report from Schweinitz showed, however, that the Tsar was

[121] Aufzeichnung, Herbert v. Bismarck, 27 May, A.A., *ibid.* Saburov is reported as saying after the reference to Haymerle's attitude towards the unification: 'Selon moi ce n'est que de la maladresse du Brn Haymerle, pas de mauvaise foi, mais que voulez-vous, nous avons nos embrailleurs tout aussi bien à St. Pétersbourg, qu'on les a à Vienne . . . si l'Autriche pose l'annexion de Novibazar comme équivalent pour la réunion des deux Bulgaries, nous pouvons traiter donnant donnant. J'ai l'idée de proposer à mon Gouvernement une rédaction, qui nous garantirait contre l'annexion de Novibazar à l'Autriche avant que la réunion des 2 Bulgaries soit consommée. . . . Je crois même pouvoir obtenir de mon Gouvernement l'admission du mot "annexion", pourvu qu'il soit expressément stipulé que cette annexion ne se fasse que simultanément avec la réunion des 2 Bulgaries. Je vais télégraphier ce soir même dans ce sens à Mr. de Giers.'

[122] Saburov's memoir not only omits any indication of his own desire to go to Vienna, but says that he told Herbert Bismarck 'that it was not my business to make any suggestion in this connection'. He also omits reference to his proposal about Bulgarian unification as a *quid pro quo* for the annexation of Novipazar (*op. cit.*, p. 243). Skazkin (p. 173) gives a full summary of Saburov's report to Giers on his conversation with Herbert Bismarck of 28 May.

[123] 'Je ne peux pas me proposer moi-même pour mener à fin les négociations, ma position est trop délicate dans cette question: si je me mettais en avant, on me le prendrait en mauvais part à St Pétersbourg et cela nuirait à l'affaire même' (Aufzeichnung, Herbert v. Bismarck, 1 June, A.A., *ibid.*). Cf. Skazkin, p. 173.

[124] 'Je regrette tellement que l'affaire n'ait pas été baclée du temps de l'empereur défunt . . .' (*ibid.*).

correspondingly anxious not to abandon the work which his father had begun, namely a triple understanding with its pivot in Berlin. How far this insistence on the Tsar's conservatism was merely tactical is difficult to say; there is no doubt, however, that St. Petersburg was thoroughly alarmed at the embarrassing situation which would arise if Bismarck abandoned the rôle of 'mediator' and either allowed the negotiations to collapse, or to end in a treaty from which he had partly dissociated himself.[125] Certainly the very last thing the Russian government was likely to do was to send Saburov to Vienna; and he was instructed on 1 June to request Bismarck to resume the direction of affairs. Bismarck's ill health was not entirely feigned; he was suffering from a 'very painful swelling of the veins'. But the illness, if painful, was also diplomatic. There were the usual reports of his anxiety to go to Kissingen. Saburov was unable for some days to see the Chancellor, and accordingly sent the Russian request to him in writing on the 7th, making it clear however that the Tsar did not wish to bind himself to the annexation of Novipazar.[126]

Bismarck's health now improved sufficiently rapidly for him to come again into action; he threw aside whatever scruples he still had about the justice of Austria's demands, blamed the whole affair on Haymerle, and called once more for his surrender. In reply to Schweinitz's despatch of 1 June he wrote on the 6th that his announcement that he was weary of the matter had referred only to Haymerle and his paltry difficulties; he was at the moment ill, but hoped to resume the negotiations, and bring them to a successful result, in a few days.[127] This message

[125] Schweinitz to Bismarck, 1 June, no. 202, Geheim; A.A. *ibid.* The Tsar annotated Saburov's despatch of 12/24 May with the words: 'The affair has to be finished, but Novipazar should not be conceded'. Skazkin, p. 172.

[126] Saburov to Bismarck, 7 June 1881, A.A., *ibid.*; *Saburov*, pp. 245–8. Kálnoky on 9 June warned Haymerle that the Tsar thought the Austrian draft 'trop vague' and preferred Saburov's: Kálnoky retorted that he could not see how the essential point could be stated more clearly. Giers said: 'Il faut avouer que le mérite du Prince Bismarck pour la réussite de cette importante négociation et la situation favorable qui en résulte pour nous tous, est immense. Cette entente est d'autant plus importante que tout fait croire qu'un danger immense menace l'avenir de l'Europe entière: c'est la révolution sociale' (Kálnoky to Haymerle, tel. no. 59 and despatch no. 6, 28 May/9 June, W.S.A., G.IV). See also *Schweinitz*, ii, 164–5; 166.

[127] Bismarck to Schweinitz, 6 June, no. 70, Geheim, A.A., *ibid. Schweinitz*, ii, 164–5; 166.

for Giers was a face-saving formula which preluded his final abandonment of Haymerle's interests. When Saburov's letter to Bismarck was presented on the 7th Limburg-Stirum promised that Bismarck would shortly resume activity.[128] A fresh German invitation to Haymerle to send a draft of the appendix was telegraphed on 8 June, in terms which called for an acceptance of the Russian position over Novipazar; and once more Haymerle capitulated. The Austrian draft which reached Berlin (apparently on the 11th) was found to accept the declaration of 13 July 1878 on this point. This was Haymerle's draft.

Eventualités sur lesquelles les trois Cours Impériales sont tombées d'accord.

Bosnie et Herzégowine. L'Autriche-Hongrie se réserve de faire tels changements dans la situation politique de ces deux provinces que la défense de ses intérêts exigerait.

Sandjak de Novi Bazar. La déclaration échangée entre les plénipotentiaires Austro-Hongrois et les plénipotentiaires Russes au Congrès de Berlin en date de 13/1 Juillet 1878 reste en vigueur.

Roumélie Orientale. Les trois Puissances sont d'accord pour envisager l'éventualité d'une occupation soit de la Roumélie Orientale, soit des Balcans, comme pleine de périls pour la paix générale. Le cas échéant, elles emploieront leurs efforts diplomatiques pour détourner la Porte d'une pareille entreprise.

[first amendment][129] à moins que la Porte ne se trouve en état de légitime défense contre des attaques partant du territoire de la Bulgarie ou de la Roumélie Orientale contre une des autres provinces de l'Empire ottoman.

[second amendment] bien entendu que la Bulgarie et la Roumélie Orientale devront de leur côté s'abstenir de provoquer la Porte par des attaques partant de leur territoire contre les autres provinces de l'Empire Ottoman.

[Bulgarie.][130] Les trois Puissances ne s'opposeront pas à la réunion éventuelle de la Bulgarie et de la Roumélie Orientale dans les limites territoriales qui leur sont assignées par le Traité de Berlin, si cette question venait à surgir par la force des choses. Elles ne feront rien pour accélérer cette réunion et tâcheront de maintenir le status quo actuel.

[Attitude des agents en Orient.] Afin d'éviter les froissements

---

[128] Memorandum by Limburg-Stirum, 10 June, A.A., *ibid.*

[129] These two 'amendments' were offered by Haymerle as alternatives.

[130] This and the next title were not included in Haymerle's draft.

d'intérêts dans les questions locales qui peuvent surgir, les trois Cours Impériales muniront leurs représentants et agents en Orient d'une Instruction générale pour leur prescrire de s'efforcer à aplanir leurs divergences par des explications amicales entre eux dans chaque cas spécial, et pour le cas où ils n'y parviendraient pas, d'en référer à leurs Gouvernements.[131]

Bismarck, for some unexplained reason, sent his son Herbert on the 10th to ascertain privately what amendments Saburov still desired, and then on the 11th sent Limburg-Stirum (who was supposed to be unaware of this private transaction) to Saburov with the amended text. The inexorable Russian ambassador deleted the few words and phrases in which Haymerle had departed from the Russian text, and was able to tell Giers that 'as final result, it is our draft, pure and simple, as it had been approved by the Emperor'.[132] This was not, however, quite the case. He deleted the word '*diplomatiques*' from the paragraph on Eastern Rumelia, and the sentence 'they will do nothing to hasten the union, and will endeavour to maintain the present *status quo*' from the Bulgarian paragraph; he argued that this sentence merely said twice over what had already been promised at the beginning of the paragraph, and that 'this insistence could only offend us'. He offered, however, certain rather flimsy counter-concessions, and these Bismarck gathered together in one final majestic attempt to sweep aside Haymerle's remaining scruples.

He set out his arguments in a despatch which went off by courier to Reuss on the evening of the 12th.[133] He described it as a last attempt to reach an agreement; if it failed he would be unable, owing to his exhausted strength, to go any further with the matter, and would have to ask Haymerle to agree to an invitation being sent to St. Petersburg for Saburov to continue the negotiations in Vienna. He then said that in return for Haymerle's acceptance of the Novipazar clause, Saburov had offered five counter-concessions. (1) He was authorized to

[131] This draft is taken from a copy in a folder of documents entitled, 'Protocole annexe betreffend' (W.S.A., G.IV).

[132] Saburov, pp. 248, 250–2; Memoranda by H. Bismarck, 10 June, and Limburg-Stirum, 11 June, A.A., *ibid.*

[133] Bismarck to Reuss, 12 June, nos. XI and XII, Geheim, W.S.A., G.IV, copies handed to Haymerle.

agree to a direct reference in paragraph I to the annexation of Bosnia and the Hercegovina. (2) He accepted the second Austrian amendment to the paragraph concerning Eastern Rumelia. (3) He accepted the first sentence of the Austrian wording in the Bulgarian paragraph ('Les trois Puissances . . . force des choses') and (4) instead of the indefinite second sentence offered the following:

Les trois cours sont d'accord pour détourner les Bulgares de toute agression contre les provinces voisines et pour leur déclarer qu'en pareil cas ils agiraient à leurs risques et périls.

He was also authorized to add the words 'nommément la Macédoine' after 'provinces voisines'. Bismarck argued that this was a considerable concession, as there was no reference at all to Macedonia in the Austrian draft. (5) Finally Saburov was willing to accept Haymerle's wording of the last paragraph, concerning the attitude of agents in the East, without alteration, and to omit the last phrase of the Russian draft ('et suspendre toute action locale jusqu'à la réception de nouveaux ordres').

Bismarck defended what he called the 'solitary deletion' of the word 'diplomatic', which Saburov had demanded, and argued at some length that the Russian counter-concessions had not been easy to secure. In reality Saburov had merely offered as 'counter-concessions' points which had already been authorized by his government. Saburov had also suggested that no attempt should be made in the treaty to define the 'local questions' referred to in the last paragraph, as Germany had much less interest in these questions than the other two powers who were Turkey's neighbours. This suggestion met with only one objection from Haymerle; he made a final attempt to retain the words, 'they will do nothing to hasten the union', in the paragraph about Bulgaria. But after some hasty telegraphing between Vienna and Berlin had made it clear that Bismarck and Saburov would not agree, Reuss was able to telegraph on the evening of 14 June the Austrian acceptance of the German draft.[134]

[134] Reuss to Bismarck, 13 June, tel. no. 81; 14 June, tel. no. 82. A.A., *ibid.* Haymerle to Széchényi, 15 June, Geheim, W.S.A., G.IV. *Saburov*, p. 253; *Schweinitz*, ii, 166.

Széchényi, who had played very little part in the negotiations hitherto, was authorized to sign the treaty, and at the same time to make one more attempt to secure some assurances that Russia would do nothing to hasten the union. Haymerle referred therefore to the undertaking on this point in Giers' letter of 15 September 1880, and Saburov told Széchényi in general terms on the 17th that the policy of pacification was necessary for Russia for the same reason as it was for other powers. After this a meeting with Count Limburg-Stirum completed the final revision of the text, and the treaty was signed on 18 June 1881.[135]

[135] On 15 June Haymerle sent Széchényi the text of a note to be exchanged by Széchényi and Saburov after the signing of the treaty; this attempted to define more precisely the 'questions locales' of paragraph 5 of the annex. This idea was dropped when Saburov said that he would have to refer the matter to St. Petersburg. (Text in Haymerle to Széchényi, Privatschreiben, 15 June, W.S.A., G.IV.) Saburov proposed 'sécurité' instead of 'position défensive' in the preamble: this was rejected following Széchényi's opposition. Saburov attached significance to the fact that the annex to the treaty was described, on Limburg-Stirum's proposal, as a 'protocol'. The suggestion came originally, however, from Haymerle. The fullest account of the final stages is in Széchényi's despatch to Haymerle, 18 June, ibid.: see also Saburov, pp. 253–5.

CHAPTER X

After the Concert

THE Concert of Europe—Gladstone's Concert, the diplomatic collaboration of the great powers for common ends which he had offered the world in Midlothian—did not survive the settlement of the Greek question. This does not mean that the powers were henceforth incapable of concerted action, or that they ceased to strive for peace, or to respect the 'public law' of Europe, or to seek, in their own interests, the 'objects connected with the common good of them all' which Gladstone had postulated as the basis for concerted action. The common good which all were seeking and continued to seek was the avoidance of a war into which all might be drawn, a possibility which had appeared by no means remote in 1879. But the powers could not find, and Gladstone could not supply, a conception of a continuous common danger which would produce the unity that he desired: the unity which would permanently 'neutralize and fetter and bind up' the selfish aims of each individual state. The neutralizing of selfish aims was not the same as unity in action; having abandoned 'selfish ends' in order to avoid the risk of war the powers would hardly wish to risk war in the pursuit of unselfish ones. There was an evident duality in the objectives of Gladstone's original programme— he sought both the tranquillization of Europe and the coercion of the Turks—and the powers preferred peace. Gladstone had promised to secure the first aim through the second, offering the powers a basis for amicable intercourse in combined pressure on the intransigent Turk, rather in the spirit of Saburov's cynical comment: 'to arrive at an era of lasting peace there must be victors and vanquished. That is the law of our world.'[1] But when the Dulcigno demonstration showed that the

[1] *Saburov*, p. 136.

Sultan was determined to be very obstinate joint pressure lost its midsummer attractions; the Smyrna proposals suggested serious trouble. Suppose the Turk, in a fanatical, hopeless way, decided to fight? Turkey had shown, in 1877 and 1853 and 1827, that she was capable of saying a final no to a stronger neighbour, and although Gladstone was probably right in asserting that the Sultan would never challenge the six great powers the possibility that he would do so remained.

At this point, therefore, collective pressure had lost its appeal, and indeed its purpose; mediation or arbitration, initiated from Paris or Berlin, was substituted in the Greek negotiations for active pressure from London, and the British government played a relatively minor part in the proceedings. The Greek problem had received too much publicity for the powers to ignore it, but they had no desire to involve themselves in further embarrassments; the Concert still supplied the mode of procedure, but its function was now advisory rather than minatory. And after this the Concert, in the eyes of the continental powers, had clearly exhausted its usefulness; they proceeded to make this clear to the British government in a number of cases which amounted to a deliberate rejection of the Concert procedure and of British leadership. In each of these cases Gladstone was still moved by concern for the 'public law' of Europe, even though British national interests were in some degree involved; but he showed no desire for isolated interventions. In the face of fresh crises in its domestic and foreign politics the British government was willing enough to leave on the consciences of others the responsibility for inaction.

The first of these rebuffs came in Tunis. Granville certainly had a momentary hope during April 1881 that the Concert could be brought into action in this question, but he had no encouragement from either the British cabinet or the German government. The story of the events immediately preceding the French occupation is well known, and it is only necessary to outline their course briefly here.[2] The French government had

[2] The fullest account is in an unpublished thesis by Mohamed Mustafa Safwat, 'Tunis and the Powers, 1878–1881' (1940, University of London Library). Saint-Hilaire's defence of his policy is given in his *Fragments* (B. St-H., pp. 204–30; 240–9; 306–36).

continued to hesitate throughout the winter and Granville, who disliked the prospect of an open quarrel with France almost as much as he disliked the Salisbury procedure of acquiescence and bargaining, was still without a policy. The Enfida case had brought the two governments into direct opposition for a time, but there is no reason to think that British policy in this affair was anything but hand-to-mouth. The Enfida was a vast estate in the Regency which Khair-ed-Din had decided to sell after his departure for Constantinople; the purchaser was a Marseilles company, and this fresh accession of French influence led the Bey to deny Khair-ed-Din's right to dispose of the property. Moreover a British subject, Lévy, claimed the estate under a Moslem right of pre-emption. Here were the makings of one of those exasperating conflicts in which doubtful title, French ambition, and Tunisian nerves and obstruction conspired to turn a normal commercial transaction into an international battle of concessions. With the temporary easing of Franco-Italian relations in October 1880 the Enfida case had made the British and French the main antagonists in Tunis from November 1880 to the end of March 1881. Reade, the British consul, took up Lévy's case with vigour; Granville, irritated and genuinely shocked by the French methods, supported Lévy for a time, regarding the matter as one of protecting a British subject's rights; on the other hand the French were determined to have their way, and they had doubts about the genuineness of Lévy's title which Lyons shared.[3] For a time Granville not only refused to repudiate Reade's activities, but at the beginning of February 1881, when France sent a warship, the *Friedland*, to Tunis, decided that Great Britain must do the same. So the *Thunderer* arrived in Tunisian waters. After hurried and conflicting explanations by the French, both ships were withdrawn by common agreement.[4] Yet Granville was aware of the danger that the Bey would be led to expect political support from England and be encouraged to drift into a major crisis with France; and Lyons reinforced this conviction when he wrote on 25 February that reasonable people in France could see 'that we

[3] Cf. Granville's comments to Lyons, 25 January, 10 February, and 11 March, 1881; Lyons to Granville, 22 March; G.D. 29/171.

[4] *D.D.F.*, iii, nos. 366, 367.

cannot allow our own subjects to be bullied, but the French in general do not distinguish between the Enfida case, the Tunisian questions regarding predominant influence, Italy, and so forth'.[5]

In short, the French were behaving badly, but what could Granville do? The French also, up to this point, had not decided what to do. Gambetta was still unconvinced that the moment for action had arrived; Ferry found an affair in Tunis unthinkable in an election year. De Courcel, Director of Political Affairs at the Ministry of Foreign Affairs, wrote on 13 March that Saint-Hilaire had been unable to persuade the Council of Ministers to take action.[6] This shows that Saint-Hilaire himself was won over, but does nothing to explain the rather rapid conversion of Ferry and the majority of the Council during the next fortnight. De Courcel in two long interviews with Gambetta marshalled all the arguments in favour of French intervention, but Gambetta knew the facts and his own mind too well to need any such inspiration. Gambetta did, however, decide that the moment was now favourable for action, and his decision brought round his following in the cabinet; Ferry himself had agreed by the end of March.[7] There had been no specific incident to justify this change of front; the raid by Kroumir (more accurately 'Khamir') tribesmen from Tunis into Algeria, the main excuse for subsequent action, was not known in Paris until 30 March.[8] The coincidence with the Tsar's assassination (on 13 March) is surely too close to be accidental. Saint-Hilaire had been reassured at the end of November 1880 that Bismarck intended to continue the support in Tunis that he had given to Waddington and de Freycinet, but the French government could not avoid some uneasiness at the growing intimacy of Germany and Russia, which might well reduce Bismarck's willingness to conciliate the French. Bismarck was likely to be in doubt about the new Tsar's intentions for some weeks, and correspondingly eager to turn French attention away from the possibilities of a

[5] Lyons to Granville, 25 February 1881, G.D., 29/171.

[6] D.D.F., ii, no. 401.

[7] Power, op. cit., pp. 49–51; G. Hanotaux, Histoire de la France contemporaine (1908), iv, 633.

[8] D.D.F., iii, no. 307.

rapprochement with Russia, and an anti-German policy in Europe. However this may be, the French initiative in Tunis received Bismarck's whole-hearted support, which carried with it that of Austria.[9] Ferry's application to the Chamber on 4 April for an appropriation of 6,000,000 francs to pay for an expeditionary force to chastise the raiders was soon recognized as the prelude to even more drastic steps.

Granville wrote to Lyons on 6 April that France could not be allowed to seize Tunis without the consent of Turkey or any communication with Europe. But this faint enunciation of the authority of the Concert was not a prelude to positive action. He could only advise Lyons to appear 'as mysterious as he could as to what might be our attitude'.[10] An article by Blowitz in *The Times* of 11 April revealed the gist of Salisbury's despatch to Lyons of 7 August 1878; Blowitz had been shown this document by the French Foreign Office, and the French press during the following days contained some blunt reminders of Britain's own action in Cyprus. The Italians had every reason to complain, for Ferry had not thought it necessary even to carry out his predecessor's promise to let them know before a decisive step was taken. The immediate result was Cairoli's resignation on 7 April. Turkey protested on the ground that Tunis was a part of the Turkish Empire, and there were reports that the Turkish navy would go into action; but the Sultan did not have the courage to attempt this technical miracle. The rapid success of the French forces speedily reduced the dangers, never very real, of effective opposition. Bismarck, who was determined to extract the maximum of credit for his attitude, told Saint-Vallier on 1 May that he had repulsed all attempts by other powers to bring about his interference. The Sultan, he said, would be wiser to concern himself with the Balkan Peninsula and Asia Minor, and Italy with her domestic miseries and her forthcoming bankruptcy. And he also claimed that he had flatly repulsed the British government, after Granville had sent Dufferin with special orders to seek an understanding with Germany with a view to a European mediation in the Tunisian affair.[11]

[9] Windelband, pp. 226–7.
[10] Granville to Lyons, 6 April 1881, G.D. 29/171.
[11] *D.D.F.*, iii, nos. 478, 485, 488, 495, 507, etc.

Of this British move there is no evidence in other sources. Throughout April Granville was reluctant to acquiesce in the French action. He wrote to Gladstone on the 23rd: 'Derby came out of one [Conservative] Cabinet in which he had been wrangling and said, "Occupy, fortify, grab and brag" is the whole policy of the Government. I own to jealousy of France getting an overwhelming preponderance in the Mediterranean.' But Gladstone was opposed to co-operation with Italy, and Northbrook, the First Lord of the Admiralty, was even more strongly opposed to any form of naval action, which would provide the only effective means of demonstration. The occupation of Bizerta on 1 May aroused further anxieties, but Northbrook was again unwilling to share Granville's rather alarmist views about the danger to Malta.[12] On 6 May Granville went so far as to draft proposals to Germany and Austria 'as to the position of the French in Tunis, with a view to raise the Concert of Europe in their path'. He was dissuaded from this course by Tenterden and Dilke. Dilke attributes this move to the 'wily Russian' (presumably Lobanov) who had 'got up the trouble by hinting verbally to Lord Granville that Russia would act with England and Italy in this matter'. Dilke was wrong, however, when he added, 'the proposal led to trouble three days later, for, of course, the Russians told the French in such a way as to make them believe that the idea was ours'. He was no doubt referring to a very guarded reference by the French ambassador on 9 May to a report of British proposals in Berlin for European mediation; but it was Bismarck, not Lobanov, who had alarmed the French with his report on Dufferin's alleged proposal.[13] On 7 May Granville offered mediation to the French government, but only if it were desired by both France and the Bey. The treaty of Bardo was signed on 13 May, and at a meeting on the same day Granville accepted the view of the majority of the Cabinet that the attitude of Bismarck and the other powers,

[12] *Granville*, ii, 234–5; Northbrook to Granville, 19 April, 13 May 1881, G.D. 29/137; Granville to Gladstone, 23 April, G.D., 29/124.

[13] Dilke, i, 380; *D.D.F.*, iii, 506. Dilke and Granville both denied flatly that any proposal of European mediation had been made to Bismarck. Saint-Hilaire's view was that the proposal had been an unofficial sounding but there is no evidence even of this in the available British material. More probably Bismarck was simply doing his best to widen the breach between the British and French.

Salisbury's earlier commitments, and the British occupation of Cyprus prevented interference with French plans. He limited himself to a note on 20 May in which he at least had the satisfaction of telling Saint-Hilaire that the treaty with Tunis went far beyond any question of the security of the frontier and amounted practically to a protectorate, which the British government had understood to have been disclaimed.[14]

It was, however, in the Balkans and Near East, where the Concert had been established with the deliberate aim of relaxing tensions created by the Berlin treaty, that British isolation was most obvious. The extrusion of British influence was, indeed, the one matter on which the three empires were agreed. The conclusion of the *Dreikaiserbündnis* had brought about no diminution of Austro-Russian rivalry; but the three powers were agreed in regarding British intervention as inimical to the state of ostensible quiescence which they were anxious to maintain; and while Russia and Austria had each welcomed some aspects of Gladstone's policy as advantageous to her own plans, they were also convinced that each must suffer in some measure from continued British activity in the Balkans. Russia had welcomed the British government's efforts on behalf of Montenegro, but not its interest in Bulgaria, where Austria and Great Britain had maintained some degree of joint opposition to Russian influence since the Congress.[15] And Austria, although welcoming British interest in Bulgaria, was thoroughly alarmed by the prospect of joint Russo-British activity at Constantinople, and even had reason to resent British activity in Serbia.[16]

[14] A. & P., *Further correspondence respecting the Affairs of Tunis* (c. 2887), no. 6; *D.D.F.*, iv, no. 21. Granville sought to tie down the French government as far as possible to assurances already given. These included an assurance that the Anglo-Tunisian general convention of 19 July 1875 should remain in force, and that Bizerta should be maintained as an exclusively commercial port. Later the Cabinet sought and received assurances in July that France had no designs on Tripoli. The Enfida case, and the rights of Lévy, continued under discussion for some time. After the French *fait accompli* it was not the desire of the British government that the Tunisian question should become a permanent bone of contention between the two countries, and it was prepared to take the view that the maintenance of the convention of 19 July 1875, which gave British subjects most-favoured-nation rights and defined the privileges of British consuls, was a sufficient guarantee of legitimate British interests. Cf. B. St-H., pp. 298–305.

[15] See above, pp. 62, 108–11.

[16] The Serbian government appeared for a time to favour a British as opposed to an Austrian firm in awarding the contract for the construction of the Serbian

It was a constitutional crisis in Bulgaria which now revealed that the days of the Anglo-Austrian entente and of the European Concert were over. Prince Alexander of Bulgaria, earnest and well-intentioned, but sadly lacking in resource in handling the exasperating dishonesties of Bulgarian party politics, announced on 24 May that he would abdicate unless the Bulgarian National Assembly invested him with extraordinary powers for seven years. His action was supported by the new Russian consul-general, General Hitrovo. The matter became one of international discussion during the summer; but when the Grand Sobranje met on 12 July, the proposals were voted with practically no opposition.[17]

The British government, disturbed at an anti-Liberal move which seemed calculated to further Russian influence, voiced its opposition. Odo Russell believed that the prince had been encouraged by both Berlin and St. Petersburg.[18] But none of the three imperial governments was prepared to support any British

portion of the railway line from Pest to Belgrade and thence to Nish. Sir Thomas Tancred, a representative of the British firm, sought the British government's support in March 1881. After a conversation on the 16th E. W. Hamilton wrote to Gladstone: 'His terms were the most favourable for the Servian Government and though great pressure has been put upon the "Skuptshina" to accept the offer of the Austrians he was given to understand that his tender would be accepted; if he could find the money, which they doubted. By the assistance of this country and Russia he *has* succeeded in getting the requisite sum subscribed; and has no doubt whatever that he shall now get the contract and so "bowl out" the Austrians. He attaches great importance to this politically; for the influence of Austria in Servia is already very great—the Prince being a mere puppet in her hands—and the additional influence which she would acquire by having to construct the railway would practically have established the complete ascendancy of Austria in the Principality. . . .'

Minutes on this note by Sanderson and others show, however, that Tancred had been too optimistic. It was remarked that Gould, the British consul-general in Belgrade, had interfered too actively on Tancred's behalf, and had been complained of by the Serbian government; and that the latter had already decided in favour of M. Boutoux's proposals, which were supported by Austria. Granville rejected further action. 'After what has passed, I am against giving Gould any authority to meddle more in the matter—G.' (E. W. Hamilton to Gladstone, 17 March 1881, G.D. 29/124.)

[17] E. C. Corti, *Alexander von Battenberg* (1920), pp. 110, ff.; Skazkin, pp. 230–51. Cf. Schweinitz, ii, 163–4, 116–7. A. F. Golowine, the prince's chaplain, admits (*Fürst Alexander I*, 1896, pp. 133–4), that 'anderseits war auch Fürst Alexander noch jung und besass nicht jene Erfahrung, die so nothwendig gewesen wäre für einen Mann, der sich in einer so schwierigen und delicaten Lage befindet'.

[18] Ampthill to Granville, 14 May 1881; Knaplund, p. 220.

opposition to the change, and it fell to Austria to say so. Hengelmüller, the Austrian *chargé* in London, explained to Granville that the Austrian government were of opinion that, in the cause of peace, it was most desirable that the prince should not abandon the principality, and they could not conceal from themselves that any expression of disapprobation on the part of the British government at this particular moment would greatly tend to such a result. The hint as to the unwisdom of imprudent platform oratory seems to have nettled Granville, who replied that he yet believed that 'some *mezza termine* might be found which would enable the constitution to be amended without establishing autocratic power. The British government thought the reasons which influenced the Austrian government made it incumbent upon them and the other powers to inculcate prudence and moderation on the Prince. The knowledge that this was being done would much facilitate reticence on the part of Her Majesty's Government.' It was, however, clear that the three empires desired above all to avoid the complications that would follow Alexander's abdication. An appeal addressed to Gladstone by four Bulgarian opposition leaders met with the reply that the Prime Minister was unable to carry on a personal correspondence, and although Granville expressed further doubts in conversation with the Austrian and Russian representatives as to the need for so complete a measure of autocracy, his official pronouncements in the Lords contained the admission that the British agent, Lascelles, had described the constitution in its present form as unworkable.[19] As Austria appeared willing to accept the risk of increased Russian influence it was hardly possible for the British to take further action, and the incident marked the close of the policy of surveillance and protest which the two powers had maintained towards Russian action in Bulgaria since 1878.[20]

The Armenian question had also seemed to Gladstone a suitable field for concerted diplomacy, and here too the other powers were reluctant to act. In the summer of 1880 Goschen had thought that it would 'be possible to obtain a great deal'

[19] Granville to Elliot, W.S.A., 20 June, 1881 (copy communicated by Elliot). *Hansard*, House of Lords, 955–8, 21 June 1881.

[20] A. & P., *Bulgaria No. 1 (1881)*, (c.2992), nos. 42, 52, 53, 112.

in Armenia, but the wide and impracticable demands of the Armenian patriarch, and the proportions assumed by the Montenegrin-Greek crisis, led to a postponement of any active reform measures throughout the winter, and Bismarck in January 1881 also advised postponement. The British government was in no hurry to act, and the reform programme was not revived until Goschen's successor, Lord Dufferin, arrived in Constantinople. When a conference of ambassadors met to discuss the question in September 1881 he found that the powers were prepared to show little active interest in the problem.[21] Dufferin admitted that the powers could no longer rely on material aids, but he proposed that the ambassadors should elaborate a practical project of permanent reforms, make this the basis of representations on the subject to the Porte, and urge the immediate appointment of a high commissioner as a temporary expedient, to alleviate distress during the coming winter. The Sultan agreed on 15 September to appoint within a month a high commissioner for the eastern provinces of Asia Minor, but nothing was done; nevertheless, at an audience with the Sultan on 14 January 1882, Dufferin 'deliberately kept the conversation running at a low pressure', feeling that as long as his government relied solely on persuasion no other course was open to him. The ambassadors gave their formal sanction to a scheme of Armenian reforms in March 1882, but already on 2 April the Egyptian crisis led Dufferin to avoid any reference to Armenia. The British occupation of Egypt provided employment for the British military consuls in Asia Minor, but their withdrawal had already been decided on in the previous winter.[22]

So ended Gladstone's Concert. The distinctive procedure which he had favoured—the definition of a common objective, consultation by diplomatic discussion or conference as to a programme of action, execution of plans by concerted diplomatic

---

[21] Giers wrote later: 'l'entente plus apparente que réelle des Grandes Puissances s'était fatiguée après l'issue de la négociation turco-grecque. Le Cabinet Anglais avait en vain cherché à la réveiller pour le règlement de la question arménienne. Nous n'y étions assez intéressés pour seconder activement les efforts de Mr. Gladstone.' Giers to Mohrenheim, R.E., 15/27 August 1882.

[22] W. N. Medlicott, 'The Gladstone Government and the Cyprus Convention, 1880–1885' (*Journal of Modern History*, June 1940), pp. 196–208.

pressure or by a mandatory—was abandoned; certain Liberal assumptions about a common European consciousness and idealism had to be laid aside, and the solution of various outstanding difficulties, particularly in the Near East, was shelved. There is no reason to think that any of the European governments saw anything particularly momentous or significant in this transition; and although Gladstone was often to talk about his faith in the Concert he did not again seek to establish it on the ambitious lines of his 1880 programme. The British government, as Granville was willing to admit, was as anxious as any other in the early months of 1881 to avoid the embarrassment and distractions of fresh crises in the Mediterranean and Near East, and what in fact came to an end in the summer of 1881 was not so much the Concert of Europe as a phase of British activity; there was no suggestion that as a means of international action the Concert itself might not be revived in the future in appropriate circumstances.

Some continental Liberals retained their faith in Gladstone. The search for guarantees of security through peace continued from time to time to revive interest in the essential Gladstonian plan of the collective guarantee of common interests; the line of development through British and American idealism to the League of Nations charter and beyond, the influence of Gladstone on Woodrow Wilson and many American Liberals, and the pacifist movement from the late nineteenth century onwards, all found some inspiration in the Concert of 1880. But there is little evidence that the programme was taken seriously, or at its face value, by many contemporaries either in England or on the continent. Most of them saw it as an oratorical flourish, useful in British electioneering, which would soon have served its ends; if the more kindly saw in it unpractical idealism, and the more cynical a clever diplomatic manœuvre to secure British interests, all were agreed that its life would be short. Gladstone himself regarded it as he regarded domestic reform; it was a step in human progress which could not be forced; it must be postponed if it was unwelcome. He still had faith in it. On the other hand he was a sufficiently good politician to know the embarrassing possibilities of public ridicule, and the ways in which his own distinctive policies were susceptible to it.

In the ridicule of its critics, and the somewhat apologetic commendation of its supporters, the Concert was now replaced by the more conventional diplomatic ties. Public opinion on foreign affairs in England during the next few years proved as embarrassing to Gladstone as it had been to Disraeli, and supplied no very sympathetic climate for the Liberal ideas. In April 1880, while Gladstone was still hesitating as to the assumption of the premiership, a pamphlet entitled *The Caucus Parliament* proposed a ministry which indicated plainly enough the rich possibilities of future criticism.

Prime Minister	Joseph Chamberlain
Home Secretary	Ginx Jenkins
Foreign Secretaries	{ William Ewart Gladstone
	{ Prince Gortschakoff
War Minister	John Bright (until a suitable
	woman be found)
Lord President	Charles Dilke

Mr. Parnell was to be Irish Secretary; Ismail Pasha, Chancellor of the Exchequer; the First Lord of the Admiralty, Puffer Popoff, and the Minister of Education, Orton Tichborne. Some verses in the same pamphlet show how small an impression Gladstone's carefully qualified denunciations of Turkey had made:

When Russian gold hatched fatal plots against Bulgaria's life
A cry of pious horror rose above the awful strife—
'From Turkey drive out every Turk with execration's yells,
And drive them "bag and baggage" across the Dardanelles'.[23]

Criticism of the Liberal government ran on these lines throughout the history of the ministry, and the long record of military activity in Afghanistan, Egypt, South Africa, and elsewhere produced a not unreasonable comparison between the pacific professions and the violent actuality of Gladstone's foreign policy. Similar inconsistency was discovered in the attacks which Gladstone had made on Austria during the election, and which certainly appeared likely to destroy the good understanding between the two countries that had existed under Beaconsfield. In spite of his willingness to withdraw his remarks, popular attacks on his conduct at once appeared. The anonymous author of *The Gladstone Rule* wrote:

[23] *The Caucus Parliament* (London, 1880), p. 15.

I said in my haste, O Karolyi! what now I've forgotten I uttered—
I wish not a soul to remember the eight-thousand-odd words I
   spluttered.
It's really not fair that a Premier should answer for gibes he out-
   flung,
When he was but a soldier of fortune, and his sword was his
   venomous tongue.

This incident, and the rebuff to Goschen on his arrival in
Constantinople[24] disturbed the atmosphere of goodwill essential
to the type of diplomacy that Gladstone wished to cultivate,
and neither incident was forgotten by the opposition. 'This
disgraceful language' wrote a 'Working Man'[25] in September
1885,

              . . . displayed animosity
And disclosed the exuberance of his own verbosity;
So abusive was he in his phraseology
That he had to retract and make an apology.
The Emperor of Austria the insult rejected,
And Gladstone's *own words* on his head were reflected.
Just fancy the leader of a great nation
Subjecting the country to humiliation!

Gladstone in opposition had made full use of the convention
that the prime minister was the omniscient director of all
government policy, and it is not surprising that the opposition,
adopting the same assumption, half convinced themselves that
the warlike policy of the peaceloving premier really was due
to hypocrisy or worse. This became perhaps the most popular
line of attack, and Gladstone was assailed with such epithets as
the 'Grand Old Mystery' and the 'Mahdi of Midlothian'
throughout the later years of his ministry.[26] A slightly kinder
line of attack was to assume that differences between theory
and practice were due rather to naivety and mistaken idealism
than to more sinister motives. It was explained that the 'Concert of Europe' was a standing joke on the Wilhelmstrasse and

[24] See above, p. 91.
[25] *Remarkable Funny Facts*, by a Working Man (Redhill, 1885).
[26] A good example from the pamphlet literature of the time is *Buzwell's Gludstone,
Tales at Hawhawden*, by James Buzwell. ' "Why, Sir, because they say that yours has
been the most slaughtering Ministry of modern times. Attila was nothing to you."
"This is some fantastic nonsense," he said' (pp. 42–3). See also *Gladstone's Garland*
(1880).

Bismarck was particularly severe on it; the six powers, he had said on one occasion, were like six old maids shut up on an island with a single man, and the burning question of the day was, who should have the one man? 'I fear it would not be decided by a conference', had been Bismarck's comment. 'Only the most parochial of Liberals', says one writer in quoting this anecdote, 'who has passed through a severe course of Mr. Cobden's early pamphlets and become saturated with the delusion which pervades them, that the universe revolves round Manchester, could ever have been misled by the crudest of all shams "the united voice of Europe".' Another remark of Bismarck's, that Gladstone 'had played so long with words that now the words played with him', represented the genuine belief of many of his opponents, and at least some of his friends.[27]

Some reference to these popular criticisms of Gladstone's foreign policy after 1880 may be considered relevant to an examination of the Midlothian policy, for Gladstone had staked everything on his ability to carry through a programme based primarily on popular support. It was an experiment, and it failed; and the failure helps to account for the very abrupt transition to a more reticent policy which appears so soon after 1885. By the end of Salisbury's ministry in 1892 the new method had been established; and the tacit agreement to regard foreign affairs as outside the sphere of party controversy was already producing as its corollary a withholding of information on many important points.[28]

Due weight must be given in this connexion to the reaction of the majority of English politicians to the violence of both Disraeli and Gladstone over matters of foreign policy, and to the concentration of attention in the middle 'eighties on Irish affairs; but the ultimate cause must be sought in a consciousness of the growing tension of European diplomacy, a condition analogous to the sinking of party differences in time of war and one already observable, though not formally established, in the action of the official opposition between 1875 and 1878. Dilke summed up Liberal opinion when he wrote in 1887 that the

[27] Anon., *The Mahdi of Midlothian, 1880 and 1884* (London, 1884), p. 9. C. Lowe, *The Tale of a 'Times' Correspondent* (London, 1926), p. 132.
[28] *Dilke*, ii, 570.

German annexation of Alsace-Lorraine 'must be considered the real cause of that predominance of force-considerations which has been noted since 1878', so that the treaty of Berlin 'which ought to have been the basis of a long-standing if not of a permanent settlement in Europe, became the opening of a period of despair to the disciples of Richard Cobden'.[29] The consciousness of this tension had already got on the nerves of the British electorate by 1880, and helped the Liberal party to victory at the polls; when the new government had discovered that it possessed no heaven-sent prescription for a Concert of Europe it settled down to an uneasy imitation of the self-defensive policy of its predecessors, showing anxiety in Asia Minor, South Africa, and India to withdraw from embarrassing commitments, entering with apparent reluctance on fresh commitments in Egypt, and repeatedly refusing either to accept the opportunity of extending the British protectorate over unappropriated portions of Africa or to facilitate the extension of other powers in the same direction. This appeared to some observers an unnecessarily timid policy and very different from the robust self-assertion of Lord Beaconsfield, but the instinct of both governments was possessive and defensive rather than acquisitive, and the difference in method became less pronounced when Salisbury succeeded to office, temperamentally disposed to favour a quieter policy than that of his former chief.

In the summer of 1881 Bismarck had remoulded Europe as near to his heart's desire as his invincible pessimism allowed to be practicable; his two basic problems, the neutralizing of French and Russian hostility to Germany, had been at least temporarily solved. England alone had offered since the spring of 1880 an ostensible alternative to his plans, and the British initiative had been tolerated, flattered, obstructed, secretly derided and, at last, openly opposed, until Gladstone had withdrawn from the arena. Gladstone failed to perpetuate the Concert procedure because his specific solutions of immediate problems had not carried conviction; and because he had quite failed to create in any continental breast the warm, exalted sense of a European society which would lead the member states

29 C. Dilke, *The Present Position of European Politics* (London, 1887), pp. 2–3.

to subordinate their own interests with a good grace to the common good. Bismarck took it for granted that the great powers had lost (if they had ever possessed) the capacity for compromise and mutual concession on the major problems that separated them in Europe, although they could still give and take in colonial affairs. Accepting this view, his foreign policy reduced itself to military and political measures of defence and to diplomatic manœuvring which would provide continuous postponements of threatened crises; the basic causes of these crises he regarded as irremovable.[30]

This attitude, while it led him to deride as naive or utopian any thoroughgoing solutions of European difficulties, produced an extremely energetic pursuit of short-term objectives which was at times confusing and even alarming to his neighbours, even though it has been the subject of many eulogies by his admirers. 'The treaty was indeed a masterpiece', writes Professor Langer of the Three Emperors' Alliance,[31] and many historians have echoed this judgment. Yet it may well be doubted whether Germany was really in a stronger position *vis-à-vis* her two allies after the treaties of 1879 and 1881 than she had been before, or whether a revived *Dreikaiserbündnis* without an Austro-German dual alliance would not have served her ends better. It has already been remarked[32] that Bismarck's position before 1879, although it brought him little thanks from either Russia or Austria, had the merit of corresponding to the facts: he had not promised more than he could fulfil, and the desire for friendship with both had been affirmed by the agreements of 1872–3. The rôle of mediator or honest broker, which had been assigned to Germany under these agreements, had been in no way inconsistent with the peaceful and passive line in foreign policy that he professed to desire for the new Germany. Russia and, in a more discreet way, Austria had grumbled at his lack of effective help during the Near Eastern crisis of 1875–8, but neither could have afforded to sacrifice his

---

[30] This was clearly his view with regard to the Alsace-Lorraine issue, Italian Irredentist claims against Austria-Hungary, and Russo-German tension on the Polish frontier; probably also with regard to Russo-Austrian rivalry in the Balkans (see p. 115).

[31] W. L. Langer, *The Franco-Russian Alliance, 1890–1894* (1929), p. 18.

[32] See p. 42 above.

passive friendship or to side with France against him. There seems no reason why, if he had done nothing to weaken belief that his friendship, though passive, was impartial as between Austria and Russia, he should not have been able to revive something of the older relationship when passions had cooled a little after the Near Eastern crisis. But by signing the dual alliance he gave a preferential position to Austria that destroyed this possibility in Russian eyes. The result was not merely the perpetuation of Russian distrust, but, as a direct consequence of this distrust, Bismarck's backing and encouragement of Austria's resistance to Russia in the Balkans, which in turn perpetuated the Austro-Russian struggle there.

One reason for this new course, and one which must certainly not be underrated, was that he was temperamentally unsuited for the thankless rôle of honest broker; the unobtrusive patience and genuine goodwill of the true mediator were singularly lacking in this forceful, dominating, ever-suspicious master of action. The free hand of the warmaker of the 'sixties had meant freedom in action; the free hand of the honest broker of the 'seventies could mean inaction, while his imagination tortured itself with all the possible plots that his neighbours might be hatching against him. His personality pushed him towards as tight a control of Europe as he had achieved inside Germany. It may well be, as Dr. Eyck has suggested,[33] that herein lay a reason for his choice in October 1879 of Russia instead of England as his second alliance partner; he knew that with its world-wide interests and dependence on public opinion the British government could never accept completely the Bismarckian system of cabinet diplomacy. Russia, on the other hand, if she entered an alliance at all, would do so on terms which accepted his personal predominance, or at least provided the maximum possibility of self-assertion. Yet these personal considerations, and the flexibility of aims which they imply, suggest a freedom of manœuvre hardly compatible with the traditional interpretation of his policy in 1879, and in turn cast doubt on the need for the new course in his diplomacy. We cannot, in view of the paucity of evidence as to his more immediate or conscious reasons for concluding the dual

[33] Eyck, iii, 246.

alliance,[34] decide finally between two hypotheses. Either he was stampeded by genuine fear of Russia into the dual alliance and then tried to attenuate its effect on Russia by concluding the triple alliance of 1881; or the dual alliance was a deliberate and irrevocable choice for Austria which he strove to conceal from the Russians by the triple alliance. But clearly the dual alliance involved the risk of a permanent deterioration in Russo-German relations, and if it was due to fear of Russian attack was justified only if those fears were justified. It is certain today that Bismarck's alarm was false, although it is less easy to say how far he was unaware of this fact.

Historians have usually accepted Bismarck's account of the events of 1879 at its face value, but this is because the wisdom and indeed the inevitability of the Austro-German alliance have been taken, rather too readily perhaps, for granted. The alliance provided a working compromise between *kleindeutsch* and *grossdeutsch* positions which satisfied German nationalist sentiment for two generations, and it is, therefore, easy to read back into the past the later events of middle European history. At the time, however, it appeared to be, and was, a guarantee of the Austrian Empire against the immediate possibility of a Russian attack arising from the Near Eastern issues in which Bismarck claimed to be impartial. It fits so closely into his domestic German policy at this time that he could perhaps have given it a German-Conservative or even pro-Catholic justification which would have avoided the sharp challenge to Russia that it contained; and one must indeed ask whether his continued stressing of the anti-Russian aspect of the treaty may not have been due to the desire to conceal its domestic implications. But however this may be, Bismarck never sought to conceal its predominantly anti-Russian character. In a famous passage of his *Reflections and Reminiscences* he wrote in 1896:

The treaty which we concluded with Austria for common defence against a Russian attack is *publici juris*. An analogous treaty between the two powers for defence against France has not been published.

[34] It must be remembered that the published German documents are completely silent for the critical period January–August 1879. A full study of Bismarck's Austrian policy, based on the unpublished German and Austrian documents, is one of the greatest needs in Bismarckian studies. See p. 13 above.

The German-Austrian alliance does not afford the same protection against a French war, by which Germany is primarily threatened, as against a Russian war, which is to be apprehended rather by Austria than by Germany. Germany and Russia have no divergencies of interest pregnant with such disputes as lead to unavoidable ruptures. . . .[35]

But by this date the damage was done, and Bismarck could only repeat advice about the treatment of Russia which he had never succeeded in following very successfully himself.

. . . if in deciding between the Russian and the Austrian alliance I gave the preference to the latter, it was not that I was in any degree blind to the perplexities which made choice difficult. I regarded it as no less enjoined upon us to cultivate neighbourly relations with Russia after, than before, our defensive alliance with Austria; for perfect security against the disruption of the chosen combination is not to be had by Germany, while it is possible for her to hold in check the anti-German fits and starts of Austro-Hungarian feeling so long as German policy maintains the bridge which leads to St. Petersburg, and allows no chasm to intervene between us and Russia which cannot be spanned.[36]

When he wrote this the Three Emperors' Alliance was long since dead and buried, and the attempt to bridge the Russian chasm with the Reinsurance Treaty had failed to convince Bismarck's successors, who could see no point in trying to restrain Austrian fits and starts with a treaty of whose details Austria was ignorant.

Thus the timing of the signature of the dual alliance in 1879, and the fact that its terms, although not its existence, were unknown to the Russians, made impossible a restoration of the peculiar relationship between Germany and Russia which had existed since 1863. Perhaps it would be more accurate to say that the October treaty destroyed *belief* in the possibility of such a restoration, for the friendship had admittedly been under a heavy strain as a result of Bismarck's hostility to Russia during the first nine months of 1879. It vindicated the suspicions, if not the policy, of those Russians who had convinced themselves long before of his untrustworthiness. Bismarck abandoned his

[35] *Bismarck, His Reflections and Reminiscences* (London, 1898), ii, 272.
[36] *Ibid.*, 272–3.

traditional mediatory position still further when he sought in the summer and autumn of 1880 to separate Austria and Great Britain: henceforth, if Austria resisted Russian designs, it could only be (in Russian eyes) because she relied on German encouragement. The battle among Russian diplomats between the French and German schools, which was to lead within Bismarck's lifetime to the victory of the former, was already joined in 1879. All Russian ministers felt bound, until they had very precise evidence to the contrary, to regard him as they regarded Austria and as he regarded them—as in some measure a potential enemy in a phase of quiescence. Giers and the ministers who worked with him took the view, which was accepted by the Emperors Alexander II and Alexander III, that alliance with Germany was necessary to neutralize Bismarck's hostility; but they had no reason to think that the mere signature of the Three Emperors' Alliance would give them more positive support.

Much of this was due to his general incapacity to leave things alone; the attempt to pile precaution on precaution certainly placed Germany in a highly equivocal position towards all her allies during the next decade. His desperate efforts in 1880 and 1881 to square the circle and to convince the Russians (and perhaps himself) that no such position existed are reflected in the strange course of the *Dreikaiserbündnis* negotiations. His tactics were determined by an exaggerated fear of Russia which made necessary her isolation and dependence solely on himself, but he wanted her to believe that after the new triple understanding had been concluded Austria would have no preferential position. The most obvious proof in his eyes of Russia's continued untrustworthiness was the retention in office of Miljutin, although after the latter's retirement in April 1881 he found fresh cause for alarm in other appointments, such as Ignatyev's. But at this stage, and perhaps to the end of his life, he also did not entirely trust the Austrians, and his assumption that a direct Austro-Russian agreement would bring into power in Vienna elements unfriendly to Germany made it necessary to prevent bilateral negotiations between Vienna and St. Petersburg as far as possible. In spite of much talk about his desire for European peace and an amicable arrangement between his two neighbours in the Balkans he continued to show the greatest alarm and suspicion when anything of the sort was seriously proposed.

Accordingly he was careful during the treaty discussions to ensure that the Russians should negotiate only through him, and not directly with Haymerle: Saburov's eagerness at the end of May 1881 to go to Vienna was obviously one factor hastening Bismarck's recovery and resumption of the negotiations. Gladstone in April 1880 had appeared to offer Russia another escape from Bismarck's clutches; Bismarck had shown his alarm by denunciations, which even the Russians found unconvincing, of the revolutionary potentialities of English Liberalism. He was willing for Austria to maintain some vague understanding with Great Britain sufficient to avoid the danger that Gladstone would be thrown into Russian arms—apprehensions which were quite unnecessary, for the Russian government did not intend to alienate the central powers by forming an alliance with Great Britain, and Gladstone did not intend to form alliances with anyone. His exasperation and alarm reached its height in the early days of October 1880, when it appeared that Russia and England might, with Italy, separate themselves from the central powers in the Smyrna demonstration. France also had to be kept out of Russian arms, and the diversion of French interest and energies into North Africa served therefore, in Bismarck's eyes, a double purpose: the obvious one of turning French attention away from the lost provinces, and the rather less obvious one of turning her attention away from Russia. But he seems to have been genuinely unable to understand why the Russians should regard the dual alliance as proof of his underlying hostility, and his attempts to persuade them through Saburov that no special favour to Austria existed explain his extraordinary handling of the Austrians, who were forced to give way on every disputed point. Even on the few occasions when he made some initial attempt to resist the Russians' demands on Austria he soon surrendered to pressure.

Each of the two had accordingly to be deceived in some measure about his commitments to the other. He assured Haymerle on various occasions in 1880 and 1881 that the real basis of the dual alliance was to be found not only in the text of the

October treaty but also in the conviction that neither power would leave the other in the lurch.[37] This amounted to a conception of Austria as the natural friend and Russia as the natural enemy of the new Germany, and Haymerle was expected to regard German concessions to Russia as tactical moves on the diplomatic battlefield which automatically demonstrated Bismarck's loyalty to his Austrian ally. Haymerle chose to regard them more crudely as progressive surrenders of Austrian interests; if he had lived sixty years later he would doubtless have remarked that appeasement never pays. His wrangling with Bismarck as to the exact nature of the *casus foederis*, his argument that the position of Austria-Hungary would not be effectively defined unless the possibility of indirect Russian aggression against Rumania were covered, and his refusal to accept Bismarck as a mediator, all show his concern lest the protection promised by Germany in October 1879 should melt away under the new arrangements. All he secured was the secret ministerial guarantee of the October treaty, which gave him no more than he had before, and apparently did not remove his doubts.

Bismarck told Saburov on the other hand that after the signing of the triple agreement no such preferential position for Austria would exist. When Saburov asked point-blank whether Haymerle was willing to enter the triple alliance because he believed Austria to be sufficiently protected by the alliance with Germany, Bismarck flatly denied this. According to Saburov he said explicitly, 'our interest orders us not to let Austria be *destroyed*, but she is not guaranteed against an attack'. This was a direct contradiction of the essential terms of the October treaty, and it satisfied Saburov: he was now sure that after the signature of the Three Emperors' Alliance Bismarck would have no obligation, and probably no desire, to come automatically to Austria's assistance in an Austro-Russian war. Some weeks later Bismarck remarked to Saburov that the only power not likely to keep an engagement was Austria; that was

[37] 'Unser Bündniss von 79 beruht nicht bloss auf dem Buchstaben des Textes, sondern auf der politischen Überzeugung, dass wir einander nicht im Stich lassen können.' Bismarck to Reuss, *G.P.*, iii, no. 525, 1 February 1881. See also p. 271, fn. 63 above.

why, with her, 'a triple alliance is better than an alliance between two'. Saburov, in reporting this to Giers, exclaimed, 'it seems to me that we have there the most eloquent funeral oration on what was done at Vienna last year!' Again, on 26 January 1881, Bismarck made the bold statement that he could make with Russia a treaty exactly like the Austro-German treaty, without Austria being offended by it. He explained this by saying that Germany must see that neither Austria nor Russia 'is completely defeated. They are both necessary for us.' Here again he appears to assert, quite contrary to the facts, that Germany would not be obliged to intervene in an Austro-Russian war in the early stages, and when she did so would be moved only by her own interests.[38]

The historian who finds his way through all the turns and twists and blind alleys of such labyrinthian negotiations must be prepared for surprises; all too often the hesitations, blunders, and short cuts of earlier travellers seem difficult to reconcile with the acclaim that greeted their achievement of the goal. Very little was known about these negotiations until recent years, and the effect of the very restricted publication of documents was to strengthen the picture of Bismarck as the master-diplomat, reconciling his quarrelsome and mediocre allies with deft, assured gestures, and indeed with an economy of effort. The tedious story of prolonged, exasperating argument with the Austro-Hungarian Foreign Minister that emerges from the full correspondence does not leave any very convincing impression of his intellectual dominance or moral ascendancy. There is clearly some justification for Saburov's complacent self-congratulations on his success in entangling Haymerle in argument with Bismarck, for he and Bismarck, while distrustful of each other, seem to have founded a working friendship on a basis of mutual deception. Saburov believed, and Bismarck allowed him to believe, that by manœuvring Haymerle into prolonged argument with Bismarck he had effectively weakened the friendship between Berlin and Vienna. But Bismarck, it seems clear, allowed himself to be deceived by Saburov, and to

[38] *Saburov*, pp. 173–4, 195–6, 207–8, and the discussion in my article in the *Transactions of the Royal Historical Society* (vol. xxvii), 'Bismarck and the Three Emperors' Alliance, 1881–7', pp. 70–5.

assume that the Russians were more accommodating than in fact they were. As a result he was badly out-manœuvred over Novipazar. He had hints in September and October 1880 that Russia would prove difficult over this question; but as Saburov refrained from raising it during the winter Bismarck evidently lost sight of it. When it was finally raised in May 1881 his apprehensions over Alexander III's policy made it impossible for him to risk a prolonged struggle over the point.

Bismarck's achievement needs therefore to be defined somewhat carefully. It is certainly an exaggeration of his rôle to say that he brought the Austro-Russian tensions over the Near East, aroused by the events of 1877–8, to an end: Austria and Russia were both ready, and without any persuasion from Bismarck, to postpone further crises. He had been unable, and indeed made no attempt, to revive the friendly Austro-Russian co-operation over Balkan affairs of the later years of the Nicholas-Metternich era, which had had an Indian summer in the Gorchakov-Andrássy intimacy of 1873–6. Indeed the disparaging comments on Russian and Austrian policy which he made to Haymerle and Saburov respectively could only serve to keep alive the hostility between them, although his criticism of the Russians probably revealed genuine apprehensions, whereas his criticism of the Austrians was intended to conceal the extent of his commitment to Austrian interests. The alliance at the time of its formation, was, in the eyes of all three, an armistice; it accepted the existing position of the Berlin treaty as it had been modified by the events of 1878 to 1880, and made provision for those developments—Bulgarian unification and the annexation of Bosnia—which were regarded as inevitable in the near future, and about which neither Austria nor Russia wished to fight; it even provided a basis for a more permanent reconciliation. But it was not animated, in either Berlin or Vienna, by sufficient trust of Russia to allow this reconciliation to be completed. Bismarck's academic talk of a division of spheres in the peninsula, and even of his willingness for a Russian control of the Straits, must not conceal the fact that the treaty contained no provision for these vast changes, as the Russians knew perfectly well. We have seen that in January and February 1881 they had decided not to seek at that stage anything more than a minimum programme of advantage in the Balkans. The discussion also reveals, however, clearly enough, their hopes of future advance. Yet apart from the provision for the eventual unification of the two Bulgarias the treaty gave Russia no positive advantage. Bismarck's admirers have praised his tactics for the very reason that he secured so much while giving Russia so little. In reality this absence of a genuine *quid pro quo* for Russia was the weakness rather than the strength of the treaty. Under Article I Russia had to remain neutral even if Germany attacked France; but Germany would not remain neutral in the event of a Russian attack on Austria. Austria's rear, moreover, was protected in the event of an Austro-Italian war. It has been argued that Russia secured in return a free hand in Asia, where her opponent, if she fought a great power, would be Great Britain. But as Russia had no desire to fight Britain in Asia or anywhere else she could hardly regard this as a substantial gain, and it certainly did not involve any sacrifice of advantage on Germany's part. In any case an Anglo-Russian war, if it occurred, would probably be fought in the Near East, where in almost any circumstances in which such a war might arise, Russia would have first to come to terms with Austria.

Yet Bismarck's conduct in 1880 and 1881 does not make sense unless we assume that he wished not only to reduce Russia's capacity for mischief by isolating her but also to regain her confidence. His deliberate, almost ostentatious favours to Russia throughout the alliance negotiations, and the hopeful tone of his comments at the time of the signature of the treaty,[39] can only mean that he believed that a genuine *détente* in Russo-German relations was possible. Some of Saburov's triumphs were on mere points of drafting that had little general significance, but in refusing to extend the *casus foederis* of the October treaty, and in abandoning so readily Austria's

[39] Cf. his comments on the treaty to the Emperor. 'Da der Kaiser Alexander für einen Monarchen gilt, auf dessen Wort sicher gebaut werden kann, so dürfen wir den Frieden unserer beiden Nachbarn auf Jahre hinaus als gesichert ansehen. Ausserdem aber wird für Deutschland die Gefahr einer französisch-russischen Koalition vollständig beseitigt und dadurch das friedliche Verhalten Frankreichs gegen uns so gut wie verbürgt; ebenso wird den Versuchen der deutschfeindlichen Kriegspartei in Russland, Einfluss auf die Entschliessungen des jungen Kaisers zu gewinnen, durch das gegebene Wort des letzteren der Boden entzogen.' (Bismarck to Kaiser Wilhelm I, 15 June 1881, *G.P.*, iii, no. 531.)

case over Novipazar, Bismarck shows plainly enough that he was not proposing to support Austria at this stage in any forward policy in the Balkans in defiance of Russia. He was to this extent, and in his own way, seeking to promote the relaxation of European tensions which had also been Gladstone's aim. He hoped that Russian hostility to Germany would be removed or rendered innocuous: in return he would do nothing to encourage Austria. But when he discovered, all too soon, that Russian behaviour fell sadly below expectation he could see no alternative but to build up Austria's position in the peninsula as a counterpoise to Russia.

This development, which can be traced from the beginning of 1882, means that the Russo-German honeymoon was short-lived; and that the Three Emperors' Alliance, as an attempt to counter-balance in Russian eyes the preference given to Austria in the Dual Alliance, was a failure almost from the start. The meeting at Danzig in September 1881 of the Russian and Austrian Emperors, and of Bismarck and Giers, went off well, but by December 1881 Bismarck was showing concern at the growing hostility of the Tsar towards Austria, and at the continuing hostility of Germany's critics in Russia towards Giers' policy. He was bitterly disappointed that the conclusion of the *Dreikaiserbündnis* had not been followed by any modification of the threatening attitude of the 'anti-German war party' in Russia. Although Miljutin's successor at the Ministry of War was a professional soldier, General Wannovski, the new Chief of the General Staff was General Obruchev, a 'political' general who had been regarded in Berlin as an enemy of Germany since his mysterious negotiations in Paris in 1879. The Russian troop concentrations on the Polish frontier, and the building of strategical railways, continued; the Russians spoke of them as routine dispositions, but Bismarck chose to regard them as continued expressions of distrust and hostility,[40] and periodic alarms during the next four years kept his apprehensions alive. Skobelev's extraordinary speech to Serb students in Paris in February 1882 (in which he named Germany as the enemy of Russia and the Slavs) was hastily disavowed in St. Petersburg, but confirmed gloomy views in Berlin as to the

[40] Windelband, pp. 247–8.

Tsar's precarious hold on the discipline of the army. So depressed was Bismarck at this point that he remarked on 4 May 1882 that only the unbalanced budget held Russia back: '*good Russian finances mean war*'.[41] All this strengthened his tendency to draw closer to Austria, although she was merely the most important element in the defences that he strove to erect against the anticipated Russian aggression. An immediate result of the Skobelev affair was his decision that earlier scruples against a treaty with Italy must be abandoned.

A study of Bismarck's correspondence leaves no doubt that the triple alliance of Germany, Austria, and Italy, signed on 20 May 1882, was the direct consequence of his conviction that 'at the present time Russia appears to be ahead of France on the precipitous path to war', as he wrote to Reuss on 16 March 1882. As late as 31 December 1881 he had maintained the opposite view: in order not to strengthen the hand of Germany's enemies in Russia it was inadvisable to join Italy in an alliance. Now war seemed to him to be sufficiently near to necessitate the alternative policy of binding Italy to the central powers in order that Austria should not find herself between two fires. The circumstances leave no doubt that the triple alliance of 1882, like the dual alliance of 1879, was due directly to the policy of isolating Russia when she appeared to threaten war; to bring about the alliance he had to induce Kálnoky not to address Italy in the tone which had proved so irritating to the Balkan states, and he had to give Italy what was, on paper perhaps, the better of the bargain. Italy secured the support of Germany and Austria-Hungary against a French attack; she would support Germany if France attacked her, but promised only benevolent neutrality in the event of an attack by Russia alone on Germany and Austria-Hungary. But this gave Bismarck all he wanted. A few weeks later, when the Egyptian crisis reached its climax, he gave Russia no encouragement to intervene against British proceedings in Egypt; in both cases he followed his established policy of isolating France, but his immediate preoccupation was to give Russia no opportunity to make trouble.[42]

[41] *Ibid.*, p. 312.
[42] *Ibid.*, pp. 316–18; 355. A. F. Pribram, *Les traités politiques secrets de l'Autriche-Hongrie* (Paris, 1923), i, 223–8.

All this can be praised as a triumph of the diplomatic art; and if the danger was real the triumph is considerable. But as the danger was exaggerated the hostility to Russia, which could be only imperfectly concealed, meant that he had abandoned very hastily the attempt to regain the confidence of an uncertain friend, and it certainly makes nonsense of the view that the *Dreikaiserbündnis* had restored Bismarck's position as an impartial mediator between Austria and Russia. His object now was to encourage Austria to build up a strong defensive position in the Balkans; the year 1883 saw his final abandonment of the rôle of honest broker, although he continued to use fair words to the Tsar and Giers.

On all suitable occasions he was careful to repeat his belief in the desirability of Russo-Austrian division of influence in the peninsula, but he did nothing to hasten the process, and the Russian government appears to have underrated even his efforts to give it a free hand in Bulgaria. It was, on the other hand, unaware of the full extent of his secret encouragement of Austria. In the struggle for influence in the peninsula Austria, as Giers had anticipated in February 1881,[43] undoubtedly had the advantage. Rumania, Serbia, and Greece were encouraged to look to Austria as their defender against any extension of the Bulgarian frontiers.[44] The negotiations with Serbia that led to the secret Austro-Serbian treaty of 28 June 1881 were unknown to Bismarck for some time, but he supported Austria in her diplomatic pressure on Rumania in 1881 and 1882, and Germany acceded promptly to the secret Austro-Rumanian treaty of 30 October 1883. Under this treaty Austria undertook to come to the assistance if Rumania were attacked without provocation, and Bismarck had thus agreed to the extension of the *casus foederis* of the dual alliance of 1879 which he had refused Haymerle in 1881. Haymerle's successor, Graf Gustav Kálnoky, had every reason to regard the position with satisfaction, and he told Reuss on 20 August 1883 that Russia's influence on the new Bulgarian state would be rapidly weakened if the unification of Bulgaria and Eastern Rumelia took

[43] See above, p. 264.

[44] A. F. Pribram, 'Milan IV von Serbien und die Geheimverträge Osterreich-Ungarns mit Serbien, 1881–1889' (*Historische Blaetter*, 1922), pp. 478–83; Lhéritier, iv, 160–1, 178–94. Skazkin, pp. 212 *et seq.*

place: for this reason he was not in general opposed to the union. Bismarck took the same view.[45]

The attitude of the two governments was clearly shown in their opposition to Saburov's plans in 1883 for changes in Russia's favour in the terms of the Three Emperors' Alliance, which became due for renewal in June 1884. During the early months of 1883 Bismarck again showed extreme alarm over the military situation, and in June 1883 the German Emperor agreed to a strengthening of the German forces on the eastern frontier; even this did not remove Bismarck's apprehensions. He now felt that he could trust only the Tsar and Giers, and who could say that the one would be allowed to live and that the other would not be supplanted?[46] Nothing therefore was more calculated to create alarm and despondency than Saburov's energetic attempts to realize the ambitious plans that he had tried to force on his government in January and February 1881. He now sought to persuade Bismarck and Kálnoky and the Tsar that the opportunity should be taken in the renewing of the treaty to provide for the eventuality of the break-up of Turkey, in the spirit of the Reichstadt agreement of 1876 and Bismarck's own numerous sphere-of-influence proposals. Kálnoky's opinion in September was that the tracing of a line of demarcation would benefit no one but Russia, and would leave Turkey completely powerless; Bismarck agreed, and his only concern was to ensure that if a Russian offensive in the Near East took place the brunt of it should fall on other powers than Austria. The issue was postponed, for Giers was too pessimistic to have any belief in the achievement of Saburov's plans, and it was Giers who secured in the end the ear of the Tsar. Yet the position was paradoxical, for it was Saburov who earned Bismarck's hostility through a continued belief in Bismarck's goodwill; Bismarck's confidence in Giers was increased, although it was Giers who was certain that Russia could expect nothing from the treaty except a postponement of conflict. The treaty was renewed with only verbal alterations in March 1884, after Saburov's recall in February.

[45] A. F. Pribram, *Les traités politiques secrets de l'Autriche-Hongrie*, i, 40–47. *G.P.*, iii, nos. 584, 585, and chapter vii generally.

[46] Windelband, p. 414.

Giers' comments in 1883 and 1884 on Russia's isolation form a convenient epitaph on the dead hopes of European concord, which both Gladstone and Bismarck had striven so recently to quicken with their own peculiar inspiration. He had occasion at this time to send several surveys of Russian foreign policy to the Russian embassies, and all reveal his belief that Russian adhesion to the *Dreikaiserbündnis* was a precaution against Austro-German hostility, and that a breach with England was undesirable as it would increase still further Russia's dependence on the central powers. Russian policy was one of peace and internal reform, he told the Russian ambassadors in a notice circulated 'in view of recent events' on 18 August 1883. 'This is not the first time that Europe has been disturbed when Russia has left it to its own devices. We also saw it after the Crimean war. The Italian, Austrian, and French wars were the result.' The aim of the Tsar's present policy was to continue as long as possible the state of peace which Russia needed to restore her strength, and which was no less necessary to the great powers in view of the universal political, social, financial, and economic tension. 'That is why the Imperial Cabinet has joined the entente established between Germany and Austria. Our adherence has given it a negative and defensive character which has blunted the point that was ultimately directed against us, and has made it, for the moment, a guarantee of peace. That is also why we have greeted calmly the entry of Italy into that alliance, although we have reason to believe that it was conceived in a spirit of hostility to us. It consolidates peace at the present time without seriously compromising the future. In the event of war Italy will act according to her own interests.' A rupture between France and England would be particularly unfavourable for Russia, for it would leave her isolated to face the Austro-German alliance.

This explicit statement was a warning to the ambassadors against the adventurous policy of Saburov, with its reliance on Bismarck's goodwill; but it also made clear that there was no thought of a French or British orientation. This limited faith in the German, and rejection of the French, alliance was too negative a position for Russian governments to hold indefinitely, and it was Bismarck's failure to find means of winning Russia's confidence with positive demonstrations of goodwill that doomed his alliance policy to ultimate failure. The feeling that the existing situation could not be indefinitely maintained, but that its alternative was an open quarrel with the central powers, underlay all Giers' comments, and his conviction that Russia was in a disadvantageous position in the economic struggle in the Balkans increased his pessimism.

In the centre of Europe the situation is dominated by the Three Emperors' Alliance, which Italy has just joined and which has as its aim the maintenance of peace. It suits the necessities of the moment, everyone having need for repose.

It is to our interest to maintain it as long as possible. It guarantees us against Germany and preserves us from an immediate conflict with Austria.

But there lies its most thorny side.

The Vienna cabinet is compelled to check its invasion of the Balkan peninsula. But nothing can prevent it from preparing the way by industrial and commercial pressure, as well as by Catholic propaganda. The railway lines whose construction it is promoting towards Constantinople and Salonica, in accordance with the treaty of Berlin, are powerful means of influence. On this ground the struggle is a most difficult one for us! To the advantages acquired by Austria through her geographical position and her industrial and commercial resources we can oppose only attempts to develop our commercial relations with those countries, to provide ourselves in Bulgaria with a railway which offers a counterweight to those acquired by Austria, to foster national feeling and the ties of sympathy that unite us to the Slavs of the East, and to bring the Sultan to a *rapprochement* with us.[47]

This extract shows that in 1883 as in 1881 Giers understood far better than Saburov the essential difficulties that faced Russia in any peaceful competition with Austria in the Balkans. It was not merely that Bismarck's fears or Germanic sympathies led him to view with satisfaction any Austrian gains at Russia's expense; it was also because, as Skazkin has pointed out,[48] Russia was economically incapable of monopolizing even the Bulgarian market in which she was politically dominant.

[47] Giers to Mohrenheim, 6/18 August 1883 (covering letter and Notice, R.E. archives: briefly referred to above, p. 59).
[48] Skazkin, pp. 161–2.

Russian capital—the Russian capital that was behind the new Russian nationalist policy of the 1880's—would not go to Bulgaria; it could not compete with its western European rivals even with the artificially created advantages that the Russian government was prepared to secure for it, and it preferred new exotic markets where no competition existed. It found these in Asia. To Bulgaria went a different kind of capital, connected with big railway concessions, guaranteed by the government; the kind that succeeds by its skill in securing official backing rather than by ability to beat a rival in open competition. But this meant in turn that the Russian government was forced to maintain its economic influence by constant political pressure which did much to turn both Prince Alexander and the Bulgarian politicians against their protector; it meant that Russia was faced with the painful alternatives of destroying her own popularity or abdicating her interests.

And yet this situation, irritating though it was to the Russians, might have been accepted if Bismarck had used his influence more judiciously and demonstratively on Russia's side. Mere economic advantage in the Balkans was not a major interest of Russia; the intense animosity aroused by the Bulgarian question, which was to lead to the destruction of the Three Emperors' Alliance in 1887, was due to two very different apprehensions. One was that Prince Alexander's defiance of the Tsar from 1883–6 was due to Austrian and German instigation; the other was that Austria, encouraged by Bismarck, sought thereby to frustrate Russia's defensive plans for the Straits. Bismarck was innocent on both counts, but there was little in his policy and bearing since 1879 to give genuine assurance on these points.

And there is, indeed, little to justify the view that the system of close alliance which he had imposed on Europe between 1879 and 1882 had increased the prospects of European peace, in the sense of preventing existing animosities from degenerating into ultimate war. Although Gladstone's Concert had discredited itself through its surprising violence in application it had pointed to the one faint possibility of escape from the consolidation of mutual suspicions: it was an appeal to the six great powers to relax, to trust one another sufficiently to solve problems like the Eastern question by discussion, concession, and a due regard for the interests and ambitions of others (including the Balkan peoples). It was an appeal for a sense of proportion and of restraint—incidentally Gladstone's attitude to Austria and Russia was correct in its assumption that Austria, although the weaker, was the more stubborn, ambitious, and selfish of the two. Bismarck, in seeking security for Germany by his method of balanced antagonisms, had done nothing to remove, and was indeed doing much to perpetuate, the sense of irrevocable antagonism which after a certain point seemed to paralyse all capacity for constructive negotiation. He had made a deadlock and called it peace.

APPENDICES

I

Text of the Austro-German-Russian Treaty of 18 June 1881

Les cours d'Autriche-Hongrie, d'Allemagne et de Russie, animées d'un égal désir de consolider la paix générale par une entente destinée à assurer la position défensive de leurs états respectifs, sont tombés d'accord sur certaines questions qui touchent plus spéciale-ment à leurs intérêts réciproques.

Dans ce but les trois ont nommé [names of the plenipotentiaries Széchényi, Bismarck, Saburov follow], lesquels munis de pleins-pouvoirs qui ont été trouvés en bonne et due forme sont convenus des articles suivants:

ARTICLE I

Dans le cas où l'une des hautes parties contractantes se trouverait en guerre avec une quatrième grande puissance, les deux autres maintiendront à son égard une neutralité bienveillante et voueront leurs soins à la localisation du conflit.

Cette stipulation s'appliquera également à une guerre entre l'une des trois puissances et la Turquie mais seulement dans le cas où un accord préalable aura été établi entre les trois cours sur les résultats de cette guerre.

Pour le cas spécial où l'une d'elles obtiendrait de l'un de ses deux alliés un concours plus positif la valeur obligatoire du présent article restera dans toute sa vigueur pour la troisième.

ARTICLE II

La Russie d'accord avec l'Allemagne déclare sa ferme résolution de respecter les intérêts qui découlent de la nouvelle position assurée à l'Autriche-Hongrie par le traité de Berlin.

Les trois cours désireuses d'éviter tout désaccord entre elles s'engagent à tenir compte de leurs intérêts respectifs dans la pénin-sule des Balcans. Elles se promettent de plus que de nouvelles modifications dans le statu quo territorial de la Turquie d'Europe ne pourront s'accomplir qu'en vertu d'un commun accord entre elles.

Afin de faciliter l'accord prévu par le présent article, accord dont il est impossible de prévoir d'avance toutes les modalités, les trois cours constatent dès à présent, dans le protocole annexé au traité, les points sur lesquels une entente a été déjà établie en principe.

ARTICLE III

Les trois cours reconnaissent le caractère européen et mutuellement obligatoire du principe de la fermature des détroits du Bosphore et des Dardanelles fondé sur le droit des gens confirmé par les traités et résumé par la déclaration du second plénipotentiaire de Russie à la séance du 12 juillet du congrès de Berlin (protocole 19).

Elles veilleront en commun à ce que la Turquie ne fasse pas d'exception à cette règle en faveur des intérêts d'un gouvernement quelconque, en prêtant à des opérations guerrières d'une puissance belligérante la partie de son empire que forment les détroits.

En cas d'infraction ou pour la prévenir si une pareille infraction était à prévoir les trois cours avertiront la Turquie qu'elles la considéreraient, le cas échéant, comme s'étant mise en état de guerre vis-à-vis de la partie lésée, et comme s'étant privée, dès lors, des bénéfices de sécurité assurés par le traité de Berlin à son statu quo territorial.

ARTICLE IV

Le présent traité sera en vigueur pendant l'espace de trois ans à dater du jour de l'échange des ratifications.

ARTICLE V

Les hautes parties contractantes se promettent mutuellement le secret sur le contenu et sur l'existence du présent traité aussi bien que de protocole y annexé.

ARTICLE VI

Les conventions secrètes conclues entre l'Autriche-Hongrie et la Russie et entre l'Allemagne et la Russie en 1873 sont remplacées par le présent traité.

ARTICLE VII

Les ratifications du présent traité et du protocole y annexé seront échangées à Berlin dans l'espace de quinze jours ou plus tôt si faire se peut.

En foi de quoi les plénipotentiaires respectifs ont signé le présent traité et y ont apposé le sceau de leurs armes.

Fait à Berlin, le dix-huitième jour du mois de juin mil huit cent quatre-vingt et un.

L.S.	Széchényi
L.S.	v. Bismarck
L.S.	Sabouroff

PROTOCOLE

Les soussignés [etc. . . . .] ayant constaté conformément à l'article II du traité secret conclu aujourd'hui les points touchant les intérêts des trois cours dans la péninsule des Balcans sur les quels une entente a déjà été établie entre elles sont convenus du protocole suivant:

1. BOSNIE ET HERZÉGOVINE

L'Autriche-Hongrie se réserve de s'annexer ces deux provinces au moment qu'elle jugera opportun.

2. SANDJAK DE NOVI-BAZAR

La déclaration échangée entre les plénipotentiaires austro-hongrois et les plénipotentiaires russes au congrès de Berlin en date du 13/1 juillet 1878 reste en vigueur.

3. ROUMÉLIE ORIENTALE

Les trois puissances sont d'accord pour envisager l'éventualité d'une occupation soit de la Roumélie Orientale soit des Balcans comme pleine de périls pour la paix générale. Le cas échéant elles emploieront leurs efforts pour détourner la Porte d'une pareille entreprise bien entendu que la Bulgarie et la Roumélie Orientale devront de leur côté s'abstenir de provoquer la Porte par des attaques partant de leurs territoires contre les autres provinces de l'empire ottoman.

4. BULGARIE

Les trois puissances ne s'opposeront pas à la réunion éventuelle de la Bulgarie et de la Roumélie Orientale dans les limites territoriales qui leur sont assignées par le traité de Berlin, si cette question venait à surgir par la force des choses. Elles sont d'accord pour détourner les Bulgares de toute agression contre les provinces voisines nommément la Macédoine et pour leur déclarer qu'en pareil cas ils agiraient à leurs risques et périls.

5. ATTITUDE DES AGENTS EN ORIENT

Afin d'éviter les froissements d'intérêts dans les questions locales qui peuvent surgir, les trois cours muniront leurs représentants et agents en Orient d'une instruction générale pour leur prescrire de s'efforcer à aplanir leurs divergences par des explications amicales entre eux dans chaque cas spécial et pour les cas ou ils n'y parviendraient pas d'en référer à leurs gouvernements.

6. Le présent protocole fait partie intégrante du traité secret signé en ce jour à Berlin et aura même force et valeur. . . .

Fait à Berlin, le 18 juin 1881.

L.S.	Széchényi
L.S.	v. Bismarck
L.S.	Sabouroff

II

Bismarck on Gladstone, February 1884

THE following is a despatch from Bismarck to Schweinitz of 26 February 1884, and forms a fitting conclusion to the story of the unrelenting hostility to Gladstone that we have traced in this book. It was not used by Windelband; if he saw it he was prevented from referring to it in his book by the ban of the German Foreign Office on its publication.[1] Bismarck, in some alarm at a report of Giers' willingness to show some consideration for the Gladstone government in its difficulties in 1884, hastens to supply Schweinitz with arguments against an Anglo-Russian *rapprochement*: he was inclined to regard Gladstone as insane, and he believed with Palmerston that he would die in a madhouse.

Auswärtiges Amt   A 1226
Abschrift   Friedrichsruh, den
           26 Februar 1884

Seiner Excellenz dem Kaiserlichen Botschafter
Herr von Schweinitz
St. Petersburg
No. 124
Vertraulich

Von Euerer Excellenz gefälligem Berichte No. 40 vom 18. d.M. habe ich mit Interesse Kenntnis genommen. Ich glaube, dass die

---

[1] The following note is attached to the despatch. 'Zu: A 1226. Der Erlass Bismarcks an den Botschafter von Schweinitz vom 26 Februar 1884 Nr. 124 i.a. I.B. 10 ist zur *Veröffentlichung* nicht freizugeben. Berlin, den 3. April 1937. FRAUEN-DIENST.'

Merw'sche Angelegenheit in England unter der egyptischen Prä-
occupirung in den Hintergrund tritt. Wenn ich aus Ihrem Berichte
ersehe, dass das russische Kabinet und auch Herr von Giers auf das
Ministerium Gladstone in dieser Sache haben Rücksicht nehmen
wollen, so möchte ich Euere Excellenz noch um eine Äusserung
über die Motive bitten, welchen Sie dieses Verhalten zuschreiben.

Ich kann mir kaum denken, dass der Gedanke, Gladstone als
einen *Russenfreund* zu schonen oder zu halten, dabei noch mass-
gebend war, und möchte lieber annehmen, dass die notorische
Unfähigkeit des Herrn Gladstone, ein Land wie England zu
regieren, als nützlich für die russischen Interessen angesehen wird,
und dass man aus diesem Grunde, weil die ungeschickte englische
Regierung nützlich für Russland ist, die Verlängerung der Existenz
dieses Cabinetts mit günstigen Augen betrachtet. Man kann ja bis
zu einem gewissen Maasse annehmen, dass eine nach Aussen
schwache und ungeschickte englische Regierung für die russischen
Interessen im Orient und in Asien nützlicher ist, als eine kräftige.

Auf der anderen Seite aber fragt es sich, ob die Gesammtinter-
essen des monarchischen Europa, und also auch die der russischen
Krone, überhaupt gewinnen würden, wenn England durch un-
gemessene Fortdauer des Gladstone'schen Regimentes innerlich
zersetzt und republikanisirt wird. Dass die Republik in England
Fortschritte macht, wird nicht nur durch sachkundige Berichte
bestätigt, sondern liegt in der natürlichen Consequenz der radikalen
Regierungsprinzipien, welche ihre Spitze gegen die bisher dort
herrschende Oligarchie zerstörend einsetzen; das Englische
Königthum wurzelt mit seinem Bestande in dem Boden dieser
Oligarchie, von welcher das Königliche Haus einen wesentlichen,
aber doch nur einen Bestandtheil bildet. Euere Excellenz sind mit
den Zuständen Englands Selbst hinreichend bekannt, um meinen
Gedankengang ergänzen zu können bis zu dem Schlusse, dass jeder
Monat Gladstone'schen Regimentes das britische Reich der Republik näher bringt. Wenn gleichzeitig die britische Machtstellung in
solchen Lebensfragen, wie es die irische, und im Gefolge derselben,
die schottisch-englische Agrarfrage, die egyptische Angelegenheit
und die sozialpolitische Stellung Indiens sind, in einer ungeschickten
und albernen Weise untergraben wird, so kann dies zu grossen
Katastrophen des britischen Reiches führen, aber auch zu grossen
Gefahren für das übrige Europa, wenn die grossen Machtmittel
dieses Reiches aus ihrer Gebundenheit in's Freie fallen. Schon
allein der wirtschaftliche Rückschlag, der auf alle Länder der Welt
stattfinden würde, wenn die Ordnung, und damit der Wohlstand,

und im internationalen Verkehr die Kaufkraft aller der heutigen Bestandtheile des britischen Reiches wesentlich geschwächt wird, würde auf die Zustände der übrigen europäischen Länder in bedauerlicher Weise zurückwirken. Ein so wesentliches Glied der europäischen Gemeinschaft, wie England, kann nicht in schwere Krankheit und Zuckungen verfallen, ohne ganz Europa in Mitleidenschaft zu ziehen. Die jetzige englische Regierung, an deren Spitze ein Mann steht, dem ausser seiner verhängnisvollen Gabe der Beredtsamkeit jede Eigenschaft eines Staatsmannes in dem Maasse fehlt, dass ich geneigt bin, ihn als geisteskrank anzusehen, wird mit solchem Ungeschick geführt, dass es, wenn die Möglichkeit dazu überhaupt vorläge, nützlich sein würde, jenes grosse Reich zur Wahrnehmung seiner Interessen unter eine Curatel der übrigen Christenheit zu stellen.

Ich sehe die zunehmende Erkrankung der englischen Zustände nicht ohne Sorge; schon die chronischen Krankheiten, denen Frankreich seit bald einem Jahrhundert verfallen ist, wirken wie schwere Schäden auf die übrigen europäischen Länder zurück. Die zunehmende Verarmung Frankreichs, und das Schwinden seiner Kaufkraft infolge dessen, betrachte ich als den geringsten Theil der Beeinträchtigung der Ruhe und Wohlfahrt der übrigen europäischen Länder, welche von Frankreich ausgeht. Geräth England in gleiche Bahnen, wie ich das bei fortgesetztem Gladstonianismus befürchte, so werden alle jene Schädigungen, die wir bereits durch Frankreichs innere Krankheit erleiden, in progressiver Steigerung zunehmen.

Ich würde Euerer Excellenz dankbar sein für eine Äusserung Ihrer Ansicht über diesen Punkt, und Ihrer Meinung darüber, ob die dortige Rücksicht auf Gladstone der Überzeugung entspringt, dass England's Schaden und selbst sein schliesslicher Untergang ein zu erstrebendes Ziel sei, oder ob man irgend welche Hoffnungen auf die Freundschaft jenes Mannes setzt, von dem Lord Palmerston die Überzeugung aussprach, dass er im Irrenhaus sterben werde.

(ges.) von Bismarck.

Index